REFUSING CARE

REFUSING CARE

FORCED TREATMENT
AND THE RIGHTS
OF THE MENTALLY ILL

ELYN R. SAKS

THE UNIVERSITY OF CHICAGO PRESS
CHICAGO AND LONDON

Elyn R. Saks is the Orrin B. Evans Professor of Law and Psychiatry and the Behavioral Sciences at University of Southern California Law School and a research clinical associate at the Los Angeles Psychoanalytic Society and Institute. She is the author of *Jekyll on Trial: Multiple Personality Disorder and Criminal Law* and *Interpreting Interpretation: The Limits of Hermeneutic Psychoanalysis.*

The University of Chicago Press, Chicago 60637
The University of Chicago Press, Ltd., London
© 2002 by The University of Chicago
All rights reserved. Published 2002
Printed in the United States of America

11 10 09 08 07 06 05 04 03 02   1 2 3 4 5
ISBN: 0-226-73397-1 (cloth)

Library of Congress Cataloging-in-Publication Data

Saks, Elyn R., 1955–
   Refusing care : forced treatment and the rights of the mentally ill / Elyn R. Saks.
      p. ; cm.
   Includes bibliographical references and index.
   ISBN 0-226-73397-1 (cloth : alk. paper)
      1. Involuntary treatment.   2. Mental illness—Treatment.   I. Title.
   [DNLM: 1. Commitment of Mentally Ill—United States.   2. Mental
   Competency—United States.   3. Mental Disorders—diagnosis—United States.
   4. Restraint,   Physical—United States.   5. Treatment Refusal—United States.
   WM 33 AA1 S271 2002]

   RC343 .S245 2002
   362.2′0973—dc21

                                                        2002020403

For Will Vinet

CONTENTS

ACKNOWLEDGMENTS

Writing this book has been an important experience. Even more than my first two books, this book has deep personal meaning for me. I have worked in mental health law for years: as a legal advocate for the mentally ill, as a volunteer at a psychiatric hospital, as a therapist, and as a teacher. I care about the issues immensely. And I find them very difficult. What follows is my attempt to come to terms with these issues.

Many people have contributed enormously to this project; I can't thank them enough. I thank first the dean of the University of Southern California Law School, Matthew Spitzer, for making USC a wonderful place to work. I am very grateful to several reference librarians at the USC Law School, including Amy Atchinson, Laura Cadra, Corrin Gee, Jennifer Murray, Lee Neugebauer, and Jessica Wimer. I thank my assistants, Rosemary Hendrix, Sheri Butala, Maureen Navarette, and Keith Stevenson, for their wonderful secretarial aid.

For reading drafts and making many helpful comments, I thank Scott Altman, Thomas Lyon, Michael Shapiro, and Christopher Slobogin. One's colleagues always help make one's work much better than it would have been. I am especially grateful to Scott and Michael for continuing to read my work even though I am no longer a young academic.

My youngest reader has been Adam Fraser, who, at fourteen, gave me very helpful comments. I am also grateful to Gladys Topkis for her expert editorial assistance.

Several students furnished wonderful research assistance, including Vishta Farahani, Amy Feicht-Kay, Jennifer Hermann, Christopher Hopkins, Karala Jenkins, Cory Johnson, Bryan Kelly, David Pierce, Gregory Shamo, Heather Spragg, Carey Stone, Saji Thomas, Nadine Youssef, and Teri Zimring. I am most appreciative of their help.

I also thank the people closest to me for being there: my parents, Barbara and Bert; my brothers, Warren and Kevin; my closest friends, Steve Behnke, Kenny Collins, and Esther Fine; my many other close friends; my analysts, the late Martha Harris, the late Stanley Jackson, Melvin Lansky, and Malcolm Hoffs; and finally, the person to whom this book is lovingly dedicated, Will Vinet. Will has added a dimension to my life that I never thought possible, and I owe him the deepest debt for so enriching my life.

INTRODUCTION

It has been said that how a society treats its least well-off members says a lot about its humanity. Our treatment of the mentally ill says that American society is inhumane. Sometimes the mentally ill are treated with extreme measures that the patients do not want: psychosurgery, electroconvulsive therapy (ECT), and unwanted medication with very serious risks and side effects. In addition, their liberty is taken away, sometimes for many years. Thus Kenneth Donaldson, for instance, was hospitalized for more than fifteen years, although he was dangerous to no one and able to hold down a good job; the prevailing standard allowed hospitalization for those simply in need of treatment.

The pendulum then swings and the mentally ill are utterly neglected. The hospital wards are opened, and people are discharged with no care available. Many want treatment but are turned away from the hospital. Some blame the lawyers for a blind commitment to liberty rather than care. The real culprit is society for not providing less restrictive care in the community. The will to help those who want help is not there. Consider, when evaluating deinstitutionalization, that in 1983, in Oxford, England—a city of 125,000—there were forty-three group homes for deinstitutionalized patients. In New Haven, Connecticut—also a city of 125,000—in that same year there was one halfway house. *Of course* deinstitutionalization will fail without the needed resources in the community.

In addition to swings between overintervention and neglect, there is widespread prejudice against the mentally ill. These are not unrelated phenomena, of course: we treat the mentally ill badly, one way or another, because we do not value them sufficiently as people.

Stigma has been reduced for many other conditions and statuses: homosexuality, cancer, AIDS. People talk openly about these situations; they join together in support groups; they write books and appear on television.

This is not to say that stigma is nonexistent for these other statuses and conditions, or that some people with mental illness are not just as open as people in these other categories. Still, there is a qualitative difference in the perception and treatment of mental illness and these other cases.

"Mental illness" is among the most stigmatized of categories.[1] People are ashamed of being mentally ill. They fear disclosing their condition to their friends and confidants—and certainly to their employers. Society is openly hostile to, scornful of, and frightened of the mentally ill. The media use terms and make comparisons that demean sufferers. Even in these days of political correctness in the classroom, students speak of "wackos," "crazies," "nutcakes," "loonies"—even though they have been warned that some of their classmates probably have an illness themselves or have a loved one who does. People who would not dream of saying something racist or sexist in conversation with their friends say the same kinds of things.

In the arena of mental illness the battle rages on, partly because the stigma is so great that people don't come forward, partly because its sufferers are sometimes unable, as a result of their disabilities, to come forward, partly because society rationalizes that people with mental illness simply *are* different and deserve to be treated differently.

This book explores the rational treatment of the mentally ill in contexts in which they say they do not want treatment. That is to say, it explores the "overinterventionist" pole of the swing in the way they are treated. It also tries to be mindful of the stigma that attaches to mental illness, thus asking when (if ever)—and why—sufferers should be treated differently than their non–mentally ill counterparts.

Why, in this day of too little rather than too much intervention, do I study overintervention? There are a number of reasons. First, although the neglect of the mentally ill who want treatment is a huge problem, it is not a problem about which a law professor has much to say because it involves not theory but political will—the decision to use our resources in a humane and giving way.

Second, in a world of limited resources, it makes sense not to impose treatment on those who should not be treated against their will. Dollars inappropriately spent on these people cannot be used to deliver services to people who truly want them or ought to get them. A rational policy of health care services requires that we think about these issues too.

Third, although it is widely thought that insufficient care for those who want it dwarfs the problems of overintervention in the lives of those who do not want it, it seems to me that that has not been established by empirical studies. It is certainly true that there are many, many people who reject treatment offered them: they don't go along with the Project Help types who come to see them on the streets; they don't sign into hospitals; they insist on hearings to challenge their hospitalization; they bring further hearings after the automatic ones; they refuse treatment and force their treaters to establish their incompetency in court. In short, there are many people being treated today who do not want to be treated. The question then becomes pressing: When should we treat those who don't want treatment, and when should we respect their choices? That is the subject of this book. I look at three kinds of unwanted treatment—hospitalization, medication, and restraints and seclusion—and try to establish in each case a standard for when we should impose treatment over the patient's objection.

Throughout—so as not to contribute to marginalization and stigmatization—I ask whether the mentally ill should be treated differently in these matters than the non–mentally ill and, if so, why. I recommend standards that should apply, when the relevant conditions are met, to the non-ill as much as to the ill.

The three meta-lessons of this book are these: first, there can be no principled paternalists or autonomy theorists in this matter of forced treatment; we must balance, and we need to find a rational way to do so. Second, the balance I perform results in standards that are both more protective of patient autonomy *and* more paternalist than current law. I try to justify these standards in the body of the work. Third, it is possible and desirable to be mindful of the desideratum not to discriminate against the mentally ill. And so I propose standards that, as much as possible, apply to the non–mentally ill as well as to the mentally ill. We simply must cease treating the mentally ill as different in a way that derogates their humanity.

DOCTORS AND LAWYERS:
WHY CAN'T WE ALL JUST GET ALONG?

Nancy, thirty-five years old, was undergoing a hearing to decide whether she should be allowed to refuse psychotropic medication. She had been brought to the emergency room by the local police. Some time ago she had lost her job and had subsequently been evicted from her apartment. That night, she was caught trying to break back in. The police did not detain her, but they found her several hours later by the railroad tracks nearby, huddled by a fire she had built to keep herself warm.

Nancy's stay in the hospital was difficult. She resisted being there, denied that she was mentally ill, and wanted no part of treatment. Although she had no history of previous psychiatric treatment, her family reported that she had been troubled for a long time. In addition to her bizarre behavior the evening of her confinement and her uncooperative behavior on the ward, Nancy admitted that she heard voices. She was committed to the hospital. She continued to refuse treatment, however, on the grounds that she was not mentally ill, did not need medication, and in any case preferred not to take medication of any kind. Nancy's treating psychiatrists sought to medicate her involuntarily via an order of the court.

Nancy's case—a real case—raises many difficult issues. My purpose in describing it is to explore why the typical psychiatrist seeks treatment in cases of this kind and why the typical lawyer seeks a disposition that upholds the patient's right to refuse treatment.[1] That is, I am interested in the fantasies and fears that underlie the psychiatrist's and the lawyer's commitment to their different stances.[2] What stories do they tell themselves to form the basis for their positions? At this point, I must somewhat stereotype the mental health professional's and the lawyer's response to this case; later I will add some depth to this picture.

The psychiatrist's theory is fairly straightforward. He tells himself that Nancy is seriously mentally ill. She behaved bizarrely—not to mention dangerously—on the night she was brought to the hospital. According to her parents' report, she has a long history of troubled behavior. Recently she lost her job, suggesting that she is unable to function effectively in society. She denies that she is ill—and therefore "lacks insight"—and does not cooperate with treatment or the ward routine. Finally, and perhaps most important, she admits to hearing voices.

If Nancy is seriously mentally ill, the psychiatrist tells himself, she needs to be treated. That's what doctors are for: to cure people—or at least to help them. Nancy's refusal of help is but a symptom of her mental illness. Mentally ill people often deny that they are ill, even when it is obvious to everyone. And of course if one does not think one is ill, one is not going to think that one needs treatment. Because Nancy lacks insight into her condition, she is in no position to make a reasoned choice concerning what to do about it.

The doctor's fantasy continues: imposing treatment on Nancy will promote her well-being. She will stop hearing voices. She will relate better to those around her. She will behave better. She will be able to be more productive. Finally, she will feel happier and have a greater sense of well-being. Serious mental illness is extremely painful and debilitating, and Nancy, if she responds well to treatment, will be restored to health. The benefits to Nancy may be matched by those to her loved ones—and to society itself. If Nancy recovers completely, she may no longer need treatment and may go on to live a happy and healthy life.

The doctor realizes, of course, that forcing treatment on Nancy does just that—it *forces* her. And being deprived of choice is itself unpleasant. But surely, he reasons, it would be less unpleasant than the fate Nancy would otherwise face. The benefits justify the costs. Indeed, the costs to autonomy can be justified in other ways. Perhaps Nancy is not truly autonomous. After all, she is impaired, so improving her functioning will serve her long-term autonomy. Indeed, perhaps she is not even truly herself when she makes the unwise choice. When restored to her true self, she will be grateful—*that* is her autonomous expression of her interests, and *that* is the choice we should respect.

If the doctor tells himself a hopeful story about the benefits of treatment, even if it is forced, he also tells himself a bleak story about the risks of nontreatment. If Nancy is not treated for her psychiatric disorder, she may progressively deteriorate. Her behavior may become more bizarre and unmanageable; she may begin to voice delusions as well as hallucinations; her hallucinations may become more frightening, her speech incoherent. Nancy may become totally out of control and even violent to herself or others. At that point there will be no choice but to medicate Nancy, whatever her preference.

If Nancy's condition does not become more acute in this way, it may, after a certain point, become irreversible. Nancy may become a chronic patient. Her bizarre behavior and preoccupation with her hallucinations may then make her unable to work ever again, her relationships may become strained if not nonexistent, and her self-care skills may deteriorate. She may become homeless. In addition, Nancy's family may suffer all of these losses as well—and society itself. At best, then, Nancy may lead a horrible life; at worst she may be dead after a short time.

Of course, the doctor will think, nontreatment will jeopardize not only Nancy's well-being but also her autonomy. Nancy's illness may cause her autonomy to become progressively attenuated. She may become so ill that her autonomy is irretrievably lost. At that point she will have no real choices left.

In short, the doctor's fantasy is that he will cure his patient; his fear, that she will decline and die. Treatment, even forced treatment, will serve not only the patient's best interests but also her long-term autonomy. Nontreatment will disserve both the patient's interests *and* her autonomy. What else is a reasonable doctor to do but to force treatment? Given these hopes, fantasies, and fears, it is not surprising that the doctor wants to force treatment. The lawyer, then, must have a very different set of hopes, fantasies, and fears, because *she* wants to allow the patient not to be treated. What is going on in her mind?

The story she tells herself may have more branches to it, as it were (or different branches may appeal to different lawyers). For example—in a move more popular in earlier days—she might entirely repudiate the notion of mental illness. Nancy, to be sure, is undergoing certain problems in living. She has lost her job and been evicted from her apartment. She is probably angry. She is responding in an angry and somewhat antisocial way—trying to break into her apartment, making a fire in a residential neighborhood. But in no way does this behavior suggest that she is *ill*. To do so only medicalizes ordinary human conflict. Of course, Nancy does hear voices, but so do religious mystics. Hearing voices is outside of the norm, but can't people be unusual or different without being labeled mentally ill?

Of course, if Nancy is not mentally ill—if there is no such thing as mental illness—forcing medication on her is abominable. The lawyer will point out that if we do so she will suffer all the risks, known and unknown, of these powerful chemical agents and will derive no benefit from them. Perhaps worse, the medication may have the effect of changing Nancy's most intimate self—her thoughts, feelings, and behaviors—solely to make her more like us. That is state intrusion at its most vulgar. Finally, treating Nancy against her wishes is a serious assault on her dignity, made all the worse because she is a fully autonomous agent.

Not many people these days, not even lawyers, think that mental illness is just difference—although we will see in the next chapter that how it is anything more is a vexed question. Accordingly, not many today think that treatment is just a form of mind control.

Many lawyers, on the other hand, might agree with this one's next possible posture in this case: that, although mental illness is real, Nancy may not herself be mentally ill. The reasoning about her behavior would be the same as in the previous condition: Nancy is angry, wants to get back into her apartment, and is sleeping rough by an outdoor fire because she has no choice. Her family is now *reading* a lot of her prior behavior as symptomatic of illness rather than of interpersonal difficulty. The voices she is hearing are a little harder to deal with, but maybe more people hear voices than admit to it, or maybe there has been some misunderstanding. In any event, Nancy is thirty-five years old and has worked most of her adult life. If she were truly psychotic, one would expect earlier and unequivocal signs. At the least she has many resources.

It is clear, of course, that if Nancy is not mentally ill, she should not be forced to receive treatment. There would be no point to the treatment—and she could be seriously damaged. In addition, as above, forcing treatment on Nancy is a serious erosion of her autonomy.

Lawyers often argue in the alternative, and the lawyer here may believe that Nancy should not have treatment imposed on her even if she is mentally ill. The medications may damage Nancy both physically and psychologically. The risks of antipsychotic medication are well known (I discuss them in chapter 4). Nancy could develop an irreversible, disfiguring movement disorder. She could even die from the treatment.

The lawyer may also point out that the psychological risks are not insignificant and may outweigh the benefits to Nancy's mental state—if the medications work. For example, accepting that she is mentally ill may irreparably harm Nancy's self-esteem, and it may be better for her to resist the label even if it truly applies. Think how well she has functioned so far. Worse yet, Nancy may come to accept the mental illness *role* even when she need not do so. She may stop seeking work, feel disabled, and become helpless. Forcing treatment may cause her to feel resentful and angry toward her treaters and thus may deter her from ever voluntarily seeking treatment in the future. And the treatment may even be less likely to work if forced—so she gets all the costs and perhaps none of the benefits.

Not only may treating Nancy involuntarily not redound to her well-being, the lawyer will point out, it certainly does not serve her autonomy. Nancy is somewhat mentally ill, according to this theory, but she is not incompetent.[3] And competent people ought to be able to decide their own fate. The idea that her autonomy may be impaired is beside the point; absent incompetence, we serve someone's autonomy by letting him or her decide free of interference by others. That is what we are *not* doing with Nancy. Medicating Nancy may increase her long-term autonomy, but so long as she has minimal autonomy now, we let *her* decide if she wants that. And the idea that we serve Nancy's autonomy when we support the choice of the grateful Nancy is no more than sleight of hand—who's to say who the "real" Nancy is?

If forcing medication on Nancy is full of risks, according to the lawyer, allowing her to refuse promises considerable benefit. Negatively, it avoids all the potential harms enumerated above—for example, risks to her physical well-being. Positively, it may provide numerous potential benefits. First, Nancy may recover spontaneously. Illnesses sometimes remit without treatment, and when they do, the patient is spared all the costs associated with treatment, while preserving her self-esteem and sense of agency. Indeed, such preservation may give Nancy added motivation to recover under her own steam—and motivation is important to recovery. Second, even if Nancy continues to be mentally ill, allowing her to make her own choice has the benefit of making her feel listened to and valued. It gives her dignity and self-respect. Nancy may prefer dignity and self-respect to being mentally healthy, and, if she is not incompetent, she may have the right to have this preference honored.

Third, whatever we may imagine, Nancy herself may feel happier remaining mentally ill than being forced to become mentally healthy. People have idiosyncratic preferences. Perhaps Nancy prefers the symptoms of her mental illness to the side effects of her medication or to the diminution of self-esteem that afflicts many who take medication. Or perhaps Nancy prefers the symptoms of her illness because they tend to dull her sensitivity to a bleak and painful life. She may wish not to know, so to speak. The lawyer will wonder who we are to tell Nancy which is the better life for her; surely she knows best.

Finally, the lawyer may imagine that, if we only give Nancy the dignity of her own choices, she may eventually come around to taking the recommended medication of her own volition. Doctors forbidden to force medication have an incentive to *talk* to their patients—to engage in persuasion—and they may ultimately persuade Nancy to do what the lawyer, in this posture, feels would best serve Nancy's interests. The advantage now is that there will be no infringement on autonomy, and the medication may work better to boot; cooperative patients are much likelier to benefit from treatment than uncooperative ones.

If allowing Nancy to refuse treatment may serve her best interests, the lawyer will continue, it also preserves her autonomy. Once again, autonomy is served if one retains freedom to make one's own choices. And one may remain autonomous in the most important senses even though one is impaired. Indeed, giving the impaired patient freedom to choose may bolster her ability to choose well and wisely. The less than fully autonomous agent may *become* more autonomous when she is *treated* as though she were autonomous. Of course, greater autonomy makes one feel better, too, so we count the benefit of increased self-respect when considering the patient's well-being.

In short, the lawyer tells herself a very different story about Nancy than does the doctor. She believes that supporting Nancy's right to refuse treatment may serve both her best interests and her autonomy. The lawyer's secret fantasy is that all the gloomy talk about Nancy may be a terrible mistake—or worse yet, some abuse of power. Maybe Nancy is not mentally ill after all, and if not, she certainly should not be treated against her will. Even if the lawyer concedes that Nancy is mentally ill, she will still tell herself that forcibly medicating Nancy threatens to harm her both physically and psychologically, whereas allowing her to refuse may enhance her well-being as she sees it. And of course this tack furthers Nancy's autonomy.

The doctor and the lawyer, then, have very different ideas about Nancy. With involuntary treatment, the doctor predicts cure and restored autonomy, with no treatment, deterioration and diminished autonomy. By contrast, with forced treatment, the lawyer imagines psychological and physical damage, as well as insults to autonomy, with upholding the right to refuse, good psychological effects and a preservation of or increase in autonomy.

I have of course purposely picked a case that is ambiguous as to the correct course—that is on the border. And both doctor and lawyer will temper their predictions somewhat in more obvious cases. For example, if the patient has a long history of nonresponsiveness to the treatment or even ill effects, the doctor is not likely to be so sanguine about the benefits of treatment. Similarly, if the patient becomes and remains extremely resentful and hostile as a result of a long history of forced treatment, the doctor is not likely to predict thanks.

By contrast, if the patient has a long history of crippling mental illness, the lawyer is going to find it harder to imagine that it might all be a mistake—that the patient is not really ill, just having some difficulties. Similarly, if the patient has a long history of responding to treatment and feeling more empowered as a result—as well as of deteriorating when allowed to refuse—the lawyer is not likely to be so confident about the benefits of allowing her to refuse or so concerned about the dignity costs of forced treatment.

Still, even in these less borderline cases, the typical doctor is likely to support treatment and the typical lawyer the right to refuse. The doctor will reason that it is better to be on medication and thus mentally healthier, even if one is still impaired and however angry one is about the forced treatment, than it is to be in a more seriously ill state. Similarly, forced treatment will ultimately serve the patient's autonomy because the drugs render him more autonomous, even if only a little.

By contrast, the lawyer will reason that there remain important benefits to allowing the patient to refuse. We should not underestimate the value of dignity and self-respect, even at the cost of some well-being, conventionally conceived. Unless she is completely incompetent, we should trust the patient to make that judgment for herself. And although the healthy patient might make a different judgment, we should respect the ill patient's autonomy as much as the well patient's—we should not be in the business of choosing selves. Indeed, the patient must have a reason for choosing at times to discontinue her medication; even the well self must have some ambivalence about the benefits, for her, of being medicated into health.

Even in less ambiguous cases than Nancy's, the doctor and lawyer come down on exactly opposite sides of the argument. How can they come to such completely different conclusions? In what remains of this chapter, I try to describe how this could happen. I then examine more carefully whether doctors and lawyers actually differ in these ways.

Doctors and lawyers may think they are serving the well-being and autonomy of the patient by taking radically different actions because, in part, they use different concepts of autonomy and they measure well-being in different ways. The doctor employs a robust concept of autonomy that requires many abilities, as well as an authentic choice; he can thereby endorse the choices of the healthier self and focus on that self's long-range autonomy. For the doctor, this course best serves the patient's true autonomy. The lawyer, by contrast, employs a minimalist concept of autonomy, one that maximizes people's freedom, eschews choosing among selves, and values noninterference with the patient's choices *now.*

By the same token, the doctor measures well-being in objective terms—such as the absence of pathology—whereas the lawyer measures it in more subjective terms—such as the patient's self-professed sense of well-being. In addition, the lawyer more greatly values the benefits of dignity and self-respect than does the doctor, who is willing to sacrifice them to improved functioning.

Doctors and lawyers also take such different stances because they have radically different fears and fantasies and make radically different empirical suppositions and predictions. Doctors are committed first to health and are immensely worried about the risks of decline and death. Not diagnosing or intervening may be a dreadful error. Their fantasy is that treatment will help and nontreatment will lead to disaster. They also imagine that all patients share their values, so that the patient with different commitments must be so minded because of his illness and will be grateful when restored to health. Even though the doctor will concede that some patients do not fit this pattern, he will think that most do. He will therefore err on the side of assuming that he is dealing with the usual kind of patient. Even when, as in our example above, history strongly suggests the opposite, the doctor will be hopeful that this time will be different.

The lawyer, by contrast, is committed first to freedom. That is why he wants the patient to be free to decide and why he takes his role to be vigorous advocacy of what the client wants. He is a professional skeptic and is very much aware of the possibility of mistake, abuse of power, state hostility to any kind of deviancy, efforts to enforce majoritarian norms, and disenfranchisement of the weak and powerless. He is first and foremost an advocate and dreads the risks of loss of liberty and autonomy. He is less than sanguine about the efficacy of treatment but is optimistic about the benefits of empowering the patient and supporting her self-respect. He imagines that the patient shares *his* values and thinks we risk the greater error by supposing otherwise. Even when the lawyer is confident, because of a long history, that there is no mistake or abuse, he cares more about autonomy than long-term health. And if the patient, by history, acts differently than predicted, the lawyer imagines that this time will be different.

As this discussion makes clear, however much the doctor and the lawyer profess to be serving both well-being and autonomy, when push comes to shove, the doctor will favor the former and the lawyer the latter. That is, when they use all their terms in the same way, the doctor must confess that, in a conflict, he will sacrifice autonomy in the lawyer's sense for well-being—indeed, he *must* do so if he is to favor forced treatment. And the lawyer will sacrifice well-being in the doctor's sense. (Unlike the doctor, the lawyer is not obliged to make this sacrifice and may retain the hope that it will prove unnecessary.) In short, the doctor cares more about health and the lawyer more about self-respect and freedom from interference.

Perhaps training contributes to their differences in commitments and suppositions. Each, for instance, is socialized into a different role: the doctor into the role of the healer and the lawyer into the role of the advocate. Each sees his central job differently. And each is trained into a different vision of human nature. The doctor is taught that patients care about health, want to and will defer to expertise, and want ultimately to be taken care of. In the legal context, where a shared goal is not so taken for granted, the lawyer is taught that people have multifarious goals, so that he must listen carefully and defer. He is the client's tool—her "hired gun." She wants to be respected and heeded—not tended to.

Lawyers and doctors may also be different kinds of people. That is, different character types may be drawn into the different professions. Doctors may be both more caring and more authoritarian, whereas lawyers may be both more aggressive and more respectful of people. Whatever accounts for this general difference in orientation, it seems clear that the difference exists.

Or does it? Is it simply a caricature to say that doctors value well-being over autonomy and lawyers value autonomy over well-being? There is some truth to the claim, as I will show, but it is certainly not the whole truth. The history of medical practice suggests limited concern for the patient's right to decide his own fate. The Hippocratic Oath makes no mention of informed consent—the patient's prime exercise of autonomy—even for nonpsychiatric patients. Historically, although consent to treatment was necessary, no effort was made to inform patients. Even then, consent to one procedure was often taken as authorization for others. Lawyers fought for a right to *informed* consent, yet doctors still often invoke exceptions to the doctrine in order to serve patients' well-being more than their autonomy. (Consider, for example, the notion of therapeutic privilege.) Competent patients at times have been bullied into treatment, as well as misinformed of their right to refuse procedures and to leave a hospital against medical advice. Doctors had theories justifying their paternalism, of course, but that they sacrificed autonomy to well-being is clear.

The traditional medical posture with respect to psychiatric patients is even more stark. Psychiatric patients not only had no right to informed consent but also had no right to *bare* consent or refusal. It was all up to the doctor. The theory was that their judgment was too impaired for them to make decisions in their own best interests and that doctors could be trusted to make judgments for them. Hospitalization authorized any and all treatment.

The legal landscape of medical practice has changed today, but old habits die hard. Some doctors still resist informing even competent patients to some extent—always on grounds of beneficence—and many believe that mental patients should not be entrusted with decisions about their own care. Consider that in many if not all relevant lawsuits, the American Psychiatric Association has filed an amicus brief opposing the right of competent psychiatric patients to refuse treatment. Thus, doctors have fought to preserve the old regime, which values well-being more than autonomy. Similarly, doctors have been known to manipulate laws to serve this end; thus they are quick to read a situation as an emergency, so justifying forced treatment. Anecdotal evidence abounds that some doctors simply violate laws they do not like. They may use coercive mechanisms to get patients to "consent" to interventions. And they certainly complain among themselves about the new regime. All these behaviors suggest that, despite laws designed to foster autonomy, doctors remain committed to an ethos that prefers well-being to autonomy.

What about lawyers? Is there any evidence that they value autonomy more than well-being? According to lawyers' code of professional ethics, their fundamental duty is to advocate what the client wants, not what the lawyer thinks he needs. Lawyers do counsel clients as to what they think best, but ultimately they defer to the clients' judgment. Even with clients having a disability, the code is very committed to the value of autonomy. Lawyers must continue to respect and consult the client as much as possible. They must also be mindful of the dilemma posed by the need to appoint a guardian, possibly prejudicing the client's interests and subjecting him to considerable stigma and humiliation.

Most lawyers agree that in the civil commitment context in particular the lawyer should vigorously advocate for what the client wants. He should not prejudge the case. There are enough people looking after the client's presumed interests. And so the client is entitled to someone who will advocate for *him*, showing him the respect of being a fully human agent who is worthy of being listened to. Indeed, so ingrained is the lawyer's commitment to not second-guessing what is best for the client that there is considerable legal literature advocating that lawyers should do what the client wants even when the client is a child and so less than fully competent. That is simply the lawyer's role. Nor do lawyers finesse the issue, as many mental health professionals do, by deciding that they know better than the client what he truly wants. He wants what he says he wants.

In addition to their professional commitment to vigorous advocacy in the attorney-client relationship, lawyers are frequently engaged in projects that strengthen protections of the individual against others who are more powerful. Laws equalize people no less than they contain the power of the state. And so lawyers are committed to developing and defending rights—essentially trumps against the interests of the majority. Once again, individual freedom prevails over best interests.

There are, then, reasons for crediting the claim that, when speaking plainly, doctors value well-being more than autonomy and lawyers value autonomy more than well-being. Their training, professional roles, and ideology predispose them to take their respective positions. Doctors value well-being perhaps because, as they might put it, what else matters? If you don't have your health, such things as dignity matter very little. Autonomy may be nice when it contributes to well-being, for example, but when there is a conflict, autonomy must yield. Indeed, as studies of patient deference to their physicians show, autonomy may be a rather mythical concept anyway; and patients give lots of evidence that they do not much value it even if it is real.

Lawyers, on the other hand, value autonomy because of a real mistrust of power and a skepticism about the ability of others to determine what is best for the individual. The powerful at best will seek to re-create themselves and impose on others their conception of the good life. But their conception may not sit well with the individual himself, so that valuing autonomy will serve his well-being as he conceives it. And who are we to say his conception is wrong? Moreover, the lawyer may value autonomy because he counts dignity and self-respect among the most important components of the good life. What good is health if one is in a demeaned and degraded state?

But is it not too simple to brush the medical and legal professions with such broad strokes? Indeed, there is evidence that doctors no less than lawyers feel considerable ambivalence about their professional commitments. Certainly, individual doctors and lawyers may do so. But perhaps even the professions as a whole do. Consider that in the new legal landscape doctors have made accommodations. Current medical ethics codes include a right of informed consent, even for many psychiatric patients. Medical students are now socialized to obtain informed consent, and writings even suggest that doing so serves medical goals by strengthening the therapeutic alliance.

There is anecdotal evidence of individual doctors in acute care psychiatric facilities supporting patients' autonomy. For example, one treatment team supported the right of a psychiatric patient to be treated with ECT despite their judgment of its inefficacy in his type of case; his experience that the treatment had helped him in the past was enough. Another therapist supported his patient's struggles to refuse medication, because he believed that the patient needed to come to terms with this difficult issue in his own time and in his own way.

Scholarly mental health writings explore the importance of autonomy not only in terms of its treatment benefits—obviously a medical concern—but also in terms of its dignity benefits. Indeed, some forms of therapy are explicitly conceptualized as being about patient empowerment—about increasing patients' sense of authority over themselves and their independence. Not only individual practitioners, then, but the mental health profession as a whole has come to value autonomy. It is simply a caricature to suggest that mental health professionals will always choose patient well-being despite any costs to autonomy.

Are lawyers, individually and as a profession, similarly ambivalent about the pre-eminence of autonomy over well-being? Clearly the answer is yes. Current ethics codes, as we have seen, try to accommodate the special situation of the client with a disability. Even though they mandate continued consultation and respect, they do allow at times that the client's wishes be overridden. The lawyer is not always just a mouthpiece.

Similarly, many lawyers do not support protecting the liberty of psychiatric patients, and even mental health lawyers are often conflicted about representing the wishes of clearly disturbed clients; they report being relieved when their clients do not prevail and often take subtle actions to undermine their clients' cases. Mental health lawyers who would never dream of subverting their patients' efforts to obtain liberty may refuse to advocate for a client who wants *less* liberty—for example, to go from a nursing home to a hospital. These lawyers substitute *their* judgment about what a self-respecting mental patient should want for the patient's. Thus one mental health lawyer refused to advocate for a group of patients who wished to ensure that the Massachusetts Mental Health Center be kept open; indeed, he refused even to suggest referrals. By such actions lawyers reveal that they do not always believe that the client knows best. They do not always wish to support his autonomy. They may have different values than do doctors—liberty rather than health—but, like doctors, they privilege their judgment over the client's.

In addition, scholarly legal writers are often very concerned about well-being rather than autonomy. A whole new school of mental health law called therapeutic jurisprudence takes as its task the evaluation of legal rules in terms of their therapeutic benefits or detriments. Although these values are conceded to be not the only values, they are deemed extremely important. Further, despite the law's professed commitment to liberty, our very statutes express extreme ambivalence about autonomy and well-being. Often, as we will see, our laws are an uneasy compromise among many values, particularly in the mental health context. It is just too simple to say that the legal profession unreservedly places autonomy above well-being.

Finally, of course, I have simplified matters by speaking as if the mental health and legal professions were monolithic, with everyone speaking in the same voice. Not only are there important differences among individual practitioners, there are also important differences among people in different schools. Psychoanalysts may have different views than do behavior therapists. And certainly psychologists and social workers may have different views than do medical doctors, on whom I have focused. For instance, the American Psychological Association files amicus briefs *supporting* the right of competent psychiatric patients to refuse treatment. The same point is true of lawyers in different roles and of scholars of different persuasions. Communitarians, for instance, are much less concerned about autonomy and much more concerned about community than is the typical legal academic. Generalizations, as always, need qualifications.

All this said, it remains true that, as a gross generalization, the typical mental health professional would support forced treatment in Nancy's case and less ambiguous cases and the typical mental health lawyer would support the right to refuse in her case as well as in less ambiguous scenarios. Each makes judgments about Nancy, about the typical patient, and about the importance of a general policy over the run of cases. Each position has virtues. It is important that lawyers and mental health professionals be able to come to see the attractiveness of the others' position. These are very hard cases. That is what this book is about.

What happened in Nancy's case? Nancy was examined in a hearing called to judge her competency to refuse treatment. The psychiatrist relayed the facts recounted above: Nancy was behaving oddly, her family reported a history of troubled behavior, and she admitted to hearing voices. On examination by the state's attorney—the *state's* attorney—it emerged that, by "hearing voices" Nancy seemed to mean she had internal conversations with herself about issues she was facing. Those were her voices. Although one can never be sure, it seemed that by "voices" Nancy was referring to what other people would call thoughts. Nancy was permitted to decline treatment. Perhaps a mistake was made by the psychiatrists, and Nancy was not mentally ill. Or perhaps she *was* ill and would now decline and deteriorate. These cases are often hard because we cannot predict the future. Part of the point of this book is that they are often hard even when we can.

MENTAL ILLNESS:

MAKING MYTHS OR GENUINE DISORDERS?

No discussion of whether mental illness is real could occur without mention of Thomas Szasz, whose *Myth of Mental Illness* (1974) set the tone of the debate over mental illness for years.[1] At the time of his first writing, there was considerable scholarship responding to his views.[2] Even today, when the biological view of mental illness is clearly in the ascendancy, scholars continue to respond to Szasz, some defending and some critiquing his work, and some using his ideas as a launching point for a discussion of the controversies surrounding mental illness.[3]

Law students in the seventies were said to give Szasz rave reviews. All were believers: there was no such thing as mental illness. Today, law students tend to take the opposite position. *Of course* mental illness exists. We see it on our streets every day. New brain research is showing the biological bases of these devastating afflictions. How could anyone ever deny that mental illness is real?

Because Szasz's work is so prominent in this debate, I shall have a few brief things to say about him before moving to a fresh exploration of the issues. Szasz's attack on the concept of mental illness proceeds on two fronts: his critique is both ideological and conceptual. The ideological critique is somewhat based on the conceptual—if there is no such thing as mental illness, we shouldn't civilly commit the mentally ill and we shouldn't excuse them for their crimes. But his ideological critique also stands on its own. There may be normative reasons why we shouldn't commit people even if there is such a thing as mental illness.

Some of the ideological claims Szasz makes are beyond reproach. For instance, mental illness ascriptions are often used to diminish people. This is a clear abuse. And we are often guilty of medicalizing ordinary human conflict, when what we should do is work hard to get along better. The rest of this book addresses many of the normative issues involving the mentally ill that Szasz addresses—for example, when we should commit and when we should force treatment. This chapter addresses the conceptual issue of whether the predicate for such state action—the person's mental illness—is a concept that makes sense and can withstand hard scrutiny.

In this chapter I address Szasz's prime conceptual argument: illnesses are physiologically based and mental illnesses aren't. If it should turn out that they are, then they would no longer be mental illnesses; they would be physical illnesses under the jurisdiction of neurology.

There are at least two responses to this argument. First, we could concede that illnesses should be physiologically based but assert that we have reason to think that mental illnesses are so as well. Much more so than when Szasz first wrote, most psychiatrists now think that mental illnesses involve some kind of biochemical or structural abnormality. For instance, schizophrenia involves faulty dopamine processing. Indeed, it is commonly believed today that all mental events are grounded in biological events, so it would be surprising if mental illnesses didn't involve some biological anomaly.

But what of Szasz's claim that, once the defects were discovered, mental illnesses would no longer be mental illnesses, in the domain of psychiatrists, but physical illnesses, in the domain of neurologists? This move is somewhat implausible. There is good reason to say that physiological defects that disrupt higher mental functions such as perception, belief formation, and affect regulation are in the purview of psychiatrists. Indeed, organic brain syndrome and mental retardation are clearly physical yet are considered mental illnesses and treated in psychiatric hospitals and hospitals for the mentally retarded. (Note the word: *mentally* retarded.)

There is also, however, a wholly different response to Szasz: to deny that illness involves some physical lesion or defect. According to this view, it is of course conceded that mental symptoms are grounded biologically, just as a desire to watch a movie is, but the *meaning* of illnesses is suffering disability or distress as a result of some internal condition. (The latter clause is necessary because one can suffer disability or distress as a result of economic conditions, others' actions toward one, and so on—and we wouldn't call these illnesses.) This definition does face some hard cases: Why isn't mourning a mental illness? Why isn't holding fanatic religious beliefs a mental illness?

Both of these moves, however, have problems, as we shall see. For instance, some behaviors thought to be illnesses today are not thought to have a biological basis, and in any case the hope for biological grounding is just that—a hope. On the other tack, some conditions involving increased disability and suffering are not illnesses and some that do not involve these things are illnesses.

Below, in teasing out the difficulties surrounding the concept of mental illness afresh, I bring out the difficulties in all the moves that can be made to respond to Szasz and others of his ilk. One of Szasz's most troubling arguments is that, whereas physical illnesses involve a deviation from a biological, anatomical norm, mental illnesses involve a deviation from a social, ethical norm.

If it is hard to distinguish mental illness from bare deviancy, this is a serious problem because our society is committed to principles of freedom and autonomy, including the freedom to live according to one's own lights, even if that means living unconventionally. Our commitment to autonomy rests on a presumption that people know their own best interests—they know themselves best and care about themselves most—and that, even if they do not, interference with life choices is a grave insult to human dignity. But if certain choices in themselves lead to a label of mental illness with all its stigmatizing consequences, we are threatening our commitment to liberty and autonomy.[4]

In what follows I present five vignettes to illustrate some of these problems—vignettes that occur in one of the leading mental health law texts and that I present to my students. I raise questions typically asked of the students that are intended to focus the problem, particularly the problem of distinguishing unconventionality from mental illness. After that, I discuss in more detail some of the themes that emerge from the vignettes; I consider whether mental illness and health are on a continuum; I examine some of the factors that may be invoked in the attempt to distinguish mental illness from unconventionality; and I suggest why we should retain a concept of mental illness notwithstanding all the problems. I do not expect to *solve* any problems here but simply to explore some of the complexities that must be addressed in an effort to deal with the problems.

John works at a 7-11; he is very quiet. One of his co-workers discovers that, each day after work, John spends several hours in the closet. When questioned about this, John says: "I've been doing it for three or four months, you know, it's where my mother used to put me." When asked what he does there, he explains: "I'm talking with Martians. They left me here to teach Earthlings about Mars. I'm also a rock star you know, but I'm getting smaller every day and pretty soon you won't be able to see me."

Sam wants to set the world record for number of days on top of a flag pole. At the present time, he has been on a platform on top of a pole for 33 days. Although he is malnourished and dizzy from lack of food and sleep, he says he will not come down until he has stayed on the pole a total of 73 days, which will be a new record.

Mary, a lawyer, says she feels hopeless and worthless. When asked why, she says she is single, has no good friends and no family, and thinks her work is meaningless. She is barely able to go to the office in the morning and in the evening she goes straight home, watches TV and falls asleep by 8 P.M. She cries frequently and sometimes wishes she were dead. She resists any attempt to "cheer her up" or get her involved socially.

Cecilia goes to all-night worship at her fundamentalist church. During the service she claims to hear voices talking to her, often speaks in tongues, and occasionally behaves in a wild way so that others have to restrain her. The monthly meetings are the only times she acts like this.

Sarah is 21 and living with her parents. She says she has no idea what she wants to do with her life. She has been put on probation for shoplifting. She will hole up in her room with piles of junk food for days. When her mother or father tries to talk to her, Sarah often explodes with anger and usually retreats to her room. Recently, she has taken to sticking safety pins in her skin and letting them hang. (Reisner and Slobogin 1990, 329–30)

I would suggest that law students typically want to see John as definitely mentally ill, Mary as troubled and possibly mentally ill, and the other three as clearly not ill. Mental health professionals, on the other hand, could in some circumstances conceive of all of these people as mentally ill, although with Sam, on certain assumptions, this claim would be somewhat of a stretch.

If we press ourselves, however, for the most part we will find that there is little basis for saying that any of these people is mentally ill in a way that turns on something other than their deviancy or unconventionality. And if we can't distinguish mental illness from plain unconventionality, that is problematic (as we will also see below). In what follows I press questions about each case without necessarily providing any answers. The questions are meant to bring out the difficulties in making the required distinctions.

JOHN

Consider, first, John. At first glance, John seems to have some kind of psychotic disorder, although he is managing to hold down a job and to socialize with others to some extent. But let us change the facts a little, taking each of John's unusual behaviors in turn to see if each, individually, would be enough to warrant a diagnosis of mental illness.

Suppose John's only symptom were that he had been spending several hours a day in the closet for several months, explaining that "it's where my mother used to put me." Would this be enough to call him mentally ill? Sitting in a closet several hours a day is strange. But perhaps John simply has unusual preferences. Do people who keep their curtains closed all day have a mental illness?

One could say that it matters what John *does* in the closet. For example, perhaps he meditates or works on math problems in his head. One of my colleagues, for example, retires to a small, bare shed every night for several hours to try to remove distractions so that he can get some writing done. Yet who are we to judge what John does in the closet any more than we should judge his simply going to the closet? Why doesn't *he* get to decide whether to sit in the closet and what to do there?

Does it matter that John cites his mother's putting him in the closet as a reason for his behavior? Perhaps he is reenacting some early trauma. Perhaps his behavior has a compulsive quality. At the least he should want to be treated so that he can understand *why* he feels the need to keep doing this. Yet maybe he simply wants to. Many a surgeon, say, is reenacting his own frightening medical treatment when he was an ill child. That does not make surgeons mentally ill.

If John's closet behavior is equivocal, surely his unusual beliefs are a sound basis for deeming him mentally ill. But take his beliefs one at a time. Does believing that one is talking with Martians and has been assigned to teach Earthlings about Mars make one mentally ill? Many people in our society claim to have been abducted by aliens. Even more claim to have seen UFOs. Are all these people mentally ill? What about people who simply believe that there *are* such things as UFOs? What about people who believe that there is intelligent life on other planets? Simply life on other planets?

As these questions make clear, judging a belief to be a delusion is a very tricky business. When many people believe something, it's hard to maintain that the belief is a delusion. More important, when a belief could be *true* it is hard to do so. A number of the beliefs mentioned above are thought by many people to be quite probable—for example, that there is life on other planets. But even the ones that are less probable *could* be true. And what could be more unfortunate than calling mentally ill someone who has the truth when the rest of us are in darkness?

Of course, the problem is that anything *could* be true. The philosophers have long established that even our belief in a material world may be delusion. Given that there is no way *really* to establish any factual belief as true or false, beliefs become more or less conventional. False beliefs are deemed false by their very deviance.[5]

Indeed, mental health professionals probably have different standards than do ordinary people on this score; law students, for instance, typically don't want to call alien abduction beliefs crazy, but mental health professionals typically do.

In any case, even if John's beliefs about Martians could be within the realm of the normal, his beliefs about getting smaller each day surely could not—again, notwithstanding what the philosophers say. Even then, perhaps John is simply speaking metaphorically: he has diminished self-esteem each day. Then we might say not so much that he suffers an impairment in his ability to assess evidence as that he refuses to play by the ordinary rules of conversation. Once again, this would mean he was deviant, not ill.

SAM

On the face of it, Sam does not seem mentally ill, and most people, including mental health professionals, would deny that he was ill. Most people can understand doing something somewhat risky to earn a world record, although most people would probably not care enough to do it.

People can also want to do something risky for other understandable reasons. For example, people climb Mount Everest for the thrill of it or the satisfaction of mastery. Presumably for the love of the work Justice Robert Jackson continued to work as a Supreme Court justice despite his physicians' warnings that he would die unless he took it easy, and he did die. Doing hard, risky things for the sake of understandable goals is perfectly normal.

This case raises significant issues, nevertheless. First, although we invoke the understandability of Sam's and these other people's goals, who are we to judge their goals? Suppose Sam's reason for being on the flagpole was precisely *in order* to become dizzy and malnourished, or in order to fulfill a hankering for sleeping in an uncomfortable place and giving himself pain? Such a goal might be much less understandable to us, but why cannot a person want something we do not want? Thus cases like this raise in sharp relief the problem of prescribing conventional goals when we make judgments of mental illness.

But perhaps the reason Sam does not seem ill is not that his goal is understandable—if he wants discomfort, more power to him—but that his means of achieving it seem appropriate. John Hinckley thought Jodie Foster would come to him if he killed the president. Quite apart from the fact that his means were objectionable, they were not well suited to achieve his ends. No reasonable person would think that Foster would come to him because he had committed a murder. On the other hand, Sam's means of achieving a world record are perfectly appropriate, provided that the record was indeed less than seventy-three days. If Sam were staying on the flagpole so as to be elected president—his only claim to the office—we might not judge him so healthy.

But is this reasoning sound? First, consequences of one's actions are always unpredictable. If it is possible that there is not a material world, it was also possible that Jodie Foster would come to Hinckley as a result of his desperate act. Perhaps she would go mad too and think herself back on the set of *Taxi Driver*. Perhaps the world would go topsy-turvy, and something very unpredictable would happen. If this is right, Hinckley is entitled to judge the probabilities very differently than we would and still not be crazy. Perhaps more important, he is entitled to tolerate a much lower likelihood of his desired outcome happening than we would; that is simply a choice. (Of course, I do not mean in any of this to approve of Hinckley's act; it's just that it might be simply bad instead of mad.)

But if, in order to judge other people's sanity, we can't judge their goals or their likelihood of coming to pass, can we judge the reasonableness of the risks they are willing to incur? We don't have all the facts in Sam's case, but it would seem that dizziness and short-term malnourishment are not very grave risks. (On the other hand, malnourishment over a period of weeks and the risk of falling from dizziness *are* pretty serious.)

Do our judgments change as the risks increase? Suppose it were very probable that Sam would die if he remained on the flagpole for seventy-three days, and we knew that he had no intention of coming down? Suppose it were nearly certain that he would die? Analogously, imagine someone who built a machine in which he proposed to fly. What if the machine were one that almost certainly wouldn't work? What about a person who jumps off of a building and spreads his "wings" to fly?

These cases, too, are far from clear. Like the Supreme Court justice, people sometimes take serious risks to achieve desired ends. We might take a more favorable view of a hunger striker risking death for very noble goals than of Sam, who simply wants to achieve a trivial world record. But again, who are we to judge another's goals? We might think that if the risk becomes too high, the person is selecting means not well suited to achieve her ends. But we have seen the problems with judging the suitability of a person's means. We might think that willingness to risk or suffer serious injury or death *must* be madness. Was, then, Justice Jackson mad? Are all martyrs mad?

Does the concept of "bad judgment" have any purchasing power here? Perhaps if Sam is incurring serious risks, he is showing bad judgment, typically associated with mental illness. But there are problems with this association. Is it not possible, for example, to have poor judgment and *not* be mentally ill? How do we distinguish bad judgment that is a result of mental illness and bad judgment that is not? Moreover, we might think judgment bad because it misevaluates some state of affairs; but we have already seen that reality is something hard to grab hold of. Finally, to call judgment "bad" is already a value judgment, and the person we've evaluated might have different values.

But what about judgments that do not involve risks in this way? Take the case of Mike, who couldn't understand why his wife was upset when he pushed their child down and kicked her leg; he attributed her upset state to having watched a violent television show. Or take the case of David Harris in the movie *The Thin Blue Line,* who could not understand why a man would try to kill him, knowing he had a gun, after he had escaped with the man's wife and child; indeed, he called the man "crazy." Surely these people are so far from being able to appraise reality—their judgment is so skewed—that they are mentally ill.

Yet here again the case is not so clear. These people may have been dissembling their true understanding for a reason: Mike may not have wanted to admit—either publicly or to himself—that he had acted in a harmful way that upset his wife and hurt his child. Moreover, if they didn't understand, that may have been a function of lack of empathy or dullness of intellect. The apparent lack of understanding may have simply reflected a difference of values: Perhaps David Harris would never have risked *his* life to save someone else, so he couldn't imagine anyone else doing so. Finally, even if this was simple obtuseness, why does being obtuse make one ill? One is once again simply outside the norm.

To return to Sam: Suppose we could treat his desire to do what he is doing? Does that make it an illness? People can come to believe and do all sorts of things because of interventions—physical and psychological—into their lives, but that does not make their prior states pathological. Consider that, in fact, certain changes are undesirable. Patty Hearst, for example, was changed into a terrorist. Does that make being a college student heiress an illness? Hallucinogens make one hallucinate. Is the person who *cannot* see imaginary colors and figures impaired? Even when the changes are salutary, the prior condition might not be an illness; although certain pills can make one lose weight, surely not all conditions of being overweight are illnesses: some people are just plain greedy.

Sam, then, is probably not mentally ill. And it is hard to justify calling mentally ill people whose means, methods, and goals are even less understandable.

MARY

Most mental health professionals would conclude that Mary has some kind of depressive disorder, provided that her state lasts more than a minimal amount of time. When law students hear this vignette, however, they typically say that Mary is experiencing a perfectly normal reaction to a horrible situation—being a lawyer!

Although this reaction is given with tongue in cheek, it raises an interesting problem. Perhaps Mary's situation is as bad as she says it is, and what she is feeling is normal, appropriate sadness in response. If she felt guilt and grief because she had committed a crime harmful to others, would we judge her ill? Suppose she had a serious illness? Of course, we might think Mary's response to *her* situation excessive. But again, who are we to judge her values, according to which her life might be truly terrible?

Consider also that normal grieving—for a parent or spouse, say—shares many features with depression, yet it is not ordinarily judged an illness. Is that because we judge this the worst loss? Some might find an empty life worse. Or is it because most people suffer such reactions to such losses? But one wonders, first, about other understandable reactions that are not exempted from the illness category: how many people with terminal illnesses, for example, *don't* become depressed? And one wonders why being like everyone else makes one normal and being different makes one ill. Again, is illness just deviation from some norm? Are all different people ill?

If Mary's "mental illness" may be simply a normal response to a terrible situation, calling it a mental illness may prevent her from taking the steps that will improve her situation. She may go to therapy or take drugs instead of changing careers and looking for some friends. Indeed, she may spend the rest of her life in a thankless job with little social contact, able to function because of the therapy and drugs but not really fulfilled. And even if the drugs make her feel better, continuing as a lawyer may not be the best use of her life. Calling her mentally ill may deprive her of the best life she could have and deprive us of the contributions she could otherwise make. And it makes her dependent on the ministrations of others rather than empowering her to change her life in a direction she wants. Of course, sometimes therapy and drugs enable people to make these changes, but sometimes they don't. Herein lies the problem Szasz identified: medicalizing human conflict and misery.

But what about the possibility that therapy and medication can help such conditions? Once again, therapy and drugs can change all kinds of things—as can other interventions—without those things being illnesses.

Finally, law students often hesitate to call Mary mentally ill because most of them have spent at least some days feeling as she does. If everybody feels this way sometimes, how can it be a mental illness? In essence, the students are very uncomfortable with the stigmatizing consequences of calling someone mentally ill, especially when they identify with that person.

CECILIA

Most law students are very reluctant to label Cecilia mentally ill, but it is somewhat unclear how most mental health professionals would react. Hearing voices, speaking in tongues, and behaving in a wild way can all be symptoms of mental illness. What if the behavior included head-banging or hair-pulling? Are such behaviors symptoms of mental illness in this context? And what is the significance of context if they are not?

There is no evidence that Cecilia is disabled in her ordinary life. She acts in this way only once a month. Would the outcome change if she did this every night? Suppose she spent every waking hour doing it? Why would this not make her simply *very* religious? Are monks who take a vow of silence and spend their days in prayer mentally ill?

Cecilia is part of a recognized religious group; she is not alone in her beliefs and behavior. Does this matter? What if Cecilia's behavior were wild even for her church? In general, what is the significance, normatively, of sharing one's beliefs and behavior with others in a group? On the face of it, there can be clear group psychoses: witness the Branch Davidians. On the other hand, not sharing one's behavior with a group may simply make one very unusual—and one may also be *right:* the first person to believe the world was round was not crazy. Did Einstein's belief in his theory of relativity make *him* crazy? Indeed, the very idea that the more widely shared the belief, the less likely the holder is mentally ill, again trades on the role of conventionality. And we have seen how problematic that is.

The psychotic-like symptoms are troubling, but if hearing voices and seeing visions were always signs of mental illness, we would no doubt be forced to call all saints mentally ill. Indeed, we might have to call all religious people mentally ill, on the grounds that their belief in an all-powerful, all-benevolent God is supported by no evidence and thus meets the ordinary definition of delusion. If mental illness is hard to distinguish from unconventionality, it is equally hard to distinguish from religiosity, unconventional or conventional.

SARAH

Many if not most mental health professionals would say that Sarah probably suffers from borderline personality disorder. Law students, by contrast, tend to say she sounds like an ordinary teenager—like a lot of their friends when they were growing up, or even themselves.

Of course, Sarah is twenty-one. Is her behavior a form of mental illness at her age? On one hand, Sarah may just be slow developmentally—immature—but not suffering from an illness. On the other, perhaps being *this* slow developmentally *is* to suffer from an illness. Indeed, a teenager with this many problems perhaps has a mental illness.

Or does she? Perhaps Sarah simply has problems. She is impulsive and unmotivated to do anything with her life. She doesn't get along with her parents. She has conflicts and troubles in everyday life. This is someone with problems. But is it someone who is mentally ill? Once again, if we call her that, we may abrogate any distinction between illness and difficulties—even badness—and we may lessen people's responsibility to get their lives together through their own efforts. In the same way, we may be absolving Sarah's parents of responsibility for being unhelpful parents (assuming they are). She may be reacting appropriately to very unpleasant circumstances.

But what about sticking safety pins in her skin? Is that not an unequivocal sign of mental illness? Even to that question we must say "it depends." A number of students have remarked that they did the same thing as youths: there is no pain or damage if one stays within the first layer of skin. Doing this is simply a mild lark—amusing, cool, like running one's finger quickly through a flame.

But suppose Sarah actually jabs the pin in so that it hurts? Would it matter if this were some ritual that was required in order to join a sorority? What about people who get tattoos? Surely they hurt no less than this. Getting tattoos and being initiated into fraternities are social, culturally sanctioned behaviors, but do we not want people to be able to be idiosyncratic?

Suppose Sarah engaged in really serious self-violence such as cutting off her hand. When asked about this, suppose she says, "It's my body, and I can do whatever I wish with it." Is really serious self-harming behavior always a sign of mental illness? Surely not: we do not assume that everyone who kills himself is mentally ill. One's life may be so pain-filled—and likely to end so soon anyway—that suicide seems an understandable choice. And if killing oneself needn't be a sign of mental illness, then serious self-harm would not be.

I will return to the question of self-harming behaviors in chapter 3. For now we can say, perhaps, that self-harm is not an unequivocal sign of mental illness. But is this so? The understandable suicide is both *understandable*—ordinary people can identify with the reasoning of the suicide and can imagine doing it themselves—and it is certain to accomplish the person's ends: the alleviation of his suffering.

But cutting one's hand off seems to be neither of these. Yet are we not once again imposing our values on the person? Given her values, her behavior may be completely understandable. Perhaps Sarah likes pain. Perhaps she feels that the act is a just response to her shoplifting. Similarly, judging the likelihood that her act will achieve her ends runs into the same difficulties we saw in judging means earlier: conventional understandings may be wrong, and she is entitled to tolerate any degree of likelihood that her means will be effective that she wishes to tolerate.

In short, classifying Sarah as mentally ill presents as many problems as do the other cases—perhaps even more, because her behavior, though maladaptive, is common and may be seen in large measure as a matter of choice.

• • •

These vignettes underscore many of the problems connected with the concept of mental illness.[6] I raise three issues connected with this exercise and then discuss why we should be so concerned about the difficulties of distinguishing mental illness from unconventionality, problems related to considering illness and normality as being on a continuum, and ways we could perhaps cope with the problem of distinguishing illness and unconventionality.

First, note that the vignettes do not give many facts. A mental health professional making a diagnosis would have many more at her disposal. Sitting in a closet several hours a day might be a sign of mental illness in one person, a sign of unique preferences in another; we would need to know more about these people in order to decide. So the fact that we can say different things about all these vignettes may simply be a function of the paucity of information provided.

Yet I am not convinced that knowing more facts would solve the problems I have identified in discussing these vignettes. Many of the issues identified remain contentious even with all the facts in the world. Take, for example, Sarah. Suppose that, along with a history of early childhood abuse, she had a long history of similarly impulsive, angry, self-mutilating behavior—indeed, that she met *all* the symptoms of Borderline Personality Disorder (BPD) in the *DSM-IV-TR*.[7] Most mental health professionals would then feel quite comfortable making a diagnosis of borderline personality disorder. Yet many members of the public who do not accept the mental health profession's worldview would still see simply a person with problems making unfortunate choices. All the difficulties of distinguishing mere problems in living or, worse, eccentricity from mental illness would remain, no matter how elaborate the factual picture. This should be clear from the discussion; every move that was made for individual symptoms could be made for an entire package of symptoms.

Second, when asking whether any of these five individuals is mentally ill, we should really ask a further question: "Mentally ill for what purpose?" Mental illness (like almost everything else) is not something that has an independent essence; different contexts may call for different judgments. Thus we might be willing to say that Mary is mentally ill for purposes of her friends advising that she seek treatment, but not for purposes of institutionalizing her against her will. By contrast, John might be regarded as mentally ill for purposes of forcing treatment on him. And Sarah might be mentally ill for purposes of a research protocol involving classification schemes but not for purposes of treatment; we might want to encourage her to take responsibility for her life instead of becoming dependent on a therapist. Context is everything.

Third, people's willingness to apply the "mentally ill" label may depend on their appreciation of the consequences, intended and unintended, that follow from the application. Law students—like members of the general public—are especially sensitive to the stigmatizing consequences of calling someone mentally ill: his liberty may be taken away, he may suffer job discrimination, he may be treated as subhuman. At the least he will be scorned and humiliated. Such sensitivity explains their reluctance to call Mary mentally ill: what a horrible thing to say about someone with whom we identify.

Another unwanted consequence of such a diagnosis, as noted, is that the person so labeled may abdicate responsibility for his problems and come simply to depend on his treaters—or on a pill. In a society increasingly alarmed by the excuses people make, there may be fear that the "mentally ill" label may become just another rationale for failure to live up to one's responsibility.

Mental health professionals, by contrast, are socialized into appreciating the benefits of a label of mental illness. A person who has been properly diagnosed can be properly treated. True, there is stigma. But surely the remedy is public education, not leaving a person to suffer. Much more afraid of a false negative than a false positive, mental health professionals will see illness where the public sees health, because they see mental health interventions as entirely benign. That's how they've been trained.

Although my examples are somewhat incomplete, my question somewhat misleading, and people's approach to answering the question complicated by a number of factors, there is a real problem in distinguishing mental illness from simple unconventionality or eccentricity. We saw above why this is an important problem. That the issue is deviancy is clear from the case of religion. It is impossible to distinguish religious beliefs from delusions using all ordinary criteria, yet no one wants to call religious people mad. Of course, the beliefs may well be true—I do not deny that they are—but so may "ordinary" delusions. Presumably we don't call the religious mad because so many people share the views—they are *not* deviant.

Assuming that we can give content to the concept of mental illness apart from deviance, there is another problem: many of the thoughts, feelings, and behaviors characteristic of mentally ill people are also experienced by people we would call mentally healthy. For example, a desperately ill person may consent to participate in nontherapeutic research secretly believing—even though he has been told otherwise—that the intervention being researched will help him. Another patient may unconsciously believe that his surgeon is omnipotent and will protect him from all harm. These beliefs may be said to be delusions, albeit unconscious, but everybody has *some* distorted beliefs. What difference does their unconsciousness make? Why are these people not showing symptoms of mental illness? More typical examples include dreams, daydreams, and reveries. In a sense, these are mini-psychoses. Why are we all not psychotic at night, when we dream? Finally, we all show pockets of loose thinking or bad judgment; are we all, then, mentally ill?

One might respond that the difference between the truly mentally ill and the mentally healthy person is flexibility in moving back and forth between primary process thinking and secondary process thinking. (Primary process thinking is unconscious-driven—illogical, magical— whereas secondary process thinking is logical, organized, and reality-oriented. See Kaplan and Sadock 1998.) The person in a reverie can snap out of it when the phone rings. The dreamer can awaken in an emergency and often will tell himself he is dreaming if things become too frightening. Great poets and artists may have more access to primary process thinking than does the average person, but they, too, can switch it off. The mentally ill person, by contrast, is "stuck" in his primary process way of thinking; he can't get out of it.

But even this is a matter of degree. There are mentally healthy people who spend considerable periods daydreaming. And it is well known that some mentally ill people can snap out of it if need be: very deteriorated catatonic schizophrenics will exit a hospital ward when there is a fire on the ward. Similarly, many patients are able to shift from crazy ways of thinking and talking to sane ways if there is a need to do so. The difference between the healthy and the ill in terms of flexibility of movement between these modes of thinking is clearly one of degree.

This observation suggests a point that complicates matters yet further: mentally healthy people often have pockets of "psychosis," and mentally ill people often have pockets of sanity. Moreover, they can be quite sane in many areas of their lives. Mentally ill people whose illnesses are relatively isolated from other aspects of their lives can function normally in a wide range of arenas; only if the specific area of their madness is triggered will they appear at all unwell. They can work at high-level jobs, have families and friends, and be quite happy. Even people whose illnesses affect more of their functioning—are more global—can have long periods of remission in which they function highly. And globally affected people may appear perfectly sane; while feeling globally crazy, they can keep it under wraps, as it were, and appear perfectly normal. Mentally ill people can lead full, rich, busy lives.

What is the significance of all this? If mentally healthy people share qualities of mentally ill people and vice versa, then these are not two different categories. Mental health and mental illness must at least be on a continuum, and distinguishing them presents significant problems. Even if psychosis is distinguishable from unconventionality, everybody is a little psychotic, and locating the line between health and illness becomes a serious problem. We saw above one effort to do so—trading on the presumed flexibility the healthy have in detaching from the psychotic processes in them—but that, too, was at best a matter of degree.

Furthermore, qualities that appear psychotic or mentally ill can be quite adaptive. Is "workaholism" a mental illness? Gene Sperling, who served as President Clinton's assistant for economic policy, was said in the *New York Times* to have one problem: he is a workaholic. But is it really a problem to be a workaholic if it lands you a high-level government position in your thirties? And what about FBI agents who have higher-than-normal suspiciousness on paranoia indexes? Surely their "pathological" trait is quite adaptive in this context.

What are we to make of the fact that putative signs of mental illness can actually be quite adaptive? Does this mean that context is everything—that someone who is ill in one culture could be completely healthy in another? The idea that the same traits could be signs of illness in one context and signs of health in another is at least troubling. In short, the concept of mental illness presents us with considerable challenges.

To me, the most significant is the problem of distinguishing mental illness from mere unconventionality: once again, mentally ill people are commonly said to be out of touch with reality, but who gets to say what reality is? Similarly, many people we do not want to call mentally ill have unusual ideas. How then do we distinguish the mentally healthy from the mentally ill?

Let us make one final effort to find ways to distinguish mental illness from unconventionality. One reason for thinking them different, as we have seen, is that there is evidence that mental illness has a biological basis. Yet we have also seen that everything has a biological basis—certain neurons are firing when someone says something eccentric—and many things we want to call illnesses do not involve, say, observable lesions. If all illnesses involve biological defects, how does one draw the line between a defect and a difference? Presumably, eccentric beliefs involve eccentric biological processes. Finally, it is far from clear that the meaning of illness involves reference to something biological rather than to such things as distress and disability.

A second possibility we have also considered: illnesses are conditions that respond to treatment. But many things we want to call illnesses are untreatable today. And many things that respond to interventions—we can call them "treatments"—are clearly not illnesses. This idea returns us to an earlier point: that the purpose in designating something an illness matters. For purposes of advising consultation with a certain kind of doctor, we can say that one has an illness if it is treatable by that kind of doctor. But treatability is not a good criterion for illness. Presumably, eccentricity can be changed, too.

Third, we have also seen that the uniqueness of a person's beliefs is not a good basis for calling him mentally ill. Since we are trying to distinguish idiosyncrasy—of which uniqueness is the limit—from illness, this should come as no surprise. Geniuses and discoverers have unique views, and there are many instances of group psychosis. The commonness of a person's beliefs, although suggestive on the question of mental illness, does not provide a good criterion.

Fourth, what about voluntariness or lack of control as a criterion? The eccentric person chooses her beliefs and lifestyle, whereas the ill person has them thrust upon him. But we have already seen, in the discussion of a person's flexibility in moving from primary to secondary process, that healthy people often lack a measure of control and ill people often have it. Indeed, given the prevalence of the view that all behavior is multidetermined, it may be that *no* behavior is truly chosen. Not only the eccentric person but also the completely conventional person has forces and factors in her background that lead her to be as she is. Determinism is quite likely to be true.[8]

Fifth, as we have seen, people often invoke, in connection with the concept of illness, the idea of distress or disability, including an increased likelihood of dying. But distress is not a good criterion. The eccentric person might be most distressed by his eccentricity. The ill person's illness could be completely ego syntonic; he might like it. Personality-disordered people, for example, often make life miserable for others but are perfectly content to be as they are—they think they have no problems. Manic people often like the highs. Conversely, ordinary no less than eccentric people might be in a state of distress—even, perhaps, chronic distress—without being ill. The person who unavoidably lives in terrible conditions might be most unhappy but clearly not ill.

Perhaps mentally ill people are either distressed *or* disabled: that would take care of the personality-disordered person. But some people we would like to call mentally ill are neither, for example, the personality-disordered person who is high-functioning. Or someone who often hears an isolated voice but is neither distressed nor at all impaired in his functioning. Conversely, some people who are mentally healthy are both, for instance, the person who is distressed about being an underachiever. (He might have an illness, but he might not.)

Indeed, the concept of disability, on reflection, is actually quite problematic, for what is an ability and what is a disability depends on one's values. Most people couldn't spend weeks in bed for no reason. Does a person who does this have a "skill" or a "disability"? If one values productivity and getting things done, he has a disability. If one values rest and quiet—more pointedly, *non*productivity—he has a skill. It will be obvious now that the concept of disability does not allow us to escape from the quagmire of distinguishing illness from unconventionality, for the concept of disability is itself a convention-laden notion.

There is another problem: abilities and disabilities are also context-dependent in the sense that how society arranges itself can make a difference. A depressed person might be able to do his job if allowed an afternoon nap, just as a physically handicapped person is able to ride the bus if it is equipped with certain devices that enable him to board in a wheelchair. If this is so, and if a person has a "disability" precisely because of the majority's imposing certain constraints, then once again the concept of illness becomes hopelessly entangled with majoritarian norms.

But what about the idea of an illness causing a disability in the sense of putting one at a biological disadvantage—decreasing reproductivity, being likelier to lead to death and so on? Once again, there are conditions that do this which are not illnesses and illnesses that do not do this. Homosexuality leads to reduced reproductivity, and skydiving leads to an increased likelihood of death. Both, however, are choices, not illnesses. And some illnesses do not lead to lesser reproductivity and are not at all associated with an increased likelihood of death.

Moreover, values hopelessly infect our judgment. It is only if we value reproduction as well as life that diminishing these could be taken as a sign of illness. Of course, the overwhelming majority of people do value these things. But do we want to impose majoritarian norms on a person who deviates at the risk of causing him or her to suffer the harms that may come from a mental illness diagnosis, such as stigma and loss of liberty?

Our provisional conclusion must be that we cannot salvage the concept of mental illness as distinct from unconventionality by any of these means. But I suggest that there are a number of issues that temper the foregoing points and that we should not abandon the concept of mental illness. First, all we have really established is that it is hard—perhaps impossible—to provide necessary and sufficient conditions for the concept of mental illness. But philosophers have long known that it is difficult—perhaps impossible—to provide necessary and sufficient conditions for any but the simplest of concepts. Life is simply too complicated to package neatly. That should not lead us to abandon our concepts but merely to realize their complexity.

Second, I may have exacerbated this problem by considering criteria of mental illness one by one. With each criterion I noted the problem of under- and overexclusivity. But it may be that some combination of criteria does account for mental illness in an adequate way. For example, some mental illness may involve distress or disability, whereas other instances may involve involuntariness or lack of control. It is not likely, given the last point, that we will find a *perfect* set of criteria, but we may do better by considering combinations of criteria.

Third—and an instance of the first point—the concept of physical illness is perhaps almost as problematic as the concept of mental illness. Claims about physical illnesses involve deviations from some norm no less than claims about mental illnesses.[9] High blood pressure deviates from the norm of healthy blood pressure and puts one at a disadvantage.[10] There is perhaps more agreement about what is desirable and what is undesirable in the physical realm—that which leads to disability and death is undesirable. But, though widely held, these are still value judgments.

Indeed, certain physical illnesses have no functional, anatomical consequences and yet are still considered illnesses. Take the case of the person who is unusually short. Such a person might be treated with hormones. But, although being short may have social or economic consequences in our society, it has no *physical* consequences. It is simply a deviation from a norm, and for that very reason disadvantageous. Many physical handicaps are of this kind;[11] to the extent that they lead to disability, it is only because society adheres to the norm: the steps are too steep for someone outside it.

Still, however much physical illnesses involve normative judgments, there are important differences between physical and mental illnesses. First, as suggested, there is much more agreement about what are desirable norms—and why—in the physical than in the mental arena. Second, the norms in the mental arena dictate appropriate thoughts and behaviors. Legislating such behavior, so to speak, is a serious intrusion into something much more personal than one's anatomy. It is also an intrusion into an area in which people want to make personal choices without the threat of intervention or stigmatization. Restrictions of freedom matter more the more freedom one has, and one has more freedom over one's values and behaviors than over one's body. Ironically, Szasz's point that "mentally ill" behavior is something one does has some purchase here.

The idea, more specifically, is that mental illness judgments implicitly restrict the realm of behavior that is acceptable; the scope of physical illness judgments is much more narrow. One must conform to much more in the way of sanctioned behavior to avoid being labeled mentally ill than to avoid being labeled physically ill—when conformity is under one's control, in the case of the latter. Hence, imposing the label of mental illness is much more troubling if there is no good way to distinguish mental illness from mere difference.

Thus, there are important differences in this regard between physical and mental illnesses. First, as noted, although in the physical sphere value choices are involved, they are much more widely shared. Life is good and death is bad. In the mental sphere there is much more room for people to make different value choices, and therefore limiting their choices is a much greater affront to their autonomy. Second, physical anomalies are less subject to a person's control; people's freedom of choice is infringed less by a negative valuation; they don't have choice anyway. Third, the scope of possible negative valuations is much broader in the mental than in the physical realm. Potentially anything a person chooses or does could get him in trouble, so to speak. Once again, freedom of choice is potentially much more subject to restriction in the mental than in the physical sphere.

Despite these differences, it cannot be denied that physical illnesses also involve deviations from norms. Mental illness may involve more of the person, and more things under the control of the person, than physical illness, but it is really just a question of degree. If importing the notion of deviance from things we value is problematic, it is problematic for physical illnesses as well as mental ones. No one would therefore deny that these are illnesses or that they are real.

If the importation of values into our judgments is unavoidable, it is also probably not objectionable unless it touches on individual liberty and autonomy in a significant way. That is where the question "Mentally ill for what purpose?" is important. It is perhaps only when we confine someone involuntarily—literally infringe on his liberty as a result of his mental illness (deeming him mentally ill for *that* purpose)—that imposing our values becomes truly problematic. Thus, we aim to do such things only to people about whom there would be no disagreement—who are clearly and unequivocally ill. There may, on the other hand, be disagreement about someone a mental health professional would call borderline and law students would call difficult, but simply labeling someone mentally ill, and therefore visiting some stigma upon him, does not *really* prevent him from exercising any choice. Thus the political consequences of using a concept that involves importation of majority values are generally not grave.

It is possible, of course, to overstate this point. Is it worse, for example, to spend two weeks as an involuntary patient at a hospital or to lose one's job or housing because of stigma? The point, however, survives this cautionary statement: a simple negative valuation may not be all that problematic unless it has collateral consequences of import to the person. I reconstruct the nature of this argument in a little more detail below.

In all, then, that values infect our mental health judgments is not an overwhelming problem. Values probably affect most of our judgments about most things—including physical illness—yet we are not about to stop discoursing.

A third response to the problems raised concerning mental illness turns on the fact that we have hewn pretty closely to a rigorous skepticism about most things. All beliefs may or may not be true. The notion of an ability or a disability depends largely on our values. Values are simply a matter of individual preference. We have taken the posture, in other words, of the skeptical philosopher. But nobody lives that way in real life. Although we may not be able to prove the existence of the material world to Berkeley's satisfaction, we are all convinced that there is a world independent of our ideas. Certain beliefs—like John's that he is getting smaller every day and will soon disappear—just *have* to be false. And if one holds a belief so obviously false, one lacks an important ability—the ability to assess evidence—and is not merely unconventional.

Similarly, values—and judgments about abilities based on values—may be more than individual preferences. At the least there is very widespread agreement about some things. These include matters in the realm of mental health no less than physical health. Thus, valuing life, except in certain extreme circumstances, is widely shared. And who could value being unable to move more than being able to move? By contrast, valuing staring at a single tree all of one's life, say, is so idiosyncratic as perhaps to betray some fundamental failure in the ways one responds to things, and not just eccentricity—more like lacking a sense organ than like disliking chocolate.

At least in the case of beliefs, if not also in the case of values, once we take off our philosophers' hats, we can feel much more comfortable with the concept of mental illness. Since we all live in the world and not in our classrooms, we should be content with our practical understandings in practical realms—the realms in which mental illness judgments are made. (Indeed, the point can be made more strongly if we think that values are not merely conventions, for then psychiatric illness might be partially constituted by objective, absolute, or "critical morality." It may have a definition and set of criteria apart from deviations from convention.)

Fourth—and related to the point above about pragmatism—given our rough-and-ready understandings of the world, there are some people whom *everybody* (except perhaps Szasz) would conclude to be mentally ill. That is, there is widespread agreement, and has been through the ages, that certain forms of behavior betray an illness. Severe schizophrenia or manic depression, say, could not be mistaken for anything else. This is not to say that there are not many categories about which there would be disagreement—about which people comfortable with a mental illness paradigm would find a mental illness and those who are not would find simply problems in living or mere eccentricity. That there may be disagreement about some cases should not lead us to deny that a concept has *any* use.

Finally, I am persuaded that a concept of mental illness is useful and necessary because I have seen what is called mental illness at close range. Most people with serious mental illnesses seriously suffer. They are in pain. Not only are they distressed and disabled but they lack the ability to change by their own efforts. They need help—often medication—and receive help when they are treated. Having a concept of mental illness probably does more good in the world than abandoning the concept, notwithstanding that the concept is fuzzy at the edges, so that some people will be wrongly stigmatized and others wrongly limited in their freedoms. True, as a lawyer I have seen the suffering that such infringements of autonomy cause—that merely labeling someone as mentally ill causes. And we will see more of this in subsequent chapters. Yet as a mental health professional, I have also seen the profound suffering caused by mental illness and the relief that treatment can provide.

Before concluding, I would like to reconstruct briefly my argument in this chapter concerning values,[12] to draw together many of the points I have been making, and to set the stage for what follows: (1) Mental illness is a value-laden or convention-dependent concept. (2) Imposing values or conventions is especially problematic in mental health concepts because to escape the stigma or other negative consequences of being labeled mentally ill one must conform to social values and practices, thus restricting one's freedom. (3) To some extent, such restrictions are necessary in order for members of society to exist in coordination, and are therefore justified. (4) But restrictions that are unnecessary for coordination or justice, or substantial restrictions on liberty, stand in need of justification, and no satisfactory justification has yet been provided.

Although we should doff our philosophers' hats and embrace a concept of mental illness, that concept raises significant problems. Even more serious than the negative valuation are the consequences that a mental illness judgment sometimes allows us to visit on a person. I turn now to one very substantial limitation on liberty, namely, the context in which it is permissible involuntarily to confine someone in a mental hospital. When if ever is it permissible to do this, and what are the justifications we may offer for this practice?

CIVIL COMMITMENT:

HOW CIVIL?

Kenneth Donaldson was committed to the Florida State Hospital on January 3, 1957, after his father petitioned the court, complaining that his son was delusional. The county judge told Donaldson that he was being sent to the hospital for "a few weeks" to "take some of this new medication," after which, the judge said, he was certain that Donaldson would be "all right" and would "come back here." Donaldson was diagnosed as a paranoid schizophrenic at the hospital, and, despite making numerous requests to leave, was not discharged until almost fifteen years later, after filing suit in Federal District Court. Donaldson's requests for release were, in addition, supported by responsible persons—including a halfway house—willing to provide him with any care he might need.

Donaldson posed no danger to himself or others during or prior to his confinement. Indeed, one of the hospital doctors acknowledged that Donaldson could have earned his own living outside the hospital, as he had done for fourteen years before his commitment; and in fact immediately upon his release, he secured a responsible job in hotel administration. The hospital justified Donaldson's confinement on the grounds that he was mentally ill and in need of care and treatment.

The Supreme Court held that Donaldson's confinement was wrongful; it was not permissible to confine, without more, a nondangerous person who could survive safely in freedom on his own or with the help of willing and responsible family members or friends. There would be no more Kenneth Donaldsons. (O'Connor v. Donaldson, 493 F.2d 507 [5th Cir. 1974], 422 U.S. 63 [1975])

On October 28, 1987, members of Project HELP forcibly removed Joyce Brown, also known as Billie Boggs, from the place she had staked out on Second Avenue between 65th and 66th Streets and had her admitted involuntarily to Bellevue Hospital. As the New York trial court put it, the street was "her bedroom, her toilet, her living room." She hadn't always lived on the streets, having come from a middle-class home in New Jersey and worked as a secretary for more than ten years before her sister found it necessary to hospitalize her. After that she came to New York.

The hospital psychiatrists diagnosed Brown as a paranoid schizophrenic and said she was incapable of caring for herself, citing her tendency to run into oncoming traffic and the fact that she tore up or burned paper currency, as well as her hostility, aggressiveness, and abusive, obscene language, which they feared might provoke others to cause her harm.

Brown contested her hospitalization, and the New York Civil Liberties Union psychiatrists found her to be nonpsychotic, nondelusional, and logical, not tangential. Her destruction of money was a way of retaliating when the money was thrown at her insultingly. Jaywalking is common among New Yorkers, and she had never been hurt. Brown was not suicidal or homicidal—or in any way dangerous to herself or others.

The trial court found the state's evidence on Brown's mental state neither clear nor convincing. It also found that she was not dangerous to herself or others. She was also able to meet her essential needs of food, clothing, and shelter: "Joyce Brown has been on the street nearly a year. She has survived, she is physically fit. She may indeed be a professional in her lifestyle. . . . It cannot be reasoned that because Joyce Brown is homeless she is mentally ill. What must be proved is that because she is mentally ill she is incapable of providing herself with food, clothing and shelter. Yet, though homeless, she copes, she is fit, she survives" (In the Matter of the Retention of Billie Boggs, unreported trial opinion).

The appellate court reversed the disposition. The NYCLU doctors examined Brown after she had had time to reconstitute. It was "against the weight of the evidence" that her homelessness was the result not of her severe mental illness but of lack of housing for the poor. (Boggs v. New York City Health and Hospitals Corp., 523 N.Y.S.2d 71 [1987])

These vignettes give some sense of the terrible dilemmas we face when deciding whether to involuntarily hospitalize the mentally ill. For many decades the standard was whether the prospective patient was mentally ill and in need of care and treatment.[1] Such a standard allowed the fifteen-year hospitalization of Kenneth Donaldson. Since O'Connor v. Donaldson, the standard has generally been whether the patient is mentally ill and either dangerous to himself or others or "gravely disabled." (There are additional minor variations among the states, but this is the basic standard.)[2]

Under that standard, Kenneth Donaldson would not be civilly commit-table, and whether Joyce Brown would be is a close case, as can be seen by the division of the two courts on this question.

The subject of this chapter is what the standard governing civil com-mitment should be.[3] A central concern throughout is why and in what ways mentally ill people should be treated differently from other citizens. Ad-dressing this concern is a crucial part of justifying any standard we adopt. We do seem to treat the mentally ill and the non–mentally ill differ-ently—at least so the stated law says—and we need to be able to say why.

THE MENTALLY ILL VERSUS THE NON–MENTALLY ILL

The Current Standard   We treat the mentally ill and the non–mentally ill differently, at least on the books. Take the current civil commitment standard of "mentally ill and dangerous to self or others or gravely dis-abled." We generally do not confine people who are not mentally ill even when they are dangerous to themselves or others or unable to care for themselves.

We generally confine healthy people who are dangerous to others only *after* they have committed a crime. A person can be extremely dangerous, but until he acts there is nothing we can do about it under our current ju-risprudence. We respect people's choices and hope they will be deterred by the sanctions of the criminal law. Similarly, we recognize all too well the hazards of predicting violence; even a hardened criminal who has committed many violent crimes may desist when he is let out of prison this time.[4]

In addition, we generally permit healthy people to make choices dan-gerous to themselves without intervening in their lives. For example, we allow people—even people with lung cancer—to smoke, we allow people to have unsafe sex, we allow people to skydive. It is nowhere a crime to at-tempt or commit suicide.[5] It is black-letter law that a person may refuse treatment such as a blood transfusion that would certainly save his life and without which he would almost certainly die. Similarly, people may insist that life-sustaining treatment be withdrawn.[6] Finally, when people do not provide for their essential needs for food, clothing, and shelter as a result of a choice or poverty, we do not force help on them.

As we shall see, our commitment to permitting people to take self-harming and other-harming actions is somewhat tempered in certain situations—in ways that are both interesting and complicated—but it is at least the black-letter law that we do so.

Competence   What, then, is so special about mental illness that we do confine mentally ill but not mentally healthy people against their will when they are dangerous to others or to themselves or gravely disabled?[7] One obvious basis on which to treat mentally ill people differently is that they are more likely to be incompetent. Theory and reason suggest that incompetency is highly relevant to whether we intervene against people's wills. Only competently made choices deserve respect. Incompetent people are not in a position to decide: they cannot understand or evaluate information that is relevant to their choices or they cannot help choosing as they do. We do not denigrate autonomy values by denying respect to incompetently made choices.

Yet many mentally ill people are not incompetent.[8] Incompetency is a very low standard, and many if not most mentally ill people are competent in many if not most areas of their lives. If incompetency were to provide the rationale for civil commitment, we would have a very different standard for civil commitment.

Autonomy   The second basis for treating mentally ill people differently is that they are not fully autonomous. Different concepts of autonomy have been proposed.[9] Some are little different from "possessing competency," whereas others are quite robust. Autonomous choices must, for example, reflect one's considered judgment about the kind of person one is and would like to become. Alternatively, a fully autonomous person is true to her freely chosen values and preferences—authentic no less than unconstrained in some gross way.

Many mentally ill people are not fully autonomous. The problem with a robust autonomy standard is that many *non*–mentally ill people are also not fully autonomous, so that we cannot justify civil commitment of the dangerous mentally ill and not the dangerous non–mentally ill on this basis. Very few people, and very few choices of those people, meet a robust standard of autonomy.

Impairment   The third basis for treating mentally ill people differently is that, though generally not incompetent, they are generally quite impaired with respect to their abilities.[10] A significantly mentally ill person is likely to have impaired cognitive abilities; he may suffer from misperceptions, if not frank delusions, and his judgment may be wanting; he may be disorganized in his ability to think or to execute actions; he may have problems with controlling himself because his ego lacks a certain amount of integrity. Virtually everybody lacks full autonomy, but very few people are this impaired, and those who are, are usually mentally ill.

There are, however, counterweights. Impairment is a matter of degree, so where to draw the line will be a difficult question. Unless the line is drawn fairly low—in which case more than a trivial number of mentally ill people won't meet it—there's a risk that too many non–mentally ill people will meet it. And, even if the standard is fairly low, what about people who meet that standard but are not mentally ill? For example, people may be quite impaired as a result of low intelligence, inexperience, physical disabilities—even lack of love. Why should we not civilly commit them as well when they are dangerous?

Finally, the idea that we should not respect the choices of people who are impaired in their abilities is inconsistent with other areas of law. We do not, for example, excuse people for their crimes unless they meet a strict insanity test.[11] Nor do we forbid them to leave wills unless they meet a strict testamentary incapacity test.

Impairment, then, is not a sufficient basis for treating the mentally ill differently.

Different Persons   The fourth possible basis for treating mentally ill people differently is that they are not themselves when they act: mental illness makes them different persons. A shy, timid, reserved person, for example, might become outgoing, impulsive, even inappropriately seductive under the sway of a manic attack. Why should we respect his manic choices? They are his mental illness speaking, not himself. The mentally ill person who "chooses" to be dangerous is not the true self; should we let him impose his choices on the real person? Similarly, the mentally ill person who declines to go to the hospital for treatment may be a "person" whose character has been entirely distorted by mental illness; he's not the real person.[12]

This rationale makes some intuitive sense.[13] Take the most extreme case: a person whose personality has been altered by mental illness decides to kill herself. If she were not mentally ill—if her true personality were at the forefront—she would certainly not opt for this irrevocable course. Should we let someone choose to die when she has made the choice only because she has been transformed by mental illness?

Although plausible, the "different person" view is not without problems. First, merely to say someone is a different person is not to say which person to prefer. If someone is passive and compliant when mentally ill but a menace when sane, should we lock him up as non–mentally ill and dangerous to others as a result? He is, after all, a different person when non–mentally ill. Why should we prefer the healthy self to the ill self? If we say health is better, we are imposing our values and thereby attenuating our commitment to autonomy principles.

Second, many mentally ill people do change in being ill but do not become different people. Their values, preferences, likes, and dislikes remain the same. Physically ill people also change in being ill, but we would hardly deny that they were the same person.

Third, it is extremely difficult to determine when a change in preferences and so on is a result of the mental illness—that is, which preferences are the mental illness speaking. It is hard to determine what choices a non–mentally ill person's values would lead him to make—that is one reason we reserve the choice to him. How much harder under conditions of change, as when mental illness strikes; perhaps, for example, the person has simply changed his mind about an issue.

Fourth, people's values, preferences, likes, and dislikes may change as a result of things other than mental illness—for example, stress, exhaustion, religious conversion, or therapy. How, again, do we justify treating mental illness differently? Do we want to say that none of these later selves can speak for the earlier self? Moreover, whereas some of these changes can be permanent—a potential problem for the different self theory—some are also as temporary as mental illness can be.

Fifth, some mental illness is not temporary. The changes the person undergoes are permanent. He has a chronic illness and stable changes in personality. Although we could try to justify not listening to the unhealthy self if the healthy self is likely to return—notwithstanding the value problems mentioned above, we may feel comfortable taking the healthy self as the true self, authorized to make choices for the person—we cannot make this move if the unhealthy self has simply become the real self. Why can he not now choose for the person?

Sixth, it is something of a *façon de parler* to speak of a different self: mentally ill people do not literally become different selves by ordinary criteria of personal identity. Their bodies and their memories generally remain the same. This means that we are speaking of more or less of a change in a person. Then the question of where we draw the line becomes a problem. What change is enough before we say someone is a different person?

If all this is right, it is problematic to justify civilly committing the dangerous mentally ill and not the healthy on the basis that they are transformed by their illness into different people.

Heightened Dangerousness   The fifth possible basis for treating mentally ill people differently is that they are simply more likely to be dangerous than healthy people. But the jury is out on whether mentally ill people are indeed more dangerous than non–mentally ill people. Most of the evidence suggests that, with the exception of certain categories such as psychopathy, mentally ill people, when their illnesses are active, are only modestly more likely than the general public to be dangerous. And although mentally ill people, when they are symptomatic, are likelier to be suicidal than the general public, when a non–mentally ill person is suicidal, why should we not commit her?

The point is that if mentally ill people are more likely to be dangerous than non–mentally ill people, and if dangerousness is the issue, then more mentally ill people will be committed as dangerous. But this is not to say that we should commit all and only dangerous mentally ill people. Indeed, if increased likelihood of dangerousness is enough reason to commit the dangerous mentally ill, it should also be enough to commit the dangerous, youthful male, who is likelier to be violent than the general public–and much more so than the symptomatic mentally ill.

Perhaps the point is not that the mentally ill are more dangerous but that it is easier to predict their danger. Hence, if someone is mentally ill and apparently dangerous, he is likelier to be actually dangerous than someone who is not mentally ill and apparently dangerous. But predictions of dangerousness are notoriously difficult—studies have tended to show that two of three long-term predictions are wrong, although more recent studies are finding better predictive ability—and I have seen no evidence that these predictions are any more accurate as regards the mentally ill than the healthy. Indeed, they seem to be best in the case of people who have actually committed violence in the past, but we do not lock up violent offenders who have served their sentences on the basis that their future violence is especially easy to predict.[14]

Or perhaps the point is not that it is easier to predict the danger of the mentally ill but that the mentally ill are in fact more *unpredictable* and difficult to defend against, hence the public fears them more. But it is difficult to know what to make of this. If this means that the mentally ill surprise us more when they act dangerously but cause no greater or lesser injuries than others, it is not clear that this matters. Isn't the danger—and harm to which it leads—what counts, and not whether we can predict it? On the other hand, if, say, the mentally ill are as dangerous as others, but less predictably so, perhaps that means their victims are hurt more; but why do we not hear about more harm to victims at the hands of the mentally ill? Indeed, is it *true* that the mentally ill are more unpredictably dangerous, or is that just a myth or prejudice?

In short, stigma may be driving this argument. Even if it is not, it is difficult to know what to make of the argument, because it would appear that actual danger is more important than public concern about danger— which is not to deny that the latter is important, too. But when someone else's long-term liberty is at stake, is it important enough?

Suffering and Treatability   It is argued that mentally ill people are suffering and treatable; therefore dangerous mentally ill people are likely to benefit from confinement, whereas dangerous healthy people will be simply restricted and confined. The mentally ill, then, receive a quid pro quo for the relaxation of their right not to be confined on the basis of dangerousness unless they commit a crime.[15]

The problems with this rationale are, first, that some mentally ill people do not consider themselves to be suffering and indeed prefer the mentally ill state to what they regard as health. To them, being hospitalized confers not a benefit but an additional detriment. Second, some mentally ill people are not at all treatable, and many are treatable to only a modest degree. In addition, we generally do not require all people who are hospitalized to accept treatment, so they will not receive a quid pro quo of treatment and alleviation of suffering. Finally, physically ill people who are dangerous to themselves or others are generally not confined against their will even though they would receive a quid pro quo in the form of treatment, too, so why should mentally ill people be?

Perhaps the point, then, is that the mentally ill are likely to benefit from their treatment in part by becoming no longer dangerous. Society therefore benefits as well. This factor distinguishes the mentally ill from most dangerous physically ill people. It also means that we needn't confine them forever on this rationale, as would be necessary with some healthy dangerous people; we can make the mentally ill no longer dangerous and then release them.

Yet as we have already seen, some of the mentally ill are treatable only to a limited degree, and we may not be able to force the very treatment that will render people nondangerous. In addition, we could change other things about people that would render them less dangerous, violating people's civil liberties in furtherance of this end. We could, for instance, civilly confine poor youth until they are older and therefore less dangerous, but we wouldn't dream of doing that. There have to be other bases for restricting liberty than liking the way the changed person is changed.

Suggestions That Mental Illness Cuts the Other Way None of these rationales alone justifies civilly committing dangerous persons with mental illness but not the dangerous persons who are healthy. Does mental illness ever cut the other way? Does it correspond to some trait that means we should respect the choices of the ill *more* than those of the healthy? If so, we would need to take that factor into account when formulating an appropriate civil commitment standard.

There are a number of ways in which mental illness *does* cut the other way. The first is a risk-of-error issue. Mental illness is highly stigmatized in our society.[16] For example, we have seen that mentally ill people are believed to be significantly more dangerous than non-ill people, but this is simply not true. Similarly, although many mentally ill people are impaired, lack judgment, and are less in control than are healthy people, many do not have these characteristics. To suppose that simply because someone is mentally ill he is also so impaired is merely a prejudice. Indeed, even when a mentally ill person genuinely gives the appearance of being impaired, he may simply be refusing to play by our rules, so to speak, or refusing to admit certain unpleasant things. Similarly, his differences may look maladaptive, but he may be able to reach his goals by alternative routes. Because there is so much temptation to find deficits in the mentally ill where none exist, we may want a standard through which we bend over backwards not to treat the mentally ill differently from the healthy or even to treat their choices with more deference.

In addition to the problem of underestimating the mentally ill, when we estimate their deficits accurately, treating them paternalistically may actually increase those deficits by further marginalizing them, reducing their self-esteem and sense of agency so that they become less capable of caring for themselves and living responsibly in the world. Consider, as an extreme instance, the large literature on institutionalization;[17] if we hospitalize people long enough, they become much more incapable of caring for themselves. Conversely, by respecting these patients' choices, we empower them and give them a sense of dignity and self-respect. In addition, we may enable them to feel strong enough to seek help in a way that does not threaten what for some is a fragile sense of self-worth; and of course, the more willing the patient, the more he benefits from our treatment.[18]

Where does all this leave us? It appears that none of the characteristics of the mentally ill that might justify treating them differently actually does so; each provides only a problematic basis for a difference in treatment. In addition, some characteristics of the mentally ill might be cause for giving them more deference and respect, not less.

CONDITIONS FOR COMMITMENT: A COMBINATION OF FACTORS JUSTIFYING DIFFERENTIAL TREATMENT

If none of the factors discussed above alone justifies commitment, is there some combination of factors characterizing the mentally ill that does so? And when—under what conditions—do they justify differential treatment? Must there be danger, or is relief of suffering enough? This, of course, depends in part on the costs of not intervening as against the costs of intervening.

There are significant costs in the civil commitment context of not intervening. These costs fall along a range. At one end is the suffering the ill person undergoes. In addition, his illness may disable him in some way—he may not be thinking as clearly, may be unable to concentrate as well on his work, may lose some social skills. He may experience more or less permanent losses: he may lose his job or reputation, or he may alienate his wife, children, parents, and friends. Moreover, an illness that could have been checked at an earlier stage may become chronic. At the other end of the spectrum, the person may completely lose his self-care skills and be unable to provide essential food, clothing, or shelter for himself. Worse, he may become violent and seriously injure himself or others.[19]

These are weighty consequences, but of course they must be balanced against the costs of intervening. Hospitalization is itself costly, and involuntary hospitalization involves what the Supreme Court has described as "a massive curtailment of liberty."[20] Most hospital wards are locked, so there is drastically reduced freedom of movement. One cannot go to a job. Other people regulate one's life in many ways, large and small, telling one when to rise, when to shower, when to eat. Opportunities for education and recreation may be limited. Indeed, one of my professors at Yale Law School, the late Joe Goldstein, used to say that he would rather be in prison than in a mental hospital: prisons have gyms, libraries, long periods of private time, paid employment, better employability after release, and many other advantages over mental hospitals. Perhaps most important, one is not scrutinized as closely as a defective, for whom fear and pity are the appropriate responses.

Liberty, of course, includes autonomy, and a severe cost of involuntary hospitalization is the loss of respect for one's self-regarding choices. The blow to autonomy represented by civil commitment and its attendant overregulation may have very high psychological costs in terms of lowered self-esteem, resentment, anger, unwillingness to seek treatment voluntarily in the future, and so forth. Patients will then lose out on the advantages in the way of increased dignity and self-respect—and perhaps empowerment—that come from respecting choice.

I have just now focused on the empirical and psychological correlates of an autonomy violation, looking at liberty from a consequentialist perspective. But the failure to show equal concern and respect—and the imposition of dignity loss generally—as an abstract and not a psychological matter is also important. Consider as an analogy showing a picture of a naked person to three Siberians he will never meet. Suppose further that it will never get back to him that this happened, and there will be no psychological costs to him. But hasn't his privacy still been violated?[21] In the same way, deprivation of autonomy is a severe degradation even if there are no psychological costs to the person himself.

There is also a risk-of-error problem involved that leads to a compounding of prejudice against the mentally ill. Doctors often overcommit.[22] That is, their prejudices may incline them to see the probability of harm as justifying treatment where no harm will come to pass. We should hesitate to risk *this* error, too. To compensate for our propensity to stigmatize and underestimate the mentally ill, we should treat them differently only in the most exigent circumstances.

Given the costs of intervening and not intervening, what combination of factors would justify civil commitment? As we have seen, being mentally ill does not equate, in and of itself, with any particular characteristic that would justify differential treatment, and the costs of intervening are high. Yet given the costs of not intervening, a combination of factors correlated with mental illness, when they are present, may be enough.

The characteristics of the mentally ill that together justify differential treatment are serious impairment, transformation into a "different person" (loss of characteristic state of mind), and, in certain circumstances, amenability to treatment. I would have a two-tiered system of additional factors—one standard for first psychotic breaks and one for subsequent cases.

Why are these characteristics important? Although impairment is not incompetence, it does detract from the integrity of the person's choice; it is being less than fully competent, and therefore less worthy of respect. Being a different person is also important, notwithstanding all the difficulties of applying that notion. For one thing, it likewise detracts from competency: character-based theories of accountability say that choices that do not reflect one's character are not worthy of respect. For another, people are likely to feel less "ownership," after the fact, of choices that are the different person's. It was not they who decided, and they may mind less that the other's choice wasn't honored. Treatability is important in giving the confined person a quid pro quo in return for the curtailment of his liberty. It also provides some assurance that we can remediate the problems that make confinement necessary, and so helps guarantee that the confinement won't be too long-lived.

Simply having an illness, then, is not sufficient grounds for committing the mentally ill and not the non–mentally ill in the same circumstances. But when the mentally ill person is also impaired, not herself, and, in some circumstances, treatable, confinement may be warranted, under certain circumstances to be specified. These characteristics diminish the costs of involuntary hospitalizations: they mean that the hospitalization is less damaging to our commitment to autonomy and, in certain cases, offers additional benefits that other potentially confinable people wouldn't receive.

Given the costs of intervening and not intervening, a range of circumstances justifying commitment for the impaired, transformed, and possibly treatable person is possible. The standard I recommend would hospitalize this person on a first psychotic break[23] solely to treat his illness and subsequently only when serious danger is present, or he is incompetent and would have wanted treatment if competent, or he has self-bound after a first break to a different course.

HOSPITALIZATION ON THE FIRST PSYCHOTIC BREAK

If Joyce Brown Were Your Sister   What would you do if Joyce Brown were your sister? Imagine that this is her first psychotic break: you find her huddled up against the hot-air vent on Second Avenue. Would you want her to be hospitalized even if she were not dangerous to herself or others or unable to provide for her daily needs?

Of course, the first thing most of us would (or should) do is try to persuade our sister to get treatment, with all the means at our disposal: we would reason with her, beg, cajole, make her feel guilty about our parents' feelings, bring her closest friends out to talk with her. But if she wouldn't budge, what would we do?

Most of my students say they would have their sister hospitalized. They say that they couldn't bear to see her suffer and risk further deterioration, not to mention serious injury. They know that if their sister were in her right mind, she wouldn't want to live this way—she would want help. That is, they trust that this is not their sister's autonomous choice; it is not she who is speaking. They are hopeful that she will get better and will be grateful for their intervention.

In essence, students' intuitions about this case show that they share the fantasies enumerated by the psychiatrist in chapter 1. Indeed, the costs of not intervening are those the psychiatrist fears. In the case of a sister on her first psychotic break, we fear the consequences of doing nothing and are hopeful that intervening will have the effect the psychiatrist predicts.

But what does it say about us as a society if all (or most) of us would not let our sister deteriorate on the streets but are willing—even determined—to let strangers do so? We justify our position by invoking the notion of rights, but if our sister's rights are not important compared to her other interests, why are a stranger's rights important?

Perhaps we *should* treat strangers and our families differently. Family members know each other better than do strangers—each knows what the others would want in their normal states of mind. (Or at least they think they do.) They also care about their family members more. Thus, they take the time to try to persuade their ill sister; they don't simply act in her interests with total disregard for her wishes. But this is precisely the point; shouldn't we at least try to care for and about strangers as much as family?

Another difference is that we trust family members' motives more than we do strangers'. A person hospitalizing her sister is probably not doing so to spare strangers the discomfort of seeing illness on the streets. On the other hand, family members may have their own ill motives: sparing the family embarrassment, preventing a family member from spending money they'd like for themselves, assuaging guilt for unhelpful behavior on their part in the past, retaliating against a family member who is making them feel guilty. But since I am recommending hospitalization only on the first psychotic break, most of the ill motives family members sometimes develop will not have had time to develop.

If this thought experiment helps justify forced treatment on the first psychotic break, what about later ones? I ask my students to imagine that their sister, Joyce Brown, was reconstituted after her first treatment but spoke of the incident to them as follows: "I am now well and happy that I am well, but not in the least happy about how I got that way. Please, don't you *ever* do what you did to me again, no matter how much you think it's in my interests. I will not forgive you if you do." What do my students want to do in that case? Here they are much more ambivalent and, when pressed to take a position, tend to split into two groups. Some say that they would forcibly hospitalize their sister again nonetheless: she recovered the first time, and they could not bear to see her ill on the streets; her post-illness judgment about what she would want in the future is not as important as her well-being; and the risk that she will be angry at them is worth the potential benefits.

The second group takes precisely the opposite position: when their sister recovered—was in a healthy, intact state of mind—she expressed her preferences clearly. As painful as it would be to allow her to be ill on the streets, they would have to respect her autonomous choice. In that state, she is the best judge of her interests. Others express the more pragmatic consideration that losing the relationship with them could, in the long run, be more detrimental to their sister than lack of treatment. With the relationship, there is always a hope that she will respond to their caring efforts to help. If she rejects them, on the other hand, then even if she is helped a second time, she is bound—like Joyce Brown—to absent herself wholly from their sphere of influence in the future.

This is a difficult question, but I am persuaded by the second group of students: in the scenario envisioned, I would not forcibly hospitalize my sister although I would redouble my efforts to persuade her and offer her whatever help I could.

Finally, I ask my students what they would want if *they* were Joyce Brown on the first psychotic break. Most say that they would want intervention, even if it meant disrespecting their wishes. Others say that they know how angry they are when not listened to; they hope and trust that they would eventually be persuaded, but if not, it would not be worth the cost to be so disrespected and demeaned.

The most interesting cases are those in which students say they would intervene if Joyce Brown were their sister but wouldn't want intervention if they themselves were Joyce Brown. Some are not being inconsistent: they say they would want intervention if someone in their family were making the decision but not if a stranger were involved. They trust in the benevolence of their family. Others, perhaps, are making different assumptions about their sister than about themselves: perhaps they are especially sensitive to insult, and they imagine that their sister would prefer to be treated. But some are violating the principle of treating others as one would like to be treated. They wouldn't like the intervention into their lives, but they will recommend intervention into their sister's. Perhaps these people are imagining their own feelings as the helpless bystander: they would feel too guilty to do nothing, too scared about the outcome, too angry at the helplessness their sister is causing. This position, though understandable, is not really defensible.

This complex thought experiment lends intuitive support to the idea that on the first psychotic break, we should intervene solely so as to treat the person;[24] most would want such treatment for both themselves and their sister. On subsequent breaks, a different, stricter standard should be used, unless the person gives consent in advance to being treated the same way on subsequent occasions: most would not impose treatment on their sister the second time if she was not happy about the first time.

Why Intervention Is Warranted on the First Psychotic Break   I shall try to formulate in more theoretical terms what justifies treatment on the first psychotic break and not on subsequent ones. The case I have in mind for first-time treatment is a person who has suffered his first psychotic break (or a later one, provided that he has never been treated before) and it is a serious one. This person must also be impaired, not himself, and treatable. That this position is plausible is underscored by our intuitions in the case of Joyce Brown.

But why is it justified? Such a person may actualize the fantasies of the psychiatrist discussed in chapter 1: he will be treated, with treatment he will recover, and on recovery he will be immensely grateful to the therapist. Alan Stone has called this the "thank you" theory of civil commitment. And so the theory goes that without treatment the patient will deteriorate and, never having realized the benefits of treatment, will never appreciate that he would really like it. The costs of not intervening are potentially high, and the costs of intervening, since the person is impaired, not himself, and treatable, are lower than they would otherwise be.

This predicted outcome would justify the forced intervention. Health is better than illness, and the person himself later ratifies our choice. Although it is an imposition of our values to prefer the healthy self to the ill self, it is unduly skeptical not to take this position. Health is better than illness, however much this represents a value choice and however committed we may be to respecting others' values.

I recommend hospitalization in this case only on the *first* psychotic break (or the functional equivalent) because, after the person has become ill and been treated, we can *ask* him his preferences for the future: If you become equivalently ill in the future, do you want us to hospitalize you again, or do you prefer forced hospitalization only if you meet our commitment criteria? Before the episode and the treatment, the person may be making decisions based more on fear than on knowledge. After the treatment, the person will have experienced what it is like to be psychotic—he will know how he feels about that state. He also will have experienced the treatment and its results. He may or may not have improved; he may be grateful that he was treated against his will given the outcome or wildly resent how he was treated, even if he improved considerably. We should let the person himself, now healthy (or healthier) and in possession of much better information, decide about his own future.[25]

This is so even if he decides — perhaps against our better judgment — that he doesn't want to be helped then: if we take the healthy self's gratitude as justification for our prior intervention, we must take his resentment as a sign that the intervention was misplaced. Not to respect *both* decisions about the future would be to impose our values, not only by preferring the healthy self but by preferring the healthy self *only when it agrees with us.*

Treating on the first but not later breaks in these circumstances, in short, makes sense because the first time we can hope that the psychiatrist's fears and fantasies will turn out to be true. But if the person does not self-bind to future treatment in this circumstance, we must presume that the lawyer's fears and fantasies have come to pass, at least in the mind of the patient — which is what counts.

I recommend commitment in this case only on the first *psychotic* break and when that break is serious, for two reasons. First, serious psychosis is among the most crippling and uncomfortable of the mental illnesses. It is also among the most threatening to decisional capacities. Thus, whereas (say) severe depression without psychosis is very painful, it is only if the person is psychotic that we should be concerned about his ability to reason adequately. Serious psychosis also usually radically transforms the personality — it makes one a different person. We should require impairment and transformation of personality in addition to the presence of psychosis, but its presence is further insurance that we are committing the right people.

Second, serious psychosis is also among the most treatable of the mental illnesses. Someone with mania or depression that has reached psychotic proportions is likely to respond to mood stabilizers (and perhaps antipsychotics) fairly rapidly. Similarly, many psychotic disorders respond well to antipsychotics. In certain thought disorders, such as schizophrenia, there may be some residual impairments, but the florid symptoms are likely to remit with treatment. By contrast, other disorders, such as borderline personality disorder, although they can be severely impairing, are longstanding conditions that do not respond to circumscribed treatments. We have less reason to hope that a time-limited course of treatment will allow the illness to remit, restore the person to her former personality, and leave her grateful for our intervention.

Some Counterweights   If all this is so, there are, however, some counter-weights to hospitalization on the first, serious psychotic break. First, without a more definable standard than "serious psychotic break" there are going to be considerable line-drawing problems and perhaps massive overcommitment. This is a legitimate concern, and we would want a more rigorous criterion than we have provided. For instance, we would want a "serious psychotic break" to involve hallucinations or profound delusions or incoherence (a slight loosening of associations would not be enough). We would require it to involve significant disability or distress, to be documented in measurable ways. There should also generally be a risk of further detrimental consequences, such as alienating colleagues, losing one's job, spending much money, becoming homeless, or becoming chronically severely ill.

Even with a more precisely defined standard, however, is there not a risk of massive commitment under my proposal? In fact, the percentage of the population with a first, serious psychotic break each year is not great.[26] My proposal, then, would not result in massive confinement. Indeed, the numbers committed each year might decrease because, after the first break, I propose perhaps more rigorous interpretations of the commitment standard than are currently practiced.

A related concern is that some people will be committed under the proposed standard who would be better off if they could avoid hospitalization altogether. I am thinking of people like Kaye Jamison, the manic-depressive psychologist at Johns Hopkins University School of Medicine, who, although she certainly suffered from psychotic manias, was able to avoid hospitalization all her life by relying on caring and helpful friends who looked after her interests when she was ill.[27] Surely it is better that Jamison never had to be hospitalized and suffer the considerable associated risks and stigma. And there is a possibility that some physicians would have insisted on hospitalizing her on her first psychotic break notwithstanding the presence of helpful friends, on the grounds that if something went wrong, they could be sued.

I agree that it is desirable for someone like Jamison not to be hospitalized. I therefore propose that a person *not* be committable on her first psychotic break if she has responsible friends or relatives who can ensure that, with her cooperation, she receives the treatment she needs and who are reasonably able to protect her from the damaging risks associated with her illness (for example, job loss).

Third, some people who would have volunteered for hospitalization if given enough support and encouragement will be civilly committed under this rubric because doing so is perceived as cost-effective. Such commitments would not be necessary if enough time had been taken with the patient.

Voluntary admissions are desirable for a number of reasons. They avoid the use of force and thus spare the patient the denigration that force involves. They also allow the patient to be treated in a way that will prove less stigmatizing in the long run; appearing before a tribunal can come to haunt one later. In addition, a voluntary patient feels that she is treated with more dignity and respect. Indeed, she is given more rights in the hospital—for example, she can refuse medication in more circumstances. Finally, there is substantial evidence that people who are willing patients are *better* patients; they are more cooperative, more motivated to get better, and more successfully treated.

The concern that my proposal would diminish voluntary admissions to the hospital is reasonable, and I would therefore require that it be documented in the person's chart that persuasion was attempted and failed. Doctors would need to make a serious effort at persuasion, for I would allow a cause of action if persuasion were not attempted in a careful and earnest manner—resulting in an action equivalent to false imprisonment. I would also allow for considerable damages, even though the injury is mostly dignitary.

Fourth, a perhaps more fundamental concern is that my proposal would justify all sorts of interventions into people's lives. Many people, for instance, have a difficult time giving up smoking. They find the discomfort—or the prospect of the discomfort—of the nicotine withdrawal so great that they cannot stop (or don't even try). But suppose that we simply abducted smokers and put them in a program that deprived them of access to cigarettes? All would lose the nicotine craving within a matter of days. They would be free of the habit. Many of these people could be predicted to be enormously grateful that they were forced to go through the withdrawal and no longer felt they *had* to smoke. Surely, though, no one would propose that we confine all smokers for several days on the prediction that they would then recover and be grateful.

I certainly agree. But this case is different from that of the first psychotic break in important ways. First, the harms incurred through smoking are much more remote in time than the harms incurred through psychotic breaks. If harm is remote, people can be given the time to come to their own decision. Second, mentally ill people are believed to suffer significant impairments in their decisional abilities whereas smokers are not. But is this true? It is unclear that smokers are making free, autonomous choices. They may be as little able to choose not to smoke as the patient is to choose treatment (the significance of the fact that many do stop being somewhat unclear). Still, the range and depth of impairment are much greater in the psychotic person.

Perhaps most important, the proposed intervention is not likely to *work* in the case of smokers. The most important thing in ceasing to smoke is motivation. If someone is taken from his home against his will and made to stop, he may not only be very disgruntled, he may also not develop the required desire not to resume smoking. Forcing someone through nicotine withdrawal will not a nonsmoker make. Perhaps another way of saying this is that stopping the physical addiction to nicotine does not transform a person to his former, nonaddicted self. By contrast, motivation is not nearly so important in the case of recovery from mental illness, and the treatment does often restore a person to his former self.[28]

The fifth concern with my proposal is that it seems to depend on assumptions that might not be true. For example, it supposes that it is at least somewhat likely that, with forced treatment, the patient will recover and be grateful. But many patients may not get any better. And many may be most resentful of their forced treatment. That is, the lawyer's fears and fantasies, not the psychiatrist's, may prove true. If so, the proposal I have recommended does not make good policy sense.

This concern, however, is somewhat misplaced. There is empirical evidence that this assumption is true.[29] For instance, experience suggests that many people benefit considerably from treatment, even forced treatment, and that untreated people do much worse.[30] Moreover, there are many anecdotal reports of grateful patients and even a few studies. One suggests that a little more than 50 percent of patients are indeed grateful that they were treated against their will. Another suggests that, at least on quantitative questions, a majority of patients report positive experiences of being treated. On how people think they *would* react, there is the evidence, albeit not systematic, that I receive each year from students. My impression from questioning my classes for a dozen years is that my proposal is consistent with what most people would want for their sister and for themselves.

We certainly need more systematic study of all these issues, but this factor should lead not to the rejection of my proposal but to a plan to conduct further empirical research about such questions as what percentage of people recover or improve considerably as a result of forced treatment. What percentage are truly grateful? What percentage, given thought experiments of the kind described above, would want to treat the patient forcibly if she were their sister? A second time, if she reacted poorly to forced treatment? If they themselves were the patients? What percentage of patients self-bind to treatment in like circumstances when given the opportunity?

Prior to obtaining the results, however, we need to do *something*. This is an important point. If, assuming that there is not enough evidence to support the view that we should hospitalize patients on their first psychotic break in part because they will be helped and be grateful, there is also not enough evidence that waiting until people meet stringent commitment criteria is most consistent with people's preferences and needs. Doing nothing is doing something, and we have as little reason—in terms of empirical evidence—to support the status quo as we do to change it.

But why should the something we do be what I propose? We do have evidence of what people prefer. But consider that, although about 50 percent of patients are grateful, after the fact, about their forced treatment,[31] about 50 percent are not. Why should we not attend to the preferences of the ungrateful?

A number of things may be said in response. First, even if the 50 percent figure is found accurate with more study, it seems to me that the costs of not acting are greater than the costs of acting. The cost of acting is that 50 percent of people will be unhappy who may nevertheless be improved clinically. The costs of not acting are a large percentage unimproved clinically together with the forgone gratitude of the 50 percent who would have been pleased. In either case, only 50 percent will be pleased. If treatment is imposed, 50 percent will be retrospectively happy; if treatment is not imposed, 50 percent will be gratified that their choices were respected. But in the first case those who give up retrospective gratitude also give up considerable treatment benefits, whereas in the second those who give up being pleased (the ones unhappy about their forced treatment) don't give these benefits up. They do give up the benefit of having their choice respected, but that's already been counted—that's what it means to say that they gave up being pleased.

Moreover, my own belief—although this needs further study—is that the extant studies underestimate how many patients are grateful. A more indirect way to measure this would be to determine how many patients who have been forced the first time voluntarily participate in subsequent treatment by going to therapy, taking their medication, or voluntarily admitting themselves to the hospital.[32] Indeed, we may find that patients who are forced earlier on, as they would be under my proposal, are more grateful than patients forced under the current system; perhaps catching their illness earlier or relieving their suffering before it becomes ego syntonic would make for a greater number of happier patients.

The reasons for doing what I have suggested absent further evidence are the very reasons I gave above justifying the proposal of hospitalization on the first psychotic break. We have grounds to hope that the result of intervention will be a well and happy patient in this class rather than other classes of patients. We have grounds to think that this class of patients is most impaired and most transformed, thus making their choices less entitled to respect. And we have little reason to intervene after the first time, because we can then rely on the choice of a healthier person who is experienced in the ways of psychosis and treatment. Thus, before the intervention we should not rely on patients' choices, and afterward we should rely only on those choices in like circumstances.

In short, the absence of extensive empirical evidence at this point does not argue against adopting my proposal any more than any other.[33] And there are good reasons, with the evidence we have, along with certain other value choices—such as the value of restoring health—to support my proposal. These are in addition to the more theoretical reasons for adopting it.

The final concern also trades on the relative paucity of empirical evidence in this arena. What if it should turn out that patients become grateful, and reliably compliant (or at least willing to self-bind), only after two or three forced treatments?[34] Why should we not then have a "three-free-shots" rule?

To answer this question, we must proceed both absent empirical evidence and assuming its presence. As of now, there is no empirical evidence that three, or four, or two shots would do the trick. We must simply reason as best we can about what to do. And there *are* good reasons to adopt a plan of *one* free shot: before that time, the person will not have experienced either mental illness close at hand or forced treatment; afterwards, he will have. He will therefore be armed with experience that will enable him to plan for the future. In addition, if it should turn out that more experience with forced treatment will enable some people to become compliant in the future, the one-free-shot rule does not remove the chance of any other forced treatment; it only makes it harder to impose. The point is that most people will eventually get to three shots and be in a position to self-bind or voluntarily comply, so we are not losing all that much by adopting a one-free-shot rule.

Although it makes conceptual sense, then, to adopt a one-free-shot rule absent evidence, it may be that, in actuality, more shots are needed. Patients may reason that they were jump-started, so to speak, by the one free shot, and are now in a position to make a go of it on their own. Or they may have some other theory that suggests that they no longer need medication or treatment. We may someday learn that patients, on average, tend to become open to treatment only after, say, three free shots.

Should we let someone go farther down the route of impairment— with all its possible consequences—before we treat them after the first free shot if we think that three shots would make them willing? That is, if we knew that treating them according to lesser standards would, after only three occasions, lead them to be grateful and to want treatment, should we forebear after the first shot (unless the person meets our stricter criteria)?

This is a hard question. On one hand, it would arguably make sense to have a three-free-shots rule. The reasons for this are the same reasons I gave for a one-free-shot rule: the retrospective gratitude and the future voluntary compliance justify the force. And although we had reasons for thinking one free shot would be enough, it has turned out, as a matter of empirical fact, that three free shots are needed. On the other, maybe this is too fast. After the first free shot we are assuming a person who is much less impaired—and certainly competent. This person has said she does not want forced treatment that is a result of applying the lesser standard in the future. Shouldn't we respect that choice? Presumably we would have told her that some people become voluntarily compliant after three shots, but that is evidently not what she wants. Although encouraging future voluntary compliance is a good, it does not, it seems to me, overwhelm the good of respecting the competent person's choice. This is especially the case if that choice was not only competent but not impaired.

Indeed, there are other philosophical problems with preferring the choice of the person subjected to the third shot and not of his former self who declined treatment. This is actually a harder case than choosing between selves, for presumably the person who has had the first two shots was as healthy as she was after the third. So we are not simply preferring the healthier self (recognizing that there are problems with this too), but the self that makes the choice with which we agree.

It will not help to say that this is how we always work—with equally capable choices, we always prefer the most recent in time. (This is not without reason; for instance, the person who has had three shots has more experience on which to base a judgment. And indeed, if we had a three-free-shot rule and after the third shot a person who self-bound to treatment were to decline future treatment, I would recognize that choice because it is the current competent self's choice based on more experience.) The issue here is not whether the most recent competent self's choice should prevail but whether we should take our prediction that that self will make a choice we like as justification for overriding an equally competent earlier choice—that is, by allowing two further free shots (recall that on the first free shot there was no prior competent choice to refuse).

I think this is a hard question, and I am not sure how I come down on it. When a self is both later in time *and* choosing as we find optimal, it is hard not to prefer that self's choice. This may be only a pragmatic position—it might not satisfy a skeptical philosopher—but it makes some sense. On the other hand, it impinges on autonomy considerably to, in effect, manipulate the person until he makes the choice we like. So I am not sure what position we should take should it turn out that three free shots are necessary to secure voluntary compliance in the future. But for now we certainly don't have the empirical evidence that a three-free-shot rule makes more sense. The question is purely hypothetical.

The arguments against a one-free-shot rule, then, are not persuasive. Many details of this proposal, it is true, remain to be worked out. For instance, how long could patients be confined and treated? I recommend that they be confinable at least as long as it takes, on average, for antipsychotic agents to work. Some jurisdictions permit confinement in the first instance for only three days. But if the aim is to remedy the psychosis, we need to allow sufficient time to do that. (I am thinking of something more along the lines of three or four weeks.) Of course, procedural safeguards would need to be in place to ensure proper commitments under this standard. We also need sensible rules for forcible treatment with medication in the case of first psychotic breaks; I discuss these in chapter 4.

HOSPITALIZATIONS IN OTHER CIRCUMSTANCES

When should it be permissible to hospitalize someone forcibly on subsequent psychotic breaks or for illnesses other than psychosis? I believe that dangerousness combined with the characteristics typical of severe mental illness justifies civil commitment.[35] In particular, I recommend a standard that would commit those who suffer from a severely impairing mental illness that has transformed their character so that they pose a serious danger to others or as a result of which they pose a serious danger to themselves or are gravely disabled (that is, unable to provide for essential needs for food, clothing, or shelter) and—unless it is virtually certain that they will kill themselves[36]—who are likely to benefit from treatment. I also recommend that one prong of an incompetency standard be adopted here—namely, that we can civilly commit those who are incompetent to decide on hospitalization and would have decided on it if competent.

Intuitively it makes sense to commit the dangerous mentally ill who have the characteristics described above. Imagine an extremely homicidal person, with a specific victim in mind, who, although not incompetent, is severely impaired in his ability to control his behavior—he lacks ego organization and integrity and, as a result, is very impulsive, doesn't completely appreciate what he is doing, has fantasies that the victim will thank him for the killing, lacks judgment about the advisability of his act and the likelihood of his suffering consequences, is having thoughts and feelings that are alien to his usual ways of being, and is totally transformed in terms of preferences and values.

Surely we want to commit this person. We would not require that he be suffering and likely to benefit from treatment, but he probably will be. It makes sense to commit him for the sake of protecting the third party, considering that it will cause him to go into treatment and does not completely derogate his autonomy, since he is quite impaired and not himself.

Similarly, a person who will kill himself if not committed and who suffers from similar impairments and alterations of himself should be protected from this harm by civil commitment if need be. Even the person who will simply harm himself in significant ways should be committed if he has these impairments, although here I would require that he be amenable to treatment. If the costs of not committing him are not so high, we should require additional benefits in the way of the likelihood of his deriving benefit from the treatments provided.

Above I suggested that we do not confine people dangerous to others or themselves who are not mentally ill. Yet I now wish to suggest that, black-letter law to the contrary notwithstanding, our practices are somewhat more nuanced than I implied.

Danger to Others

The Analogy to Tuberculosis   Although we generally do not confine the dangerous until *after* they act, there is one interesting exception involving the physically ill. In the past, when tuberculosis was a serious health danger, we forcibly institutionalized people whose tuberculosis was active and who did not seek out treatment of their own accord. New laws are being passed, and old ones invoked, to deal with the contemporary resurgence of this disease.[37] On the face of it, maybe it is enough that the danger a person poses be coupled with an *illness* for us to confine him involuntarily in an institution; perhaps we do not need the other characteristics we have required.

But why would illness play this role? We must figure out what it is about illness—or this illness—that justifies this course. Two things stand out. First, tuberculosis is very serious—it can cause death—and very contagious. Second, unlike the person who poses a danger to others but who is not ill, the tuberculosis patient at least benefits from his confinement—he receives the quid pro quo of treatment.

I suggest, however, that although the second point does apply to the dangerous mentally ill, the first does not. The likelihood of serious injury caused by an infectious tuberculosis patient being at large is very great. The same is not true of the mentally ill person we fear to be dangerous. When the injury is less patent in the case of physically ill people, we do not confine them against their will. For instance, we do not confine sexually active HIV-positive patients who do not disclose their illness to their partners and do not practice safe sex. One of the reasons, presumably, is that the likelihood of causing infection is not so great as in the case of tuberculosis (although the magnitude of the harm may be greater).[38] Similarly, leprosy is both contagious and a very serious illness, but it is not so contagious that it is thought to warrant confinement of carriers.

If we are going to confine mentally ill people who are dangerous to others, it will have to be because they manifest the characteristics I adduced earlier: they are impaired and their personalities are distorted by mental illness—their acts do not reflect their true characters. (The fact that they are likely to benefit from their confinement is an added benefit but presumably not necessary; we would confine tuberculosis patients even if their illness were untreatable.) Giving such impaired choices less respect is to affront less the personhood of these actors.[39]

Of course we lock dangerous mentally ill people up principally to protect ourselves—we cannot trust other means at our disposal to restrain them—but also in recognition of the fact that they need help restraining themselves. Most people would prefer to be helped to prevent them from seriously injuring others if they are having difficulty restraining themselves, both because they would be distressed to hurt another and because they would prefer short-term mental hospitalization to long-term imprisonment. Thus, even though the person may not receive treatment benefits from his confinement, he does receive some benefits. In short, it is permissible to commit people who are dangerous to others.

The Degree and Likelihood of Danger to Others   What degree and likelihood of danger should we require? Clearly it is enough if there is an extremely high likelihood that the person will cause serious physical harm—death or grievous bodily injury. This case is justified in the same way and for the same reasons that it is justified to confine the infectious tuberculosis patient or perhaps the person accused of a heinous crime: the danger is patent, and we must protect ourselves.

I am also willing to commit the mentally ill even when the danger is less likely or serious than in the above cases because serious impairment and transformation of character make the threatened act less entitled to respect. The physical harm to others would not need to be virtually certain—as in the case of the tuberculosis patient—but it should be serious. Breaking (or posing a serious risk of breaking) someone's legs or beating him to a pulp would count, but not simply getting into (or posing a risk of getting into) a fight. The standard would be similar to the one in the criminal law of homicide or aggravated battery (or of posing a serious risk of such) and not simply battery. Similarly, I would not count property damage.[40] Nor would I count simply the harm caused by assault (except insofar as it betokened a prediction of actual and serious battery)—that is, the harm of causing fear to the assaultee would not count, although perhaps aggravated assault should.[41]

But why do I insist on such a high standard of harm? Harm is still *harm* and can, indeed, be quite significant. So why not take steps to prevent it? The idea would be that the costs of involuntary hospitalization are so high that it should be imposed only when failing to do so is likely to be very costly itself.

Is It Wise to Divert the Mentally Ill to Jails and Prisons? The reader may wonder, however, how we protect ourselves against dangerous mentally ill persons who threaten less harm. The answer must be that we do so in the same way we protect against dangerous non–mentally ill persons who do so: we arrest them when they actually commit crimes (which include such things as harassment, threats, and property damage). We may give them the choice to go to the hospital for treatment, but we are not entitled to civilly commit them on this basis alone.

But where is the wisdom in sending people to jail rather than a hospital? With a stricter dangerous-to-others commitment criterion, more people will be diverted from the mental health to the criminal justice system. Thus the person committing assault can be found guilty of a criminal offense but not civilly committed, and he could spend more time in jail than he would have spent in a hospital. Or a person found screaming on the streets might spend time in jail for breaching the peace. Do we really think it a good thing to put people in jail rather than treating them in a hospital? Many say that the result of more stringent commitment criteria has been the criminalization of mental illness.[42] Indeed, it is well known that the Los Angeles County Jail is the biggest mental hospital in the country.

But surely, the reader will say, it is not a good thing that so many mentally ill patients are being diverted to the criminal justice system. They do not receive adequate—if any—care there. They may be given criminal records. They are forced to associate with other criminals, who may take advantage of them in their vulnerable state. How could it possibly be desirable to let this happen?

The answer, I think, is that people may prefer the costs of being jailed to the costs of being involuntarily committed and they will have expressed this preference when they are in a healthy state of mind, after they have seen and felt the miseries of mental illness and the potential benefits of treatment (recall that patients are asked to self-bind after their first treatment). They may prefer the greater freedom from observation in a jail. They may feel that they will be treated with more dignity and respect. They may feel that it is more stigmatizing to be a mental patient than a criminal—and they may be right. Finally, they may believe that they will be confined for less time in jail than in the hospital—and again, they may be right. Whatever their reason, they are making this choice, and we should respect it. They may never have experienced jail before, but they can always make a different choice after that experience if their view changes.

I would like to make one qualification to this position. Some police may take the mentally ill person to jail irrespective of whether he would consent to treatment in a hospital. I believe that patients who are willing to accept treatment ought to be provided with treatment. The police ought to give the person a choice. It is certainly an undesirable outcome if someone who wants treatment is diverted to the criminal justice system for a petty crime.

The reason police may bring some people to jail without seeing if they would prefer treatment may underscore a problem with my whole approach. I have been focusing on patients who don't want treatment. But the central problem facing the mental health system today is not treating unwilling patients but failing to provide treatment to willing patients. There is simply not enough care available for those who want it.[43] That is the real problem.[44]

More specifically, public institutions these days may accept for treatment only patients who meet civil commitment criteria.[45] That is why the police don't bring some patients to the hospital; they will not be admitted, because they are not dangerous. It does not matter whether they want treatment; they will not get it.

But this is not a problem with my commitment standard. It is a problem with the policy governing admittance to public hospitals. If someone is seriously ill and wants treatment, he should be entitled to receive it. It is irrational to admit only those who meet commitment criteria. The best use of resources might be to admit those who want help. And it is certainly a sensible use of resources. Similarly, current policy no doubt leads to much shading of the truth among patients and doctors alike: say the magic words, or you won't be admitted. The point is that this policy should not lead us to adopt a different commitment standard; the policy should change.

Danger to Self and Grave Disability   What about the "dangerous to self or gravely disabled" prong of our commitment statute? In what follows I review the law in action (rather than the law on the books) in the case of the physically ill to suggest that there is precedent to intervene to help the person even when the person is not incompetent; I try to identify the precise circumstances in which we can do so; and I discuss recurrent examples of self-harm to see how they fare under my proposal.

The Case of the Physically Ill: The Medical Analogy   Let us look, first, at the case of the physically ill. The black-letter law, as noted above, is that we do not require physically ill people to be treated without their consent, even if failure to treat them will cause considerable harm. We also allow them to ask that treatment once given be withdrawn.

Our practices, however, show considerably more ambivalence, particularly when life or serious disfigurement or impairment is at issue. A friend of mine, for example, suffered what might have been appendicitis. Trying to decide whether he wanted to incur the costs of surgery, he was informed by his doctor that the doctor would not allow him to leave the hospital without the surgery. This was probably just "doctor talk"—if my friend had insisted, the staff would probably have let him leave (after signing many releases, no doubt). But the talk may have effectively coerced the patient.

Similarly, Bo Burt in *Taking Care of Strangers* recounts the case of David G., a severely burned patient who wanted the doctors to cease treating him because of the immense pain caused by the treatment. Psychiatric evaluation found the patient perfectly competent, but the doctors refused to abide by his wishes and forced treatment on him. The patient lived, and although he reported that he was now glad to be alive, he also reported that he wished the doctors had respected his choice to die; he resented how they had treated him.

Patients are, of course, permitted to refuse lifesaving treatment or ask that it be withdrawn when we are certain that this is a rational choice— when, for example, they have only a few months to live and are likely to be in severe pain or permanently to lose consciousness. In two California cases, the courts extended this holding to less severely ill people who were asking that *nonextraordinary* means of treatment—feeding tubes—be withdrawn.[46] In many jurisdictions this would probably not have been the outcome of the cases.

Moreover, even in California, one imagines, if the patient had a very minor illness, the outcome would have been different. Suppose a patient had treatable tuberculosis and a feeding tube. If he asked that the tube be withdrawn, thinking this an opportune time to commit suicide, it probably would not be permitted. It is unclear what the courts would say—after all, we do not even force-feed all hunger strikers in prisons—but it is likely that the doctors would not comply in any case.

This brings up an important point. Even though the California courts allowed the feeding tubes to be withdrawn (although both patients changed their minds once given the opportunity to have the tubes withdrawn), doctors in California and other jurisdictions are said routinely to force lifesaving treatment on people for whom death is not an obviously rational choice. Although the black-letter law allows competent patients to refuse treatment, patients have little recourse when their doctors ignore the black-letter law, for when these cases do come up in the courts, courts tend to hold that patients are not *injured* when their life is preserved, even against their will. There may be dignitary damage, but it is small. The rule that competent patients can refuse such lifesaving treatment, then, is probably honored more in the breach than in the observance.[47]

Examples of patients' wishes not being honored include violations of do-not-resuscitate orders,[48] Jehovah's Witnesses blood transfusion cases,[49] and putting people into nursing homes without their consent.[50] Doctors and courts alike have a hard time allowing people (except the terminally ill in certain cases) to refuse treatment that will save their lives.

Does all of this mean that there is ample precedent for confining the mentally ill who pose a danger to themselves precisely because they are ill? The answer is no. For though our treatment of the case of the physically ill reflects some ambivalence, when we try to understand this case better we see that it does not offer good precedent for confining the self-endangering psychiatric patient without more. Consider that we probably interdict the choices of the physically ill when their life is in danger precisely because, in an emergency with serious consequences, we want to be sure the patient truly is competent—more, is unimpaired—and is also making a choice representative of his true self (so that his self has not been distorted by his physical illness). Even if a patient appears intact psychologically, we don't have time to really convince ourselves of that in an emergency, so we presume that he is not; the alternative—here, irreversible consequences—is too stark.

Second, we do not always intervene in the lives of the physically ill as we are justified in doing—and sanctioned for not doing—in the case of the mentally ill. The very black-letter rule that we respect competent patients' choices will induce some, if not many, doctors to allow patients to refuse even lifesaving treatment. In addition, some courts may, at least in principle, award considerable damages for the dignitary harms suffered by these patients, even when they don't find prolonging life a harm; the risk that this may happen might motivate some doctors to respect patients' choices. Finally, whereas in emergencies life-sustaining treatment can be forced on the unwilling patient without much cost to the forcer, in nonemergencies that require ongoing treatment, the patient has recourse to the courts before the treatment is imposed; presumably, if the courts are convinced that the patient is competent, he will be able to leave the hospital, even if that means he will die.

In short, although we sometimes treat the physically ill in a way that would justify similar treatment for the mentally ill, we don't do so in theory, we often don't in practice, and the explanation for the instances when we do is often parasitic on the explanation in the case of the mentally ill: physical illness often impairs mental capacities by virtue of the increased fear, helplessness, and regression it causes. Nevertheless, we are not wholly departing from our practices when we confine the mentally ill who are dangerous to themselves.

The Rule for the Mentally Ill   The case of the physically ill, then, is to some extent precedent for confining mentally ill people who are dangerous to themselves or gravely disabled. Note that it is not precedent for confining mentally ill people simply because they suffer and are treatable—so are all manner of physically ill people whom we wouldn't dream of treating against their will. There is ample reason in the case of the mentally ill formally to require—in addition to the danger—impairment, transformation, and (unless death is certain to occur) treatability: the injuries in the case of the physically ill tend to be life-threatening and fairly certain to occur, but we would not require such a high degree of gravity or likelihood in the case of the mentally ill. We have also seen that these characteristics (impairment and so on) are often the implicit basis for intervention in the case of the physically ill.

As noted, I would also require, unless death is virtually certain, that the person be likely to benefit from treatment.[51] This does not mean that the person must be likely to be cured. But his condition must at least be likely to be somewhat ameliorated. Otherwise, he will remain seriously mentally ill, impaired, and in an uncharacteristic state, and his danger to himself will not abate. This means that his confinement will probably have to be for a very long term, and its sole benefit will be to prevent the danger. He will not receive the benefit of alleviation of his suffering in return for the relaxed standard of intervening. The benefits of his confinement will not justify the costs. Since he is the only one who will incur these costs—it's not as if he threatens harm to others—we should not force him to incur them without this additional benefit. By contrast, saving him from virtually certain death is benefit enough to justify the costs of confinement; death is the single greatest harm a person can suffer—and there is no going back.[52]

How Much Danger Is Enough? Some Examples   What level of self-harm should we require before permitting involuntary hospitalization as a danger to oneself? Clearly we should permit commitment if the potential harm is serious—death or grievous bodily injury—and is virtually certain to occur. Once again, we often permit intervention even for the non–mentally ill, at least in emergency circumstances, when these factors combine.

We should not, on the other hand, permit civil commitment when the threat or actuality of nonextreme self-mutilation occurs. Many patients injure themselves for a wide variety of complicated reasons—with no intention or likelihood of killing or damaging themselves extremely. They cut in nonlethal ways. They burn. They scratch. Most often the harm is fairly minor.[53]

This behavior is extremely disturbing to others (and to the patients themselves), but it is only because it is so far outside the ken of ordinary people—so upsettingly deviant—that we would risk forcing treatment on the person who does it. Our reaction to such patients is visceral. It is not completely rational because we do not intervene in the case of people who take less blatantly self-harming actions that actually threaten more

damage—overeating, smoking—or that interfere with their bodily integrity—tattooing, piercing. We intervene in the case of self-mutilation
only because the behavior violates deeply held norms of behavior. We are
acting out our prejudices against those who are different. The point is not
that the patient's behavior is not distressing to her or something with
which she cannot be helped. It is that the behavior is not so harmful that
it warrants intervention against the patient's will.

Perhaps I am being too hasty. Perhaps people who self-mutilate in
minor ways are almost bound to escalate their behavior so that they will
come to self-mutilate in very major ways. Perhaps they will kill themselves
if we do not intervene. This is an important point, and certainly research
needs to be done. But my understanding of the evidence to date suggests
that it is not true. Many patients report that they have no intention of
killing themselves. Theories about why patients do this—for example, to
interrupt the numbness they are feeling, to organize themselves, to alleviate guilt—suggest that serious injury and serious pain are not necessary and not to the point. Again, more research is needed. But I am not
convinced that it will support forced interventions into these patients'
lives, at least without further evidence that the individual patient is likely
to escalate.[54]

Consider, finally, that there are objectively much more serious harms
that we allow patients to incur without civilly committing them: homelessness, squandering of family resources—at least after the first break.
On "objective" measures, these seem worse than minor self-injury. I suggest that we are tempted to intervene in self-mutilating patients' lives only
because they so blatantly violate a deeply held taboo. What will they do
next? This is a natural fear, but it is not completely rational in light of the
evidence.

Although I do insist on a threat of really serious self-injury before
civilly committing someone, I do not require that the self-harm be a result of intentional acts. Suppose, for example, that an impaired mentally
ill person with a serious case of diabetes is unable to regulate his insulin
level. He eats all the wrong foods and forgets to take his insulin regularly.
Suppose this person has been rushed to the hospital in a diabetic coma
several times. If his behavior is the result of his impaired thinking, we
would be justified in trying to restore him to wellness so that he could
manage his condition safely. This person is risking death or serious dete-

rioration. The risk is a result of his illness. And we might be able to restore him to a state in which he does not pose these risks to himself.[55]

What about unsafe sex? People have unsafe sex all the time. Prostitutes have it promiscuously. Teenagers think they are invulnerable. Yet we do not lock up teenagers who are having unsafe sex. The question here, I think, is, in part, how unsafe the person's practices are. If a person is having passive anal intercourse with multiple unknown partners a day, and if that exposes him to a very high risk of conversion to HIV, then perhaps he could be civilly committed.

The difference in the case of ordinary citizens who have the same degree of unsafe sex is that they are not impaired as I require the mentally ill person to be. Similarly, teenagers are said to think much as adults do by the time they reach the age of formal reasoning (around fourteen). They are presumably not as capable of judgment as adults—they simply have less life experience—but they are clearly more intact psychologically than most seriously disturbed psychiatric patients. In addition, teenagers would have to be locked up for an awfully long time to prevent the feared harm.[56]

What about an impaired mentally ill person who, as a result of his behavior, is likely to provoke others? The question here would be how likely he is to do so and what degree of harm he is risking. For example, one patient, when he became manic, would wander through bad neighborhoods antagonizing others, suffering many beatings as a result. On one occasion he so provoked others that they surrounded him and threatened to push him onto the subway rails. One could predict with a high degree of confidence that this patient would come to significant harm within a short time after becoming manic. So long as the harm is serious and its likelihood of occurring high, this case presents as much of a basis for civil commitment as do others in which there is a high likelihood of serious harm. It is somewhat troubling that we must confine the victim and not the perpetrators of harm toward him, but law enforcement cannot be in all places at all times. In addition, we should try to address this problem by imposing especially severe sanctions against someone who harms a mentally ill person precisely because of his vulnerability—that is, who exploits his condition of mental illness.

To take one more example: a person's mental illness renders him homeless, and his homelessness exposes him to a certain degree of harm.[57]

This person could be construed as dangerous to himself or as gravely disabled. Indeed, imagine that the person, if he recovered from his illness, would be able to work and support himself—and a home. This is a difficult case because homelessness in and of itself is a horrific experience, and there are all sorts of concomitant harms: infection, injury, exposure.

In this case, it seems to me, the question should be twofold: is the person's homelessness truly a result of his mental illness or is poverty the culprit? And is the person protecting himself from harm, notwithstanding his homelessness, more or less as well as most homeless people do? The real question is, What is the likelihood that harm will befall the person, and what kind? I would require serious harm—that the person be extremely malnourished, at risk of dying from exposure, or frequently beaten up. I would also require a significant likelihood of the harm. Because this type of situation does not present acute risks, it is possible to be more certain of the likelihood of harm: the person demonstrates over time her inability to care for herself in important ways.

This is a hard case because homelessness is an unenviable situation, to put it mildly, and if we could restore the person to health and enable him to obtain permanent shelter, wouldn't that be a good thing? Three points may be made. First, we generally don't know what the result of our ministrations will be—we can't be sure that the person's homelessness is the result of his mental illness and that our treatment will enable him to get a place to live.

Second, if the harms the person is suffering are less significant than death or serious bodily injury, then, even though the illness is causing his homelessness, that is arguably not a severe enough harm to justify the loss of liberty involved in civil commitment. We don't round up other homeless people who are exposed to more minimal injuries yet managing well enough and force them into homes or shelters. The Supreme Court in *O'Connor v. Donaldson* said that a person could prefer the comforts of his home to the comforts of an institution—although that was before the time of massive homelessness. One could also say that one could prefer the comforts of the streets to the comforts of an institution.

Third, we should allow homeless mentally ill people who want to receive treatment to receive it, even if, again, they don't meet the commitment criteria. Similarly, we should make much better provision for low-cost, supervised housing for the mentally ill. It would be perverse to lock up the homeless mentally ill in hospitals because they were homeless when it is less costly to provide them with halfway houses or supervised apartments.

Of course, if a homeless mentally ill person is unable to provide minimal protection for himself from the elements and from malicious people and no less restrictive alternatives are available, we should be able to civilly commit that person until he can care better for himself, provided that he is impaired, transformed, and treatable. It seems correct, then, to say that the person is dangerous to himself or gravely disabled—he is exposing himself to more than the usual harms from being homeless, and he is doing so as a result of his mental illness.

Incompetent to Decide on Treatment The last prong of my commitment statute refers to the patient who is not only impaired but incompetent to decide on hospitalization[58] and who would have decided on hospitalization if competent.[59] Although many civil commitment statutes do not provide for this case, I believe it is justified. Presumably the idea of these other statutes is that it is reasonable to assume that a competent person would want hospitalization only if he met commitment criteria. But I reject this view: many people volunteer for hospital treatment because they are suffering and want to be helped. And doing so is certainly reasonable.

One could object, however, that the question is not whether competent people ever volunteer for hospitals when they are not civilly committable but whether competent people would want to be forced into hospitals when their refusal was incompetent. I think the answer is yes, at least sometimes. The point is, we can ask this question in the case of each incompetent patient—is there good evidence of what *she* would have decided if competent? Indeed, I propose that we *do* ask patients treated on their first psychotic break that very question, and I expect that at least some of them will ask for just such involuntary treatment on subsequent breaks.

When incompetency leads a mentally ill person to refuse the hospitalization that would help alleviate his suffering, then, we should not respect that choice. Incompetent choices are not deserving of respect, and we do not dilute our commitment to autonomy when we do not respect them. Mental illness is a serious burden, and an incompetent person is not in a position rationally to weigh the costs and benefits of treatment.

Maximal respect for autonomy would counsel us to override the person's choice only if he would have chosen hospitalization if competent.[60] Absent expressed preferences, we judge that a person would have wanted hospitalization if he were competent only if it is in his best interests *and*, given what we know about what he thinks, hospitalization is consistent with his other preferences.

But why *should* competency matter so much that its absence wholly justifies overriding choice? Take for example the following situation:[61] you arrive on a strange planet and are captured by the inhabitants. They speak an alien language. They appear to be offering you a choice between two contraptions whose function you cannot recognize and to be explaining in their strange language what each of these does. You can't understand them. *They* know that one device will instantly cause you an agonizing death and the other will grant your every wish. Does it really show respect for your autonomy to let you choose? Would it not be better to let some benign other—who *does* understand—choose for you?

The point of this thought experiment is to underscore how important competency is. Incompetent choices are not worthy of respect for a number of reasons. A person who does not understand the issues at stake in a decision cannot determine which choice is most likely to serve her values; she cannot make the calculations that will enable her to choose so as to achieve her goals. She may make *bad* choices, as if the person in the strange land chose the contraption that would torturously kill him. If her choices would not serve her interests as she perceives them, they would also, in a sense, not be her choices; they would not represent her values and needs.

A question, however, arises with this prong of the proposed civil commitment statute: why is the provision for self-binding not adequate for telling us who, in effect, would have wanted forced treatment if competent—namely, those who have self-bound to it? The answer is threefold. First, patients who are not seriously psychotic are not subject to forced treatment the first time according to my proposed standard. And some of these patients are incompetent and would have wanted treatment if competent. They simply have not been given the opportunity to self-bind.

Second, some who have formally self-bound to nontreatment may have given clear indications that they have changed their minds but have not gotten around to formalizing the change. Because this prong can be abused, however, I would require the finding that the patient would have wanted commitment if competent to be based on absolutely clear evidence that he would—evidence beyond a reasonable doubt.

Third, some patients may have concerns about committing themselves in advance—conflicts about self-binding—but in fact if they saw their state now, they would have wanted treatment if competent.

In short, there is a need for this prong of our statute, and its underlying commitment to furthering autonomy makes good sense.

CONCLUSION

This chapter has focused on the problem of the unwilling patient rather than the willing but unserved patient because, as noted in the introduction, the first is a problem for legal scholars and the second is not. Our legal system is committed to protecting negative liberties—freedom *from* unwanted intrusion—and not to supplying positive liberties—the right *to* be provided for. Thus, legal scholars are not likely to get far by suggesting avenues to force society to provide care for others—say, through constitutional arguments. That is a matter of politics and of our commitment to this population. What is needed in this area is not scholarly writing but lobbying and other forms of activism. Money is the key.

Society should give wholehearted endorsement to providing adequate mental health care to all who need and want it. But this is not to minimize the autonomy needs of those who do not want it. It is common to say that the former problem—at least when it comes to hospitalization—dwarfs the latter, but I am unaware of empirical research: Are more people who volunteer for hospitalization turned away, or are more people who do not want hospitalization forced? It would be interesting to have data on this question. Whatever the data show, it is clear that there is a considerable group who care most about their liberty and autonomy, and it is worth exploring how the legal system should meet their concerns, especially since there are scholarly, legal arguments that can help in this pursuit.

Perhaps more important, protecting the rights of those who do not want treatment need not detract from the rights of those who do want it. So long as we separate the provision of treatment in public hospitals from commitment criteria—as we should—people who want treatment can be given it. The current link between these two items has nothing to do with the agenda of civil libertarians; there is nothing in rights ideology that says we shouldn't give treatment to willing people unless they meet civil commitment criteria. Indeed, rights ideology would rather say that we *should* give treatment to patients who want it. The real culprit responsible for our not treating people who want treatment is not a strict set of commitment criteria but a lack of resources.

Of course, unwilling patients also have treatment needs. And to try to meet the concerns of those who want to protect these treatment needs and of those who want to protect patients' autonomy, I have proposed a two-track system of civil commitment. I have tried to justify the complex standard proposed and have shown how it applies to various recurring cases. In a sense, the standard defers to the intuitions of *both* the doctor and the lawyer in chapter 1—of the doctor, in the case of first psychotic breaks, and of the lawyer thereafter. Each may be right—only at different points in the person's treatment trajectory.

4

THE RIGHT TO REFUSE MEDICATION:
WHEN CAN I JUST SAY NO?

Psychotropic medications, discovered serendipitously in the 1950s, have revolutionized the treatment of the major mental illnesses.[1] There are drugs for psychoses (antipsychotics), manic-depressive disorder (mood stabilizers), depression (antidepressants), and anxiety disorders (anti-anxiety drugs). Whereas anxiety rarely has caused someone to be hospitalized, the first three disorders frequently have, and the drugs have enabled many of the afflicted to live happy, functional lives in the community. The drugs, particularly the antipsychotics, also have significant side effects: they can lead to uncomfortable pseudo-Parkinson's symptoms, restlessness, apathy, depression, and even, in rare cases, death. Perhaps the most problematic risk is the development of tardive dyskinesia, an irreversible neurological disorder that can cause serious, disfiguring movements of the mouth, tongue, lips, and extremities.[2] Newer drugs are appearing that promise to be equally or more efficacious with fewer serious risks and side effects. Mental health professionals tend to see these drugs as the salvation of most patients and most refusals as a product of the patients' illness; lawyers often speak of patients' autonomy in making the very sensible decision to refuse. They also raise the specter of mind control. Finally, some decry the growing overreliance on chemicals in Western society.

THE PROPOSED STANDARD

Before addressing doctors' and lawyers' visions of this issue, I shall address more abstractly what the standard governing refusal should be,[3] comparing the costs and benefits of medication with those of civil commitment and remaining mindful of what, if anything, is special about mental illness.

What factors might justify medicating involuntarily committed psychiatric patients against their will?[4] First—and unique to this context—the state might have an interest in medicating someone who would otherwise need to be civilly committed. Second, as with civil commitment, the state might have a police power interest in preventing danger to the patient himself or to others. Third, and also as with civil commitment, the state might have a *parens patriae* interest in alleviating patients' suffering and disability.

The first seems an illegitimate reason to medicate someone against his will. Although forcible medication is less costly than civil commitment, cost, it seems, is never a sufficient justification to abridge so important a right. Many choices people make—for example, choosing to smoke—are costly to society, yet we don't force them to behave otherwise. Avoiding civil commitment might also be thought to be justified by the fact that the intrusion on liberty is greater than with forcible medication. But this is not clear; I consider this issue below. More important for present purposes, why should we not let the patient decide what he would prefer? If he prefers confinement to forcible medication, then the latter is the greater intrusion. This claim is complicated by the patient's impairment; I also discuss this issue below.

Moreover, the focus on civil commitment might serve as a proxy for serious mental illness, suffering, and disability. If the illness becomes so bad that confinement is necessary, then forcible medication is permissible. But then this rationale reduces to the third: it is not that we want to avoid civil commitment for the patient but that we want to ameliorate his illness and suffering. I address that rationale below when I consider the third reason for forcibly medicating patients.

If we should reject the idea that patients can be medicated over their objections for the sake of preventing or shortening involuntary civil commitment, what about preventing physical harm to self or others? Danger sufficient for hospitalization would not be sufficient for medication under this rationale if the hospitalization itself sufficiently mitigated the danger. But someone who is imminently dangerous *within* the hospital—for whom hospitalization does not suffice to abate the danger—conceivably could be forcibly medicated. I discuss this rationale in chapters 5 and 6, in which other emergency interventions designed to prevent danger—such as seclusion and restraints—are also discussed.

The third rationale for involuntarily medicating someone is to alleviate his suffering and disability; we should also include a seriousness requirement, possibly to be indicated by some objective measure such as meeting civil commitment criteria. Be that as it may, I already noted in connection with medication instead of civil commitment that there is a question as to why the patient should not decide. Why does the state get to choose medication—with all that that entails—rather than suffering and disability? If alleviation were enough to justify forced treatment, there would be no reason not to force treatment on the physically ill as well. Yet we let the physically ill decide whether they will accept treatment.

This returns us to the inquiry of chapter 3, namely, Why should we treat mental patients differently? What is special about them? As in the case of civil commitment, we could treat them differently, on one extreme, because their suffering compels our action, and on the other, because they are incompetent. In the middle is the view we adopted in the case of civil commitment: many if not most mental patients are impaired, not themselves, dangerous, and likely to benefit from treatment.

Which tack should we take in the context of the right to refuse medication? I argue for an incompetency standard. In effect, this means that psychiatric patients are treated no differently than physically ill patients, whose choices are also not honored when they are incompetent. I show that the intermediate standard is not appropriate here (as it is in the civil-commitment context) and that therefore the more liberal standard is even less appropriate. But I also argue that there should be one free course of medication as there should be one free shot in the case of the seriously ill patient who would benefit from civil commitment.

Why is a competency standard more appropriate than the mixed impairment-cum-altered-personhood standard I proposed in the case of civil commitment? To answer that question, let us compare the two contexts. At first blush, one might think that the case for compulsion is easier to make for medication than for hospitalization and that therefore it should be permissible on a lesser showing, not a greater. Consider that taking medication is less stigmatizing than being civilly committed; it is between the patient and his doctor. By contrast, civil commitment is a public affair, right down to the existence of a public record.

Furthermore, medication has less effect on one's liberty, at least in its grossest manifestations: it does not confine the patient to a particular place, regulate whom he can see and when, and so on. Finally, medication

has much more beneficial effects on one's mental status than hospitalization. Medications are real treatments, whereas hospitalization is at best a
safe haven—rarely does it result in the remission of mental illness. (One
need only reflect on the census in mental hospitals before and after the
advent of psychotropic drugs to see that this is so.)

There are arguments on the other side, however, and I am persuaded
that they are stronger. Compulsion, that is, is harder to justify in the case
of medications, and therefore it should be permissible only on a greater
showing—namely, actual incompetency. Although medications are less
stigmatizing than hospitalization, they are also far riskier to one's health.
Death itself is a possibility, as are considerable discomfort and an irreversible, sometimes grotesque movement disorder.[5] Indeed, the latter
makes medication potentially far more stigmatizing than hospitalization,
because people who develop the disorder look mentally ill to all the world.

And, whereas hospitalization involves greater restrictions on one's
liberty than does medication, the latter in a sense involves greater intrusion into one's person. It changes one's mental state—one's very thought
processes—and in a way that can't be resisted by any effort. People probably care more about their freedom of mentation than their locomotor
freedom. Therefore, we should abridge this freedom only on a greater
showing.

Also, medication is more beneficial in terms of one's mental health
than civil commitment, but the latter, given the extreme circumstances
under which it would be permitted, is more beneficial in total. Civil commitment, as I would allow it, is designed to prevent extreme harm to oneself or others. Avoiding death or grave physical injury would seem to me
to be a greater benefit than restoring one's sanity, however great a benefit
the latter is. I can imagine someone preferring the nonmedicated state to
the medicated state, given the risks and side effects of the medication and
perhaps the gains to the person of the ill state. I cannot imagine many
people preferring death or grievous physical injury to hospitalization.

It is true that our predictions may have been faulty and the person is
in no real danger of these severe harms, whereas he is definitely suffering
from his mental state. But the intent is that such predictions be made with
caution. Moreover, our predictions of benefit from medication may be
equally flawed.

Finally, giving patients a more robust right to refuse has benefits for
the therapeutic relationship that strengthening their right to avoid hospi-

talization does not. A patient who is entitled to do the latter leaves; he is no longer subject to the influence of the doctor. Nor does his behavior provoke changes in the doctor that might serve the therapeutic relationship. On the other hand, allowing patients to refuse medication may have benefits for the therapeutic relationship. It gives patients not only self-esteem but also a chit with which to bargain with doctors. We also have the luxury of trying to persuade patients to take the medication—or, more important, of trying to bring about the changes in their personal dynamics that will reconcile them to the medication. The situation is not so urgent, because they are in a safe enough place (whether hospital or home) to allow us to obtain their consent instead of using force.

If I am right, then, that it is harder to justify forced medication than forced hospitalization, why do I also suspect that most patients (at least those with experience of both) would sooner be medicated than hospitalized? Of course, this is only an intuition—I don't have empirical evidence—but it is a strong one. A number of things may be said. First, some people might prefer medication to hospitalization but not forced medication to forced hospitalization. That is, they might prefer one to the other, given a choice, but prefer less to be forced to have the former than the latter. To put it yet another way, when people reject medication (or contemplate rejecting it), it might be more of an affront to them to force it than when they reject hospitalization.

A significant number of people refuse medication in hospitals, knowing that the refusal will prolong their stay, or refuse it as outpatients, knowing that this makes them likely to be committed. At least these people are showing unambiguously that they value their nonmedicated state more than their very liberty. Of course, this says nothing about the relative numbers whose preferences go the other way. Still, those whose preferences lead to refusal might simply *care* more about avoiding the forced intrusion.

Finally, the real question is not medication versus civil commitment but medication for the sake of alleviating one's disturbed mental state versus civil commitment for the sake of preventing extreme harm to self or others. I suspect that many might prefer medication to hospitalization, but they might prefer hospitalization designed to keep them alive, say, to medication designed to make them better. That is, I suspect that most patients would see civil commitment in the circumstances in which I envision it as more of a benefit than medication.

The reader may insist that, if we compare *like* circumstances, hospitalization emerges as more restrictive. But I disagree. I think if we could prevent serious danger by either forcibly medicating patients in the community or hospitalizing them, we would choose the latter; indeed, that is precisely what we do now.[6] I also think that if hospitalization did cure people, we would hospitalize before involuntarily medicating them; all the considerations raised above in connection with medication—for example, risk to health, intrusion into the person—argue for that option.

Thus I contend that compulsion is harder to justify in the case of medication than of institutionalization and therefore the former can be done only on a greater showing of impairment. The principal point is that the benefits of being restored to mental health are not so great as the benefits of one's very survival, when that is at stake. The first involves alleviation of pain, suffering, and disability; the second, possibly the preservation of life. The pain, suffering, and disability of mental disorder are not irreversible and do not generally lead to a *seriously* increased likelihood of death or severe bodily injury. Improvements in mental state are less tangible than preservation of life. Indeed, for a long time, courts did not even recognize purely mental injuries as actionable under the law.[7]

Moreover, although I have conceded that being restored to mental health is a benefit, some might actually prefer the ill state. Indeed, the benefits of mental health are the subject of much less agreement than the benefits of survival. More to the point, some might even see mental health as a lifestyle choice. Some patients like their mental state. For these patients, charges of "mind control" may be compelling.

If this is right, we should not forcibly medicate people for the sake of restoring them to mental health solely because they are impaired, not themselves, and likely to benefit from treatment. We should do so only if they are incompetent to decide on medication, and then only if they would have decided on medication if competent. (I discuss what competency means in chapter 7.)

I propose one exception to *parens patriae* medication of involuntarily committed psychiatric patients only if incompetent—an exception consistent with my position in chapter 3: patients with first-time, serious psychoses may be medicated involuntarily if medication is likely to benefit them. The same reasons that justified hospitalizing these patients justify even more involuntarily medicating them; it is the medication that promises to alleviate their suffering and disability—which cry for attention—

and to restore them to their former selves. If they are then grateful for our intervention, our act will have been justified. After the first course of medication sufficient to reconstitute the patient, he can decide for himself, in a now-intact (or more intact) state, what he wants for the future.

But I have just said that compelling medication is more problematic than compelling hospitalization. So how can I justify forcibly medicating someone on such a low showing? I argued above only that compelling medication for the sake of alleviating someone's symptoms is more problematic than compelling hospitalization for the sake of protecting him from severe physical harm or death. Here I am suggesting that it is permissible to use the same standard to compel medication *for the same reasons and on the same showing* on which we compel first-time hospitalization—namely, to benefit the patient's mental state. Indeed, there may be greater reason to compel medication than hospitalization for the sake of treating someone, since it is more effective *as* a treatment. Finally, my position—that forced hospitalization is permissible for first-time, serious psychoses—would be utterly pointless if we could not then treat the patient in the only effective way we have. The upshot is that if the reader was convinced by the discussion in chapter 3, he should be accepting of my position here.

Although I am persuaded that imposing a course of medication on someone suffering his first psychotic break makes sense, I am nevertheless mindful of the insult to autonomy that the use of force causes. Moreover, there is evidence that consensual treatment is more effective.[8] As a result, I would be much happier if the patient himself consented to the treatment. Because he is in the safety of a hospital ward, moreover, we can afford the time to *try* to elicit his consent. In addition, many people do consent to medication over time who had initially refused.

Imposing a mandatory waiting period, however, does not make sense. If the medication is automatic after, say, a couple of weeks, patients will either find out about this and realize that they have no real choice or they will learn of it at the time of the medication and feel tricked. In addition, doctors may not take the trouble to try to persuade the patient if they know they can eventually use force.

My view is that there should nevertheless be an incentive for doctors to try to persuade patients, and here, as in the case of civil commitment, I would require doctors to make serious efforts to persuade patients. Indeed, we should arguably require doctors to prove that they made earnest efforts to obtain their patients' consent before they forcibly medicate them.

Once the patient has had the first course of medication, he will be in a position to judge whether he wants it imposed in the future even if he is competent, though impaired. He can self-bind to treatment or to no treatment, or he can decline to self-bind. Patients should be encouraged to think about their future health care even if they reject the option to commit themselves to a particular course in advance. (I discuss potential problems with self-binding in chapter 8.)

In any case, although patients may be concerned about self-binding, some will make a choice about future treatment, and that choice should govern caregivers' response. The default rule, however, will be to medicate patients for the sake of their mental health only if they are incompetent and would have chosen medication if competent. There will be a need for a default rule precisely because some patients won't self-bind to treatment and also because some who self-bind will change their minds, and this change of mind will be of questionable competence.[9] That is, we will not know which choice to respect, and so we will need a default rule to govern our response. I would, however, allow this course only when there was a real basis for suspecting the later choice to be incompetent.

The foregoing represents my position on the right to refuse medication in mental hospitals.[10] I also think that even nonhospitalized patients should sometimes be forced to take medication, namely, when they, too, are incompetent and would have wanted the medication if competent. Many jurisdictions do not involuntarily medicate patients when they are not in the hospital because such medication is hard to enforce; patients may simply not show up for treatment. Indeed, so-called outpatient commitment has been something of a failure for this very reason.[11] Yet I believe that this problem can be surmounted with sufficient commitment. A health worker can simply go to the person's place of living to administer the medication, or a guardian can arrange for him to receive the medication at a treating facility.

Perhaps another reason outpatients are not treated against their will is a desire to keep to a minimum those against whom the state intervenes. If only hospitalized patients can be medicated against their will, fewer people will be receiving involuntary medication. There are many ways in which we could limit the number of patients involuntarily medicated—

for example, by their hair color—but I believe it is desirable to limit only *wrongful* involuntary medication and that people incompetent to decide on medication are *not* wrongfully medicated. Medication is often good, and these people are prime candidates to receive it for very sound theoretical and policy reasons.

Moreover, civil commitment can be done on a lesser showing than forcible medication, and these patients are not even civilly committable. But it is possible for a person to be incompetent to make medication decisions while being nondangerous and not gravely disabled—or not incompetent to make hospitalization decisions. Indeed, the "greater or lesser showing" I have mentioned refers primarily to the patient's degree of impairment, and these outpatients are as impaired in the relevant respect as the inpatients for whom I would allow involuntary medication.

A final reason for limiting forcible medication to inpatients might be that, once one is in the hospital, one has already lost one's liberty; and some think—wrongly, I believe—that hospitalization is the greater intrusion, so that it makes sense to do something lesser to *prevent* this greater intrusion. That something is medicating the patient. But I have already argued that it should be impermissible to medicate someone forcibly for the sake of sparing him hospitalization. And, indeed, this would be an argument for medicating outpatients no less than inpatients—only different ones than those who are incompetent, namely, those who are at risk of involuntary hospitalization. Finally, loss of one important liberty is no argument for allowing loss of another.

Thus, there is a place for forcing medication on outpatients. First, there is just as much reason, as I have argued, to force medication on outpatients who are incompetent and would have wanted medication if competent as on inpatients in the same circumstances.[12] These are patients who cannot be expected to protect their interests, and it respects their autonomy to honor what we determine to be their competent wishes. Second, those who self-bind to future forced medication when psychotic and impaired may be forcibly medicated in those conditions as outpatients as much as can inpatients. Treatment in the community, even involuntary, is permissible in these circumstances.

But what of formal "outpatient commitment,"[13] which allows, in some places, commitment if the patient, among other things, is not dangerous but can reliably be predicted to deteriorate to dangerousness if not treated?[14] Here, of course, the patient is subject to coercion despite not meeting civil commitment criteria—the net of state control is widened. And the rationale of the treatment, at least in part, is to avoid civil commitment once one reliably becomes dangerous. But did I not say that that is not a permissible basis for forced medication?

I did, but other stances are possible here. For instance, it might be impermissible to force medication to avoid (or shorten) commitment but not impermissible to give the patient a choice between forced medication and forced hospitalization. Indeed, I said above that the patient might prefer hospitalization to forced treatment. With my proposal, we are simply putting that preference to the test. Forcing medication may intrude too much into the person to be allowable in nonemergencies absent incapacity. But giving someone a hard choice—medication or hospitalization— may be permissible in order for us to protect ourselves from eventual danger (and of course we cannot predict with certainty when or how it will come) and possibly to save the cost of hospitalization should the patient choose medication.

I don't, finally, accept this position as a general rule, but I would allow one free shot of outpatient commitment, so to speak. But why don't I accept the general rule? Isn't there overwhelming evidence that outpatient commitment helps? It reduces hospital recidivism in a significant percentage of cases if combined with aggressive treatment and prolonged six months or longer, and it results in a greater likelihood that the patient will voluntarily remain in treatment once the commitment period is over.

On the other hand, all the results are based on only a couple of data sets, and the studies need to be replicated. Moreover, there are studies with opposite results. Perhaps more important, these good outcomes must be weighed against the costs of outpatient commitment—all the patients coerced to no good end. And we must study more systematically whether aggressive outpatient treatment—for example, outreach workers going to people's homes when they don't show up for appointments—wouldn't be a better use of resources.

Finally, although giving a choice is preferable to forcing medication to avoid hospitalization, it is still a coercive choice, and it is unclear why competent people should be forced to make it. For these reasons, I would not, as a general rule, allow outpatient commitment to avoid hospitalization.

I would, however, allow one free course of outpatient commitment, under certain specified conditions. For instance, the patient would need to have a record as a revolving-door patient, so that we know we are coercing those who indeed reliably deteriorate into dangerousness. In addition, the patient, though not incompetent, would need to be psychotic and impaired, at least at the start of the commitment. I would allow the commitment to last six months, or however long the best evidence suggests is necessary to get patients to become voluntarily compliant. Indeed, I judge the outcome of encouraging future voluntary treatment a big plus of a limited use of outpatient commitment.

If patients are noncompliant during the period of outpatient commitment, what should the consequences be? Some jurisdictions allow the person to be rehospitalized only if he or she meets inpatient commitment standards. Others allow unjustified noncompliance to suffice. It may seem that the former gives no teeth to the outpatient commitment: one must comply or one will be committable only under the circumstances under which one would have been committable anyway. In fact, however, there are some consequences: the person may be returnable by the police to the health facility, where he will be evaluated and an effort made to persuade him to take his medication. At the very least one comes to the attention of the authorities much sooner.

In addition, some patients probably comply because they think they have to. If this is simply a matter of respecting a court order, that seems to me fine. If the patients are under the mistaken impression that they have to take the medications or they will be forced to take them, then that is not so fine. Some of the evidence suggests that some patients are under this misimpression, and some doctors encourage it. Patients should be aware of the real consequences of their noncompliance—greater likelihood of hospitalization rather than forced medication in this scenario.

It seems to me that if patients really knew that all they risked from noncompliance was greater scrutiny of their behavior, they may not have much incentive to comply. I would therefore allow, on the one free course (or subsequent self-bound courses) that noncompliance itself, unless appropriately justified, should itself be a basis of civil commitment; again, patients should be given the choice of medication or hospitalization.[15] The advantages in the way of encouraging compliance in the future by giving patients six months of doing well on medication—and perhaps coming to appreciate it—may justify the costs.[16]

But why isn't the one free shot of medication in the hospital sufficient basis for the patient to self-bind? If she hasn't chosen to do that, surely we must wait until she becomes incompetent or dangerous before we medicate her. But some may not appreciate the benefits of treatment *in the community* without forced treatment there for six months. They may have failed to self-bind because they deluded themselves that they could survive in the community without medications, or they may have mistaken the unpleasantness of being hospitalized for that of being medicated. In any case, one free shot of consistently doing well in the community for six months may be what makes the patient want to maintain her gains.

Indeed, after the one free shot of outpatient commitment, I would allow the patient to self-bind not only to future treatment but also to continuing or future outpatient commitment, even though it would not otherwise be required. A patient might feel she would be likelier to comply continuously with treatment if she were under coercion for an extended period. Under self-binding principles she could be required to be treated, but not for so long. And in any case, the patient might prefer to self-bind to a coerced choice than to literal forced medication; she might think that course most consistent with both her autonomy and her well-being.

In short, forced outpatient medication should be allowed if the patient is incompetent; if the patient has self-bound to it; and under limited circumstances in the "preventive commitment" context. But the latter should be forced only under a "one free shot" regime, with the ultimate hope being to induce the patient voluntarily to accept treatment in the future.

THE PROPOSED STANDARD IN LIGHT
OF PATIENTS' REASONS FOR REFUSING

Doctors and lawyers are divided about patients' typical reasons for refusing psychotropic medications.[17] Psychiatrists, for instance, often think that a right to refuse makes sense only if patients invoke the right using the language in which lawyers speak of it—for example, protection of mentation (a First Amendment concern) or protection of liberty (a Fourteenth Amendment concern). Not surprisingly, patients generally don't speak this way. But a careful evaluation of the language they do use suggests that they are implicitly invoking rationales that can be put in such terms.[18]

Perhaps more important, psychiatrists often think that the reasons patients give for refusing treatment are products of their mental illness and therefore are not to be respected.[19] I disagree. Patients' reasons may sometimes be related to their illness, but they are not usually symptoms of the

illness. Psychiatric patients tend to have the same kinds of reasons for refusing as do physically ill patients—whether they are fully aware of them
or not—and we do not deprive the latter of their right to refuse. These
motives, moreover, though sometimes regrettable, are completely understandable and perfectly sound reasons for refusing.

Finally, the reasons patients refuse treatment do not generally change
as a result of forced medication.[20] With the exception of certain fears they
may have—of how the drugs will change their personalities, of effects
and side effects—subjecting them involuntarily to the drug treatment
will not allay their concerns. Patients' issues and conflicts concerning
taking medication are prime targets of therapy; force will do little to help.
Patients are sometimes accused of wanting a quick fix, but doctors can
sometimes be accused of wanting to give a quick fix. Certain issues are re-
solvable only through painstaking therapeutic work.

The typical reasons patients refuse medication generally do not reflect
incompetence and are worthy of respect. Lawyers get this point right, and
doctors are misguided. I nevertheless believe that it would be better for
most patients if they could overcome their conflicts and take the medication. Some lawyers get this wrong, and doctors get it right. Indeed, some
lawyers characterize medication as mind control—in which case it should
arguably not be permitted at all—but I will show that this characteriza-
tion is misleading; doctors' denials that it is mind control also miss the
complexity of this issue. In any case, I believe the best way for patients
to overcome their conflicts and be induced to take their medication—
indeed, the only sensible way—is for psychiatrists to work with them in
therapy. Thus, the standard I have proposed makes good policy sense. I
shall have some things to say about our increasing reliance on medication
to control psychological problems in the last section.

How could I possibly know why patients refuse medication? There are
discussions of the question in the literature.[21] In addition, I have considerable anecdotal evidence from my own patients and clients. Finally, I
speculate about reasons on the basis of my understanding of human nature, particularly when compromised by disease. I confine myself here to
reasons that, as I shall show, are probably competent. I do not include reasons based on delusions and hallucinations.[22] Table 1 lists some typical
reasons patients refuse medication.[23]

The never-medicated patient may have profound fears of the effects,
side effects, and risks of the medication—both physical and mental. Will

Patients Who Have Never Been Medicated	Patients Who Have Been Medicated
Fear of taking the medication: Fear of physical side effects Fear of risks Fear of mental side effects Fear of change generally	**Preference against taking the medication:** Dislike of physical effects and side effects Dislike of mental effects and side effects Other fears may remain the same (if somewhat moderated)

Preference for the mentally ill state:
As a result of primary gain
As a result of secondary gain
As a result of identification with the ill self
As a result of a desire to punish oneself
    with illness
	Same (but may be somewhat moderated
	    if the patient is currently on
	    medication)

Desire to avoid narcissistic injury:
Rationalized as a belief that one shouldn't
    rely on crutches
Rationalized as a desire to improve on
    one's own
	Same

Denial:
Patient thinks he is not really ill
Patient thinks that, if he is ill, he can
    control his symptoms volitionally
Patient thinks that, whatever was once the
    case, he no longer needs medication
	Same (the first may be somewhat moder-
	    ated, the second and third stronger,
	    if the patient is currently on
	    medication)

Reactivity:
Patient controls distance of caregivers
    through refusal
Patient is annoyed or angry and acts out
    by refusing
Patient seeks negotiation through refusing
	Same

TABLE 1. TYPICAL PATIENT REASONS FOR REFUSING MEDICATION

he perhaps be one of the unlucky ones who die? Will he contract a disfiguring movement disorder that will brand him a mental patient forever? Will the motor restlessness or muscle spasms be unbearable? Mental side effects, such as impaired concentration, may be of equal concern to him. Perhaps more important, the patient may fear the intrusion into his mental state. He understands that these drugs will change the way he thinks and feels. Even though the psychiatrist tells him that the drugs will simply restore him to his former self, how can he know that for sure? Perhaps the psychiatrist is minimizing the power the drugs will give her over her patient. Perhaps the drugs will change him into someone unrecognizable to himself. No matter what reassurances are given one can never know how one will be changed by mind-altering drugs until one takes them, and then it may be too late. One may like the transformed self—a self that would be abhorrent to one's current self.

All patients—even the highly functioning analytic patient[24]—are somewhat resistant to change because the familiar is, well, *familiar:* it is comfortable to be as one is and scary to contemplate change. If psychoanalytic patients have these fears, how much more do patients to be treated by medications, which are not resistible in the way that talk is— or at least so we imagine. The first cluster of reasons for refusing medication, then, can be quite powerful.

The second cluster is perhaps more recalcitrant to change. These all involve a preference for the mentally ill state. Why, one might ask, would anyone prefer to be mentally ill? So-called primary gain involves benefits the patient derives from the very symptoms of his illness—mainly by the relief of anxiety and pain to which the symptoms are a response—as opposed to secondary gain, which involves benefits the patient derives from others' responses to his illness. The high of the manic state might help the manic patient avoid his pain; that is primary gain. The omnipotent state of psychosis might help the psychotic patient avoid his pain. Indeed, these states may be highly gratifying to patients, even though they often can't admit that to themselves. Secondary gain involves collateral benefits of the ill state, principally the gratifications of adopting the patient role— of being taken care of. Patients may like being nurtured by caregivers, not having to go to work or earn a living, being fed and clothed. They may even get a thrill out of being pursued, so to speak, when their doctors are trying to convince them to take medicine. Being chased may, for some, have sexual connotations. Patients might also prefer the mentally ill state because their "normal" life is unutterably bleak. The pain of the illness is preferable to the misery of their life. This may be a matter of either primary or secondary gain or both.

Another motive in this cluster is that the patient may identify his ill self as his true self. The never-medicated patient may feel that this is who he really is—that he would be betraying his true self by taking medication that will change him. This may be a powerful motive for refusing medication.

Finally, the patient may wish to punish himself through his illness. He feels guilty for something or many things, and his superego takes revenge by refusing medication and keeping him ill. Psychoanalysts have discussed this kind of dynamic as the negative therapeutic reaction in neurotic analysands as well. It is a powerful reason people resist getting better.

The third cluster of reasons for refusing medication involves a desire to avoid the narcissistic injury that comes from admitting that one needs the help of a chemical agent to be in an intact state of mind. It is profoundly hurtful to one's self esteem to admit the need for help of this kind. One feels damaged, inadequate. The medication is a daily reminder of one's defective state. The illness is a wound, and the medication exacerbates that wound. Sometimes the motive to avoid further narcissistic injury—which may actually be behind some of the other motives (see below)—manifests itself as a belief that one shouldn't rely on crutches or one should improve by one's own efforts. The crutch imagery graphically brings home the point that the narcissistically vulnerable patient feels damaged and rejects the offer of an external means of propping himself up.

The fourth cluster of reasons is related to the third: one refuses the medication because one is in denial to one degree or another about one's illness (probably in the service of sparing oneself narcissistic injury). The never-medicated patient may think he is not really ill. He is experiencing difficulties, he is feeling bad—but it's not an illness. Or the patient admits that he is suffering symptoms of illness but thinks that he can control them volitionally; if only he would exert more effort, he could feel better. His symptoms are in that sense a choice. Finally, the patient may admit that he has been ill in the past but he feels fine now and no longer needs the medication; he may feel these things even though he remains quite ill—but just feels a bit better than before.

The final cluster may be thought of as reactive. The patient refuses in order to control the distance of people he perceives as too close or too remote. Generally, he will want to bring caregivers closer when he refuses his medication (he may even want them to chase and dominate him). Or patients may become annoyed or angry and respond with one of the few things in their control: whether they put the medication in their mouth.

Some patients are chronically angry about their fate and lash out by refusing medication. Finally, patients may refuse in order to promote negotiation about the kind and dose of medication; refusal in this case is a gambit in a game of interaction.

Do patients who have been medicated in the past or are currently on medication have the same kinds of reasons for refusing? If they do not, or if they cease to refuse once they are medicated, we would have a powerful (if still problematic) reason for forcing medication: such patients would have a good chance of recovering and would be grateful for their recovery—so grateful, indeed, that they will now continue on the medication of their own accord. We will see, however, that most of the reasons patients have for refusing continue postmedication. Thus, although some patients will be compliant after being forced, many will not; force is a very unstable solution.

It is the first cluster of motives for refusing, involving the fears of risks, effects, and side effects, as well as the fear of change in general, that is most likely to be affected positively if patients simply take the medication. Once they do, they will know the effects and side effects of the drugs. They may now refuse because they know the effects and do not like them. However, some who refused initially on this basis will find the effects and side effects not too aversive—indeed, will be pleased by the medication's primary effects.

Some fears may remain. Fear of risks will not be allayed by knowledge of the effects and side effects of the drugs. Still, many patients will be reassured when the risks don't materialize from their current treatment—they may have overestimated their likelihood (and may now be underestimating it). The patient who is no longer on medications, even though he has experienced the changes they have wrought in the past, may nevertheless fear them now; fear of change—especially in one's mental state—may persist even if one has experienced similar changes in the past. Indeed, this patient may have some residual fear of effects and side effects; things could be different this time.

It remains true, however, that most patients lose their fears of the drugs once they have taken them. In addition, the effects and side effects of these drugs, given in moderate doses, are generally not very aversive—certainly not so aversive as the symptoms of the illness. Most patients therefore do take their medication, although there are pockets of noncompliance. Some medication practices, on the other hand, are rather substandard, and in high doses or with an incorrect drug for a particular person, the side effects can be—and have been described to be—unbearable. Similarly, some people may find even moderate side effects terribly aversive. But most patients, provided their doctors take their complaints seriously—as a robust right to refuse will encourage them to do—can be medicated in a way that is not too unpleasant.

If the first cluster of reasons may respond to forced medication—although persuasion is the better course—the remaining reasons are not likely to do so. The second cluster referred to a preference for the mentally ill state, as a result of primary or secondary gain, patient identification with the ill self, or a desire to punish oneself with illness. A patient who has been forced to take medication and remains on the medication may miss the gains of being ill. She may be tempted to refuse because she is starting to feel symptoms (for example, of psychosis or mania), even without realizing it, and finds the symptom picture seductive. Or she may feel guilty about being in a well state—as if she were betraying her true self. Many patients on medication feel that, since their mental state is not a product of nature, so to speak, it is not authentic. They are not themselves when on medication and should return to being themselves. In addition, they may feel as if they are cheating. Patients on medication may also have an unconscious desire to return to the ill state in order to punish themselves.

Yet the person currently on medication will probably be subject to these motives in a less compelling way than the never-medicated person who feels them. The person in a medicated, healthy state has the experience of health to counterpose to his experience of illness. Though he may have derived primary or secondary gains from his illness, he may derive enormous gains from being well. Likewise, he may be tempted to identify with the healthy self rather than the ill self, and any desire to punish himself may be moderated. Indeed, in many people these factors will overwhelm their preference for being in a mentally ill state. But in some cases the gains they receive from being ill may simply be too compelling. And almost certainly the person who has been medicated in the past but is not now on medication (and is ill again) is likely to have just as strong motives in this category as the never-medicated person.

The third cluster of reasons, centered around a desire to avoid narcissistic injury, is likely to be as potent for patients who have been medicated in the past—and have either continued or discontinued their medication—as for never-medicated patients. Patients often feel considerable shame about the need to be on medication, and there is no evidence that being on the medication mitigates that shame. Indeed, using force to compel patients to take medication in the first instance is likely to increase the feelings of shame and degradation. I suspect that this motive for refusing medication may be the most powerful. It fuels the patient's denial. It may be behind reactive motives; a patient may be enraged by his defective status and therefore lash out against his caregivers by refusing medication. And it may result in a stated preference for the mentally ill state, as a kind of reaction formation. It is also, as we shall see, likely to be behind physically ill patients' noncompliance with medication regimes. If narcissistic injury is the most compelling motive for refusing treatment, it is as compelling—or more so—after the patient has been medicated as before.

The fourth cluster of reasons for refusal—based on denial—is also likely to motivate patients who have been medicated in the past, although with different force than in the case of never-medicated patients. Patients are likely to be in deepest denial when their symptoms are most active; the denial is a kind of protest. Thus, previously medicated patients who remain on medication are likely to be in less denial than symptomatic patients, such as those who have been medicated in the past but have discontinued their medication. Still, many will have a hard time admitting to their illness, and they may refuse medication to bolster their conviction that they don't need treatment.

On the other hand, patients currently on medication are likely to have stronger reasons than never-medicated patients to think that, if ill, they can control their symptoms volitionally. Patients may concede that they have an illness, but they may also accept their mental states as their own and feel that they exercise some degree of choice over their symptoms— at least they can do things to intensify and diminish them—and over what they allow people to see of their symptoms. As a result, patients may have a sense that they can control their symptoms entirely by force of will. This effect may be intensified when they are in a well state and exercising more volitional control generally—and perhaps having distorted memories of their ill state, in the service, again, of avoiding narcissistic injury. Similarly, patients in a medicated state may have a stronger reason to think that, whatever was once the case, they now no longer need medication. Patients who are asymptomatic on medication often begin to think they are now well. They can't believe they have an illness and at the same time feel so good. Perhaps the illness has gone away. Perhaps they no longer need medication. Patients who have never been on medication before may feel better than at first, and so hold this position, but patients who are asymptomatic on medication have the best reason to do so. Presumably, being in an asymptomatic state is a common reason for noncompliance with all kinds of medication regimens, psychiatric and nonpsychiatric.[25]

The final cluster of motives for refusing medication—the reactivity-based reasons—is as powerful after the person has been medicated as before. There is some chance that medicated patients will have more adaptive means to control distance, express anger, or prompt negotiation. But medication may not translate into developing more mature and adaptive defenses of these kinds. And patients in closed institutions such as hospitals often have little scope to exercise more mature defenses. That is, the situation itself promotes regression, and the patient is so powerless that he may peremptorily exercise whatever power he can muster—for example, by controlling what goes into his mouth. In fact, forcing medication on patients is likely to exacerbate these trends; the patient is likely to feel even more powerless—and he will see that the caregiver, whom he is trying to control, cares deeply about this issue. Lack of force seems the wiser course here.

What lessons can we learn from this catalogue of motives patients have for refusing medication? First, as I have already implied, the only class of reasons likely to be affected by simply forcing the patient to take medications is his fear of effects and side effects. To the extent that refusal is based on fear—often pronounced in the psychoses—medicating the patient, even against his will, is likely to change that. Of course he may then refuse on the basis of what he *knows* rather than what he *fears*. But most will find the effects a decided improvement—at least those treated properly—and will come retrospectively to consent to the medication.

The second cluster of reasons may be impacted somewhat by forcibly medicating the patient. But I do not see reason to expect that great change will be accomplished merely by medicating the patient and restoring him to health. It is, in a sense, a health-illness issue to choose illness rather than health, but it is primarily a preference issue. In any case, it is not a health issue that can be addressed by medication. Forcible medication is not likely to make a significant impact on the third, fourth, and fifth clusters of reasons. Robust denial, which may be mitigated by the patient's being brought into a healthy state, may be an exception; but it also may not.

If this assessment is right, forcible medication will not lead to a stable solution. The patient retains many motives for discontinuing his medication that survive his emergence from psychosis; once forced, he may later discontinue his medication. Force also adds insult to the already severe narcissistic injury of being ill and needing medication. It is disrespectful, and it leads to lower self-esteem and to passivity.

What the refusing patient needs most is talk, not force. This is true even of the acutely psychotic patient whose reasons are in the first cluster. It is an immense advantage—from the point of view of both therapy and dignity—to obtain the patient's consent in advance of medicating him. True, the acutely psychotic patient is unlikely to be amenable to any kind of in-depth therapy. Still, he may be able to hear concern and respond to gentle persuasion. If his fears revolve around the effects and side effects of the medication, he can be carefully educated—even hearing the testimony of other patients.

If the patient does not respond to talk, however, I would allow force for one course of medication-treatment while the patient is hospitalized, both for the reasons given in chapter 3 and for reasons that emerge from my classification of motives for refusal. First, some patients will be too afraid of effects and side effects, and at the thought of intrusion into their minds, to consent. Physically ill patients do not have that fear. Moreover, psychiatric patients have at least impaired competency and are not themselves. Some patients, as a result of medication, may come to appreciate the benefits of health and identify with their healthy self. And indeed, it may be that the patient comes to be restored to health, grateful for treatment, and unambivalent about continuing it. Given that possibility—and the fact that I think it justifies the intervention if it happens—I would allow one course of treatment for acutely ill psychotic patients on their first break.

But then treaters will have to turn to noncoercive treatment to induce future compliance. Once the patient is on medication, a very serious effort in therapy ought to be made to help him explore the issues that are leading him to refuse his medication. Patients need help to be brought to see that a part of them likes being ill or the collateral consequences of being ill. Their grief and rage over their illness needs to be addressed, as well as their shame. Therapy can be used to encourage the patient to self-bind to treatment in the future if he insists on discontinuing his medication or, better yet, to come to be reliably willing to resume medication if and when he becomes ill again or to be compliant continuously. Therapy, not force, is the key.

There is much medical literature on the various medications. In my view, a significant literature on psychotherapeutic means of encouraging compliance needs to be developed. This is a neglected area of research— people have come to rely too readily on force.[26]

Of course, my suggestion is costly, and some may think it unnecessary. Even if forcing medication is an unstable solution because patients retain various reasons to resist taking the medication even when they are no longer psychotic, there is a simple solution to that problem: continue to force them to take their medication indefinitely. Don't give them the option of ever refusing. Use a form of outpatient commitment that simply requires continued medication. This solution, however, is most problematic. How can we justify medicating a patient rendered completely healthy— not only competent, but completely nonimpaired—by his medication? Presumably, we would do this only with patients who reliably deteriorated once off medication. But forcing someone who has the full power of reason to take medication is offensive to our notions of personhood. We may think we know better than the patient what is good for him, but we may well not. For example, it may be true that a particular person is better off mentally ill than healthy given the bleakness of his life and the unlikelihood of its changing—and given *his* unique response to his circumstances.

If effectively forcing a nonimpaired person to remain on medication for life is not an option, what about medicating the person once he reaches the psychotic state again? That is, we would require not incompetence, merely psychosis. But although this approach is better than the one proposed just above, my reasons for thinking the standard should be incompetence remain. Moreover, although this person has not self-bound—perhaps he has conflicts about doing so—his continued refusal may be a statement that his competent self prefers the ill state; after all, he discontinues the medication while he is competent and keeps doing so.[27] And perhaps, again, he knows better than we do what is good for him. Note also that we should encourage self-binding so that such situations do not arise; Wthe healthy, competent person's choice about future impairment is what should control.

Finally, if we can't simply keep someone on medication indefinitely, the use of force remains the very unstable solution I said it was. If we use force, patients can eventually thwart our efforts to medicate them indefinitely because of the persistence of the motives identified above coupled with the high threshold before we involuntarily medicate. With a lower standard (say, psychotic and likely to deteriorate), the solution is still unstable in the sense that patients can engage us in a game of cat and mouse: first they refuse, then they deteriorate, then they are forced again, then they refuse again. They may spend as much time off medication, and ill, as on.

It is a much better solution to focus on serious therapeutic efforts to help patients come to terms with being on medication; the hope is that they will then continuously consent instead of riding a roller coaster of force-refusal-force—along with the corresponding fluctuations in mental status. We must, of course, remain open to the possibility that therapy will not induce self-binding or consent—and, that whatever we think is likely to be the case, that might even be better for the patient.

In this discussion of clusters of reasons for refusal, along with the effect of once using force, I have added some complexity to the picture of the treated patient being restored to his former self and thanking us. The picture was of a person who was now well and committed to staying well. He would continue with treatment if that was what it took to stay well, because staying well was what he wanted. Of course, even if he stayed in treatment, there would be a chance that under stress he would have some recurrence of symptoms—that is why we discussed self-binding in the first place—but he would remain the grateful patient, at least while well, and continue to accept our ministrations.

But this picture lacks nuance. We now see that even people who are cured and grateful may remain conflicted on a conscious or unconscious level about their illness, their treatment, and their need for treatment. Medication is no treatment for most of the issues that spur noncompliance. As I have stressed, careful therapy is necessary.

But this means that we should be less sanguine about the effects of forcible treatment. I continue to believe that one course of forced treatment for serious psychoses makes sense: some patients will be permanently restored and committed to treatment and many others will wind up in a place in which skillful and careful therapy can be undertaken. Since it is reasonable to expect that this will happen with many patients, the intervention is justified. But I cannot overstate how limited such intervention is as a long-term solution.

The reader may wonder why we should regard most of the clusters of reasons I suggested as acceptable bases for refusal in the first place. Surely the psychiatrists are right when they say that most refusals are illness-based. Granted, persuading patients and helping them to consent through therapy are preferable; still, if these avenues are unsuccessful, force is permissible under the principles argued for here: incompetence justifies overriding the patient's preference.

I wholeheartedly disagree that these reasons demonstrate incompetence. I undertake a complete discussion of competency in chapter 7. For now I make just a few simple points. First, everyone will agree that knowledge and fear—of effects, side effects, and risks—are perfectly permissible bases for refusing treatment. That is the reason most people refuse all kinds of treatment, or at least so they say and think. And I argue that robust denial in the face of flagrant symptoms is, in fact, not a basis for an incompetency finding.

The other reasons patients give for refusing are clearly competent. Each is a reason that physically ill patients might have for refusing or being noncompliant with treatment, and no one would question their competency. A physically ill patient might derive secondary gain from his illness (and conceivably primary gain if he likes, say, pain); he might feel identified with his ill self and guilty about forsaking it; he might have a desire to punish himself by remaining ill (second cluster). Physically ill patients also might be in denial or might think they can control their symptoms through willpower; and it is very common for asymptomatic patients to discontinue their medications because they feel they must be well now (fourth cluster). Similarly, some may use their compliance with treatment for physical illnesses in a reactive way (fifth cluster).

Most if not all reasons for refusal apply to the physically ill no less than to the mentally ill. I think that the third cluster of reasons—the desire to avoid narcissistic injury—is the principal reason most physically and mentally ill people refuse treatment. It is hard on one's self-esteem to accept the need to be on medication, especially long-term medication, for an illness. Patients feel wounded and may protest by refusing treatment. They want to convince themselves that they are whole. Mental illness may involve a particularly severe narcissistic injury, since it involves a perceived defectiveness in who one is—one's mind, one's personality—not just one's body. But physically ill people too feel wounded by the knowledge that their bodies (with which they identify) are defective. Coming to terms with the shame of having an illness, physical no less than mental, is an important step. My main point is that narcissistic-injury-based refusals are common for the physically ill no less than the mentally ill.

Indeed, there is a wide literature on noncompliance among all patients.[28] Mental patients are said to lack insight and judgment. But if so, then all patients do. One study found that patients on antihypertensive medication discontinued their medication at no lesser rate than did psychiatric patients. If psychiatric patients are incompetent because they have the reasons for refusal enumerated above, so are physically ill patients.

Of course, the reader may argue that all patients are incompetent when they refuse for such reasons. This is an extreme position that would wreak havoc with our legal norms surrounding medical treatment, and I show why it is wrong in chapter 7.

Psychiatrists may insist that even if these reasons are not incompetent, they are illness-based and therefore by definition unhealthy and only barely (if at all) worthy of respect. I deny that these reasons are products of a major mental illness. None of them is a symptom of a mental illness. Recall that physically ill people have such reasons as well. These reasons may be the result of unconscious conflicts and concerns. They may not be the most rational, in the sense of serving the patient's ultimate interests,[29] and they may respond to treatment (although not treatment with drugs). As such, these reasons can be the focus of treatment without being therefore symptoms of illness. They are perhaps better thought of as issues or problems people have. Indeed, even to say that may be wrong; preferring the mentally ill state may be just a choice, not a problem.[30]

Moreover, construing these reasons as illness-based is no reason for not respecting the choices based on them. So the psychiatrists' claim should not lead to an abridgement of the right to refuse. And perhaps it should not even lead us to value the right to refuse any less. Respecting autonomy is extremely important, and we demonstrate our commitment to it when we respect the autonomy of those whose decisionmaking is somewhat (though not grossly) compromised.

Finally, psychiatrists sometimes seem to suggest that these reasons are not the kinds of reasons the law contemplates and are therefore not so worthy of respect.[31] The claim is that people invoke legitimate bases for refusal only when they cite a reason cognizable under the Constitution. Legal advocates seek to protect constitutional rights, but patients care not a whit about their constitutional rights. If they did, those reasons *would* be a legitimate basis for upholding their choices.

But as suggested above, the kinds of reasons I have identified, though not couched in the terms of the Constitution, are just the kinds of reasons the Constitution aims to protect. Take the Fourteenth Amendment right to liberty. Fear or dislike of the medications' effects and side effects is a liberty interest; one wants to be free of unwanted intrusion into one's mind and body and free to make one's own choices based on such concerns. Avoiding narcissistic injury differs little from avoiding injurious side effects; it is within one's liberty interest to be free of this harm. Reactive refusals are exercises of a liberty interest to accomplish certain aims, such as to draw caregivers nearer. Freedom also includes the right to see oneself as less ill than one is and to try to control one's symptoms through volitional means. Finally, people may have a First Amendment right to have their mentation protected against unwanted state interference. The person who says he prefers his ill state and doesn't want it changed is exercising a right under this amendment. Thus, the reasons I have identified are the very kinds of reasons the law seeks to protect; they are not less worthy of respect because they are far from our core rights.

In short, the standard I have proposed makes sense in light of patients' typical reasons for refusing. Psychiatrists are wrong to think that these reasons are illness-based and not worthy of respect. But lawyers are wrong to think that these drugs are a form of mind control—at least in any interesting or invidious way—and therefore very suspect. I turn to that issue now.

IS INVOLUNTARY MEDICATION
A FORM OF MIND CONTROL?

The rhetoric of many lawyers and courts concerning involuntary medication states that it is a form of mind control. Psychotropic drugs are said to be not only "mind-altering" but also "thought-suppressing." This quality makes them highly suspect and may require that they be given a presumption of impermissibility—if allowed at all.[32] The rhetoric of treaters is precisely the opposite: these drugs cannot compel or suppress thoughts, and the drugs are neither mind-altering nor mind-controlling—at least, they cannot compel particular thoughts. The treaters also argue that the drugs are not mind-controlling because they are "normalizing."[33]

Neither side sees the complexity of the issue. The psychiatrists are wrong because these drugs *do* suppress certain thoughts and compel certain others. But the lawyers are wrong that the practices should be off-limits because the drugs are mind-controlling. The drugs are not mind-controlling in any invidious or even interesting way; they are so, perhaps, only in the most trivial senses. The psychiatrists are also right in pointing to the normalizing effects of these drugs, although even this claim, as we shall see, has certain complexities.

What the antipsychotics do primarily is cause psychotic symptoms to abate. The patient's thinking is no longer incoherent, say, or riddled with delusions and hallucinations. Thus, in at least a trivial sense, these drugs suppress psychotic thoughts and replace them with—compel—nonpsychotic thoughts. They compel the negation of the patient's former delusions; if asked, he will now deny that he is God. At the very least, then, these drugs are clearly mind-*altering*. They may also be said to be mind-*controlling*. They control the psychotic process by its suppression and, again, compel the production of nonpsychotic thoughts.

The question now is whether these drugs are mind-controlling in any deeply problematic sense. Consider that many things we do to and with people "control" their minds in the sense of producing changes in them, changes they cannot help. Although the rapidity and irresistibility of the effects when drugs are at issue may make them more problematic, we also "control" or "alter" people's minds with drugs for physical illnesses, and no one is concerned. Consider that giving certain drugs to someone with a severe case of gout will greatly alleviate his pain. Moreover, it may brighten his mood and lead him to undertake his formerly pleasurable activities with a renewed sense of gusto. Is this mind control in any invidious sense?

For now let us note some ways in which drugs may be mind-controlling in a problematic way and see if psychotropic drugs are of this kind. First, we might find it problematic if giving someone antipsychotic drugs could not only compel nonpsychotic thinking in general but could also compel *particular* thoughts—not only the form of the thoughts, but their content. Imagine being able to compel the thought in a patient "I shall give all my money to you" or "I will now vote Republican." The psychotropic drugs will not usually be able to compel thoughts of this kind, but they can, indeed, compel particular thoughts. As I have noted, they compel one to believe the negation of one's former delusions. As an example, they may compel the patient no longer to be paranoid with regard to his caregiver but rather to trust her in the future.

If this is enough to make the drugs' mind-controlling power invidious, then it is invidious. Perhaps, however, we need more than simply compelling particular thoughts. After all, prior to the medication, the *illness* is compelling many thoughts, too. (Indeed, people in general may have much less freedom than they believe to generate any thoughts they wish; this whole debate might not make sense to a thorough-going determinist.) Thus, what about the idea that drugs are mind-controlling in an invidious way if they can compel thoughts that are beneficial to the person who administers them—if they are such that he may use their effects to his own benefit? Causing you to give all your money to me or to vote for me in an election would be an invidious effect. Once again, although the drugs are not likely to be able to do this, they can produce changes in patients that are very beneficial to their doctors, making the patients placid, acquiescent, easily controllable, and willing (within limits) to do the doctor's bidding.

Perhaps we think this is really invidious only if the sole motive of the administerer is to benefit himself; if he wants also to benefit the patient, it is acceptable. This possibility raises several points. First, it is problematic to have to start examining the private motives of caregivers. And second, it is frightening to think of someone as having the power to administer a drug that will change someone else's thoughts and behaviors in a way that will benefit himself.

Third, we may think that psychotropics are invidiously mind-controlling if they benefit the administerer in a particular way—namely, by increasing his power. Being able to make someone vote for you or give you her estate is frightening and abhorrent. But of course, these drugs do quite often increase their administerers' power. As I noted above, they make people much more subject to others' control. Similarly, when they work, they often make people well-disposed toward the caregiver, as well as vesting him with more authority.

Fourth, psychotropics may be mind-controlling in an invidious way if they allow the administerer to make the patient over in his image. It is quite frightening to imagine someone having the power to clone himself. But antipsychotics do have something of this ability. They may change a patient into someone who shares the caregiver's values, behaves more as he does, thinks more as he does, and in those senses is quite like him.

Fifth, we may believe that psychotropic drugs are mind-controlling inasmuch as they allow the administerer to make the patient over in any image different from what the patient already is. To the extent that these drugs are identity-changing, they are troubling. Losing oneself is a huge loss, and giving certain people the power to create others anew is frightening. But these drugs can bring about so many changes in personality as to create a new self; a patient may go from being euphoric but scattered to being steady but lethargic (or vice versa); enough changes may occur that we say he is a new person.

Although each of these five ways of effecting change in a person seems problematic, I still resist saying that psychotropics are invidiously mind-controlling. We can perhaps explore why by conjuring up the kind of model that is truly frightening: a mad scientist gives someone a pill that totally alters his character. The pill gives him control over the changes— allows him to design the person he wants him to be: to implant *all* of his thoughts, beliefs, preferences, personality characteristics, and goals. Finally, via some mechanism he *retains* control over all these features and so can program the person before each election, for example, to vote as he wants him to vote.

Psychotropic drugs do not come close to having this power. A person may be altered quite a bit by the drugs, but no one can really control *how*, at least to the degree discussed above. Most people, for example, will retain all but the most illness-sensitive goals and personality characteristics. And the goals and characteristics that do change may change in totally unpredictable ways; a person may decide not to resume work as a lawyer but to become a doctor.

Indeed, all the changes I pointed to above are at best somewhat probable. They are by no means certain—they may simply not happen at all. A patient who is uncontrollable off medication may be uncontrollable on medication too, not (now) because of his illness but because he is a stubborn, irascible person. A patient may remain paranoid with regard to his doctor not now because of his illness but because there is good evidence that the doctor does not have his interests at heart. Patients who are IRS auditors will remain suspicious of taxpayers even when they are on medication; it is part of their job to be suspicious.

Finally, the pill-giver in no way retains continuous control over the person. Giving someone the pills is not like determining how he will live his life. After the pills take effect, the patient retains considerable choice over how he will live.

All this said, psychotropic drugs are mind-controlling or mind-altering in a way that comes uncomfortably close to the scary picture drawn above. Indeed, we saw that they allow all the things we found problematic to happen, though not in the cumulative and fear-inspiring way that the scary scenario does. Part of the difference is in the scope of the changes. Part is in the amount of control one has over the outcome. And part is in the control one retains over time. One could imagine that newer and more effective psychotropics could give caregivers more control in these ways, and then we would have even more reason to be concerned.

Are psychotropics, then, invidiously mind-controlling? Let us attend to another consideration mentioned above: that these drugs restore one to health or are "normalizing." This may be true in the sense that the drugs simply make one no longer mentally ill, or in that they restore one to one's true self.

The first sense is not very helpful in allaying fears of mind control. It may mean that the mind control has positive rather than negative benefits, at least if one values health. But that is the rub: the person himself may not value health. Moreover, imagine that a drug could perform the complete alteration and allow the thoroughgoing control I depicted above. Would we think this acceptable so long as the changes were in the direction of health? In other words, the drugs may be health-producing and invidiously mind-controlling at the same time.

There is a further sense, however, in which these drugs may be health-restoring that is more helpful: the drugs may remove the foreign body of the illness, so to speak, and allow the person's true self to emerge. Here the two senses of the drugs as restorative converge.

The supposition is that the person has a particular essence—his character—which, once restored, governs his future behavior; it is not the drugs controlling his behavior, but his re-emergent character. Thought experiments suggest that there is something to this line of thinking. Suppose a twenty-year-old with a very definite character is slipped a pill that totally transforms him. Would we object to giving him another pill that would restore him to his true self? My guess is that we would not.

Now part of the reason this case seems a compelling one for the medication is that we can clearly identify a causative agent for the original transformation. Moreover, there is an external malefactor who administered the agent, causing an unwanted transformation. Further still, we have hypothesized that the person's character was radically transformed and that he had an identifiable character prior to the transformation that survives the transformation in the form of a potentiality—that can eventually be restored. Finally, we have hypothesized a pill that serves as an antidote and does restore the person to exactly what he was before the malefactor appeared on the scene.

Still, in this scenario, I think most people would find it justifiable to administer the antidote. This is true, I think, even if the person now wants to stay as he is. That is, although administering the antidote is mind control—of a thoroughgoing sort—it is not invidious mind control precisely because it is restorative of the person's true self.

But if we relax some of these assumptions, we may find ourselves supporting a different outcome. Suppose there is no pill and no malefactor; the person simply wakes up one morning transformed, and that the change he undergoes is decidedly for the better—or at least that it is controversial which character is better. Further still, suppose this new character can step into a new life immediately, without feeling any loss of his old life; he wants to remain the new self and no one else suffers loss in this scenario, either. Is it clear that we should give the person the antidote? Would doing so be not only mind control, but mind control of a problematic sort?

Our first problem, then, with the position that administering psychotropics is not invidious mind control because it is restorative of the person depends on whether the psychotropic medication scenario is more like the first case or the second. There is obviously no malefactor in the psychotropic medication case. On the other hand, the changes wrought by the person's mental illness are generally not thought to be for the better. But as we have seen, there are significant difficulties in identifying mental illness in any value-neutral way, let alone justifying a preference for the healthy state; why can't the person decide for himself? Once again, these may be rather precious philosophical concerns, but they give pause.

The second point is that taking psychotropic medication is often not at all like taking an antidote to a character-altering pill. Thus some people do not change character when they become mentally ill; they were always suspicious and poorly related (although the illness may make them more so). Some of these people may be changed quite dramatically to something they have never been before: trusting and well-related. In the same way, a person may have obsessed and ruminated all his life; when he takes medication, he may simply stop doing so. This is not restoring him to something he was before but changing him into something new. Similarly, a chronically anhedonic person may brighten with these drugs. If psychotropic drugs frequently work this way, we cannot say they are not problematically mind-altering because they simply uncover the person's true self. They make a wholly new self.

One may respond that, although the person never *demonstrated* his trusting nature, or his nonobsessional or brighter nature, they were there all the time but were distorted by his illness. If this is so, the drugs do in fact restore him to his true self. This claim, however, is more than a little problematic. Why can't these things be said about *any* change? Why can't we say about LSD, for example, that the nonhallucinatory self is not one's true self, to which the LSD restores one?

It is necessary once again to invoke the troubled notions of health and normalcy. When is a state a state of health, and when is it simply something someone prefers? When is a state the normal, healthy self, and when is it a new edition? We have seen that some of the troubles connected with the notion of mental illness may be rarefied and only a function of serious philosophical skepticism. Thus most unskeptical people would agree that psychotropic drugs may restore people to their healthy selves, as LSD certainly does not. It remains the case that we are putting a lot of weight on this notion of mental illness—weight it may not be able to bear even if we are *not* overly skeptical. Indeed, in the particular examples I have given (obsessionality, lack of a zest for life), we may be dealing simply with traits of people rather than with illnesses that prevent the true self from emerging. That *is* the true self in those cases.

Nevertheless, although there are problems with the idea that restoration to the true self renders medication noninvidious mind control, this claim should finally command our assent. The thought experiments I have invoked at least *suggest* that.

Where, then, does all this leave us? Doctors and lawyers both get it wrong when they invoke notions of mind control in connection with psychotropic drugs. Doctors are also wrong in thinking that the way these drugs control thought processes is not a prima facie cause for concern. We saw that the drugs can cause changes in all the problematic ways a pill could alter one's thoughts.

But these drugs are not mind-controlling if we consider the rhetorical and affective context of the term. Lawyers are wrong in using a term that has connotations that are not present in the practice in question. Doctors are wrong, in other words, in the literal sense, and lawyers are wrong in the emotive sense. Nor are these drugs invidiously mind-controlling in *any* sense of the word. As the drugs improve, however, we will have to grapple with these issues further. The stakes may change.

Lawyers who think that psychotropic medication is mind-controlling want to control the administration of the drugs. The administration of the drugs, they may say, should receive a presumption of impermissibility. Some may think that the drugs should be disallowed outright because of their mind-controlling potential. At the very least our reasons for imposing them should be strictly scrutinized. Doctors, on the other hand, think the drugs are benign and should be allowed; they are not mind-controlling but restorative of the true, healthy self. Many think they should be forced on patients so long as the drugs are in their best medical interests.

I think a position somewhere between these two points is right. The drugs are not mind-controlling in any scary or invidious way and should not give rise to a presumption against their use. On the other hand, they should not be allowed willy-nilly, either. Reasons to administer the drugs should be given strict scrutiny, because there *is* an intrusion into the person. But no more so than *any* medical treatment, which, as we have seen, may also have effects on mentation.

Are lawyers and other lay people also barking up the wrong tree when they worry that we as a society, following the psychiatrists, are coming to depend too much on medications to solve our ills? I shall have a few things to say about that topic in the next section.

ARE WE COMING TO RELY TOO MUCH ON MEDICATION?

This chapter has been about the right to refuse medication. But throughout I have implied that doctors are right and lawyers are wrong—that medication is a good for most people. And I have implied that most patients do well to overcome their conflicts about staying on medication. But perhaps these positions are misguided. Some law students and many members of the public think that psychotropic medications are problematic because they cause dependence and allow people to take the easy way out. (According to this view, decrying this feature of the drugs is not a

matter of a defense against narcissistic injury but a true and powerful reason to object to the drugs.) Further, they allow tinkering with the mental
state, when perhaps people should be satisfied with their lot or at least
committed to changing through hard work and effort. They may create a
society of consumers of substances that will cause this effect. Finally,
drugs may eventually become more powerful than our visions of genetic
engineering.

A number of things can be said about these claims. The vast majority
of psychotropic drugs are not addictive (the anti-anxiety drugs are the exception); there is no street value for Thorazine. Although some people
may need to be on them for the long term—they create a dependence in
that sense—that is because the person's illness continues, not because his
body has come to need the substance.

Second, the idea that these drugs allow people to take the easy way out
seems misguided. Many people simply could not function without the
drugs. The diseases these drugs treat are for the most part not manage-
able without medication, and no amount of effort will change that.

I speak to the third and fourth points after the fifth point—comparing
the drugs to genetic engineering. This point harks back to our discussion
of mind control, although now the patient himself is consenting to it.
The drugs are not now close to problematic mind control when imposed
involuntarily, nor are they close to problematic genetic-like engineering
when used in this way voluntarily. The drugs are simply not that powerful; if they become so, we shall have to deal with this point then.

As noted, the third and fourth points are most problematic. Although
this chapter concerns drugs for serious mental illnesses, these drugs may
be used for less serious illnesses or for less serious symptoms in those
with more serious mental illnesses. Antidepressants like the selective
serotonin reuptake inhibitors (SSRIs), for example, may cause a subtle
brightening in the outlook of a person who has been chronically, though
slightly, anhedonic all his life. This is not a seriously depressed person
who cannot get out of bed in the morning; this is someone who is simply
a little down most of the time. Or an extremely depressed person may take
more than the normal amount of an SSRI because in high doses it helps
with his obsessional features. He may not be seriously obsessional—he
doesn't, say, take fifty showers a day—but he may ruminate some, check
locks, and have other mild features of obsessive-compulsive disorder.

Do we approve of such uses of the drugs? Presumably, individuals can decide what they want to do with their own bodies and minds. But encouraging psychotropic drug use for seriously ill people may encourage its use for less seriously ill people. There may be all sorts of pressures, subtle and otherwise, on patients to take medications for even small effects. I have known a number of patients who become obsessed with tinkering with all manner of medications so that they have no uncomfortable symptoms (feelings?) at all; they want to get the medications just right. These are people who do indeed have serious illnesses but who have been socialized into turning to medications for even the slightest problem. Encouraging the use of psychotropics may have this effect. Similarly, only mildly uncomfortable patients may be induced by their doctors—or what they have heard from their friends or on television—to take psychotropic medications. Prozac has been available for only ten years or so, and already thirty-five million people have tried it.[34]

Do we think this is a good thing? Many psychopharmacologists think it poor clinical practice to be chasing after symptoms with ever-so-subtle drug changes; it simply doesn't work. But what if it did, or, with better drugs, will? Perhaps doing this is objectionable because, if effective enough, it threatens to make us all alike or because doing this *does* take us away from our true selves. It is simply human to feel certain things (imagine a drug that did away with all mourning). And to be the particular human one is may be to feel particular things. Taking drugs to change that does objectionably alter one's very self.

There may also be issues related to merit and cheating; are the drugs performance-enhancing, as it were, like steroids? If they don't enhance performance, do they detach effort and reward in a way that is problematic?

Some of the concerns that seriously ill psychiatric patients have with respect to the drugs they take—concerns that I suggested are "problems" that need to be worked through—are also concerns that we as a society may have about overreliance on drugs for the subtle changes they may produce. This may suggest that the seriously ill patients' concerns have more legitimacy than we thought, that society's concerns have less, or both. It seems likely to me that such concerns are more prominent the more high-tech the drugs become and the more possible subtle tinkering becomes. Today, of course, most of the drugs have fairly gross effects, and concerns that we will become all alike, that we will stop expending effort to reach our goals, that we will become overconsumers of drugs for ever-more-subtle effects, or that we will be able to do the equivalent of genetically engineering ourselves and our offspring, are overstated. Thinking through these issues will take time. But the issues are significant not only in the case of forced treatment but also in the case of consensual treatment, and a practice of forced treatment exacerbates the problems involved in consensual treatment inasmuch as it encourages a positive attitude toward drugs.

CONCLUSION

Psychiatric inpatients should have the right to refuse medication sought to be administered to help them unless they are incompetent (I discuss dangerousness in chapter 6). Doctors should have one free course of treatment while patients are in the hospital, and one free course of involuntary outpatient treatment in certain circumstances, in the hope that patients' fears will be allayed and they will experience a stability that will encourage future compliance. After the free shot, patients should determine whether and under what circumstances they would like to be treated involuntarily in the future. This issue, as well as all the conflicts that taking medication raises, is extremely important to sort out in therapy, and more research should be devoted to how best to help patients work through it. The message of this chapter—as of this book—is that talk is always better than force.

SECLUSION:

THE PATH OF LEAST RESISTANCE?

In *Rogers v. Okin*, plaintiffs challenged the way seclusion was used in Boston State Hospital. The Massachusetts statute governing seclusion permitted seclusion only on a threat of extreme violence, personal injury, or attempted suicide. Seclusion was nevertheless used for such apparently nonviolent behaviors as escaping, refusing to take medications, having sex, walking nude, masturbating, talking loudly, and saying negative things about oneself. In addition, Donna Hunt, an out-of-control mentally retarded girl, was secluded for set times during the day, on different regimens designed to modify her behavior; she spent more than eighteen hundred hours in seclusion over a fifteen month period— an average of four hours a day. Eventually, her behavior became calmer. The court found that many of these were impermissible uses: seclusion was being used for treatment or perhaps punishment, not to contain or avert violence. (*Rogers v. Okin*, 478 F. Supp. 1342 [1979])

What do we think of such uses of seclusion and of the practices of seclusion and restraint generally?[1] It is the aim of this chapter and the next to sort through our reactions to seclusion and restraints and to suggest, in light of these reactions, a system of legal rules governing their use. As in preceding chapters, I first inquire into restraint practices in the case of the non–mentally ill. Then I evaluate the justifications mental health professionals invoke for using them. Finally, I propose rules governing their use.

RESTRAINT OF THE NON–MENTALLY ILL

I have suggested throughout this book that mental illness alone, even when severe, is no basis for treating people so afflicted differently from others. The mental illness must result in certain characteristics in order to justify taking action against these patients that we would not take toward the healthy. In the case of civil commitment, I suggested that dangerousness to self or others or grave disability was a basis for confining the mentally ill and not the healthy only if they were also impaired, not themselves, and in certain instances likely to benefit from treatment in a hospital. (Obviously, the healthy would never meet the last qualification.) In the case of psychotropic medication, I suggested that mentally ill patients should be treated no differently from physically ill patients: they should have the right to refuse medication unless they are incompetent and would have chosen medication if competent.[2]

I suggest in this chapter that, once again, mentally ill people should be treated no differently from ordinary citizens with regard to such emergency measures as seclusion and restraints. I point out that ordinary practices allow emergency restraint and that prisoners and the vulnerable physically ill are sometimes treated with more extreme mechanical restraints. I argue that the mentally ill should be treated better than prisoners and no worse than ordinary citizens and that no characteristics of the mentally ill justify severe mechanical restraints as they sometimes do with the physically ill. I therefore suggest changes in our current practices to bring them into accord with our treatment of non-ill citizens.

Do we ever take emergency restraint measures against the non–mentally ill? Certainly we do. Imagine that a friend in a bar is having a verbal altercation with another patron. He starts exhibiting signs of escalating to physical violence: he is clenching and unclenching his fists, his face is strained, he starts yelling more loudly. Eventually he rises and approaches the other patron, shouting that he is going to beat his brains in. The other patron responds in kind. It would be perfectly appropriate for you and others in the bar to restrain these people; indeed, in some circumstances it would be inappropriate *not* to.

The lesson of this example is that emergency restraint to prevent or contain imminent physical violence to others is completely acceptable. This is true of imminent physical violence to oneself as well; if you see someone lift a knife against himself or set his socks on fire, of course you do and should intervene. Still, there remain questions of how likely the person is to be violent, how violent he is likely to be, and what kind of restraint is permissible.

In the case of the men in the bar, the violence looked quite threatening. The likely response would be to separate the two men, keep them from attacking each other, and try to "talk them down"—placate their anger and allow them to regain control.

Of course, seclusion and mechanical restraints are a far cry from this. Seclusion involves locking someone in a small, bare room that is devoid of anything that could be used to hurt oneself or others. Perhaps there will be a sturdy mattress that cannot be torn, but there will be no magazines, no pencil or paper, no radio. There will be a light in the ceiling behind a protective shield. The window will be screened and will be made of unbreakable glass. A small, unbreakable window in the metal door will allow the staff to check on the patient. Often the patient is forced to disrobe and wear a hospital gown. There the patient will stay, with no companionship and nothing to do, until the staff releases him.

Mechanical restraints are, if anything, much worse. These days, the patient is typically tied spread-eagled to a bed with leather cuffs fastening each limb tightly to the bed and perhaps some body restraint (a net or sheet) as well. The procedure is both very uncomfortable and degrading. Other mechanical forms of restraint include straitjackets, camisoles, and wet-sheet packs (not much used these days). Most often the patient is restrained in a seclusion room and thus suffers the same deprivation of companionship and stimulation as the patient who is simply secluded.[3]

Do seclusion and mechanical restraints have any analogues in the world outside of mental hospitals? If not, are they justified there? Let's consider seclusion first. Although not the same in all details, seclusionlike practices are used outside of mental hospitals. For instance, we send children to their rooms or give them time-outs in some segregated area. And we do so for reasons similar to those in the seclusion context—to provide a cooling-off period, perhaps to allow destimulation, and to modify the child's behavior. Similarly, prisoners are sent to isolation to protect others from their dangerousness, to modify their behavior, and simply to punish them.

Seclusion in mental hospitals may involve more force than that used with children (both to get the patient into seclusion and to keep him there), as well as more lack of stimulation than most forms of seclusion in homes and prisons. In the view of some mental health professionals, it also may have therapeutic benefits—and at least a therapeutic intent; seclusion should not be used as a punishment. Whether we should make seclusion more or less like seclusion outside mental hospitals—and why—is a question I consider more carefully below.

What about mechanical restraints? Prisoners are exposed to minor forms of restraint such as hand- or footcuffs when they are a danger or an escape risk. In recent years new restraint chairs have come to be used more and more frequently when prisoners get out of control. Sometimes prisoners are tied spread-eagled to a bed. Yet from reports in the literature and the press we know that this seems less frequent than using restraint chairs and may occur primarily with mentally ill prisoners. Children are not mechanically restrained unless they are mentally ill or delinquent— and doing so would probably be considered child abuse.

Physically ill patients, on the other hand, are sometimes mechanically restrained when they are in a hospital.[4] But it is interesting to note that all of these patients are probably either mentally ill or cognitively impaired (perhaps suffering from a form of organic mental illness). Some are restrained because they are agitated or likely to get up and hurt themselves; most if not all of these people would be considered classically mentally ill. Some are in impaired states of consciousness and, not knowing what they are doing, attempt to pull essential tubes out of themselves. It seems that most often only soft, cloth restraints are used with these people—and only at the wrists. Finally, some are frail and liable to fall if they wander; bed rails may be used in such cases, or waist restraints or trays when patients are in wheelchairs.

In all, then, seclusion-like practices occur with the non–mentally ill, but mechanical restraints, especially the extreme forms, rarely do. Tying someone spread-eagled to a bed is a huge degradation. It is unclear to me why it is used or whether it is justified in prisons in the case of the healthy, and as we have seen, it seems a rare occurrence there compared to the use of restraint chairs. In any case, psychiatric patients are entitled to more dignified and humane treatment than prisoners even if such practices are justified there; certainly they can in no way be punished with restraints as prisoners arguably can.

In the case of the physically ill, more serious forms of mechanical restraint may at times be justified. For instance, sometimes confinement to a bed is necessary for physical health, so alternatives such as restraint chairs are unavailable. Given the danger to himself if a seriously ill person leaves his bed, it may sometimes be justified to restrain him at several points. The mentally ill have no such need to remain in a bed, and less restrictive and less undignified forms of restraint are available.

I would like to justify these claims. In what follows, I suggest when seclusion and mechanical restraints should be permitted in the case of the mentally ill, taking my cue from what is done with the healthy ordinary citizen. Here as elsewhere, mental illness alone does not justify different treatment; if, for example, mechanical restraints are too brutal and undignified for the healthy ordinary citizen (except perhaps in extreme circumstances), so they are for the mentally ill.

COSTS OF SECLUSION OF THE MENTALLY ILL

The costs of seclusion, though rarely discussed in the psychiatric literature, are substantial.[5] First, seclusion is a severe curtailment of a patient's liberty. His freedom to move is greatly restricted—indeed, confined to a fifty-to-one-hundred-square-foot room. His freedom to associate with family, friends, and acquaintances is taken entirely away, as is freedom to engage in any form of action except pacing. He is deprived of any and all stimulation.

Second, the patient is subject to a quite degrading process. Seclusion is something we do to children and prisoners. (Indeed, for the most part we cage only animals.) Is the patient to think that he is no better than, at best, a child, at worst, an animal? Seclusion, then, is a severe affront to the patient's dignity.

Third, both limitations on freedom and assaults on dignity may cause the patient a good deal of psychological suffering; he may become bored, panicky at his helplessness to alter his situation, scared of what is happening to him. His self-esteem may suffer. He may feel humiliated and resentful. He may also suffer the effects of sensory deprivation; many experiments show that sensory deprivation is extremely aversive, causing even quite normal people to hallucinate.[6] And there is no good evidence that psychiatric patients, suggestions to the contrary notwithstanding, may not also suffer these ill effects. In addition, other patients may come to fear or scorn the patient who has been secluded, and this may also cause him psychological suffering.

Finally, the patient may suffer physical harm from the seclusion process. If he resists the intervention and struggles against the staff, he may hurt himself or someone else. Some studies show that most staff injuries, for example, occur during the restraint and seclusion process. (This may be because these patients, as predicted, are in fact dangerous or because seclusion actually increases patients' violence potential.) Similarly, the patient may be more likely to injure himself, intentionally or unintentionally, while in seclusion, and he will be less in the staff's line of vision.

Seclusion, then, is a very costly procedure in terms of liberty and dignity interests and patient well-being, both physical and psychological.[7] But what are its benefits? How can it be justified? Four rationales for seclusion are possible:[8] first, that it provides therapeutic benefits;[9] second, that it permits containment of patient violence; third, that it preserves the therapeutic milieu; and fourth, that it is an effective punishment.[10]

The first rationale for seclusion is based on, for example, destimulation and separation of the patient from stressful interpersonal interactions. The second rationale has obvious benefits both for the target of the patient's violence and for the patient himself—including preservation of his self-esteem, no less than his relations with others. The third, benefits principally others on the ward but may benefit the patient as well to the extent that it enables him to remain in good standing with his peers. The fourth, may be in the service of modifying the patient's behavior (thus overlapping with the first rationale) or of deterring unacceptable behavior (thus overlapping with the third).

RATIONALES FOR SECLUSION

The Treatment Rationale   In addition to the side benefits of the other rationales (for example, the therapeutic benefit to the patient of preserving the good will of others), there are at least two theories of how seclusion is directly therapeutic.[11] First, the patient is separated from stressful interpersonal relations and so is permitted to reconstitute, to feel more settled. He simply takes a break—a time out—from a difficult situation. Since the patient is vulnerable and his interpersonal difficulties are magnified, this may be a useful function of seclusion that serves the patient's treatment interests.

Second, seclusion is therapeutic because of the destimulation it provides. The idea is that patients, especially psychotic ones, have a real problem with overstimulation. They have, as it were, lost their ability to filter out unnecessary detail. They feel each impression reaching their senses acutely. The experience can be totally overwhelming and completely disorganizing. Thus, placing a patient in a bare room with no stimuli to distract, impinge on, and overwhelm him can be most therapeutic. It is precisely the dull, unstimulating sameness of seclusion that helps the patient by allowing him to reorganize and reconstitute himself.

The treatment rationale for permitting seclusion would arguably allow all of the patients in the Boston State Hospital case to be secluded. Each of the patients presented either disorganized or noncompliant behavior that was at least consistent with the deterioration of their mental status and that would arguably respond to the therapeutic effects of isolation and destimulation. This includes even the patient who was frequently "saying bad things" about herself. Generally, however, patients are secluded under this rationale who are decompensating—becoming more and more agitated or disorganized—and to apply some of the uses mentioned above would be a stretch.

Are the alleged therapeutic benefits of seclusion sufficient justification for imposing the costs discussed above? My sense is that they are not. First, I think there are generally less restrictive, equally effective means to accomplish the ends of seclusion; seclusion is simply not necessary, and at the risk of being repetitious, it should not be used in the cases where it is not. Second, and more important, I question the reliability of the judgment that seclusion is a bona fide treatment; there may not be sufficient evidence of its therapeutic efficacy. Third, even if seclusion were therapeutically beneficial in the stated ways, and there were no less restrictive alternatives, the benefits do not justify the costs.

There are often less restrictive means than seclusion to separate patients from stressful interpersonal interactions and provide destimulation. Patients starting to feel interpersonal tensions acutely can be escorted to their rooms, given some privacy, or accompanied on the grounds of the hospital (which can be done in a nonintrusive way that preserves the effects of solitude). There is little need to deprive the patient of recreation; he may read or listen to music in his room, and that may calm him more than the absence of anything to do.

The second therapeutic effect too can be accomplished in a less intrusive way. The patient can be invited to go to a place in the ward, perhaps his room, where there is little stimulation. Perhaps a room can be provided that is devoid of much stimulation precisely for the purpose of allowing patients to take a break from the commotion of the ward. The room needn't be small, totally bare, or prisonlike to have that effect. And it certainly needn't be locked. Indeed, one might think the very starkness of the seclusion room would cause some people considerable agitation;[12] it would not be in the least destimulating, inasmuch as it would itself stimulate horrible fantasies and fears—and associations with jail cells.

Of course, in each case in which arguably less restrictive means of accomplishing the same putative therapeutic ends are available, the patients might not agree to cooperate, and then perhaps we *would* need to seclude them. I discuss below why these ends are insufficient to justify seclusion when patients won't cooperate with less restrictive alternatives.

My second reason for repudiating seclusion—that its therapeutic benefits have not been sufficiently established—is even more powerful. Suppose that the patient refuses to cooperate with a less restrictive alternative, or suppose that there is no less restrictive alternative that is equally effective (for example, that being alone in a bare room is better than being accompanied by a nonintrusive staff person on the grounds). Can we really feel confident that seclusion will permit the patient to reconstitute when she is suffering interpersonal stress or overstimulation? Many psychiatrists and other mental health professionals *say* that seclusion is therapeutic for these reasons and even supply clinical examples purporting to show that it is efficacious. One study, for instance, found that patients calmed down faster in seclusion than in restraints.[13] Other reports describe patients who were becoming more and more agitated, reported experiences and showed behavior consistent with overstimulation, and calmed down and reconstituted as a result of seclusion.

But that "as a result" is the rub. The patients were in seclusion, and they calmed down; but did they calm down *because* they were in seclusion? Did the patients in seclusion calm down faster than the patients in restraints because restraints are even more humiliating and unpleasant, thus causing patients to fight against them more? And would patients in neither condition have calmed down fastest of all? To my knowledge, there are no controlled studies demonstrating that seclusion does provide, for example, destimulation that helps patients therapeutically. Without controlled studies, we cannot be sure that a modality is therapeutically effective. So long as the patient is not on the verge of doing serious harm, it seems that we could do such studies. Unfortunately, history is replete with enthusiastic accounts by psychiatrists extolling many, many treat-

ments—from blood-letting to lobotomy to *years* in restraint to megavita-
min therapy—that have been proved wanting.

Moreover, although there are theoretical reasons for thinking that
seclusion is therapeutic, there are also theoretical reasons for thinking it
countertherapeutic; and of course, without controlled studies, both positions are speculative. Consider all the studies showing aversive effects of
sensory deprivation in normal subjects. Or consider that patients who are
interpersonally sensitive might become more agitated *imagining* what
others are thinking than from observing their reactions; absence of cues
might be more upsetting than their presence. Separation from others may
then exacerbate the patient's state. Without controlled studies, we simply
don't know.

In addition, psychiatrists' interest in believing that seclusion is therapeutic should also give us pause. Seclusion serves an important social
control function—even a convenience function—so thinking that it is
also therapeutic eases the conscience of mental health professionals.
Therefore, psychiatrists might not be the most reliable reporters of the
therapeutic efficacy of seclusion.

Finally—although this reasoning, I admit, is somewhat suspect—
seclusion does not *seem* like a treatment; it is too barbaric. Of course, interventions that would be barbaric were they not treatment—for example, cutting off someone's limb—are perfectly acceptable when proved
efficacious. But *this* intervention has *not* been so proved. And when interventions appear especially barbaric, they should arguably require a higher
standard of proof before being accepted as efficacious.[14] Finally, the particular intervention of seclusion has so many negative connotations—the
patient as caged beast or despicable prisoner—that it should arguably
have to cross the highest threshold before we accept it as a bona fide treatment. Consider what we would require in the way of proof if a psychiatrist
claimed that beating patients was effective therapy.

My third reason for rejecting the therapeutic benefit rationale for
seclusion is that I do not think the therapeutic benefits, even if they are
shown to be real, justify the costs of seclusion. This is partly because even
the benefits alleged are not very great. If seclusion allowed a severely psychotic person to become mentally healthy, that would be one thing. But it
actually is alleged only to calm people somewhat; they become a little bit
less upset. (Medications, for example, are potentially much more beneficial than seclusion in this regard.)

The benefits of seclusion as treatment also do not justify the costs precisely because this is such a costly intervention. Again, liberty, dignity, physical, and psychological detriments are suffered by those undergoing seclusion. Perhaps most important—given this book's concern with not unfairly stigmatizing the mentally ill—the dignitary costs of seclusion are very high. For these reasons, I simply do not believe that the treatment benefits justify seclusion.

Finally, even if the treatment rationale *did* justify seclusion, competent patients should have a right to refuse seclusion as treatment just as they have a right to refuse other treatments. Some patients for whom this modality is chosen will be so disorganized that they are incompetent—although, as an emergency measure, it may not be possible to establish this in time. But many will not be incompetent and so cannot be forced into seclusion. Seclusion for the sake of treatment, then, may have a less limited use than it has in practice even if we did permit it. But for all the reasons given above, I conclude that we should not.

The Rationale of Preventing or Containing Violence   The second rationale for seclusion is that it permits prevention and containment of violence to others. The patient is forcibly segregated from others and therefore cannot hurt them. (Of course, staff may be hurt in the process of secluding the patient, but the potential for damage is more limited than if the out-of-control patient is left at large.) This rationale would justify the seclusion of Donna Hunt when she was actually acting violently and perhaps of some other patients if their disorganized behavior were a reliable precursor of violence.

This use of seclusion, on the face of it, seems perfectly justified. We restrain people who are committing or about to commit violence all the time, whether they are ill or not. Generally, the segregation is quite time-limited and not so formal as to involve a seclusion room. But we might well separate people in different rooms in a bar (say) if they appeared to be assaultive. And of course we send fighting siblings to their rooms, and we separate dangerous criminals from the community, partly on the rationale that they need to be incapacitated.

The incapacitation of dangerous people is justified by the benefits of preventing serious physical harm to others. And we do not in this way treat the mentally ill differently. But what probability of what degree of harm do we require in order to seclude someone and to continue him in seclusion? And what less restrictive alternatives need to be tried before we should permit seclusion? Finally, what conditions of seclusion should be permissible given this rationale?

The answer to the first question is easy to state but hard to apply. We should arguably seclude only people presenting imminent and serious danger to others.[15] Clearly someone who is in the act of being violent is secludable if he cannot be restrained and calmed quickly without seclusion. Also secludable would be a person on the verge of an act of violence—say, with a chair lifted over his head or (less dramatically) his fists raised as he runs toward his victim screaming bloody murder.

These are the easy cases. Others are somewhat more difficult. Take the case of the patient becoming more and more agitated, pacing rapidly, gesticulating wildly, starting to swear loudly (although he does not seem angry at anyone in particular). If these are *reliable* precursors to the patient's attacking someone, it may be permissible to seclude the patient. We can be as confident of our judgment that danger is imminent as can friends in a bar restraining someone on the verge of violence. In a sense, he *is* on the verge. Of course, the evidence that he is would need to be substantial.

Suppose, on the other hand, that this is the first time the patient has paced wildly and sworn loudly. The case then becomes harder; what should the reasonable doctor or nurse do? This, of course, is partly a clinical question. One course is to predict imminent violence and seclude the patient preemptively. This patient seems to be becoming agitated and out of control, and the staff fears that he will attack another patient or himself. Surely we can seclude the patient before anybody gets hurt; we don't have to wait until the damage is done—especially if the damage is likely to be severe—so long as we have good reason to think it imminent.

The proponent of seclusion may claim that psychiatrists are better at predicting short-term than long-term violence.[16] It is not clear, however, that this is so; some of the violence predicted, for example, may occur during the restraint process, which itself may be violence-provoking. In addition, threats may be counted as actual violence. Finally, I am unaware of evidence that psychiatrists are better than laypeople at predicting violence or that anyone can predict psychiatric patients' violence on lesser showings than those that lead to accurate predictions in the case of the healthy.

If so, we should err on the side of caution in making predictions. We should try to avoid false positives. This would argue in the case above for not being so quick to restrain the pacing and swearing patient but trying to calm him by other means. At this point it will be clear that the question of how dangerous the person to be secluded needs to be interacts in important ways with the question of what less restrictive alternatives are.

Many agitated patients can be calmed by means other than force and, if not, their violence can be averted by less restrictive alternatives. Psychological means of soothing are always better than force, which often only escalates violence. For the patient who will not respond to soothing, redirection, suggestion, or even instruction, there are still often less restrictive alternatives that will avert harm without requiring the use of seclusion. A patient who is becoming agitated can be "staff specialed"; that is, a staff member can be assigned to be with him at all times, able to respond if violence becomes really likely. Given that many more patients are predicted to be violent than will actually be violent, staff specialing may be a good way to avoid many false positives without significantly increasing the risk that someone will get hurt. Similarly, some dangerous patients may be better served by wearing wrist restraints than by being placed in seclusion.[17]

I think less restrictive means should be tried, at least to a modest degree, even if they have failed in the past. They just might work this time. It would be unfortunate to brand a patient inaccessible to means other than force simply because he has not responded in the past. Of course, after a certain point we *can* predict with some confidence that the means won't work, and at that point it does not make sense to keep trying.

By requiring that staff try less restrictive alternatives, of course, we are increasing the probability that mental patients will be treated like others on the verge of violence: they will be talked to, stayed with, physically held back. Only as a last resort will they be locked in a room. Treating the mentally ill differently only when that is warranted is a principal recommendation of this book.

My third question regarding seclusion as incapacitation concerns what the conditions of seclusion should be under this rationale. I think that current practices are unnecessarily restrictive. If the function of seclusion is simply prevention or containment of violence—and not destimulation—seclusion in a bare room with no stimulation is far too onerous. Provided that he is not dangerous to himself (see below), the patient in seclusion should have access to items with which to occupy himself: music, paper and pencil, books, magazines. If it is thought that an out-of-control patient might be destructive in any way available to him—for example, damaging to property—or might turn against and injure himself, there is still no reason to deprive him of reading materials, perhaps music of his choice piped in, and so forth.

Perhaps this suggestion sounds heretical; the essence of seclusion is a bare room. But I am questioning the soundness of this policy. Patients should be treated as decently, humanely, and respectfully as possible. There is no reason seclusion should be depriving if its purpose is solely to contain violence. To the claim that seclusion might become too attractive—people will become violent so that they can partake of its advantages—I respond that patients should be permitted to choose seclusion if they wish; they will then have no need to become violent in order to partake.

In short, the second rationale for seclusion—to prevent or contain violence—makes good sense. It is permissible to prevent or contain actual or imminent violence, with the mentally ill as with the non-ill; less restrictive alternatives than seclusion, such as staff specialing, should be tried, especially since many patients will not in fact become violent; and patients should be permitted to read, write, listen to music, talk on the phone, and so forth while in seclusion.

The Rationale of Preserving the Therapeutic Milieu   I now turn to the third rationale for seclusion, namely, that it preserves the therapeutic milieu. The idea here is that patients on a psychiatric ward are entitled to a peaceful, predictable, inoffensive environment. When a patient behaves in a disruptive (if not threatening) way, she disturbs the peace and quiet of her fellow patients. Sometimes the only way to preserve peace in the ward is to remove the offending patient until she is able to behave in an appropriate way.

Depending on what we pack into the milieu that is to be preserved (see below), a number of the behaviors in the Boston State Hospital case would give rise to seclusion. Certainly walking around the ward nude or masturbating publicly would. At the other end of the spectrum, having sex or escaping would do so only if we define violation of any ward rules as disruption of the milieu. In the middle would be such behavior as talking loudly; the question would be how loudly, how often, and how easily escapable.

Is this rationale used for segregating non–mentally ill people? In a sense, it is. Joel Feinberg (1985) has identified not only a harm principle in the criminal law but also an offense principle. Without rehearsing the criteria he puts forward for identifying offensive behavior—including such things as whether it has any rational purpose, whether the observer has assumed the burden of exposure, and how easily it can be escaped—we can say that behavior that is upsetting, disturbing to others' peaceful enjoyment of life, disgusting, and the like would qualify as offensive.

The criminal law sanctions such behavior. Thus disturbing the peace is ground for arrest and segregation from the rest of the community. So is public nudity. The idea is that such behavior is, in its own way, harmful, and often the only way to terminate it (let alone deter it) is to segregate the offender. Often people who are disturbing to others in these ways are sent to mental hospitals—when, that is, they are mentally ill. Often they are arrested and kept in jail for a time. The point is that they are separated forcibly from those whom they are offending or whose peace they are disturbing.

We segregate children, too, who are acting in a disruptive, disturbing way. They are sent to their rooms, so that the rest of the family can preserve its sanity. Or they are sent to the principal's office at school. And a person who is becoming boisterous or belligerent in a bar or any other place may simply be asked to leave or escorted out.

The comparison to criminals and children is not meant to be invidious—and, indeed, I noted that ordinary citizens are subjected to the same sanctions informally applied. When we isolate the mentally ill if they are disruptive to others, we are treating them as we treat others. In addition, our very aim is to respect the privacy and peace of psychiatric patients other than the offender and to preserve the milieu for them when we seclude him. Mentally ill onlookers or victims of the offensive behavior of one mentally ill person are entitled to the same decent treatment as healthy onlookers or victims. Perhaps they are entitled to better treatment, for they are a captive audience.

All of that said, it should be clear that the rationale of preserving the milieu justifies seclusion on the basis of benefits to persons other than the person being secluded. Of course, he may get the benefit of better relations with his fellow patients, as well as the avoidance of some embarrassment. But the critical factor is to preserve the peace for the sake of others. (Although the violence-to-others rationale for seclusion is similarly other-regarding, the benefits to the patient are probably greater and the circumstances of the seclusion—it's a real emergency—are such that we should not require the protections I will require under this rationale.)

A number of issues remain. What should count as disruption of the milieu? What are less restrictive alternatives in this case? Should we experiment more with "disturbed wards" for the sake of greater freedom among the disturbed patient and greater tranquility among the nondisturbed? What should the conditions of seclusion be under this rationale? And finally, what if any procedural protections should surround this use of seclusion?

The question of what should count as disruption of the milieu is perhaps the most important. Three candidates exist: (1) any behavior that on the outside would count as disturbing the peace or an analogous crime; (2) behaviors that are disturbing to others but are below the threshold that would warrant arrest; and (3) behaviors that violate ward rules and are disturbing to others only in the sense of disrupting the order and predictability of a rule-bound community.

The first type of behavior should clearly count as disrupting the milieu and, under certain conditions, is sufficient justification for secluding someone. A person who is causing a severe commotion could be arrested for disturbing the peace. Part of the point of arresting her would be to preserve peace and tranquility in the community. Psychiatric patients are also entitled to peace and tranquility.

It is true that one may have less expectation of peace and quiet in a psychiatric ward inasmuch as it is well understood that disturbed patients may be disturbing. And they often have less control over whether they are disturbing than do the healthy, so that it seems less fair to penalize them. In addition, the patients who are "bystanders" in any given instance, being ill themselves, may at times become disruptive. This means that sacrificing some peace now may benefit them later when they are the disruptive ones. Nevertheless, at a certain point, the offending patient becomes too disruptive to be in the ward. Making a commotion, public nudity or masturbation, being in others' "faces"—all these behaviors would justify seclusion for the sake of preserving the milieu, provided that lesser interventions would not accomplish the same end.

Shouting or screaming alone is a somewhat harder case because, although it is disruptive, it is almost as disruptive in seclusion as on the ward. Still, the noise may be somewhat muffled by the seclusion room, patients may predictably get as far away as possible from the noise, and it reduces the fear among others that the screaming patient will escalate out of control. Finally, some seclusion rooms are outside of wards, and others are soundproof.

I have suggested that there is less expectation of calm and quiet on a psychiatric hospital ward than in the community. This implies that disturbances should be really serious before restrictive interventions are implemented. What, then, could be the rationale for the second posture above: that we can seclude patients on a *lesser* showing than would justify arrest and segregation from the community?

The argument here is that patients are captive onlookers of fellow patients' disruptive behavior and thus should be entitled to greater protection from it. According to this view, even patients who are being mildly disruptive—for example, talking or laughing somewhat loudly—should be subject to seclusion. Similarly, patients who do not bathe often enough, and thus are smelly, should be secludable, even though one cannot be arrested in the community for poor hygiene. Once again, the point is that people in the community can simply go elsewhere to avoid the smelly person, but people on a psychiatric ward cannot.

There is some merit to this claim, but it is overwhelmed by the reasons for being *more* tolerant of disruptive behavior on a psychiatric ward than on the outside. For one thing, wards are not so cramped that other patients cannot achieve some distance from the offender. For another, often the offending behavior will be just as offensive in seclusion as out. Moreover, interventions short of seclusion will ameliorate the disturbance. For instance, the staff can require the patient to take a shower. Finally, the reasons given above for thinking that patients should be more tolerant of fellow patients' offensive behavior are really quite powerful.

The third type of disruption of the milieu would be violations of ward rules that do not directly disturb the peace but do upset other patients. A less rule-bound environment is frightening to some people if they need predictability and order to feel safe. In addition, other patients may be offended by the very idea of some of the behaviors of their fellow patients, even if those behaviors are done in privacy.

Following this rationale, staff may seclude not only people who are disrupting the peace and tranquility of the ward, as by screaming, masturbating publicly, and so forth, but also people who violate any ward rule. So, for example, the patients in the Boston State Hospital case who were secluded for escaping, having sex, and not taking their medication would have been properly secluded. Similarly, patients who do not come to morning meetings or perform their daily activities could be secluded on this basis.

I believe that seclusion should not be permitted on this basis; it distorts the "preserving the milieu" rationale. Nor is it justified on the basis that it may spare patients from feeling a sense of insecurity about limits and a sense of offense at inappropriate, even immoral, behavior. For one thing, the putative psychological harms that patients are thereby spared are speculative. For another, they are probably not severe even when they do occur. Finally, seclusion is an extreme measure, given these alleged harms.

There is an analogue to this rationale in the criminal law: prohibiting and punishing behavior that causes not harm or offense but only the speculative unhappiness that comes of knowing that certain behavior is tolerated in one's community. These are so-called morals offenses—such victimless crimes as consensual adultery or sodomy in the privacy of one's home. Without entering a lengthy discussion of this class of offenses, suffice it to say that many criminal law scholars repudiate this rationale for criminalizing behavior.[18] The central point is that we should give members of society maximal freedom to act in their interests as they see them so long as they don't harm others.

The reader may respond that rules are more important in an institution like a mental hospital where people live in close quarters and where not abiding by rules may have more severe consequences, leading down a slippery slope to the violation of rules essential to order. But these fears may not be reality-based. And this rationale, so understood, is arguably a matter more important to the staff's comfort and sense of security than to patients'. Indeed, I believe that stretching the "preservation of the milieu" rationale beyond behavior that directly disturbs the peace of the ward is really to seek the staff's comfort more than patients': the staff has a need to feel in control and able to preserve order. Although staff's comfort level is important—for one thing, it may affect patients' comfort level—it is arguably not enough to justify seclusion.[19]

This last point suggests perhaps the most telling argument against reading "preserving the milieu" to include violation of ward rules. Simply put, secluding the patient in this circumstance does nothing to preserve the milieu. The patient's act is in the past. Unlike the patient who disturbs the peace, whose behavior can be checked by seclusion, the patient who, say, won't come to ward meetings does not have his behavior checked by being placed in seclusion. By definition, the publicly masturbating patient does not masturbate publicly if he is in seclusion, but the patient who won't come to group meetings won't come if he is in seclusion.

It follows that secluding patients on this basis does not spare other patients from ongoing harm, and even though it may deter rule-violating behavior in the future—and to that extent makes patients and staff more comfortable—that is a function of punishment. Seclusion here is punishing behavior so that it won't happen in the future, not stopping behavior that is happening now. In short, it is more a punishment rationale than an incapacitation-from-disruptive-behavior rationale, and I shall consider it further when I take up seclusion as punishment.

Having discussed the first question of what should count as disruption of the milieu, I turn to that of less restrictive alternatives. The answer is fairly straightforward. A patient who, say, is making a commotion should first be talked to, accompanied to his room, or taken on a walk. If all else fails, seclusion may be necessary. A patient who is nude should simply be helped to dress, and if he takes off his clothes again, he should be helped to dress again. It is only after it becomes clear that he will remain nude no matter what the staff does that he should be secludable—and then only if he insists on being in a public place. The response is similar with the publicly masturbating patient: lead him to a private place. These interventions naturally take time, but avoiding unnecessary seclusion should be a high priority.

Third, and related to the second point, we might experiment more with "disturbed wards," which would house patients who frequently disrupt the milieu, thus preserving greater freedom among the disturbed and greater tranquility among the nondisturbed. Would that be a less restrictive alternative? Seclusion, after all, is an extreme sanction for ward-disturbing behavior, inasmuch as it greatly impinges on freedom of movement and of association. So why confine the patient in a small room? Why not put her in an entire ward where she can be disturbing among others who are disturbing? Disturbing patients, of course, do not always act in a disturbing way. But perhaps patients would accept some disturbance of their peace when others on the ward are being disturbing in exchange for greater freedom when *they* are being disturbing. Alternatively, we might require large rooms for disruptive patients throughout the hospital when they were acting out. They could then return to their wards when they were well.

These are but suggestions, and they would require serious thought and research before they could be accepted. For instance, would an entire dayroom reserved for disruptive patients be too costly? Would most patients not *want* to be on a separate ward even if it would spare them from seclusion and thus give them greater freedom at times? Would wards (or rooms) full of disruptive patients increase the disruptiveness of the behavior, as by a kind of contagion effect? Would the staff become upset and demoralized and refuse to work on such wards? These are all important questions. I think they are worth addressing.

What should be the conditions of seclusion following this rationale? I think that, as in the case of seclusion for the sake of containing violence, seclusion for the sake of preserving the milieu should *not* take place in the aversive conditions in which it takes place today. The patient in seclusion should have reading materials, pencils and paper, music. Fellow patients and relatives should be permitted to visit him so long as it would not harm the patient and the visitors are aware of the patient's condition. There is no reason seclusion on this basis should have to be unpleasant.

What procedural protections should surround seclusion following this rationale? Especially since the seclusion is largely for the sake of others, we would want to be sure that patients were protected from wrongful deprivation of their liberty. We should require, for instance, that staff members actually observe the offending behavior and that patients be given an opportunity to explain themselves.

Finally, and perhaps most important, we should limit the time in which a patient could be kept in seclusion. Recall that this patient is not posing an imminent danger to anyone. He is simply making life a little less pleasant on the ward. Accordingly, he should not suffer a serious deprivation as a result of his behavior—it is simply not bad enough or threatening enough for that. Consider in this regard that crimes such as breach of the peace are considered very trivial offenses and give rise to very trivial sanctions, in part because the harm to others is limited and the disruptive behavior will probably abate in a short time.

Indeed, the staff should be required to let patients out of seclusion after, say, an hour. Even if they are continuing their disruptive behavior in seclusion at that point, there is always a possibility that the seclusion is exacerbating instead of ameliorating their condition, so that letting them out would interrupt the behavior. Moreover, the behavior is, again, not *that* harmful to others. If the patient continues to be disruptive during, say, the next hour, he could be secluded again, only to be released again in an hour. This suggestion strikes the right balance between the liberty of the disruptive patient and the comfort level of the other patients. (Of course, staff members are not required to keep such patients in seclusion as long as an hour. As soon as a patient ceases to exhibit the disruptive behavior in seclusion, he should be released.)

In short, the rationale that seclusion preserves the therapeutic milieu is justified provided that we narrowly construe disruptions of the milieu, first try less restrictive alternatives, provide decent and humane conditions of seclusion, including ways patients can occupy themselves, and surround this use with certain procedural protections, especially a strict time limit on the seclusion.

The Punishment Rationale   What about secluding people to punish them for their misbehavior? This rationale would allow seclusion in any of the instances mentioned in the Boston State Hospital case, from violence to being disruptive to escaping to saying negative things about oneself.

Punishment in the outside world serves many aims; some of these are arguably permissible within mental hospitals and some are not. Presumably, punishment *for the sake of* punishment—because the person did wrong and deserves to suffer—has no place in a mental hospital.[20] Retributive functions of punishment are out of place here; punishment in this sense is permissible only when one has been found guilty of violating some codified law.[21] This is not the case with the mentally ill, so what gives the staff the right to punish? In addition, some mentally ill people are less than fully responsible for their behavior and therefore less deserving of punishment.

Indeed, without a right to punish and a notion of desert, the concept of punishment does not apply. Does it help to think of seclusion as a form of behavior modification? Perhaps so. We may then think seclusion justified because it helps rehabilitate people, and therefore serves their treatment interests, as well as because it helps maintain discipline on the ward.[22] It will be clear that this rationale for seclusion overlaps with the treatment rationale, as well as at least one version of the "preservation-of-the-milieu" rationale.

Seclusion as Behavior Modification to Treat the Patient   Is this use of seclusion justified? Should we allow, in particular, seclusion as behavior modification on the theory that it serves patients' treatment interests? Perhaps, for instance, the patient will cease to say bad things about herself. Perhaps she will stop disrobing and masturbating publicly. Perhaps she will learn to self-regulate her affective states so that she does not keep getting out of control. Surely these goods are in the patient's interests.

Nevertheless, seclusion as behavior modification, insofar as it is conceptualized as a treatment, may be subject to many of my previous arguments. First, there will be little scope for its use, as competent patients should have a right to refuse it. Second, less restrictive and more humane alternatives should generally be possible. Third—although less so than in the case of the other treatment theories behind seclusion—there is insufficient evidence that it is effective. Finally, if it is effective, the benefits do not justify the costs, particularly if its use is relatively unrestricted.

That competent patients should be entitled to refuse the use of seclusion as behavior modification is an even worse problem in this context than in the earlier treatment context, because many patients subject to seclusion on this ground will not be at all disorganized or incompetent. Furthermore, patients subject to seclusion are likely to be at their angriest and most upset so they very probably *will* refuse seclusion, precisely at the point at which it must be imposed for behavior modification purposes. This is arguably a self-defeating form of treatment for competent patients.

Less restrictive and more humane alternatives will generally be available. Behavior can be modified by any aversive stimuli, and most are less violative of patients' basic personal liberties. For instance, patients can be deprived of a favorite activity or food, or they can lose grounds privileges, which they highly value. Many wards have a "levels" system, with greater privileges attaching to higher levels; problematic behaviors could result in a lowering of one's level. Other aversive stimuli can be applied that are less intrusive and degrading than seclusion.

But what about the patient at the lowest level, with no privileges? Perhaps he needs something even more aversive before he will respond. But patients in seclusion may also need more aversive stimuli, and we have to draw the line somewhere. Presumably most patients would cooperate if the sanction were severe enough—for example, amputation of a leg. But some aversive stimuli are too cruel to allow. Consider that we limit punishment proper on this basis—witness the cruel and unusual punishment clause of the Constitution. Even if a patient does not respond to less re-

strictive alternatives and might respond to seclusion, the potential benefits do not justify the costs.

We need better evidence of the therapeutic efficacy of this use of seclusion if we are to justify it. It is true that, unlike other treatment justifications of seclusion, an aversive intervention following unwanted behavior
at least *looks* like a form of treatment—namely, "behavior modification,"
a treatment with a long history and a robust theory underlying it.[23] Nevertheless, whether a particular aversive intervention is effective with a particular class of patients requires further study. Are other aversives as likely
to do the trick? Do seriously mentally ill people register this sanction in
the appropriate way and are they able to modify their behavior accordingly? Given the serious detriments of seclusion, I would want better evidence of its efficacy before I allowed it on treatment grounds.

Even if seclusion as behavior modification were demonstrably effective, I think this benefit would not justify its costs. Arguably, seclusion as
aversive stimulus falls at the far end of the spectrum of restrictiveness;
there simply must be less undignified forms of aversive stimuli to use. Although we do use seclusion-like interventions with prisoners and children, so it does not strike our consciences as totally barbaric, seclusion
rooms in mental hospitals are even more depriving than administrative
segregation in prisons (though not something like the "hole") and are certainly more depriving than a child's bedroom. And mental patients should
be treated with more respect and decency than prisoners or children.

What about the use of extremely aversive stimuli in homes for the seriously retarded or autistic? Such patients are not only secluded but also
sometimes shocked. Unlike prisoners and children, these are people who
have an illness. If we allow seclusion as behavior modification for autistic
and mentally retarded people, why not for people with the more typical
mental illnesses?

There are several reasons. First, there is some reason to think that,
given the cognitive or interpersonal impairments of some autistic or retarded patients, behavior modification is the only form of therapy that has
any chance of working. That is generally not the case with the mentally ill,
for whom medications are effective. Second, many if not most autistic
and significantly retarded people will be incompetent to decide on their
treatment, so that others can make the choice for them. Third, because
people with these conditions are devalued in our society, use of these

interventions with them may be a function of stigma itself. Finally, I am not at all certain what I think of the more aversive stimuli in behavior modification programs for the autistic and mentally retarded; I would want to give this issue careful thought before I invoked it to justify seclusion as behavior modification of the mentally ill.

In addition, although my hypothesis here is that such a use of seclusion is "demonstrably effective," the treatment benefits are likely to be modest, as in the case of seclusion as other forms of treatment. Behavior modification may induce people to change their behavior, but it does not give them understanding or well-being. It does not change them inside, so to speak. It is not a specific treatment for severe mental illness; it does not lessen psychotic thought processes. Given the costs, then, these modest benefits are not enough.

Finally, even if we allowed seclusion as behavior modification or treatment, we would need to impose significant limits on its use. Again, the most severe aversives may also be the most effective. In the Boston State Hospital case, Donna Hunt was secluded for eighteen hundred hours over a fifteen-month period as part of a behavior modification regime. She did get better, but she might have improved in another way, less costly to her.

Seclusion as Behavior Modification to Maintain Ward Discipline   What about using seclusion as a form of behavior modification for patients who do not follow ward rules, for the sake of maintaining ward discipline? For instance, a patient who repeatedly had sex with another patient could be secluded. A patient who kept trying to escape could be secluded. Even a patient who refused to get out of bed or go to ward activities could be secluded according to this rationale. The idea would be that the staff needs to be able to maintain ward discipline in some way. Total institutions need rules or they will devolve into chaos. If the staff cannot secure patient compliance with ward rules simply by asking, they must be able to use force. One way to force is to threaten or use sanctions if patients don't comply. Seclusion is a potent weapon in this endeavor.

In this sense, seclusion serves some of the functions of ordinary punishment. In particular, it serves general and specific deterrence. Patients see by example that if they do not observe ward rules, there will be consequences. It serves specific deterrence because the offending patient tastes the punishment and is thereby induced to avoid it in the future.

It could be argued that the use of seclusion in this way secures benefits both to the offending patient and to other patients and staff. The offending patient undergoes behavior modification as a result of the seclusion; this is the theory I discussed and rejected above. Other patients, as suggested when I discussed seclusion as preserving the milieu, will feel more secure in knowing that there is a consistent, predictable ward routine as well as sanctions if the routine is violated. The staff will feel more secure knowing that they will be able to maintain discipline.

This use of seclusion should be prohibited. When a patient is dangerous to others or is seriously breaching the peace, there is a significant enough breach of ward routine to justify seclusion. But both of these cases stand on their own—indeed, I discussed them above. In other words, we do not need the notion of behavior modification as a justification for seclusion.

Actions and behaviors that do not fall into these categories are not sufficiently disturbing to justify the use of seclusion to interrupt them. If patients are having sex, watch them more closely, take away their privileges, or transfer them to different wards. But do not seclude them. If patients are simply refusing to participate in the ward routine, talk to them, cajole them, take away their privileges, and, if all else fails, *let* them not participate. Do not seclude them. Seclusion should be seen as the severe sanction it is.

But what about the effects on other patients of seeing a fellow patient violate the rules? These effects are speculative. Perhaps patients are more pleased that staff members are flexible than fearful that they are weak. It may be more harmful for patients to see the staff as rigid or vindictive than as soft. Seclusion can be terrifying to other patients, and the world can seem cruel if it is used as a sanction for mere rule violation.

What about the effects on staff morale if they cannot maintain discipline? I agree that the staff may feel more comfortable if they have many tools in their arsenal to enforce ward rules. But I am more concerned about patients than about staff, and, unless the ward is verging on being out of control—covered by our other cases—an inability to enforce rigid discipline is simply not important enough to justify seclusion.

In short, seclusion as punishment or, more benignly, as behavior modification should be impermissible, even though it may allegedly serve patients' treatment interests and help maintain ward discipline. Given that we rejected earlier the idea of seclusion as treatment and as a response to rule violation, it should come as no surprise that adding that behavior modification accomplishes these things does not change the result. Something so closely associated with prisons and zoos should not be used so lightly.

CONCLUSION

Seclusion is a very costly procedure in terms of patients' liberty and dignity. Four rationales have been offered to justify it: treatment, containment of violence, preservation of the therapeutic milieu, and punishment (or, more properly, behavior modification). I believe that only the second and some instances of the third are permissible bases for seclusion. The other rationales are too speculative and offer benefits insufficient to justify the costs.

I note also that conditions of seclusion should be more humane than is currently the case. I suspect that they are not because mental health professionals often rationalize seclusion on more than one of the above bases. If seclusion, say, is not only containing violence but also treating by providing destimulation, it makes sense that the room should contain little stimulation. But I think, again, that rationales other than containment of violence and preservation of the milieu are implausible, and they are as implausible together with other rationales as alone. Seclusion should be as humane as possible.

All of that said, we are only at the beginning of studying seclusion, and our evaluation could change with additional data. Clearly more research is needed. One important issue is patients' reactions to seclusion. According to most studies patients find it a very aversive modality, notwithstanding their treaters' claims that it helps them and makes them feel better.[24] Some commentators have suggested that patients be educated about the benefits of seclusion.[25] A perhaps more obvious response is that treaters should be educated about its detriments from patients' points of view.

Moreover, we need more research into whether seclusion is indeed therapeutically effective. Patients secluded for other reasons—for example, danger to others or disruption of the milieu—could be studied to see if destimulation, say, helps them reconstitute or feels like unpleasant sensory deprivation and has the same effects as other forms of sensory deprivation. Do patients hallucinate more in seclusion? Ideally, controlled studies would compare secluded patients with patients for whom other modalities are tried in the same circumstances. Another interesting question is how seclusion compares with other modalities in terms of effectiveness. Are there alternative, equally effective ways to help people calm down?

Finally, seclusion as containment of violence cries out for better studies of mental health professionals' ability to predict short-term violence. Ideally, controlled studies could be done to see what percentage of patients actually attempt to engage in violence as opposed to threatening it. Is staff specialing a reasonably effective way to prevent others from getting hurt in view of the likelihood of many false positives? Or do too many people get hurt that way?

Pending results of such studies, I would allow seclusion only to prevent or contain serious and imminent violence or to preserve the milieu in the face of serious disturbances of the peace. I turn now to mechanical restraints—an even more drastic and brutal intervention.

MECHANICAL RESTRAINTS:

LOOSENING THE BONDS

Julia, a newly admitted psychotic patient, suddenly breaks a plastic spoon while she is eating lunch. She appears amused, slightly fearful, and a touch defiant. Staff suggest that she needs to be restrained. When Julia resists, six orderlies converge on her, pin her to her bed, and, despite her struggles, cuff her limbs with thick leather straps. Finally, they immobilize her torso with a body net. Tied spread-eagle to the bed, unable to move, Julia is now in "six point" restraints.

In time Julia's physical pain will increase. Her ankles and wrists will bruise, her body will ache from the forced immobility. Although she will beg for release (many patients do), Julia will neither be let go, nor told when staff plan to untie her. Alone, frightened, and in pain, she will begin to struggle again—a signal to staff that she needs to be restrained longer. (Saks 1986, 1836)

In this chapter I discuss the costs and benefits of mechanical restraints of the kind that Julia underwent. After balancing competing interests, I recommend alterations to current practices.

THE COSTS OF MECHANICAL RESTRAINTS

Patients like Julia incur significant costs when they are mechanically restrained. Such treatment produces costs in terms of the patient's liberty, dignity, physical, and psychological interests—even more so than secluding him.[1] The patient, tied at four or six points to a bed, is obviously unable to move at all; a patient in the seclusion room at least can pace the four walls of the room. Being unable to move is a drastic curtailment of freedom of the most fundamental kind. Indeed, the person constrained from moving is constrained from doing one of the most basic human activities.

In addition, and perhaps most important, the mechanically restrained patient suffers perhaps the most severe assault on his dignity allowed in a civilized society—and perhaps we shouldn't allow it for that very reason. Animals are often caged. They are sometimes leashed. But even animals are not tied down at their every limb so that they cannot move at all. Doing so would be considered cruel.

Why should it be thought undignified to be mechanically restrained in a bed? The answer is obvious. First, it suggests that one is so dangerous as not to be trusted with even so fundamental an activity as moving. It also renders one utterly helpless, and an attribute of competent adulthood is a degree of mastery over oneself and one's environment. (Infants are utterly helpless, not competent adults.) In addition, being tied to a bed puts one totally at the mercy of others—a facet of helplessness. One cannot protect oneself from others, and one must rely on others for help with such basic activities as toileting and eating. Moreover, being tied spread-eagled simply *looks* undignified: competent human adults are not meant to be in this position. Indeed, it may even call forth sexual connotations—masochistic connotations—that are most unwelcome to the patient and further humiliate him.

Mechanical restraints also subject patients to the risk of physical harm.[2] Being unable to move is deeply uncomfortable—more, painful. Patients mechanically restrained for eight to ten hours report incredible aches in their limbs. Often patients suffer circulatory problems if the restraints are tied too tightly. A significant number die in restraints, typically because they aspirate their vomit and choke to death or have a heart attack. One study identified 142 deaths reported as occurring during or immediately after restraint between 1989 and 1999. A research specialist at the Harvard Center for Risk Analysis estimated many more unreported deaths— 50 to 150 each year. That of course is 1 to 3 deaths per week.[3]

The less irreversible physical risks of restraints are fairly common. That is because patients are often restrained for long periods of time, though not everywhere. There is a different ethos in each state—and each ward—about how long is too long.[4] Thus, New York state law requires that patients be released after two hours and checked after four hours— so most patients, on average, are released then (itself an interesting fact).[5]

By contrast, in Connecticut, doctors mechanically restrained one patient most of the time for more than two years in one facility and routinely restrained patients for weeks in another. A different facility in the same Connecticut city restrained patients much more frequently, on average, but for much shorter periods. These differences cannot be explained by variations in the patient populations of these hospitals but by the ethos of the staff. The central point, however, is that if one city permitted restraints of such long duration, it is probably the case elsewhere as well that patients are often mechanically restrained long enough for the physical pain to become a significant problem.

Of course, the risk of death is the most serious physical risk—and one that raises doubts about the use of mechanical restraints to protect patients from self-harm. I return to this point below.

Finally, and not surprisingly, mechanical restraints are very costly in terms of the psychological harm they may cause. All the other harms restraints cause—to liberty, dignity, and physical well-being—have their psychological counterparts. Being unable to move—to go where one wants, do what one wants to do—can be very upsetting. Dignity violations can be very painful—the patient feels humiliated and degraded. Helplessness is also upsetting and scary. And the physical pain can be acute. Indeed, patients almost uniformly report despising mechanical restraints. In all surveys I am aware of patients report that they find them very aversive.[6] And when asked to rank medication, seclusion, and mechanical restraints, patients almost always rank mechanical restraints last.[7] Patients themselves, then, attest to the psychological harms they cause.

In addition, restraining a patient can be countertherapeutic. It can lead to an atrophy of his internal controls (as can seclusion) and thus can increase his violence in order that he can provoke further episodes of mechanical restraint. The restraints may provide immense masochistic gratification that the patient wishes to re-create. They can do the same if the patient wishes to provoke care-taking by the staff, even physical contact. Finally, the restraint process may further agitate patients, increasing their violence potential.

It should be clear, then, that mechanically restraining patients is a very costly procedure in terms of their liberty, dignity, physical, and psychological interests. Indeed, I think that mechanical restraints are worse in these regards than is seclusion. Since restraints are considerably more restrictive than seclusion, the latter should always be preferred when it would do the job as well.

THE POTENTIAL BENEFITS OF MECHANICAL
RESTRAINTS: THE LESS PLAUSIBLE CANDIDATES

Given all these costs of mechanical restraints, what are the potential benefits? As in the case of seclusion, restraints can be used to preserve the milieu, to punish—or modify the behavior of—patients, to provide treatment, or to protect patients themselves or others from harm.[8]

The first two rationales can be dismissed out of hand. A patient disturbing the peace of the ward is much better managed by seclusion than by restraints, for the former segregates him from others and so minimizes his noxious potential. Perhaps more important, seclusion is less restrictive than restraints and, since it is at least equally effective, should always be used instead of restraints.

Behavior modification is also an impermissible basis for mechanically restraining patients. I forbade seclusion for this purpose, and, again, seclusion is less restrictive than mechanical restraints, so of course I would forbid restraints for this purpose. There are simply better, more humane ways to modify the behavior of patients. Restraints are too brutal to serve as an aversive stimulus.

THE POTENTIAL BENEFITS OF MECHANICAL
RESTRAINTS: THE MORE PLAUSIBLE CANDIDATES

The Treatment Rationale What about mechanical restraints for the sake of treatment? This rationale is also not very persuasive. Indeed, the theoretical reasons for thinking that restraints might be therapeutic are less plausible than in the case of seclusion. Some mental health professionals do claim that restraints are therapeutic in that they help an out-of-control patient feel safe and therefore to reconstitute herself.[9] Nevertheless, this basis for restraining should not be allowed because there will generally be less restrictive means to accomplish this goal; the judgment that restraints are therapeutic is not very reliable; and even if it were, the benefits don't justify the costs.

If restraints help patients feel safer, other interventions may do so equally well at less cost. For instance, the patient may be staff-specialed or held for a time. Mechanical restraints are not generally necessary to avert harm; patients can be made to feel safe from harm by other methods than one so degrading and brutal. Moreover, as in the case of seclusion—perhaps more so—the reliability of mental health professionals' judgment that restraints are therapeutic is suspect. There are no controlled studies establishing (or even suggesting) that this is so. Indeed, surveys suggest that most patients find restraints very aversive—they do not report them as comforting and helpful. Moreover, there are theoretical reasons for thinking that restraints may often be countertherapeutic.[10]

Furthermore, psychiatrists have an interest in thinking that restraints are therapeutic; it allows them to justify to themselves doing something that makes them feel less exposed to liability, less called on to interact with a patient, and better able to manage the ward with maximal convenience to themselves. Indeed, even if restraints did not help them, the staff would want to feel that they were therapeutic simply because they seem so horrible a thing to do to someone. If they are therapeutic, one's conscience is eased.

Finally, like seclusion, mechanical restraints do not seem like treatment. They of course may be so, but with an intervention that so obviously serves the staff's interests, has so many degrading connotations, and is so barbaric, we should require the highest standard of proof before we accept it as treatment. And if restraints *are* therapeutic, the benefits do not justify the costs. The alleged benefits—calming down, feeling safer—are not very great. And no one claims that there are greater ones. It is not as if restraints were a specific treatment of psychosis.

The liberty and dignity costs of mechanical restraints couldn't be greater. And the physical and psychological costs are also very high. In essence, mechanical restraints call forth the image of the mentally ill as wild beasts. In fact, we do not so constrain even wild beasts. The alleged treatment benefits of mechanical restraints do not justify this degradation. Even if the treatment rationale *did* justify mechanical restraints, competent patients should have a right to refuse this treatment just as they have a right to refuse others. And if they can refuse, then mechanical restraints for the sake of treatment may have a very limited use in our mental hospitals.

The Prevention-or-Containment-of-Violence Rationale   Using mechanical restraints to prevent or contain violence seems, on its face, the most plausible use of this modality. Generally, restraints will be used on this basis because the patient is imminently dangerous to himself. Seclusion may not protect him from self-harm; he can bang his head, say, or hurl himself against the wall. So he needs to be mechanically restrained. Generally, this will not be necessary to protect others from danger: seclusion will suffice. But in certain circumstances, whether because seclusion is unavailable or because others by necessity must be around the patient, restraints might be the only option.

Danger to Self Mechanical restraints of the more serious sort should *never* be used to prevent or contain violence to the patient herself. Less restrictive alternatives are almost always available and if we allow restraints on the rare occasions when they are not, many patients will be unnecessarily restrained on other occasions, if only because mental health professionals have an interest in using restraints (they are in terror of liability, tend to seek the most convenient response, and so forth).

The reader may balk at the idea that mechanical restraints are overwhelmingly unnecessary to prevent harm to self. The psychiatrist may point to the case of an agitated patient who is totally out of control in seclusion: flailing, hurling herself against the wall, banging her head very hard. Medication will help but it takes time; in the interim, the patient may seriously harm or even kill herself. Mechanical restraints will calm her down or, in any event, prevent her from harming herself. True, there are liberty and dignity costs. But isn't saving the patient's health or life well worth it?

I take issue with both implicit premises of the doctors' claim. Patients intent on seriously harming themselves can do so in restraints almost as easily as out of restraints. To be graphic about it, a patient can bite herself hard if she is determined to bleed to death. Patients can fight so much in restraints that they die of exhaustion. They can bruise and hurt their limbs by struggling. Most important, they are at serious risk of unintentionally dying by aspirating their own vomit, strangling, or having a heart attack.

It may be that most patients are likelier to *think* of ways of harming themselves when free to move. Even so, the determined patient is as much at risk in mechanical restraints as out. More important, he is arguably at greater risk of dying in restraints than unrestrained in seclusion. This is something that needs to be studied. But the statistics about the number of patients who die in restraints are frightening. It at least needs to be shown whether more die or would die by head-banging—even if there weren't other ways to contain it. Countries that do not use mechanical restraints do not report rashes of patients dying by such actions as head-banging. And of course countries that do use them do report rashes of patients dying while restrained.

This brings me to my second point: there are almost always less restrictive ways of preventing self-harm than mechanical restraints. The image of patients going berserk and killing or maiming themselves in seclusion is not borne out by the evidence. Consider, most strikingly, that mechanical restraints have generally not been used in Britain in more than two hundred years. They are sometimes used, generally while the patient is being transported to the hospital. The fact remains that it is possible to avoid them without patients suffering grave encroachments on their health and safety.

Obviously, British patients are sometimes dangerous to themselves. What do British mental health professionals do in this circumstance? It is unlikely that they simply allow a patient who is repeatedly banging her head against a wall to continue to do so. In my limited experience with British mental hospitals, staff members try first to talk the patient down. They then stay with her to help her remain calm and in control. Physical restraint is sometimes used—that is, holding the patient so that she cannot continue to hurt herself. And medication is of course also used. In my experience, such responses always averted serious self-harm on the part of patients.

I can also imagine other responses to patients' threats to their own safety. First, all hospitals should outfit their seclusion rooms so they are maximally protective of patients; in short, they should return to having padded cells. These are no longer common, perhaps because of their connotations, perhaps because of the difficulty of maintaining them odor-free. But the connotations of being tied spread-eagled to a bed are much more offensive, and being in a somewhat smelly place is much less of an affront than being tied to a bed. I assume, in addition, that padded cells will avert serious self-harm in the case of the vast majority of patients.

For patients who are very likely to harm themselves even in a padded cell because of determined head-banging, or in institutions that have not yet fitted themselves with padded cells, patients at risk of serious head injury should have helmets locked on their heads. Mentally retarded and autistic patients sometimes are treated this way. This *is* a form of restraint, it is true. But it is much less undignified and restrictive than being tied spread-eagled to a bed. People at risk of head injuries—say, as a result of motorcycle accidents—are required by law to wear helmets. I assume that helmets will suffice to protect patients who are head-banging from most forms of serious self-harm.

For some patients, provided the danger to the staff is not too great, physically holding the patients down might be the least restrictive and most effective way to help calm them in a safe fashion. Of course, with a very big and strong patient, and staff members who are not numerous or strong enough themselves, this intervention creates significant danger to staff and so should not be used.

There are concerns about the patient's welfare with this form of intervention. For example, some may dislike being physically restrained more than being mechanically restrained. But I think these patients will be few. Some also may be more gratified by physical restraint, with the prolonged contact it involves, and then they may be likely to provoke it. Such patients should not be treated in this way. In my view, we should presume that physical is preferable to mechanical restraint, both because it will not be used as much—it is simply too costly in terms of staff time—and because, when it is used, it will be worth the costs. In essence, holding someone down is something we do to non–mentally ill people, too. By treating the mentally ill the same as others, we are treating them with more respect.

Finally, it may sometimes be desirable to give patients who are determined to harm themselves high enough doses of medication so that they lose the energy and strength to continue their efforts. I think that even heavy sedation—designed not to treat the patient's underlying illness but simply to disable the patient—is preferable to the use of mechanical restraints. The risks of certain forms of sedation must of course be compared to the risks of serious self-harm. Below I suggest ways of deciding which of these modalities should be used and when.

If all this is right, mechanical restraints should not be used to prevent harm to self. Sometimes, of course, nothing else will work. We have held the patient down as long as is humanly possible without serious risk to the staff, and we think that the medication is taking effect and she is now safe in a padded cell with a helmet. But when we are not looking she hurls herself so hard against the padded walls that she dies. Isn't this a horrible outcome? Doesn't it justify the use of mechanical restraints in cases when nothing else will suffice?

It is, of course, a horrible outcome, but the fear—and the rare actuality—of this occurring does not justify the use of mechanical restraints. Once again, the same outcome can result—may be likelier to result—from the use of mechanical restraints. Perhaps more important, if they are permitted, the outcome will be many false positive predictions of this very scenario, and therefore many unnecessary uses of this measure.

If mechanical restraints are an option, caregivers will reason that they had better use them on pain of liability if serious self-injury occurs. Inappropriately restraining someone is likely to result in no liability; most patients do not bring suit to be compensated for merely dignitary harm, since it will result in only small amounts of recovery and a public hearing will be very stigmatizing. The standard of care should therefore arguably be lessened in the case of failure to use restraints so as to create better incentives; only if a doctor of the most common understanding would have predicted serious self-harm should liability result.

This is a reasonable suggestion,[11] but the standard has not been adopted and perhaps does not go far enough. I now think that a better course is to rule out the use of serious mechanical restraints altogether to prevent self-harm: they are generally not necessary and may result in more injuries than if they were forgone. If a doctor cannot use mechanical restraints for this reason, he will not be able to practice defensive medicine in this sphere—to overuse restraints in an effort to avoid all risk of liability.

It should be clear that the predicate for this recommendation is that mechanical restraints are a brutal and barbaric way to treat people. Their benefits in terms of possibly preventing self-harm do not outweigh their costs, especially since they can cause harm to the patient and there are other ways to prevent his self-harm.

Danger to Others   What about the use of mechanical restraints to prevent violence to others? Is that use ever justified? At first glance one would think not, inasmuch as seclusion is always available and is clearly a less restrictive alternative. But in fact seclusion is *not* always available and, when it is not, restraints are arguably justified to prevent harm to others. I can think of at least three settings where this might be so: during ambulance rides to the hospital, in emergency rooms, and in limited circumstances on psychiatric wards.

On ambulance rides transporting patients to emergency rooms or from emergency rooms to psychiatric hospitals, mechanical restraints may sometimes be justified to avert harm to others. Ambulances cannot house seclusion rooms. And it would be impracticable to staff them with enough manpower so that all patients could be restrained physically.

An agitated or violent patient in an ambulance threatens significant harm. He could directly and intentionally harm the emergency medical technician (EMT) accompanying him. He could also make enough of a disturbance to distract the driver, causing an accident that might harm many other people. Most patients who are dangerous to themselves in an ambulance will not act self-destructively while in the company of another. But if they are intent on doing themselves harm, and if physically restraining them threatens harm to the EMT, then such patients should arguably be mechanically restrainable as well. Driving is simply too potentially lethal an activity to not contain an uncontrollable patient. Nevertheless, given that it is so easy to state a *prediction* that someone will be disruptive and violent, and given that mechanical restraints are very degrading, I would require there to be no reasonable doubt that the patient will become violent: there must be an overt act threatening or doing serious harm or severe agitation.

Moreover, because being tied spread-eagled to a bed or stretcher is so degrading, I would require lesser and less compromising forms of mechanical restraints; for example, simply cuffing the patient's hands and restraining him to a fixed point (by, say, attaching a cord from the restraints to the side of the ambulance) would be adequate. Police generally find it adequate simply to handcuff even extremely dangerous criminals. A scared, confused, and upset psychiatric patient should be treated no less humanely.

The second circumstance in which psychiatric patients might be restrained to avert danger to others is in emergency rooms. Some general hospitals do not have sufficient space for seclusion rooms. And emergency room doctors need to have safe access to patients to evaluate them and their need for treatment. Thus, seclusion would be inadequate even if it were available, and heavy medication does not make sense until the patient has been examined (both because it might not be needed and because the patient might become nonresponsive if too heavily medicated).

The fact that general hospitals sometimes do not have seclusion rooms in their emergency divisions is a problem. I would hope that most of them would try to have a number of such rooms, so that patients who could not be examined outside of restraints at least could be freed while waiting for a bed. It may still be true that having enough such rooms, especially in busy metropolitan areas, would be too costly, so that at times patients would need to be mechanically restrained to protect medical personnel and other patients.

What about the idea that even if the hospital has seclusion rooms, doctors need to be able to examine violent patients? I think there is some sense to this. One could say that if a patient is so out of control that he needs to be secluded or restrained, he is obviously ill. But it may not be at all clear in what way he is ill. Is he psychotic? Is he in a violent rage? Is he having a bad drug reaction? Questions must be asked and tests done to try to establish what is wrong. That said, such an evaluation can be done very quickly, so that, if seclusion is available, the patient needn't be kept in mechanical restraints for long. I would nevertheless carefully regulate use of mechanical restraints for this purpose. First, I would require a serious and overt act of violence, not just a threat. For threats, I would bring in security to stand by in case an actual act occurs (and only *then* seclude or restrain). If seclusion is available, I would use that, unless direct contact with the patient is required, which I would limit to one hour.

I would not tie the patient to a bed but would cuff him, perhaps to a heavy chair. I would require the patient to be released from mechanical restraints as soon as he stops struggling. I would tell him that he can be released then. At least once an hour I would require the staff to release such patients with oral instructions that they may remain outside restraints if they do not threaten or act in a violent way—if they show they can restrain themselves. Security may be present during these times if the patient continues to appear agitated and seems likely to need to be re-restrained immediately.

I believe that such procedural protections are necessary to minimize patient time in mechanical restraints, given the human tendency to over-predict violence. In addition, studies in New York, which requires release after two hours, show that most patients are then released, and that system seems to work.[12] Finally, without such a rule, patients might spend extensive periods in mechanical restraints; in some locales, psychiatric hospital beds are at a premium, and patients spend days in emergency rooms waiting for beds.

The third setting in which patients might be mechanically restrained to prevent violence to others is on psychiatric wards—in very limited circumstances. An out-of-control patient may need to be examined by a doctor and may be too dangerous to approach unless he is in restraints. And patients who become violent on the ward might need to be mechanically restrained in order safely to move them to a seclusion room. Finally, there might be a contagion of violence on a ward and an insufficient number of seclusion rooms to manage the situation safely.

I am not certain that the need to protect the examining doctor is a sufficient basis to restrain a patient once he is on a ward as opposed to in an emergency room. Perhaps on the first day of hospitalization the patient should be mechanically restrained for no more than an hour so that he might be examined. After that, the doctor should simply speak loudly to the patient through the seclusion room door; if blood samples need to be taken or medication needs to be given, the staff can physically (but not mechanically) restrain the secluded patient for the brief time needed to do so.

Mechanically restraining a patient to move him to a seclusion room is also a close call. I find it difficult to believe that doing so is so much safer for the staff that it justifies this barbaric modality; simply putting someone in the restraints probably exposes the staff to as much risk as physically restraining and carrying him to a seclusion room. Many hospitals follow the latter procedure. Until there is evidence that doing so is much more dangerous to the staff, I would not allow mechanical restraints for this purpose. Exceptions would be made if a hospital's only seclusion rooms were very far away from the ward.

Mechanically restraining a patient because there is insufficient seclusion space on the ward or in the hospital as a whole also troubles me. I believe that hospitals should have sufficient seclusion space. If they don't, perhaps the patient should be transported to another facility temporarily. I think this is a close call and leave it to others to debate.

In any of these circumstances on a psychiatric ward, I would require that the least intrusive amount of mechanical restraint be used. Once again, wrist cuffs should probably be tried first. Or the patient could be restrained at the wrists to a heavy chair. Tying someone spread-eagled to a bed because he is dangerous to others is a huge indignity and should not be allowed.

The reader will perhaps wonder why I allow mechanical restraints for the sake of protecting others from the patient but not the patient from himself. Practically speaking, the circumstances are much more limited. I allow it only in ambulances, emergency rooms, and very occasionally (if at all) in psychiatric wards. Moreover, I allow it only in a very time-limited fashion—not only because the time in these circumstances is limited but because I *set* specific limits. In addition, it is clearly possible to use minimal restraints in the case of danger to others: the patient simply needs to be kept separate from you and unable to hurt you. Arguably, patients who are dangerous to themselves would need to be more restricted.

Second, the showing of harm to others that I have required before mechanical restraints are permitted is greater than the usual showing required for danger to self. The patient *has* acted or attempted to act in a violent way. The patient is not secludable, so lesser means are not available. When a patient who is dangerous to herself is secluded, the danger to her is lessened considerably—there simply is not much she can do to harm herself seriously, particularly if other interventions (holding, medications, helmets) are also used. The likelihood of serious self-harm for the patient in a padded cell is much less than the likelihood of serious harm to others in the circumstances in which I would allow mechanical restraints.

Third, it is extremely important that patients protected against harm to self are performing self-regarding actions, as opposed to patients prevented from harming others. This has many implications. For one, it is arguably worse to be hurt by another than to be hurt by oneself: it is less expected and more unwanted on all levels. Thus, the harm of *not* intervening is greater, given equal degrees of physical injury. There are arguments on the other side. One may be more upset with oneself later when harm comes at one's own hands: how could one have intentionally injured oneself? But I think as a rule people will feel worse when harmed by another than by themselves; the world then seems a much less predictable and benign place—and much less under their control.

In addition, it is a worse indignity to be prevented from hurting oneself than to be prevented from hurting another. Why don't you get to decide what is good for you? Perhaps even if you wish you didn't want to hurt yourself, you feel that the harm of mechanical restraints is worse than the harm of the self-injury—and again, why don't you get to decide? The harm of the intervention—the restraints—is, for all of these reasons, greater. We should intervene, if at all, only on a greater showing than in the case of danger to others.

In short, serious mechanical restraints are never justified to prevent self-regarding harmful actions but are justified in very limited circumstances to prevent harm to others. I would prefer that mechanical restraints never be permitted. But I concede that they are sometimes allowable.

CONCLUDING THOUGHTS
ABOUT MECHANICAL RESTRAINTS

Mechanical restraints are not justified for purposes of preserving the milieu or behavior modification. Nor are they justified for treatment purposes. That each of these rationales would arguably justify the mechanical restraint of Julia, in my original vignette, underscores that those rationales are impermissible; I think it obvious that Julia should not have been restrained.

I would not permit mechanical restraints to protect the patient from her own dangerousness on a psychiatric ward, with the exception at times of such minor restraints as helmets. The fact that this view would spare Julia being tied spread-eagled to her bed for more than ten hours is, I think, a mark in favor of my view. Similarly, with respect to danger to others, since the danger she posed was minimal, my proposal would not allow her to be restrained on this basis, even though her facility lacked a seclusion room (itself impermissible in my view).

Danger to self, then, should never justify use of severe mechanical restraints on psychiatric wards. And danger to others, on a very limited basis for very limited time-periods, should be permitted as a basis for mechanical restraints only when seclusion is unavailable or a doctor needs to examine the patient at close quarters. Even then, the patient should be restrained in the most minimal way possible: in wrist restraints alone or restrained at the wrists to a chair.

Tying a patient spread-eagled to a bed should simply be abolished in a civilized country. England has largely done it. We can—and should—do it, too.

PATIENT CHOICE REGARDING EMERGENCY MODALITIES

I have written the preceding two chapters as if emergency modalities can be imposed on patients wholly without regard to their choices. And indeed, we do not ask the man escalating out of control in the bar whether and how he would like to be restrained. But mental hospitals are different from bars, and perhaps some effort should be made to elicit patient choice about the manner of restraint at a point at which it is feasible to do so (that is, before the emergency). But before considering the topic of choice among modalities, let us first consider whether patients should be permitted to request seclusion or restraints at all.

Should Patients Be Permitted to Request Seclusion or Mechanical Restraints? The short answer to this question, I believe, is that patients should be permitted to request seclusion and the minor forms of restraints but not very restrictive forms of mechanical restraints—in particular, being tied spread-eagled to a bed.

Under what circumstances do patients request these modalities, and do these circumstances yield different answers as to when their requests should be granted? Why should we permit some but not others of these modalities to be requested? And what justifies refusing the choice of a competent patient to be, say, mechanically restrained if he thinks this is in his interests? Patients may request seclusion for a number of reasons. They may sense themselves escalating out of control. They may fear that they will become violent—either to themselves or others—and want to protect against that for obvious reasons. Since patients are in a good position to know if they are getting out of control, and since the consequences of uncontrolled behavior can be serious, such requests should clearly be honored. In addition, if the patient feels he cannot be trusted to remain in seclusion, we should arguably lock the seclusion room door; this allows the patient to engage in a kind of self-binding.

Patients may feel overwhelmed by all the stimulation on the ward and may want some quiet time to themselves. I rejected destimulation as a basis for forced seclusion, but it seems a reasonable basis for chosen seclusion. Again, the patient is in a good position to know how he feels and what he needs, and such requests should be honored. There seems to be a much less compelling reason to lock the seclusion room door in this case, but if the patient will not otherwise feel safe or really secluded, I suppose that locking should be allowed.

Some patients may request seclusion who do not *need* destimulation because of their mental state but who simply want some quiet time by themselves. It may be quite pleasant then to be in seclusion—away from the hubbub of the ward, with means of occupying or amusing oneself. Should this kind of request for seclusion be honored? The staff may fear that some patients will abuse seclusion for these reasons and will spend too much time on their own, away from activities, not facing the world. Similarly, the staff may fear that seclusion will come to seem so pleasant that too many patients request it too much of the time. The demand will be so high that there will simply be insufficient seclusion space to meet the demand.

Nevertheless, I believe that most such requests for seclusion should be honored. What is wrong with wanting a little time to oneself? Shouldn't patients generally be allowed to be the judge of when they want to be alone, just as ordinary adults are allowed to do on the outside? In the face of severe harm to a patient's treatment interests, perhaps the staff should be allowed to deny the request. But there should be a very strong presumption in favor of granting it. After all, a patient intent on going into seclusion can simply act out. Of course, if seclusion space is literally unavailable, a patient requesting seclusion for time alone will simply have to wait. Based on the experience of hospitals that permit patients to request seclusion, I do not believe that overwhelming numbers of requests are likely to be a serious problem.

There are other more questionable motivations patients may have in requesting seclusion. They may want staff attention, they may want to appear macho and in need of control, they may want to be unavailable to someone with whom they are angry. Human motives are extremely varied and should be expected to be so in this context as well as others. Once again, though, it is only if such requests are persistent and seriously harmful to a patient's treatment interests that they should be denied—and then only after an effort to persuade the patient that seclusion is not now in his interests.

Patients may request mechanical restraints for a number of reasons as well. Patients who feel themselves becoming dangerous to others, for example, may choose wrist restraints because they prefer to be permitted to

162 . CHAPTER SIX

associate with others—which seclusion obviously doesn't allow—yet do not want to risk harming anyone. Similarly, patients who feel that they might harm themselves by head-banging may ask to wear a helmet in a padded cell, so they cannot harm themselves. Such requests should generally be honored.

Patients may also request more drastic forms of mechanical restraints because they believe them necessary to avert self-harm or because they have found them gratifying in the past, perhaps because they involve physical contact with staff, because they allow the patient to lose control, or because they make the patient feel safer. I believe such requests should never be honored.

But why? The kinds of reasons patients have for requesting the more severe forms of mechanical restraints are precisely the kinds they have for requesting the less severe forms or seclusion. Some of these reasons are good, some are bad—some in the patient's therapeutic interests, some not. What could conceivably allow us to deny this request and grant all the others? The severe forms of mechanical restraints are, simply, much more restrictive than the other modalities. They more drastically curtail liberty and are much more painful. They are also much less obviously necessary to accomplish their aim; other less restrictive alternatives are almost always available. This is not true of seclusion. The most important point, I think, is that tying someone spread-eagled to a bed is very degrading; it is hard to imagine a more humiliating intervention.

But even if severe forms of mechanical restraint are more restrictive in these ways than seclusion or the more minor forms of restraint, why can we not let the patient herself, particularly if she is competent, decide whether the benefits are worth the costs? Perhaps the added well-being she derives from being in severe mechanical restraints outweighs, for her, the dignitary harms. Why should we not let *her* decide?

We do not let competent people make certain choices; the choices are simply too terrible to be allowed. For instance, one cannot consent to being killed or mutilated. We would not let prisoners today choose being whipped in exchange for a less severe prison sentence—or being put in stockades or made to wear diapers. The reasons we do not allow these things, though competently and voluntarily chosen, have interesting implications for our principles of autonomy. The point I want to make here, though, is that severe mechanical restraints are too degrading to allow, even when the patient chooses them.

Second, even if the benefits of using such a severe modality in mental hospitals justified the costs when they were freely chosen, we should not permit them to be chosen precisely because we must always suspect the freedom of the choice. If the staff can't impose these forms of mechanical restraints unless patients request them, no doubt considerable staff effort will go into convincing patients to request them. Persuasion can veer into coercion fairly easily, especially in a total institution like a mental hospital.

Third, these forms of mechanical restraint may be "requested" when there is no doubt that the choice was not free; that is, even when the coercion is not subtle it may be misread as choice. Thus it is common practice for hospital personnel to surround a patient and tell him that if he does not allow himself to be restrained, he will be forcibly placed in restraints; when such patients agree, they are commonly reported to have "gone willingly into restraints."[13] Staff members are not very adequate philosophers with regard to the meaning of such notions as free will.

Fourth, if mechanically restraining someone is allowed at all, then this will inevitably suggest to other patients that it sometimes *should* be requested. Other patients will see the patient who has requested restraints receiving considerable attention; perhaps they will think such a patient special—unusually dangerous or even "cool"; perhaps such a patient will sing the virtues of this method. If we think mechanical restraints of this kind are extremely problematic, we should not want to encourage patients to request them.

This brings me to my last point. Patients *do* sometimes request the severe forms of mechanical restraints. But interestingly, they generally do not do so in countries such as England that have not used them in a long time. Patients in England do, on the other hand, ask for medication or for time in the quiet room.

There are at least two interpretations of this difference between America and England. First, patients in America have seen firsthand the virtues of severe mechanical restraints, whereas patients in England have not and cannot be expected to think of them. Second, everyone has heard of mechanical restraints or has seen examples of their use in "snake pit"-type movies. Patients in England don't ask for them not because they haven't thought of them, but because *no* patient in his right mind would ask for them; only if they are valorized, encouraged, made to seem special—that is, if the staff exerts subtle and not-so-subtle pressure on patients to want them—are they ever requested.

Most distressingly, the people who request such restraints today are probably most often the people who have been restrained in the past. This again could be either because they have seen the true benefits of restraints or because they derive some masochistic gratification from the modality, fulfillment of a need to be cared for, or pleasure from adopting staff's views—or because they have been subtly pressured or coerced. Mechanical restraints may create a need for themselves; in that sense, using them becomes part of a cycle of violence (the patient starts feeling violent so that she can, in her own mind, legitimately ask that this form of violence be practiced against her).

In short, we should not let even competent patients request the most severe form of mechanical restraints both because it is too horrible a choice to permit and because we have some reasons to doubt the bona fides of the choice.

Should Patients Be Given a Choice among Emergency Modalities?

Certain emergency modalities are as effective as certain others in preventing injury to self or others. For instance, secluding the patient and placing him in wrist restraints—especially if tied to a fixed point—are equally effective in preventing harm to others. Similarly, for patients who are dangerous to themselves, physically holding them down can be as effective as putting them in a padded cell, and the latter can be as effective as putting a helmet on a patient who is hitting his head in an unpadded seclusion room. Patients likewise can be given heavy doses of medication that will restrain them chemically; at the limit, patients can be made to fall asleep. Doing so may be as effective a modality as secluding or restraining the patient, although it may take some time to work.

I have not yet mentioned medication in ordinary doses—to treat, as it were, the patient's condition as an emergency measure. Medication may or may not be as effective as these other modalities at preventing harm to self or others. And in combination with them, it may be the most effective. Whether patients should be permitted to refuse medications designed, alone or with these other modalities, to prevent danger to self or others by treating the underlying condition—whether they should be one of the modalities patients can choose—I leave for the next section.

Assuming, say, that seclusion and wrist restraints in the community are equally effective in preventing harm to others, what is the least restrictive alternative? When I pose the different emergency modalities to my students and ask them to rank them for restrictiveness, they propose and defend all possible permutations and combinations. Here, for instance, they might say that seclusion gives greater freedom of movement, whereas wrist restraints fastened to a fixed object allow the patient to be in the company of others. On the other hand, they might say that it is humiliating to be restrained in public.

The exercise shows at least that the concept of the least restrictive alternative is fuzzy and hard to apply. But it also suggests that the most important barometer of restrictiveness is the patient herself. If *she* prefers company to freedom of motion, and will not feel too humiliated in wrist restraints, then that is the least restrictive alternative.

Thus, we should let the patient choose which modality he prefers.[14] Indeed, perhaps incompetent patients should be allowed to make such choices, because, if the modalities are equally effective, what matters most is what the patient wants; and even incompetent patients have wants. If there is no clear right choice—either as to efficacy or as to restrictiveness—who better to choose than the patient? It is his comfort and dignity that will be most affected.

This proposal seems to me to be sound. Questions of implementation would arise. For instance, it would obviously be impossible to elicit the patient's choice at the moment of the crisis. Yet asking him as he signs himself into the ward is likely to terrify him. In addition, he would have little basis to make the decision if this is his first time in a psychiatric hospital.

Questions such as these could be worked out over time—and could be studied—to see which approach is most therapeutic. A reasonable place to start would be not to mention the choice on admission, at least of first-time patients, but to ask the patient after he has been on the ward a few days, or (whichever is earlier) after the first emergency modality to which he is subjected—the staff having discretion the first time. This would frighten patients less and elicit more informed choices, yet would give patients the choice fairly quickly.

There might also be problems with the staff needing to remember patients' choices when responding to an emergency. In an emergency time is of the essence—one must act quickly and decisively to avert the harm.

So the staff can hardly be expected to look up the patient's choice; on a busy ward, how are they supposed to be able to *remember* the patient's choice? I am not persuaded that this is as severe a problem as it might appear. Most patients will make the same choice, so that it is only the outliers whose preferences must be remembered. And of course we would make exceptions if the staff cannot reasonably be expected to know the patient's choice in an emergency—say, substitute staff members who have just come on the ward.

Giving patients the choice among emergency modalities, even if they are incompetent, acknowledges that there is no right answer and shows the patient maximal respect. He is the one who will be controlled; at least give him some say about his poison. Of course, the choice he makes will have to be reasonable—as well as available.[15] For instance, a patient who poses a danger to himself cannot choose physical restraint if he is big and strong and the staff is unwilling to take the risks involved in holding him down.

Indeed, I suggest that the staff retain the residual authority to adopt another modality than the patient's choice, but only if in their reasonable judgment the patient's choice will be significantly more likely to fail to protect the patient or others from severe harm. To give an obvious example, a patient who is severely dangerous to others and who has shown himself to be able to escape restraints will need to be secluded; restraint on the ward is simply much too dangerous.

One may worry that the exception will swallow up the rule. The staff may frequently come up with reasons why the patient's choice cannot be honored. But I would hold the staff to the standard of the reasonable mental health professional, and I would require a *significant* increase in the risk using the patient's modality. Staff members who do not live up to this standard would be subject to suit just as those who fail to take adequate protective action are.

Indeed, I would somewhat alter the liability regime in this instance. Unnecessarily subjecting a patient to an emergency modality that is not of his choosing will generally be a dignitary harm, which does not give rise to significant damages. By contrast, failing to pick the right means of restraint could result in large damages if injury ensues. It is obvious what the incentives are in this regime: use the most restrictive modality. To counteract this tendency, I propose that the damages for wrongfully restraining someone in a way he did not choose be equivalent to typical damages when the staff fails to restrain in the right way and permits serious injury to occur. Only then will the incentives be in proper balance.

I noted above that large doses of medication can be used to prevent all risk of harm. Patients can be sedated to the point at which they cannot act or they can be made to sleep. These measures, once they have begun to work, are clearly as effective as segregation or mechanical restraint. Should we therefore allow this option to patients in the event of an emergency? Should we allow it if they are incompetent? Many physicians suggest that they use physical restraining mechanisms in order to avoid having to disable a patient pharmacologically. They assume that patients would prefer such restraints to heavy medication. But surveys of patients suggest that they prefer medication to other emergency modalities, and some might prefer even heavy medication. The point is that we can *ask* them whether they do.

I believe that patients should be permitted to choose chemical restraints—even extreme ones—rather than physical or mechanical ones. I would, however, reserve this right to competent patients. The choice between, say, wrist restraints and seclusion depends principally on how the patient feels in each—the differences between the two are not very weighty. By contrast, there may be significant risks and benefits of heavy chemical restraints that require a competent mind to mull over and assess. For example, certain medications in high doses may present a nontrivial risk of seizure or death, and it takes a competent patient to evaluate that risk.

I would allow this modality to be used, then, only when a competent patient chooses it. That is, I would not allow substituted judgment determinations for an incompetent patient that he would have chosen it if competent: I want him actively to choose it himself. And I would not allow doctors in their discretion to choose this modality on the theory that it best serves the patient's interests—or even that all other alternatives are much riskier. Restraining someone in a chemical straitjacket is dangerous enough, scary enough, and subject to enough abuse that we should allow it only if the patient competently chooses it.

Where medicating someone for her illness turns into heavy chemical restraint is of course not an easy question. The former as an emergency modality raises different issues, to which I turn now.

Should Patients Be Permitted to Refuse PRN ("As Needed") Medications That Could Avert an Emergency?   When I listed emergency modalities that could be substituted for one another and argued that patients should have a choice among them, I purposely excepted emergency medications because they raise important complications. The central question is whether patients should be able to choose them instead of restraints or seclusion and, perhaps more important, whether they should be able to reject them either alone or in combination with one of the other modalities.

The answer to the first part of this question is clear: competent patients should be able to choose PRN medications rather than restraints or seclusion if these medications would do the trick as well or nearly as well. Similarly, incompetent patients whose choice would have been medication if competent can do so in the same circumstances. Medication is a specific treatment for their illness, and their illness may be causing their danger. Medication is also not nearly so degrading as restraints or seclusion.

In many circumstances, medications may not work quickly enough to keep everybody reasonably safe. But in that event the staff can explain to the patient beforehand that he cannot choose this emergency modality alone; or in the exercise of their discretion at the point of the emergency they can apply another modality while the medication is taking effect. (Of course, if that is the likely course, the staff should inform the patient of this fact.)

But what about the opposite scenario? Here, the competent patient[16] decides he does *not* want medication in the event of an emergency; he prefers seclusion or a minor form of restraint, even if such seclusion or restraint will be more prolonged as a result. Interestingly, every court that has given competent patients the right to refuse psychotropic medication has made an exception for emergencies. Whether this should be the rule and why are interesting questions.

I do not think it at all obvious that there should be an emergency exception to the right to refuse when the patient has, at some time prior to the emergency, expressed a competent refusal of medication in an emergency (although I express some qualifications to this suggestion below). After all, as in the nonemergency context, it is the patient's life; she will have to suffer all the pains and pleasures her choices bring. And the fact that it is an emergency when the medication is to be imposed—though not when it was decided on—does not lessen the value of choice to the patient.

Why, then, do all courts decide otherwise? Perhaps the reason is the emergency exception in all medicine; doctors in this circumstance are given the authority to do what, in their judgment, seems best for the patient. Of course, in most emergencies time is too short to determine whether the patient is competent—indeed, whether he even *has* preferences regarding his treatment. In addition, if the emergency is acute, all the time available needs to be spent on deciding what is medically the most appropriate course of action. We lack the resources to do otherwise.

But my proposal spares doctors the need to determine if, in the heat of the emergency, the patient is competent; he will have made a competent choice beforehand. The situation then is like that of the living will or other advance directives. Of course, doctors sometimes do not honor advance directives when the patient's condition is life-threatening.

One difference between our case and the emergency exception in the case of the physically ill—if we even think doctors' behavior is justified there—is that medication is not necessary to save the patient's or others' life. Generally, the physical forms of restraint will be equally effective at protecting against harm. So why not honor the patient's choice?

One might worry that self-binding in this context is not nearly as good as a current competent choice; and once again, in an emergency there is no time to assess whether the current choice is competent. The problem with self-binding is that the patient cannot have anticipated what it would be like, say, to spend a *prolonged* period in seclusion. Although he may have thought he would prefer that to medication, he might change his mind in the circumstances; but he has no way to register that change and prove it is competent. In an emergency, given the acuity of the situation, we care only about what the patient has said in the past; we arguably cannot take account of what the patient is saying now. In addition, he may be too upset to let us know. Moreover, the patient appears more disturbed now—even though, again, he has not become less competent but has only had a change of heart. During an emergency we do not have the kind of access to the patient that would allow us to assess his current choice—or even, sometimes, that would allow him to express it.

These are legitimate concerns about self-binding, but they are no more weighty here than elsewhere; I will discuss problems with self-binding in chapter 8. It is true that the situation is emergent. But I have glossed over the fact that once the patient is in at least some forms of physical restraint, we have some access to him and can assess any changes of mind he may have had.[17]

The fact that a situation is an emergency, then, is not a good reason to prohibit competent patients from refusing medication. We need to rethink the shibboleth that doctors have free rein to make decisions for patients in emergencies in this context.

Perhaps, however, the problem is not that the situation is an emergency but that seclusion and restraints are not as effective as medication—or at least as medication in combination with these modalities—so that patients should not have a choice of these modalities alone: they are simply less effective at preventing harm. That is, the staff must be able to medicate patients or they will be unable to prevent harm effectively. Perhaps that is another reason that, in emergencies, doctors are given discretion as to how to act; they are in the best position to know what will prevent harm most effectively.

Seclusion and mechanical restraints, of course, are some guarantee of safety. But so is physically restraining someone at a cliff's edge. It is just that there are safer, more effective ways to prevent harm in the two cases. For instance, removing the person from the cliff and bringing him to a secure place is safer than physically restraining him at the cliff; what if, in a burst of strength, he gets away and jumps?

The case is similar with seclusion and restraints. Although medicating a patient who is dangerous to others is probably as dangerous to the staff as placing him in seclusion, leaving him in seclusion, without medicating him, raises other dangers. For instance, he may be so agitated that he intentionally or unintentionally harms himself. Eventually, the staff will need to make contact with him—whether to evaluate him or to enable his eating or toileting—and, without medication, he may pose a significant danger to them. Or he may simply yell and scream nonstop and so disturb the rest of the ward. With medication, by contrast, the patient may calm down much faster and his danger may diminish markedly.

In the same way, a patient is prevented from seriously harming himself much more effectively with medication than without. Although I think that padded cells, helmets, and so on are sufficient protection against self-harm that they justify banning four-point restraints—themselves quite dangerous, as I've noted—these modalities are not foolproof. Patients who repeatedly and determinedly hurl themselves against a wall, even a padded wall, are at some risk of seriously hurting themselves. With medication, there is a greater likelihood that the patient will calm down—and sooner; her agitation will diminish, and she will be less apt to really hurt herself.

Should we, then, permit emergency medication even over a refusal by a patient known to be competent on the ground that it is necessary to prevent serious harm—that the other modalities alone are not enough? I think the answer in some cases is yes, in some cases no. I would allow refusing patients who are in seclusion as dangerous to others time to calm down without medication if that is what they wish. If after, say, an hour, they remain out of control, I would permit medication to be imposed. Such patients pose a threat to the staff who have to interact with them.

What about the patient who is disturbing the peace of the ward? Again, I would allow such a patient time to calm down without medication. Commotions are much less upsetting to the person when he is out of harm's way, so other patients won't be too disturbed. And the patient may calm down without the medication that he does not wish and has a right not to take. After, say, an hour, if an extreme disturbance continues, the patient should be subject to medication; others' interests overwhelm his at that point.

The patient who is extremely dangerous to himself—hurling himself against the wall, banging his (helmeted) head against the wall with all his might—should be medicated right away. This patient is posing a significant risk to himself, and we should attempt to counteract the risk without delay. Medication to treat his agitation will probably help in this regard and is the least restrictive alternative in the circumstances.

The reader will appreciate that I am adding some nuance to the notion of the least restrictive alternative. I suggested above that the least restrictive alternative may be the one to which the patient least objects. But I also suggested—and I underscore now—that this is only the case with roughly equally effective alternatives. Seclusion and restraints in some circumstances are not as effective in averting harm alone as they are together with medication. And sometimes, of course, medication alone will be the most effective modality.

In sum, certain competent patients should have a right to refuse PRN medications, at least for a time, but others should not, principally because the medication is necessary for a reasonable prospect of safety—of the patient himself and of others. There is a final reason for thinking that even the patients for whom I granted a limited right to refuse PRN emergency medications for a time should not have this right, namely, that they will inevitably decompensate to requiring medications, so why not give them to them right away? Patients could eventually require medications either because they pass the one-hour mark or because they become incompetent to refuse.

But this suggestion is not compelling because some patients *won't* decompensate to requiring medications. For the sake of these patients, we allow others to be uncomfortable for a short time—yet also to feel respected in their desire not to have medication. And there is always the hope that more patients will be in this camp than in the camp that eventually requires medication. Actually trying this proposal would allow research into how many patients refusing in an emergency are ultimately medicated on emergency grounds.

In sum, courts that, almost without thinking, allow competent patients to be medicated in an emergency have not given adequate reasons. There are adequate reasons for medicating some patients in limited circumstances. But respecting patient dignity requires allowing other patients to refuse medications even in an emergency.

INCOMPETENCY AND IMPAIRMENT:
CHOICES MADE, CHOICES DENIED

Maida Yetter was a sixty-year-old woman who had been in a psychiatric hospital for a number of years. Her physicians recommended that she receive a breast biopsy as a result of a breast discharge she experienced. Yetter refused, at first because she was afraid of the procedure because of the death of an aunt as a result of a similar procedure (the aunt had actually died many years later for unrelated reasons); she also said that it was her body to do with as she saw best. Yetter was then described as lucid and rational and as understanding that the possible consequences of her refusal included death. For the past three months, her reasons had become delusional: she feared that the procedure would affect her genital system, interfering with her ability to have babies, and would prohibit a movie career. In court Yetter said that she was afraid that the procedure might hasten the spread of any illness and that she continued to have fears because of the death of her aunt. During others' testimony she continually interjected that if she had the procedure she would die.

The court found Yetter competent on the grounds that her original refusal was informed and conscious of the consequences and that her refusal now was based primarily on her fear of the procedure. Fear is common and, although it may be irrational, it is not incompetent. Yetter's current delusions created some doubt, but the court found that they were not her primary reason. Yetter's brother's petition for a guardianship of his sister was denied. (*In re Maida Yetter,* 62 Pa. Dec. 20, 619 [1973])

Mary Northern, a seventy-two-year-old with gangrenous feet as a result of frostbite, refused to have her feet amputated even though her doctors believed that amputation was necessary to save her life. Northern met all criteria of general competence: she could follow conversations, think and speak clearly, and make unexceptionable decisions about her life; she was, as the court said, "an intelligent, lucid, communicative and articulate individual" (205). On the specific subject of her gangrenous feet, by contrast, Northern's comprehension was "blocked, blinded, or dimmed." Her psychiatrists said that she was operating on a psychotic level with regard to her feet: "She tends to believe that her feet are black because of soot or dirt. She does not believe her physicians about the serious infection. There is an adamant belief that her feet will heal without surgery, and she refused to even consider the possibility that amputation is necessary to save her life" (204).

The court found Northern incompetent, pointing to her inability to accept what the doctors saw as the inevitability of her death from gangrene. The concurring opinion pointed out that a more appropriate basis for the incompetency finding was Northern's inability to accept *that* her doctors' believed death was inevitable, not the truth of their belief. Both opinions also pointed to Northern's other distorted beliefs about her feet to ground their incompetency finding. (*Department of Human Services v. Northern,* 563 S.W.2d 197 [Tenn. App. 1978])

These two opinions show courts struggling to decide what it is for a patient to be competent to make a treatment decision.[1] What makes for competency or incompetency is a hard question, as is the definition of "impairment." Competency is a notion that has received extended discussion; "impairment" is a term introduced in this book. I have argued that psychiatric patients generally must be incompetent before we can medicate them forcibly. And I require them to be impaired (in addition to other things) before we can civilly commit them. But what do these terms mean?

THE NORMATIVE ISSUES

In recent years, incompetency findings have ceased to be made on a global basis but are made only as to specific tasks.[2] Is one competent to be a parent? To make a contract? To write a will? The specific context may change what is required. For instance, with regard to contracts but not wills, the security of transactions is a value that must be taken into account. And of course, certain tasks are more difficult than others—for example, certain contracts are especially complex and therefore require a greater level of ability in the parties. Whether we should vary the level of competency on the basis of the consequentiality of the decision is controverted; I discuss that issue below. In this chapter I focus exclusively on competency to make treatment decisions.

Clearly, adopting any standard or instrument for capacity or competency requires careful normative analysis. This analysis is unavoidable, and it is necessary to justify the standard chosen. The most critical normative issue facing any designer of a competency instrument is how to strike the balance between autonomy and paternalism. Bioethicists may have moved beyond this simple dichotomy in many areas. But in the arena of assessing competency, this conflict remains central. This is because, at least as a broad generality, competency standards are the mechanism by which we draw the line between those who will be permitted to exercise autonomy and those who will be treated paternalistically.

Still, it is incomplete to say that in our society we strike the balance between autonomy and paternalism by holding that competent patients only have the right to exercise their autonomy. This simply pushes back the question: how we define competency is itself the pivotal determinant of how that balance is struck—requiring much in the way of competency favors paternalistic interests, and vice versa.

Perhaps more important, the definitional question itself replicates autonomy-paternalism concerns. When to decide for a patient and when to allow him to decide for himself is an autonomy dilemma. We are concerned about allowing people choice—say, of treatment or participation in research—when it is appropriate to do so. But the very definition of competency requires us to decide how much choice we will permit the decisionmaker to exercise in choosing the methods of *deciding* she will use. Are intuitive methods adequate? Must she compare all alternatives? A related question is how much scope we give the decisionmaker to choose the versions of the truth she will embrace—particularly given how contested some issues are.

What does this all mean? In adopting a competency standard, we first want to protect those who are unable to decide for themselves (our "paternalism interest"); this translates into a careful inquiry into what abilities are essential for making decisions. Second, an important purpose of our doctrines regarding competency—which must therefore be reflected in the standard we adopt—is to protect the unconventional (our "autonomy interest"); people should have the right to pursue their interests according to their own lights.

Third, we must be mindful of the discovery of psychoanalysts, psychiatrists, and psychologists that irrationality in decisionmaking is pervasive: people misunderstand statistics, overvalue vivid memories, form somewhat distorted beliefs about their doctors as a result of transference, and so forth.[3] Do we want to find many more people incompetent than our current practices do—to encompass people who are mildly irrational? If we do not make this normative choice, we must be very careful not to find incompetent those who are mentally ill but who suffer from no more irrationality in the relevant regard than many healthy people do. To do otherwise is to mistake the floridness of symptoms for sufficient decisional impairment and therefore to stigmatize unnecessarily the mentally ill (our "nondiscrimination interest"). All these, of course, are concerns that have animated us throughout this book but they become especially pointed in this context.

These are some of the normative parameters in terms of which we must measure a competency standard and instrument. Concretely, what this means is that we must justify both the abilities we require for competency as well as the level of these abilities. Are they really necessary, and if so why? Or are they nice but inessential, much as speaking a foreign language with a good accent is inessential to basic communication? Even if we think them important, do we impinge too much on patient autonomy by requiring them? And if their lack is widespread, do we risk discrimination by applying them only to the mentally ill? In short, choosing the abilities and levels is a thoroughly normative endeavor.[4] The choices will be manifest in the kinds of abilities chosen, the skill level needed in the tests of those abilities (for example, the reading level of an informed-consent form), and the level of performance required in order to be deemed competent.

There are other normative issues also raised by competency standards, for instance, in the research context, where other values (such as the progress of science) are involved. In addition, the question of whether we should adopt a sliding-scale competency approach cries out for further analysis.

Fully justifying a competency standard requires answering all these normative questions: I do not justify here the choices I make in proposing a fairly autonomy-protective standard. The reader will have to be content with knowing that the standard I propose is a sound standard *for someone who values autonomy.*

Indeed, addressing this central normative question—how do we strike the balance between autonomy and paternalism being mindful of the need not to discriminate—is the most important task facing future competency researchers. For example, the designers of the premier instruments to date, the MacArthur Treatment Competency Instruments,[5] completely eschew normative analysis, claiming that they make no normative choices. The MacArthur Research Instruments measure four capacities: understanding (in the Understanding Treatment Disclosures instrument or *UTD*); appreciation (in the Perceptions of Disorder instrument, or *POD*); reasoning (in the Thinking Rationally About Treatment instrument, or *TRAT*); and expressing a choice (a submeasure of the TRAT). The MacArthur Competence Assessment Tool-Treatment (the MacCAT-T) combines these four in a streamlined version that is more usable by clinicians.

What do we make of the MacArthur researchers' claim that they eschew normative analysis? Simply put, they must perform this analysis, and they do smuggle choices in. For instance, they suggest a level for impairment on their research instruments and for clear competence on their clinical instrument. They suggest that we should probably adopt a variable competency standard depending on a cost-benefit judgment about the patient's choice.[6] Perhaps most important, the MacArthur researchers point out that the three main research instruments seem to be picking out different populations of patients, so that a treatment capacity instrument (the MacCAT-T) should aggregate the three measures. This judgment supposes that all the skills measured by the three instruments are important for competency—something that is not at all obvious and needs to be justified.[7]

Indeed, by proposing the research instruments the MacArthur researchers make normative choices.[8] True, the instruments measure only "capacities" (abilities that go to competency) and not "competency" (a legal judgment that one's capacity is inadequate). But why would one measure these particular capacities unless one thought them relevant (critical?) to competency? One could also measure foreign language skills, but no one would bother to measure them in a capacity instrument administered in one's own language and designed to be significant for measuring treatment competency. Simply by selecting the abilities measured and measuring them down from and up from certain levels, the MacArthur researchers are making normative choices. Once again, these choices must be justified. In the meantime, the normative framework I have laid out can help us see the landscape of values in terms of which choices must be made, and my standard can be seen as an autonomy-protective one.

EVALUATING WHICH GENERAL
CAPACITIES ARE NECESSARY FOR COMPETENCY

At least four cognitive abilities seem necessary for competency: understanding the treatment information one's doctor provides (without necessarily believing it), forming adequate beliefs regarding that information,
reasoning in an adequate way on the basis of the information, and giving
evidence of one's choice. With some qualifications,[9] these abilities are
measured by the MacArthur instruments for understanding, appreciating,
reasoning, and evidencing a choice (it seems less likely that the clinical instruments are measuring these precise abilities). All of these abilities can
be normatively justified as necessary for competent decisionmaking.

Why is "pure understanding" (that is, without any necessary beliefs)
required? Comprehension of relevant information is a sine qua non of assessing that information for its bearing on how one should decide. To see
that a competency standard should require pure understanding, recall the
thought experiment concerning John. John is a captive faced with two very
different contraptions—one horrible—between which he must decide,
but about which he understands nothing, because the explanation is
given in a foreign tongue. It seems plausible to say that John is incompetent to decide between the two contraptions and that we should let benign
others decide for him; surely that is what most of us would want.[10] Indeed,
we do not need fanciful thought experiments to recognize the importance
of pure understanding: imagine being asked to make any important decision on the basis of a description in a foreign language. One is simply not
in a position to decide in that case. Pure understanding, then, is arguably
a necessary ability for competency.

But although necessary, it is not sufficient. The ability to assess evidence and form appropriate beliefs is also necessary; thus MacArthur's
inclusion of this ability in one of its capacity instruments makes eminent
sense. Consider our example again. If the captive comprehends his cap-
tor's information but does not credit it—say, because he believes the cap-
tor is delusional—he is not going to advert to this information in making
his decision. Because making a decision in one's best interests requires
assessing how those interests are likely to be affected, the patient must be
able to form adequate beliefs in order to be a competent decisionmaker.

We can think of the matter yet another way. Decisions are based on desires and beliefs. One desires x and believes that y is the way to get x, thus

one decides to y. Believing that y is the way to get x, in turn, requires subsidiary beliefs. A deficiency in one's beliefs may therefore severely affect one's decisionmaking capacity. (How deficient is too deficient is of course another question.) One forms beliefs as a result of assessments of the evidence, so that the skill tapped here is the latter; and this skill is clearly needed in some degree or another for competency.

But pure understanding and the ability to assess evidence are also not enough; one also needs to be able to reason with some degree of intactness. Reasoning allows one to put together the information one has purely understood and, having assessed it, has formed beliefs about it. Consider, at its simplest, the practical syllogism recited above. If one knows that one desires x and believes that y is the way to get x (and say that not doing y will guarantee not getting x), and if one then concludes to not y on the basis of deficient reasoning, one has clearly not made a competent choice to not y. Some level of reasoning ability is required. Thus the MacArthur instruments' inclusion of a measure of this makes sense.

Should expressing a choice also be considered a necessary skill for making a competent choice? There are two possibilities here. If "making a competent choice" means (in part) expressing a choice, then the answer is obviously yes; so much is a tautology. If, on the other hand, "making a competent choice" can include going through intact decisionmaking processes without necessarily telling anyone what one has chosen, then the answer is obviously no. Take a person who is paralyzed and unable to communicate. He may decide after careful consideration that he would like some procedure to be done. Suppose that he would be deemed competent by any (other) measure we could formulate. Does his inability to say what he wants make him incompetent? If not, making a choice and showing one's choice are two different things.

Two views are possible, then—expressing a choice is prima facie evidence of competency that is necessary for a choice to be honored, or is itself necessary for competency. It is not important which we choose, however; in either case the ability must be assessed. (In other words, even if theoretically making a choice without expressing it is the only thing necessary for capacity, unless a person expresses a choice, no one can honor it.)

All the abilities described may be thought necessary for competency. Are there others that have been omitted? For instance, practical syllogisms also refer to the person's desires, so perhaps one must be able to identify one's desires. Indeed, perhaps one must make a choice that is *true* to one's desires. More robustly, perhaps one must *be* oneself so that one can be true to oneself and one's values. Other noncognitive abilities should also arguably be required—for instance, that one not be under the sway of internal compulsion.[11]

I have argued elsewhere that we should not include noncognitive capacities among those required for competency, but I in no way think the question settled. I have doubts at least about our ability to reliably identify such deficits—but it is clearly an open question whether we should want to try to test for them. Here, however, I simply assume that a cognitive competency standard is what is wanted. Readers may regard this chapter as talking about necessary abilities for competency but taking no position on whether they are sufficient.

The four abilities discussed in this chapter are abilities that any competent decisionmaker must have, formulated at a high level of abstraction. The next question is to what *degree* the patient must manifest them. In setting the level we must pay sufficient regard to the values involved in designing competency instruments in addition to the one addressed so far: protecting the vulnerable.

THE STANDARD

I believe that a person should be deemed competent if he (1) understands (without necessarily believing) the information about his illness and its treatment; (2) forms no patently false beliefs about that information; (3) reasons in an acceptable way with the information; and (4) manifests a choice.[12] This standard is similar to that supported by the MacArthur research (as opposed to clinical) instruments in points (1), (3), and (4); it departs significantly from MacArthur in (2).

Understanding   Understanding, as we have seen, seems necessary for competent decisionmaking. The question becomes what level of understanding to require. I believe it should be fairly basic. The informing part of an effort to obtain consent should therefore be set at, say, a high school level of readability; there is no need to be very sophisticated, provided that the essential information is conveyed.

The trickiest part of measuring understanding is that tests may both over- and underidentify people as incompetent. They will overidentify them if the tests measure memory rather than understanding; one who fails to remember may have understood perfectly well and retained that understanding in memory long enough to make a decision. Tests will underidentify incompetency if, once again, they measure memory too much and understanding not enough: one can remember words and recite them back without having any idea what they mean.

The MacArthur UTD is a fairly good measure. It suffers somewhat from the problems identified above but generally does a good job of testing for understanding.[13]

Reasoning   Reasoning, as we have seen, also seems necessary for competent decisionmaking. The question, again, is what level of reasoning ability to require. I believe that only rudimentary reasoning ability is necessary. Requiring knowledge of all the rules of logic or absence of any strong emotions influencing a decision is problematic for a number of reasons. One is that it is unclear that pure or pristine reasoning plays an essential role in all effective decisionmaking; intuitive, idiosyncratic processes actually may improve decisionmaking in some cases. (Consider the reported cases in which people dream of solutions to difficult mathematical problems.) Thus, fully intact reasoning may not be necessary. Concerns about protecting the vulnerable, then, may not be implicated. Moreover, what qualities of reasoning are "good" may be open to dispute, so that to require some particular form of reasoning may be to discriminate against unconventionality.

Perhaps most important, even generally effective decisionmakers who clearly have the ability to form accurate beliefs misuse statistics, misunderstand probabilities, and accord undue weight to vivid examples. They also may be affected profoundly by irrational and unconscious factors. Thus, unless we are to declare most people incompetent, to so declare only the mentally ill who exhibit these deficiencies amounts to prejudicial discrimination.

Requiring some reasoning ability, on the other hand, seems to make sense, as I argued above: if one does not know how to put together the information one has understood, so to speak, one will not be able reach the right conclusion. MacArthur's TRAT seems to set the level of reasoning ability required at about the right place. The TRAT tests for rudimentary abilities—for example, imagining consequences and comparing possibilities—and doesn't require too much of any. For instance, in measuring probabilistic reasoning, it requires only that one understand a gross inference from the probability stated. There is a possibility, however, that the TRAT may underestimate the possession of certain reasoning skills by the way it tests for them. But the TRAT is basically a good instrument, and some reasoning ability is clearly necessary.

Belief Formation   What about the beliefs that should be required for competent decisionmaking? The ability to assess evidence and form appropriate beliefs does seem necessary. The question, again, is how much ability. What sorts of beliefs disqualify one from competency?

Deciding what beliefs a patient must have in order to be deemed competent is fraught with danger. Since decisions take effect in the world, we want the patient to come to accurate beliefs about the world. The problem is that, more often than we like to think, what is true is an open question; very few beliefs are completely indisputable. This means that requiring particular beliefs may not further our interest in protecting the vulnerable; if the beliefs we require are wrong, we are not putting the patient in a better position to decide. We should not say she is incompetent—indeed, if most of us are wrong, she may in fact be supercompetent.

Perhaps more important, freedom includes the freedom to decide what is true no less than what is good. If we require particular beliefs, we prevent the patient from pursuing the truth according to her own lights. There may be some limits on what patients can believe. But limits that are too stringent severely curtail patients' freedom to be unconventional in their pursuit of truth. And once again, patients may turn out to be right. In addition, we must be mindful of the fact that many people have distorted beliefs and make decisions on the basis of those beliefs. Unless we want to call many if not most people incompetent, we are discriminating against the mentally ill if we disable them on the basis of their distortions.

There is a range in the type of belief competency measures can require. At one end of the spectrum is the MacArthur POD, which requires essentially that the patient agree with her doctor about her illness and its treatment. At the other end is a standard that says one must not believe only impossible beliefs. I believe the correct standard is somewhere in the middle: a patient cannot hold patently false beliefs" (PFBs).

I clearly part company with the MacArthur researchers on their measure for belief formation. A subtest of the POD, the Nonacknowledgment of Disorder (NOD), measures whether patients agree with the diagnosis in their charts, the degree of severity of their symptoms as found by the Brief Psychiatric Rating Scale, and the presence of symptoms noted in their charts. The subtest Nonacknowledgment of Treatment (NOT) measures whether patients agree with their doctors' assessment of their prognosis with and without treatment.

Although the ability to assess evidence is important, the POD requires too high a level of that ability—and in a context in which we sometimes cannot decide what a high level is. In my view, the POD is seriously flawed and needs to be radically revised. Given the many contested matters in our society, an individual doctor cannot be held out as the final authority on truth. What would become of second opinions if she were?

In particular, the NOD is most problematic in its first two measures. One's doctor may be wrong about one's diagnosis. Thus, the NOD is limited by the reliability and validity of psychiatric diagnosis.[14] In fact, doctors disagree quite often about how to diagnose a patient and about the category of illness (for example, psychotic disorder, mood disorder, or personality disorder). They sometimes disagree about whether a patient even has a significant illness. A single individual cannot be made the final authority on truth. Indeed, the patient may be quite willing to believe an earlier doctor's diagnosis or even that he is seriously ill but if he disagrees with this particular diagnosis, he is counted as impaired on this measure of the NOD.

The reasons given above also counsel against making the doctor's judgment decisive. She can be wrong and it does not add to a patient's abilities to believe falsehoods. The patient should be given the freedom to decide on truth within broad limits. And mild distortions—here, mild disagreements with one's doctor—are pervasive.

Admittedly, unlike the research instruments, the MacCAT-T asks evaluators to assess the patient's reason for his denial, and the kind of reason given above would result in a full score. It remains the case that the research instruments count some people as impaired who are arguably not in the least impaired. In addition, as I discuss below, the MacCAT-T counts many deniers as impaired—for example, those who believe their symptoms are a response to stress and not an illness—who I think should receive a full score: people can have idiosyncratic ways of looking at things.

The second measure of the NOD asks if the patient agrees with the Brief Psychiatric Rating Scale in rating the severity of his symptoms.

This position also makes little sense, since patients are in no position to rate the severity of their symptoms on a common metric, given that they don't know the metric; they are not in a position to make comparative judgments.

The third measure of the NOD is more acceptable. It asks if patients acknowledge the presence of symptoms mentioned in their charts. Many of these symptoms will be grossly demonstrable. If a patient denies that he has just been frenetically pacing or hasn't slept in days, he is severely distorting reality. Some symptoms, of course, involve more interpretation. Is the patient agitated? Maybe not for him. Other symptoms essentially duplicate the illness question; patients cannot deny that they are ill and admit to hallucinations and delusions, so these types of questions should be off-limits.[15]

The NOT, which measures acknowledgment of treatment potential, is also problematic. The NOT requires one to accept a good prognosis with treatment if it exists, in particular treatment with medication, and a worse prognosis without treatment. If the patient has reasonable grounds to disagree with the doctor's judgment, a hypothesis nullifying his premise is presented, and he is again asked his beliefs. ("Imagine that a doctor tells you there is a medication that has been shown in research to help 90% of people with your problem, *even people who had not gotten better with any other medication.*")[16]

As with other measures, the doctors may simply be wrong—in this case, about one's *particular* likelihood of benefiting from treatment and deteriorating without it. For instance, some patients may become demoralized and depressed by the need to take medication and essentially stop trying, just as some may regress in hospitals and never want to leave. How patients on average do with and without a particular treatment may be indisputable, but averages don't speak to this particular patient, and he may be *right* that he will be in the 10 percent that do not respond to a particular treatment.[17]

Because no one can predict the future, it is problematic to require patients to form beliefs about a particular outcome they will experience in the future. Asking patients to understand what happens generally may make sense; asking them to believe that the general will apply to them does not.

To look at this in another way, in essence the NOT measures optimism and pessimism. Many people are unduly optimistic or pessimistic about many things. Thus, in addition to requiring patients to believe things that may be false and taking away their right to decide about truth as they will, the NOT requires patients (generally mentally ill people) to manifest a trait—optimism and pessimism when they are called for—that many people do not manifest.[18]

I noted above that there is a range in the kinds of beliefs we can require. At one end is the naive view, incorporated in the POD, that we can require the patient to believe essentially what the doctor believes.[19] The view at the other end—patients must not believe only things that are impossible in the nature of things—is equally problematic. Quite apart from the fact that virtually anything, technically, is possible, this view probably allows beliefs that are serious distortions of reality. As such they are most probably wrong, don't impinge too much on the right to be unconventional, and are not widespread. Within these extremes other standards are possible. The most plausible is to rule out delusional beliefs or, farther along the spectrum, patently false beliefs. I suggest that only patently false beliefs should lead to a finding of incompetency. The central task is to explain why.

The standard of holding a delusional belief at first glance seems promising—at least more so than the MacArthur standard. This standard would offer greater assurance that the patient's belief is false and that, even in the face of this falsity, the individual refuses to give up the belief. Unlike false beliefs, delusional beliefs are tenacious—they remain despite evidence to the contrary. Whereas laziness is sufficient for a false belief, mental illness may be a prerequisite for a delusional belief. Thus, stating that a delusional belief renders an individual incompetent is likelier to select people who are impaired while, at the same time, excluding people who simply choose to believe differently from the norm.

There are many questions about delusions that must ultimately be addressed and for which I lack space here. For instance, what are the phenomenological characteristics of these beliefs? Are they a function of conflict or deficit? Are they always in some sense restitutive? How do we distinguish delusions from unconscious and conscious fantasies? Are delusions distinguishable from fleeting thoughts with irrational content? From hopes, wishes, and fears? From unwarranted optimism and pessimism? From other affective states? How do we distinguish delusions from the other mild irrationalities that cognitive psychologists have shown to be pervasive?

The more philosophical questions concern whether we can establish necessary and sufficient criteria for delusions and, if so, whether we can reliably distinguish delusions from false beliefs and other mental products that we do not call delusions. Examples of questions include the following: Is the notion of a delusion thoroughly culture-driven, so that we are simply invoking a concept of conventionality once more? Should our definition of the delusional include people who are not mentally ill? For instance, should we call people who do not believe in physical illness and believe their "maladies" to be curable through prayer delusional? Does it matter if the person is not part of any organized religious group? If delusions are characterized by a lack of evidence, are beliefs in nonsensory entities, such as God, delusions by their very definition? And does a lack-of-evidence standard threaten an infinite regress, since we must assess the evidence for the evidence too?

Unfortunately, I cannot answer all these questions here, although an acceptable competency instrument must do so. Still, the concept of delusion, without more, is not sufficient to deem an individual incompetent for three reasons. First, beliefs that appear to be delusional may in fact be true beliefs. We don't have enough certainty about the world to know with complete certainty when a belief that is termed "delusional" is actually false. The problem is one of insufficient information. Second, given our uncertainty, it becomes all the more important to give people wide latitude in what they believe (our autonomy interest). Third, mild distortions of reality are quite pervasive—yet false. Were mildly irrational thinking to provide a sufficient basis for a finding of incompetency only of the mentally ill, we would be discriminating against the mentally ill (our nondiscrimination interest). Each of these three reasons argues against making the presence of a delusion that affects a treatment decision the touchstone for incompetency.

Stricter still is the standard I propose: patently false beliefs should vitiate competency.[20] The following example illustrates how a PFB differs from a simple delusion. Consider a patient who, as a result of her depression, feels she is a bad person. Suppose that by everyone else's account, however, she is a very good person. Her belief in her badness may be a delusion according to many psychiatrists, who will point out that her belief is typical of a certain kind of depression. But perhaps the patient knows herself better than anyone else, and she harbors mean and ugly thoughts toward others. Her belief may be delusional if it is false, but it is not a *patently false* delusional belief. If, on the other hand, she were to believe that she was the most evil person in the world because she had committed mass murder—even though there is no evidence that she had ever harmed anyone—she would then be suffering from a patently false belief. As this example shows, PFBs are beliefs that are so unlikely that even the most superficial reading of the data will indicate their falsity. Put another way, PFBs—almost, but not quite, impossible—are obviously and indisputably false. They are so unlikely that we would almost not ask *why* a person held them, because it is hard to imagine what would persuade us of their veracity.

A complete account of competency must explore the idea that PFBs impair competency in a way that false beliefs and simple delusions do not. To reach this conclusion, one would have to provide a psychoanalytic, psychological, and philosophical understanding of patently false beliefs. Questions to be answered include the following: Does a PFB impair an individual's decisionmaking capacity in a manner that a simple delusion does not? How do we determine when a delusion is patently false? Can observers reliably agree about this judgment? What criterion defines a PFB? Lack of "scientific" evidence for the belief? Lack of popular support for it? Lack of *any* support for it? Knowing that the belief is not quite, but almost, impossible? Some yet unnamed standard?

A particularly pressing challenge, which I take up only in a future competency project, will be to distinguish PFBs from unconscious fantasies with the same content. In a nutshell, the problem is that many people have unconscious fantasies that form the basis of their decisions, often these fantasies have the same content as conscious, patently false beliefs, and I have established PFBs as the criterion by which competency is deemed impaired. As a consequence, either we call many people incompetent or we risk discriminating against the mentally ill who, unfortunately for them, suffer on a conscious level from PFBs. Put another way, the problem is how to handle pervasive irrationalities—after all, many patients decide to accept treatment on the basis of an unconscious fantasy that their doctor is omnipotent and will protect them from all harm, and many subjects decide to participate in nontherapeutic research based on an irrational belief that the research has a chance of helping them. My project on competency must address the significance of a belief's consciousness.

Many questions remain, then, concerning the "patently false belief" standard. I leave these for another time. For now I want to look at typical reasons for which patients refuse treatment to see if they are best understood as PFBs. From the examples given above, it will be clear that beliefs about others' feelings and motives are not PFBs: the beliefs could easily be correct—perhaps the patient is sensing some unconscious current in another. A patient, therefore, who refuses treatment because he distrusts his doctor's motives—thinks, say, he's in it for the money—would not be found incompetent, even if his belief is a delusion; it is not a patently false delusion. A patient who believed that all of the staff were conspiring to kill him, if there were no evidence for this, would be incompetent.

Another case would be that of the patient who thinks the medication will not work because he distrusts the medical establishment; he therefore does not have faith in his doctor's latest recommendation. Such a patient might be wrong but would probably not be delusional, let alone patently delusional. What about the patient who thinks that the medication will fail and he will be able to heal himself through thinking good thoughts? This is an equivocal case, although no doubt such thinking is not that uncommon—so our nondiscrimination interest is triggered. It may also, at times, turn out to be true. On the other hand, the patient who thinks the medication is literally poisoned would be patently delusional according to my standard.

Another, more difficult, case would be that of value judgments. We saw above that a patient who felt herself to be a bad person would not be suffering from a PFB, although if she thought herself the most evil person in the world because she had killed millions (given no evidence of this), she would be. But what if the patient refused medication, saying that she is bad and does not deserve to get better? This case, I think, is a hard one. The patient may be right that she is a bad person. Could she possibly be right that, as a bad person, she doesn't deserve medical help? This belief, true, is a value judgment. And value judgments are arguably not true or false in the most straightforward way. But it is an extreme value judgment that most people in our society would not hold. For instance, it is cruel and unusual punishment under the Eighth Amendment not to provide adequate medical care for even the most vicious criminals.

My intuition is that most patients who hold this view, if probed, will reveal PFBs about what they have done and why they deserve to suffer. For those who do not, it is difficult to know how to proceed. On one hand, to punish oneself by refusing treatment seems to be a value choice that, if forthrightly articulated, seems to seriously depart from our norms of how to treat ourselves and each other. On the other, many people probably punish themselves, perhaps in more minor ways, for thoughts and behaviors about which they feel guilty. Self-punishment is quite pervasive in our society. If so, our nondiscrimination interest would be triggered if we find people who hold such views about treatment incompetent.

What about Maida Yetter and Mary Northern? Most of Yetter's beliefs are not patently false, but some are. It is not a PFB to believe the treatment she would have might hasten the spread of any cancer and might interfere with a movie career; in some scenarios it might. It is not necessarily a PFB to think her aunt died of the procedure being recommended; that belief might simply be a mistake. The belief that the procedure would interfere with her having children is considerably more suspect, because she lived in a time in which it was probably impossible for a woman over sixty to have children.

In light of this mixed picture, how the court should have decided the case is a bit unclear. For one thing, both *Yetter* and *Northern* might be cases in which we should really apply the impairment standard; see below. But if competency is the issue, the proper disposition in the *Yetter* case is unclear. Perhaps the strongest argument for finding competency is that Yetter, when she was lucid, refused the procedure; so even if incompetent now, the substituted judgment standard would allow her now to refuse.

What if she had always had the same mixture of delusional and nondelusional beliefs? Would she be competent or incompetent then? The answer turns in part on what we do in such cases. Black-letter law is that the competent reason prevails,[21] but this is not obviously right. In addition, the court's invoking the fact that Yetter's decision was based on fear of the procedure, which it noted as extremely common, is of equivocal import. Most delusions involve fear in some way. Thus, if underlying fear were enough to render a choice competent, all delusional people would be competent. Moreover, are all fears rational? What about fear that aspirin will instantly kill one in a case (hypothetical though it may be) in which it were likely necessary to save one's life or limb?

What about the *Northern* case? Here, again, it would seem that some of Northern's beliefs were patently false and some were not. Her belief that her feet were dirty and not gangrenous would seem to be a PFB. Presumably she persisted in her belief despite obvious facts such as that the "dirt" would not wash off and physiological tests demonstrated the gangrene. On the other hand, her refusal to believe that she would die without amputation is not a PFB. Indeed, there was a certain chance that she would *not* die, and she could believe that she was in the percentage who would survive. The majority opinion got this wrong. The dissent was correct to point out that the issue was not whether Northern believed she would die but whether she could acknowledge that her doctors believed she would. Believing the contradictory of this latter belief would be patently delusional. Once again, what to do in mixed-motive cases is an open question. As with the *Yetter* case, the issue here should also arguably be impairment, not incompetence (see below).

I want to conclude this section by suggesting an idea that may be somewhat radical: that, according to the "patently false belief" standard, denial of mental illness often does not disqualify one from competency.[22] I hasten to add that I have no doubts whatsoever about the reality of mental illness and the severe suffering it causes. I completely subscribe to the medical model. On the other hand, denying that one is mentally ill may have characteristics that should lead us to say that it should generally not go toward a finding of incompetency.

Let us consider why. First, a person denying that he is mentally ill may simply not be willing to admit to something that is so stigmatizing and carries such negative consequences in our society. He may be frankly lying about what he thinks, or may be conflicted about what to think, for these completely understandable reasons. In either case, a person trying to avoid the negative consequences of a mental illness diagnosis may be thought to be acting quite rationally in our society—and far from incompetently.

Second, the person who cannot admit even to himself that he is mentally ill is acting on the basis of a common, understandable, and often quite adaptive defense. Denial of difficult things is quite common. One might, through denial, be attempting to avoid the narcissistic injury of having a mental illness. People identify with—and accept ownership of— the contents of their mind; it is a big blow to feel that such an intimate part of oneself is diseased. Denial is also understandable in a way that other primitive defenses may not be. People may perhaps understand another's saying that she can't fully believe that her daughter has died or that she herself has cancer; they do not in the same way understand a person's saying he just can't help believing that someone put a transistor in his brain. In addition, denial can be very adaptive. There is evidence that seriously physically ill people live longer if they deny the seriousness of their ill-ness.[23] And there are other less striking examples of the same. A person denying that he is mentally ill might draw on resources he would be too discouraged to use if he admitted his illness.

Third, mental illness diagnoses are simply less certain than many physical illness diagnoses.[24] Unlike physical illnesses, for which there can be definitive physical findings that unequivocally establish the diagnosis, there are no physical tests for any nonorganic mental illness.[25]

Thus, even when there is considerable consensus among physicians about a particular person's diagnosis, it is *possible*—though perhaps not likely—that the consensus is mistaken. Consider seizures prior to the ad-vent of EEGs or lumps in the breast prior to the advent of biopsies. Phy-sicians could have reasonable bases for diagnosing epilepsy or cancer, but they could always be wrong. In the case of the seizures, an EEG could es-tablish with some reliability that there were no electrical charges firing and that hysterical seizures were the more likely diagnosis. Prior to EEGs, that judgment would be much less certain.

In the same way, a person presenting with the symptoms of a psy-chotic disorder might not actually have a psychotic disorder; she might in-stead have what used to be called a "hysterical psychosis" or what would be called today a "factitious disorder with psychological symptoms." Al-ternatively, she could have a less serious diagnosis, such as obsessive-compulsive disorder with bizarre obsessional thoughts that she does not quite credit and that therefore should not be called delusions. Or perhaps she is frankly malingering for some reason we have not discerned. Even such serious disorders as schizophrenia are thought by many to be a rag bag of different conditions, and sometimes what looks like schizophrenia may not be an illness at all—or at least the illness doctors thought it was.

Although psychiatrists may have reasons for preferring to say that a person has a psychotic disorder, then, they can always be wrong. In the same way, physical illnesses without clear physical findings cannot be as certainly diagnosed as those with clear physical findings. A diagnosis of chronic fatigue syndrome, Epstein Barr's, soft tissue damage, irritable bowel syndrome, even Crohn's disease, cannot be made as certainly as, say, a diagnosis of cancer.[26]

The point I am making is epistemological, not ontological. Again, I have no doubts about the reality of mental illness. In the same way, to say that we cannot definitively prove that someone has soft tissue damage is not to deny that there is such an illness as soft tissue damage or that it can cause considerable pain and disability. The two issues are different.

Now the reader may object that what I have established is only that someone's belief that she is not mentally ill is not *impossible,* not that it does not patently distort reality. Some diagnoses of mental illness are simply fairly obviously true—the person has recurrent episodes, responds well to treatment, and so on. But denial of mental illness may still not patently distort reality because, coupled with the fact that the belief is not impossible, the reasons why the patient believes as she does given her evidence may be completely understandable. People often have a hard time accepting a mental illness diagnosis because they have felt the way they are feeling now for a long time—the illness has come on so gradually, say, or feels so appropriate to their current surroundings, that it feels a part of them. Why suddenly are they called "mentally ill"? In addition, people often accept far more responsibility for their thoughts, feelings, and actions than they arguably should, so a patient may feel that she has chosen to be the way she is. (Compare the reasons people give for behaviors that are clearly a response to posthypnotic suggestion.) In short, when a belief is possible, and when the belief does not wildly depart from the evidence the patient has, we should not deem the patient patently delusional.

Fourth, many members of society are skeptical about mental illness— or at least whether particular behavior patterns or symptom constellations amount to an illness.[27] They may think that mental illness is a failure of will or consists of problems in living or is motivated by a desire to be cared for. They may attribute symptoms to stress and believe that the best response is to cope with or avoid the stress.

Many of these beliefs are not what we would call "enlightened." Some amount to frank prejudice or are at least based on ignorance. But my point is that if these beliefs are not very uncommon, then a particular patient's believing them does not represent a gross departure from ordinary ways of thinking. Once again, we don't want to penalize only the mentally ill who hold certain beliefs when these beliefs are relatively widespread in society at large. In addition, that many people think this way is further reason to hold that the patient's holding this possible belief is reasonable given his evidence and understandings of the world.

Fifth, I have suggested that it *does* represent a patent distortion of reality to deny that one is suffering from grossly demonstrable symptoms. But the patient who can admit that she is agitated, pacing, or scared has every reason to accept treatment that her doctors say will help those symptoms abate. It is not clear that we need to make the patient admit to the illness; it is almost forcing a humiliation on her to do so. In the same way, a patient who admits to abdominal pain and all the symptoms of Crohn's disease, and who understands that her doctor can recommend treatments that will help, need not admit to the disease to be in an adequate position to decide.

Perhaps, however, we should require more; patients need to accept not only that they are pacing, say, but that they have *some* condition, even if it is not the condition that their doctors say they have. Or should we require the patient to admit, say, that he has some condition that *looks* like schizophrenia, that most doctors would diagnose it as schizophrenia, and that, before the fact, it is as likely to benefit from treatment as any other similar presentation? These claims are fairly indisputable in many cases— we don't need a physiological test to establish them. And they may be an added ingredient necessary before some will consent to treatment. I think it's a close call whether we require these additional beliefs or whether simply admitting to one's symptoms and one's doctor's belief in the potential benefit of treatment is enough. An intermediate position would be to require patients to admit, simply, that "something is wrong."

All of this said, there are at least two tacks one could take: one could simply exclude most denial as a basis for an incompetency finding.[28] Alternatively, one could probe the denial further to see if the patient's reasoning is such that one can understand his denial or see it as somewhat reasonable. Perhaps he is not speaking honestly. Perhaps he is narcissistically wounded but, in his heart of hearts, knows the truth. Perhaps he thinks of his behaviors as his choice. Perhaps he shares widely held views about mental illness that lead him to think he is not really ill. In short, one would probe to see whether a given case of denial should be thought to amount to a patent distortion of reality. The implicit assumption is that if a belief is not impossible, then one must consider the patient's evidence, and reasonable interpretations of the evidence, to see if the belief patently distorts reality.

One final point about denial: allowing denial to be a basis for an incompetency finding—and thus forced treatment—is in fact fraught with danger. Not only would it permit us to force treatment on an obsessive-compulsive person who denies that he is ill—and who among us does not have some maladaptive personality traits?—but it would also allow us to characterize political dissidents as ill, and then to use their understandable denial that they are ill as a basis for their involuntary treatment, despite the fact that such denial is to be expected.

In conclusion, we should adopt a standard that holds incompetent those who cannot understand the information provided them, who form patently false beliefs concerning that information, who can't reason with the information, or who cannot manifest a choice. I have discussed these components of the competency standard and have given examples where appropriate. I turn now to the higher standard of impairment.

IMPAIRMENT

I suggested in chapter 3 that, in the case of at least one extremely important decision, decisionmakers who are impaired (among other things) should be disabled from making them. The example was civil commitment; only if the patient was impaired, not himself, dangerous to himself or others or gravely disabled, and (in some circumstances) likely to benefit from treatment should we allow civil commitment. Yet, particularly when the danger is only to the patient himself, why not require incompetency? My view was that, with these other factors present, impairment was sufficient diminishment of a person's competency to allow civil confinement, given its potential benefits.

We may generalize by saying that impairment is enough to justify forced interventions designed to help the patient herself only in the most exigent circumstances: when her choice exposes her to a serious risk of very substantial, perhaps irreversible harm.[29] In certain cases impairment will need to be coupled with other factors, such as the patient's not being herself. In others, where the danger is more patent, impairment may be enough. Cases include choices against hospitalization, refusal of lifesaving treatment, acceptance of extremely risky treatment such as psychosurgery, and acceptance of extremely risky nontherapeutic research. I discuss below having these two levels alone as triggers for forced choice.

But what is impairment? I noted above that a significantly mentally ill person is likely to have impaired cognitive abilities. He may suffer from misperceptions, if not frank delusions and hallucinations. His judgment may be wanting. He may be disorganized in his ability to think—speaking in "word salad" or at least with loose associations. He may be disorganized in his ability to execute actions. He may have problems with controlling himself because his ego lacks a certain amount of integrity. He may be overwhelmed by strong affects. His pessimism may be profound. He may be so low that he cannot execute the simplest actions.

The person I have described sounds like someone in a psychotic state, so perhaps the standard should simply be "psychotic."[30] But the standards actually are not coextensive, although there is a good deal of overlap. They are not coextensive because someone could be psychotic without her psychosis affecting her ability to make a particular decision, whereas the impairment standard requires that there be impairment of the kinds described above *regarding the particular decision or sphere of behavior of interest to the law*. In addition, one could meet the impairment standard without being psychotic—for example, someone with poor impulse control such as a borderline patient, under the sway of an overpowering mood or emotion, extremely fatigued, in terrible pain, with low intelligence, extreme inexperience, conceivably certain physical disabilities. "Impaired," as I use it, does not mean the same as "psychotic," although many psychotic people are impaired and most impaired people are psychotic.

What is the criterion for impairment, then, and how can it be established? One possibility would be to do a clinical evaluation and note the presence of the factors described above. Is the person disorganized? Delusional? Hallucinating? Impulse-ridden? One would need to take care, of course, that these impairments were involved in the particular decision at issue. Another idea would be to use the MacCAT-T to judge of impairment. Unlike the MacArthur research instruments, the MacCAT-T does not count, say, all denial as incompetent—if it has a reasonable basis (for example, a former doctor's diagnosis) and is grounded in cultural or religious factors, it is acceptable. It does, it seems to me, count too much denial as incompetent, but perhaps it counts the right amount for impairment. In a similar way, higher (but still depressed) scores on the understanding and reasoning measures than amount to an incompetence finding could be used to ground an impairment finding.

The MacCAT-T would need to be supplemented by a clinical evaluation, however. First, "impairment" covers more than impaired thinking regarding illness and treatment. Cognitive deficits concerning self-care and behavior toward self and others would also be covered. In addition, the patient must be evaluated to consider such issues as impaired judgment and volitional impairments, which the MacCAT-T does not test for. Another possibility, which somewhat combines the first two, is to use the

196 . CHAPTER SEVEN

MacCAT-T together with a measure of psychiatric symptomatology. The latter may allow an evaluation of the kinds of symptoms that go to impairment without relying so much on clinical judgment.

What are some examples of impairment? To return to Yetter and Northern, both would be deemed impaired. Naturally, their patently false beliefs would be enough to render them impaired. But the beliefs they held that were not patently delusional would also render them impaired. Thus, Yetter's beliefs that the procedure would interfere with a movie career is so implausible that it indicates impairment. Her belief that the procedure would hasten the spread of any disease probably is so as well—depending on the medical facts—as would be her belief that the procedure would interfere with her genital system. Her belief, on the other hand, that her aunt died of the same procedure some years earlier would have to be evaluated further: Is the belief simply a mistake? Was the aunt's death shrouded in secrecy, so that Yetter could reasonably have drawn the conclusion she did? We don't know. Still, Yetter's beliefs largely indicate impairment.

Is Yetter's decision, though, governed by the impairment standard? It depends on how likely her choice is to have life-and-death consequences. If most people with breast discharges are at high risk of cancer, then her choice should be taken away from her based on an impairment standard.

Northern is in the same situation. Her patently false beliefs—that her feet were covered with soot and that the doctors didn't believe she would die (assuming that she held the latter)—would also qualify her for the designation "impaired." In addition, her belief that she wouldn't die, though not patently false, may be an impaired belief. The vast majority of people in her situation do die; at least she must believe that the odds are that she will die. This is the case even though she may be one of the lucky ones who survive, so that a belief that she will survive could turn out to be true. In short, Northern is impaired, and since this is a decision that is likely one of life and death, the impairment standard would govern.

I have touched briefly here on the concept of impairment. A full account of the difference between incompetence and impairment would locate the precise points at which the two could be found on the MacArthur (and related) instruments. This account, as I have suggested earlier, remains for the future.

But why should we have only two levels at which we override patient's choices: one for decisions involving ordinary risk and one for extremely consequential decisions? Should we not, rather, vary the competency level required to correspond to many different degrees of impairment, given that decisions range along a continuum of more or less important? I turn to that question next.

JUSTIFYING A TWO-TIERED SYSTEM

I have suggested that we adopt a two-tiered system for judging when people should be allowed choice: if they are incompetent, we can override their choices in decisions involving the ordinary level of risk; if they are impaired, we can override their choices in extremely consequential or risky decisions. If we decide to have such a system, we must of course justify calling the different tiers by different names (incompetency and impairment), rather than simply saying that they refer to different levels of competency.

But there is a prior question: Why should we not have a much more highly variable competency standard—one that is adjusted up or down at many and various points to accommodate the reality that decisions are not simply ordinary or very consequential, but are risky to different degrees? In other words, why should we not have a truly "sliding-scale" competency approach that makes very fine distinctions to accommodate the fine distinctions in risk that patients face?[31]

Everyone agrees that if a task is more difficult, one must have additional abilities to perform it. This is simply in the nature of competency, which is no longer global but judged of very particular decisions. The proposal here is different—that if a patient is making a good decision, we should require only a low level of capacity, but if he is making a bad decision, we should require a high level. The reason is clear: If patients are about to choose something that has a high risk of not helping them and probably harming them, we want to be very sure that they know what they are doing.[32]

To my mind, however, there is a very serious conceptual problem with varying the level of competency: doing so is only a distant cousin to declaring people who make good choices competent and people who make bad choices incompetent—a practice that has been roundly criticized. In essence, one sets up each individual evaluator as judge of the quality of the patient's decision and allows him to substitute his judgment for the patient's. If the evaluator, for example, devalues limitations on occupational functioning to a high degree, he may disable the patient, by varying the level of competency, from making a choice that risks such limitations. But what if the patient himself does not much care about this?

One response to this charge—although not entirely satisfactory— is to stipulate that whatever level of competency we set, we are balancing well-being against autonomy, so that striking the balance differently when well-being is likely to be affected more seriously makes perfect sense. That is, we as a society choose a particular level of capacity required as the place at which autonomy will be preserved because we judge that most such people, when allowed to choose on their own, make good choices. But this again is to set ourselves up as the authorities on what choices are good.

Two responses are possible. First, in setting the general level of competency (to the extent we have) we may be making a judgment that certain skills are needed for particular tasks, given the nature of the tasks, rather than making the judgment that people with those abilities make what we consider good choices. Yet this response is not entirely persuasive, because we judge skills for a certain task adequate in light of a judgment about adequate performance of the task—does it do well enough what it sets out to do? (For instance, someone lacks the capacities to build a house if the houses he builds all fall down.) So this is not an entirely satisfactory response. On the other hand, to return to the decisionmaking context, to the extent that we judge choices made at particular levels of ability good choices, we may be basing our judgment on people's satisfaction with those choices, not our opinion that they are good choices.

Second, there is an important difference between saying that one must have certain abilities, as a general matter, in order to take responsibility for one's own choices and saying that one must have more abilities when *we* judge one's particular choices bad. The first may be based on the abilities we think are needed (see above), rather than a judgment of whether an individual choice is good; and the first does not involve particular judges making particular evaluations concerning every choice a person makes. Arguably, competency doctrine should not allow evaluators to be continually resetting the balance, as it were; in this way, we avoid allowing evaluators to second-guess patients' decisions and setting someone else up as a judge of what is a good choice; isn't that up to *her*?

The picture, then, is complex. There are reasons to vary the standard of capacity involved and counterweights to those reasons. It seems to me that a reasonable compromise is to have a two-tiered system and to call disabilities at the different levels by different names ("incompetency" and "impairment"). Such a system recognizes that, when decisions are very consequential, we want to be sure that the person making them knows what he is doing. Yet it avoids the worst excesses of allowing individual evaluators to determine competency, in part, based on their evaluation of the person's choice.[33] It does so in two ways. First, it reins them in by articulating precisely when a higher level of capacity is required, namely, when decisions expose the decisionmaker to a very high risk of very substantial, perhaps irreversible, harm. Second, it allows only two levels, instead of fine-grained judgments about individual choices. Such judgments are more offensive in that they allow the evaluator to substitute his judgment for the patient's. They are also more subject to abuse.

So I recommend a two-tiered system instead of a sliding scale. (In fact, this is something of a misstatement. There are rare occasions when we do not allow even competent, nonimpaired people to make choices, namely, when the choices are horrible: for instance, no one can consent to being maimed or killed or to entering unconscionable contracts. Similarly, there are occasions when we let plainly incompetent people make choices, namely, when the choices are completely trivial and benign; for instance, we let young children decide what flavor ice cream to buy and "generally incompetent" demented people make small purchases of "necessaries." The vast majority of decisions, however, will not fall in these ranges, and so, for our purposes, speaking of a two-tiered system makes sense.)

If I am recommending a two-tiered system, why not simply talk about two levels of competency, rather than incompetency and impairment? I prefer the latter for a number of reasons. First, it is too easy for evaluators to lull themselves into a sense of complacency about abrogating people's choices—a really terrible thing—by telling themselves that the person is incompetent; if he is incompetent, we are not derogating from principles of autonomy in overriding his choice. Evaluators should be mindful that they are sometimes overriding competent people's choices, and they should make those judgments with extreme care.

Second, I am not sure that it makes sense to speak of varying the level of competency depending on the consequentiality of the decision. That is, the logic of the term "competency" may be such that one level is all there is. Either you can do something well enough or you can't. One might have a realist ontology with respect to competency and think that there is something objective to which the term refers—and, again, that that is either there or not. But one needn't go so far to take this position; it may simply be a matter of common usage that it doesn't make sense to speak of varying the level of competency based on the consequentiality of a decision.

In conclusion, it makes sense to have a two-tiered system referred to by different terms, and I have tried to give some content to the concepts of "incompetency" and "impairment."

CONCLUSION

"Competency" and "impairment" are terms of art that I have tried to give some content in this chapter. I have also given examples of how these terms should be used and tried to justify a two-tiered system of incompetency and impairment.

Many questions remain. Most prominently, the normative justification of having a standard that is quite protective of autonomy awaits a further treatment, as does development of instruments to measure competency and impairment.[34] Still, my hope is that the discussion in this chapter gives the reader some sense of how to think, tentatively, about these concepts.

SELF-BINDING:

ULYSSES AT THE MAST

Self-binding has made a strong showing in the medical arena. There are probably few in our country who have not heard of "living wills." And many people these days sign them or use other self-binding mechanisms such as durable powers of attorney—designating someone to make health-care decisions in the future if they are incapable.[1]

There has been less of a movement to employ advance directives (ADs) in the mental health context, although commentators have debated their advisability here. In this work I envision a large role for self-binding in the mental health context. Patients are civilly committable and treatable with medication the first time their psychosis manifests itself to health professionals absent dangerousness or incompetence, provided they are psychotic, suffering, impaired, not themselves, and likely to benefit from treatment. Doctors get "one free shot," so to speak. After that, patients will only be civilly committable and treatable by forced medication under much more stringent conditions—*unless they self-bind* to future such treatment in like circumstances. Naturally, they are permitted to self-bind when they are in an unimpaired state (as I define the term "impairment" in chapter 7).

But is this proposed policy good?[2] Should we allow such extensive self-binding in the psychiatric context?[3] The reader will be aware that the rec-ommendation of extensive use of self-binding in the psychiatric context is not the only controversial aspect of this proposal. More controversial, per-haps, is that it allows imposition of the self-bound choice even when the patient is not incompetent but is impaired. I attempt to justify that choice below. (Indeed, it is hard for me to see why self-binding when the second choice is incompetent is at all controversial. Most commentators who are autonomy-protective favor a substituted judgment standard—what the patient would have wanted if competent—when faced with an incompetent patient. What better way to find out what the patient would have wanted if competent than by his deliberately saying, when competent, what he will want in the eventuality of incompetence?)[4]

What are the reasons that commentators disfavor self-binding in the psychiatric context? Rebecca Dresser has written one of the more important articles on this issue.[5] Her essential argument is that, despite the potential benefits of so-called Ulysses contracts, they entail too great a risk of the erroneous deprivation of liberty. In more detail, Dresser notes three important differences between the contract of Ulysses himself—when he instructed his crew members not to release him from the mast when he heard the sirens call—and Ulysses contracts imported into the psychiatric context. First, it is much more difficult in the psychiatric context to determine that the person is incompetent to choose; Ulysses clearly was. Second, the patient in the psychiatric context does not face a danger to his life and the dangers he does face may not materialize.[6] Finally, Ulysses' agreement was a private contract and did not involve the intervention of the state. Self-binding in the psychiatric context would.

Dresser also notes related problems. For one thing, it might be hard to tell when the behavioral indicators triggering the contract have really been met: Is someone spending a lot of money in a manic state or—this time—has he simply made a choice to purchase something he really wants or needs? For another, how do we prevent overreaching by doctors as they try to convince their patients, now grateful that they are well, to enter these contracts?

Despite these problems with self-binding in the psychiatric context, it seems to me to be a good idea under the conditions stated above. Dresser's observations of the difference between Ulysses' contract and Ulysses contracts in general leads her to want to reject them. I acknowledge the differences but do not accept the conclusion. Essentially, Dresser's argument amounts to a risk-of-error argument: we risk too many false positives by using Ulysses contracts here. But every time we make judgments about someone's mental state we risk such errors—in the civil commitment context as now constituted or in the proposed new self-binding context. We tolerate such risks because the potential benefits are so great.

I admit at least two differences in these contexts. First, the person subject to ordinary civil commitment has to be much sicker, and so we are less likely to err. But this ignores the fact that the ordinary civil commitment context involves making some judgments in areas where errors are rife—for example, future dangerousness. It also ignores the fact that, in the most acceptable Ulysses contracts, objective behavioral indicators will be built into the contract based on someone's actual history. Second, the potential benefits are greater in the ordinary civil commitment context, because the person is prevented from suffering severe harm. But this ignores the fact that, in the Ulysses contract scenario, the patient herself is saying she finds the consequences of her illness so aversive that she wants to self-bind.

All of that said, if we adopt Ulysses contracts in this context, there is a greater risk of false positives for the simple reason that *more* people will be subject to evaluation and confinement—people who today are immune. The most important response to this is, again, to point to the immense benefits of Ulysses contracts. There *is* a risk of false positives with them, but there are also significant benefits.

It is also worth noting that the arguments against Ulysses contracts that have been adduced are "second-best" arguments—given the way the world is, the test is hard to apply accurately. The arguments are *not* that Ulysses contracts don't make conceptual sense assuming the ability to apply them reliably. The response to these arguments may be to build in more safeguards to allow for reliable application and not to reject the device out-of-hand.

I have argued against Dresser's claims by invoking the potential benefits of Ulysses contracts. But what are these benefits? Ulysses contracts allow mentally ill people to avoid all the often terrible consequences of being in an actively ill state. These include events that are not sufficient to justify civil commitment but that everyone would find dreadful: going through hundreds of thousands of dollars; alienating family and friends—indeed, losing them; losing one's job; becoming homeless; suffering medical conditions that, though not life-threatening, could nevertheless be very troubling; and—last but not least—suffering tremendously.

The person who signs a Ulysses contract can avoid all of these problems. Indeed, she may in any case become dangerous enough that she is civilly committed eventually—but only after she has wreaked havoc in her life. Why not take steps now to prevent all of these harms? A Ulysses contract allows the person greater ability to plan her life. It gives her more mastery over her fate. Surely these are good things—good enough to justify Ulysses contracts despite the risk of false positives.

In any case, the person drawing the contract thinks so. Which brings me to the next point. Ulysses contracts, while derogating from autonomy in one sense, serve it in another. When honoring a Ulysses contract, we are respecting the choice of the self who made it. We are also respecting the earlier self's right to bind his later self.

In fact, we self-bind all the time: we make promises, we enter contracts, we start projects we need to finish. It is true that we are not contracting to lose our liberty, but is it not up to the individual herself to decide what choices she later wants taken away from her? Indeed, the recognition of advance directives in the ordinary medical context suggests that medical treatment is among the things we feel entitled to make advance choices about—and the treatment or rejection of treatment to which we self-bind can be much more consequential than a short-term loss of liberty. In other words, allowing self-binding is to respect the self in one sense—the earlier self. It is true that we then do not respect the self whose choices are paternalistically taken away. But we have reasons for thinking that the earlier self is the better self—the less impaired self, perhaps even the true self. Allowing self-binding, then, is a strange mixture of autonomy protection and paternalism. Essentially, we allow a person to engage in self-paternalism, which is the most autonomy-protecting kind.

Still, it should be clear that enforcing a Ulysses contract is a form of paternalism. We are letting someone else—the prior self—choose for the current self. We are doing so because we think that the prior self is in a better position to decide—knows better, so to speak, than the current self what its interests are. Indeed, we think that the prior self knows better inasmuch as we imagine it—not least because it is unimpaired—to be the true self. Of course it's going to know the self better than the imposter.

But this needs to be unpacked a little. Is the issue that the prior self is unimpaired or that it is the true self? Yet it is hard to say when a new self has come into being (rather than simply being a changed self) and when the new self has *become* the true self or is simply a temporary aberration. Most likely we identify the prior self as the true self *because* it is unimpaired. But if the status as unimpaired is what is important, we are simply flagrantly imposing our values as to what is better. I concede that this is true but do not find it altogether problematic. Surely a self that is unimpaired is in some sense "better" than a self that is impaired. It has more skills and more options. Impairments are limitations, and, all else being equal, it is better not to suffer limitations. Value choices are problematic in some ways, but some value choices seem so right and good that we should feel fine about making them.

In short, Ulysses contracts respect the better self, and although they are paternalistic to some degree, they are more autonomy-protecting than other forms of paternalism.

We now face the hard issue of allowing the second self's choice to be overridden in favor of the prior self's, *even though the second self is not incompetent.* How can we disallow a competent person to make his own choice? True, it's different from the prior self's. But cannot people change their minds? Even in the case of contracts, say, one cannot force someone to keep working for one, although one can force him to pay damages if he won't. We don't require all contracts to be honored even though the person has, in a sense, self-bound.[7]

To make this position more graphic, I would like to tell a story about myself in college. It was during exam period. I was studying hard. I would take a break each evening and go to one of my friend's dorm rooms to shoot the breeze and unwind. She would offer me cookies, and I would gladly partake. Trouble was, I was also on a diet. So one night I told my friend that I was on a diet and I wanted her not to offer me cookies. What is more, if I requested cookies, she shouldn't give them to me. Further still, if I said I *really* wanted cookies and I had changed my mind about her not giving them to me, she should still decline to offer them. She said she understood and she agreed.

The next night I went to her dorm room. I eyed her cookies with some intensity. My friend, true to her word, did not offer me any. I then asked her for some cookies and she said no. Getting frustrated, I then said I remembered what I had said last night, but I had changed my mind, and I now wanted her to ignore my previous instructions and give me some cookies. She said I had said last night not to listen to such pleas, and I reiterated that I had *really* changed my mind and I wanted some cookies. She refused. I left, furious, and trudged a mile in the snow to a food store to get a pack of cookies, all of which I ate when I got to my room. I eventually talked to my friend again but was cross for a long while. And I never asked a friend to join me in a self-binding contract again.

The lesson of this story is clear: the self may change its mind. The later self, if competent, arguably deserves to be respected, too. Certainly the later self may feel fury if its wants and needs are not heeded, even given

206 . CHAPTER EIGHT

the prior self's choice—the same fury it feels when anyone *else* imposes her views of what is good for it.

Does this story establish that self-binding should not be allowed when the second self is not incompetent? A number of points can be made. First, in the cookie example my subsequent self was not only not incompetent but probably not impaired, either.[8] I would not allow imposition of the prior self's choice when the subsequent self was not impaired. We then have no reason to choose one self rather than the other; even if we prefer the prior self's choice, it is frank paternalism of the worst sort to impose that self's choice because *we* like it. Why do we get to say? Doing so is what preferring the prior self amounts to.

Second, my story traded on the fury I felt when my friend did not honor my choice. But the fury a person feels when her choices are not respected may be as great when the subsequent self is incompetent as when it is not. Of course, later the person may understand why the anger was a necessary evil when her incompetent choice was overridden, whereas if the choice is not incompetent she may not; certainly I never came to understand that in the case of my choice for the cookies.

One question, then, is how the person will feel when the subsequent self was impaired. This will partly turn on whether overriding impaired people's choices in favor of choices their unimpaired selves had chosen is justified, and the person so treated can come to see this. I think it is. Impairment, as I define it, involves a fairly high degree of disability. The person's cognitive, affective, and volitional aptitudes may not be intact. Although not strictly incompetent, the person is not in *as* good a position to decide as if he were not impaired. In addition, the person who self-binds will realize—and accept—that the self-bound choice will be imposed if he becomes impaired, even if he then changes his mind.

It may also be advisable to have an "importance" criterion for triggering imposition of self-bound choices. That is, we might say that if we (or the state) refuse to abide by the subsequent self's act, it should only be in cases in which the stakes are high. For we are engaging in an act of paternalism, and we should arguably only do so in cases of significant importance. For instance, rage may in some circumstances be stronger when minor choices are not allowed—not allowing them is much more humiliating.

Now arguments could be made that drawing lines will be hard and will invite evaluators to make fine distinctions preferring one self's choices to another's because it is ever so slightly more intact. But this need not happen. Because being impaired as I define it is a fairly gross departure from the norm, there is little risk that small departures would result in an impairment finding and allow imposition of the self-bound choice. We will not, as a result of this proposal, be allowing many instances of evaluators imposing their will and their preferences (if only by choosing to respect the prior self's choice—which is of course to prefer the prior self, if nothing else).

Of course, even if it is justified to choose the prior self over the impaired, subsequent self, there may still be rage, both at the time and after. This is something we will simply have to tolerate, given the benefits. It is important to keep in mind, however, that this may well be the response of the person treated in this self-paternalistic way. And therefore we should be mindful of this fact and impose self-bound choices only when we are sure that the specified conditions have been met.

If it is justified to allow self-binding, to be implemented when the subsequent self is impaired, we must put procedures in place to ensure that the self-binding is done properly.[9] First, we must be sure the consent to self-binding is informed, voluntary, and competent. Perhaps the "voluntariness" requirement is the most problematic in this context. A patient has just been treated against his will, perhaps on the "one free shot" protocol described for hospitalization and medication above. Perhaps he is feeling vulnerable. Perhaps scared. Perhaps overly grateful to his doctor. Perhaps afraid to hurt the doctor's feelings. Perhaps as if he must acquiesce in what the staff want if he is ever to be released. Do we really trust the choice of the patient in such circumstances to be his true choice? What can we do about this problem?

I suggest that this is a real problem. But there is little that can be done, at least on the first occasion in which the patient may consent. Certain procedural protections can be put in place. For instance, perhaps a patients' rights advocate can be present during the process of informing the patient and obtaining his consent. Or at least another doctor can be there. Perhaps someone other than the treating doctor should suggest this procedure, so that the patient feels less coerced. One might also verbally inform patients, then give them a written informed consent form, and then give them several days to think about the issue.

On the other hand, these methods may overdeter patients. Perhaps we *want* patients to choose based on their feelings of vulnerability and gratitude: they have just been there, so to speak, and are in the best position to know they don't want to go there again. Yet again, the methods proposed above are not so onerous that they are likely to deter many people.

Whatever we do at the initial consent stage, there should be follow-up when patients are feeling less vulnerable, less grateful, and less coerced. That is, patients should be required to reaffirm their consent to self-binding at some later time—say, three months after they are released from the hospital. It might be well to try to procure patients' consent every three months after their release for the first year, and perhaps yearly thereafter. This is a weighty choice. The mechanics of obtaining patients' consent—writing a letter, telephoning—requires further study: we want to have as many responses as possible without putting undue pressure on the patient.

Other procedural protections would need to surround the self-binding process. For instance, it is important for the parties involved to try to operationalize criteria for when interventions will be allowed. The patient must clearly be impaired. Presumably she must also have relapsed. How are these terms to be understood? Must the patient also face risks of certain kinds, and what kind and to what degree? All of this must be spelled out in as much detail as possible.

Another procedural protection that should be required is an independent check on whether the contract terms have been met. That is, the treating doctor alone should not make this decision. In addition, provision should be made for the patient's revoking of the contract when she is not in a relapse and of settling the dispute equitably if the parties cannot agree whether she is in a relapse. What should be prescribed when the contract conditions have been met should also be spelled out. It seems advisable in this regard to allow for only a short course of treatment during which, say, medications can take effect—on the order of a few weeks at most (and much less if the patient has a history of fast response).

Moreover, if a person agrees to self-bind to coercive treatment in the future, the instrument in which he does so may not be available to the treating physicians or the courts; he may have executed the instrument at another hospital or his attorney's office. Presumably such issues could be resolved by setting up a central registry. The privacy issues around such a registry are significant, but in this instance the person himself is agreeing to be part of it. No doubt other practical solutions are also possible, particularly in the case of people with involved significant others.

One final issue must be discussed. We have talked about the case of someone self-binding to treatment on a lesser showing than is required today for involuntary hospitalization or medication. But what about self-binding to no treatment? This could occur when someone meets involuntary treatment criteria but has previously decided in her nonimpaired state that she doesn't want it. In the right-to-refuse-medication context, she says she does not want medication if she becomes incompetent to refuse. In the civil commitment context, she does not want to be committed even if she becomes incompetent to decide on hospitalization.[10]

How do we feel about allowing people to self-bind to no treatment in the contexts described above? A thoroughgoing commitment to autonomy would perhaps treat this case the same as the case of self-binding to treatment. The nonimpaired self, which has experienced illness and its treatment, has decided it does not want them again.[11] Its considered decision is to have no treatment. This has been decided by a self fully informed of the situation and in a nonimpaired state. How can we not respect that choice, particularly if we respect the choice of the prior self to accept treatment on behalf of its later self?

Let us distinguish two scenarios here: first, the prior self self-binds to no treatment and the subsequent self agrees; second, the prior self self-binds to no treatment and the subsequent self wants treatment.

The first scenario seems to me a perfectly appropriate use of self-binding. One could raise concerns that the prior self is not the same as the unimpaired self now, who perhaps would have wanted the treatment. But one can make the very same argument in the case of self-binding to treatment: the current unimpaired self would not want it, even though the prior self and the current impaired self do. We do not let this argument persuade us in the latter case, and there is no good reason to let it do so in the former. It is true that we generally think no treatment a worse choice than treatment; but we are committed to not imposing our own values as much as possible, and here we have both the unimpaired self and the current self in agreement.

What about the case of the person who self-binds to no treatment, and then, in the situation in which he is impaired, asks for treatment? What do we do then? In the analogous case of the person who self-binds to treatment, and then, in the situation in which he is impaired, rejects it, we honor the prior self's choice. For consistency's sake, should we not do that here too? Whatever we decide of the case in general, there are certainly cases in which we would respect the prior self's wish for no treatment. Suppose, for instance, that the treatment involves a risk or side effect that the unimpaired self strongly disfavors. It makes his hands shake, say, and he is a concert pianist. Similarly, even if we sometimes permit impaired people to assent to treatment when their nonimpaired self self-bound to no treatment, we should do so only in cases where the treatment is clearly the best choice in terms of risk-benefit ratio. If someone says in an unimpaired state that he doesn't want psychosurgery, and then in his impaired state says that he does, we should not allow it. This is because only with nonexperimental treatments that are clearly likely to benefit a person is the person's suffering likely to be alleviated—the whole point of giving the treatment. In addition, if there are serious risks, we want the unimpaired self to evaluate them.

Now these caveats might well make us wonder whether all prior treatment refusals should be upheld on the basis of similar reasoning. I gave examples of disfavored side effects and risky treatments that might lead someone to refuse. But presumably even if we do not know what a prior refuser disfavors about treatment, there is something he disfavors. Perhaps we do best by presuming that he has his reasons, and they are, for him, as good as the reasons invoked above. (Indeed, these may be his reasons; he may just not have articulated them well.)

This is an important point. There is a real tension between our desire to respect the choice of the nonimpaired (the "better") self and yet to provide needed, and in this case wanted, treatment. It seems extremely difficult to deny someone treatment when he is suffering, could benefit from the treatment, and expresses a wish for the treatment. But why is this any different from the prior consent situation? It is also hard to deny someone the right to refuse treatment when that is what he wishes. These cases may seem different, but why? In each case we would be withholding what the current self wishes and imposing the choice of the former self.

Do we think the first case (the prior refusal case) is on a different order of magnitude because we favor treatment rather than nontreatment? But this would be an example of a bald imposition of our values and preferences on someone who is unwilling. He may favor nontreatment. Why do we get to decide? Perhaps the point is not treatment versus nontreatment—recall the choice of psychosurgery—but a good choice versus a bad one. But this is perhaps worse, because we are second-guessing an unimpaired decisionmaker's own evaluation of his choices.[12]

Perhaps the difference between the prior-consent and prior-refusal cases is that in the latter, disregarding the prior self's choice and assenting to the current self's confers an added benefit to simply listening to the current self: it provides needed treatment.[13] By contrast, listening to the current self in the prior-consent case provides only the benefit of not treating a self that currently does not want treatment. Unfortunately, this observation either simply repeats the first two points, which I have rejected, or makes the same mistake as they: it is only if you favor treatment that you see the provision of treatment as an added benefit. The same error? What gives us the right to decide what is a benefit? The patient herself, at least in her unimpaired state, disagrees.

There is another reason that we might wish to provide treatment despite prior refusal given the current self's desire for it: it might be too difficult for *us* not to provide currently wanted treatment when we can help alleviate someone's suffering by doing so. We may not want to be complicit, so to speak, in someone's suffering and declining when he says he wants help. It's too awful to watch a person who wants his suffering ameliorated to go untreated.

If this is so, the idea is not that in the one case we agree with the choice. It's that we feel too bad about not helping someone not suffer. We are then bystanders who are not helping when help both could be given and is wanted. It goes against the grain of the good Samaritan.

But this claim needs exploring. If it is too painful to watch someone suffer when he wants treatment and we decline to give it to him, why is it not too painful to watch someone suffer when he doesn't want to be treated and we decline to respect his choice? Perhaps we think suffering from an untreated illness is worse than suffering from having a choice be disregarded. But why do we get to say that? Perhaps the person who now wants treatment and doesn't obtain it suffers doubly, both from not being listened to and from not receiving treatment. But the person who now doesn't want treatment and receives it also suffers doubly, both from not being listened to and from having treatment. Unless we impose our evaluation of what suffering is or which is the worse suffering, the cases are the same in this regard.

Maybe the most persuasive thing is that we simply feel worse not giving treatment when we can than we do about disrespecting choice when we can. It seems so cruel. But we may think this, if we do, because we think it's good to have treatment when you're sick but not good to have no treatment when you're sick, even when you don't want it. This is a value judgment and is arguably out of place here. More important, even if we are saying that we think it good to use our medical skills to minister to sick people—it's not that they're making a better choice but that their choice coincides with what it feels good for us to do—this argument may be impermissible in another way. For why should we get to use people as instruments to make us feel good? Doing so may violate the norm of not treating people as means.

Now the reader may pull back from the thrust of these arguments. She may point out that we are not *simply* favoring what we think is the good choice. For I conceded above that if both the prior and the current selves decline treatment, we should respect that choice, even though we may think treatment may be best and even though we feel sad to watch someone suffer, perhaps needlessly. So perhaps our principle is that if *a* self of the person accepts treatment, making a good choice, we respect the choice for treatment. But at least *a* self must do so. We are thereby protecting both the patient's treatment interests and his autonomy interests—in the form of respecting at least one self.

An immediate response to this suggestion is that it allows wholesale paternalism: if a person *ever* expressed a desire for treatment, this principle would allow us to treat him. So the principle has to be modified: if either a person's unimpaired self or his current self makes a choice for treatment, and the choice is good, then we should treat him. Unfortunately, this is simply adopting a principle that accommodates some of our intuitions without justifying it. My efforts above went to trying to justify it, but were all problematic.

If this is so, we should arguably not give treatment to one whose unimpaired self self-bound to no treatment, even when her current self asks for it. There are, however, at least two considerations that genuinely cut the other way. First, someone who self-binds to no treatment may not have thought what it would be like if his current self wanted treatment. If he had thought of that, he might have said that, in that circumstance, treatment should be imposed. An obvious way to circumvent this problem is to explicitly mention this scenario to the self-binder, asking him what he wants us to do if his impaired current self wants treatment. An effort should be made to help the person imagine what it would feel like to be the later current self wanting treatment.[14]

Now, one might not be entirely satisfied with this scenario. Even if the person has been asked, if he has never experienced wanting treatment but being bound to his prior self's refusal of treatment, he may not be able to imagine what it would feel like or what he, if he were there at the time as the unimpaired self, would want done. If we think this is a real problem, however, we can simply allow a second free shot, so to speak, in this scenario: treat the consenting self, and when it becomes unimpaired, ask it what it wants the next time it is in this situation—a situation it has now experienced. At that point there would be little choice but to respect its prior choice.

But there is a second, more important consideration that may argue for *not* respecting the prior choice for nontreatment: it is arguably an irreversible choice, and perhaps we don't want to respect irreversible choices when the self later changes its mind. Take the case of someone who self-binds to no life-saving treatment in the event of certain physical ailments accompanied by incompetency or impairment. When a person self-binds to no life-prolonging measures, and then, when he is incompetent, decides he wants the treatment, we give it to him. This is not necessarily because we think the treatment option is the best choice for him. He may endure incredible suffering. It is, rather, that we are committed to not being complicit in a loss of life when someone says he doesn't want it (recall my point above about our suffering from the patient's suffering) and that the decision to die is irreversible.

In the same way, if someone self-binds to sterilization and then, in an impaired state, says she doesn't want it, we are inclined to respect her later choice, because sterilization is permanent. Or if she self-binds to no sterilization, and then changes her mind and wants it, we respect the prior choice: again we avoid doing something irreversible when someone is in a mixed state about what she wants.[15] The reader will appreciate that it is the irreversibility, here, that is most crucial, and not necessarily our agreement with the no-sterilization option: we may think in fact that sterilization is very much in the patient's interests.

If this is so, there may be reason not to allow self-binding to no treatment when the current self wants treatment because the no-treatment option practically guarantees that the person's condition—mental illness, impairment—and therefore his choice will be irreversible. By contrast, self-binding to treatment is not irreversible in this way. Once one is treated one will likely regain one's unimpaired state and can then repudiate one's Ulysses contract.

The claim that the no-treatment choice is irreversible, however, is somewhat overblown. People do sometimes spontaneously recover from mental illness without treatment (although such a person would have more, not less, reason to self-bind to no treatment—he turned out not to need it). In addition, the person can arrange, so to speak, to get himself hospitalized by evincing dangerousness to others. In the same way, I allowed some emergency medication for dangerous patients who do not calm down after a time or who are harming themselves. So a patient who self-binds to no medication could eventually get herself medicated under this alternative rubric. Indeed, to be somewhat cynical, the patient need not even regress to a more dangerous state; she can simply act that way or say the right words.

Patients, of course, need to know that treatment is permissible under these rationales, but they can be told. It is a little disingenuous not to abide by the current self's choice but give her the means herself to circumvent her earlier choice. On the other hand, it is also quite respectful of both her prior self's choice and her current self's. And it leaves it up to her to decide how far she will go to have her current wishes respected.

How we come down on where the irreversibility consideration should lead, then, is a difficult question. The choice of no treatment, although perhaps difficult to reverse, is not strictly irreversible. Thus, it does not belong in the category of truly irreversible choices such as refusing life-saving treatment. As such, it should arguably not be a basis for allowing disrespect of the prior self's choice. This is a close question, though, which deserves more careful scrutiny.

Where should we stand on this position, then? Patients who are self-binding should be told that they may change their mind at the time of the choice and be asked what they would like to have done in that case. When patients have never had the experience of being denied their current choice of treatment, they should be treated once more and asked what they want the next time, now that they have experienced changing their mind about treatment. We are less concerned about the parallel scenario of self-binding to treatment for a couple of reasons. First, most of these people will have experienced their current choices having been overridden in the past—they will have been treated on "one first shot" grounds. Second, even when this is not so, not treating someone closes more options than treating him, even though it does not lead to a strictly irreversible situation.

After the second free shot, self-binding to no treatment should be respected. After all, the patient may have good reason, articulated or not, for not wanting treatment. If we are committed to respecting the choices of the unimpaired self, we must respect choices that we think bad for it as well; we should let the self decide.

Self-binding in the psychiatric context, then, makes eminent sense. It returns choice to the individual. It allows people more mastery over their fate. It has achieved widespread acceptance in the medical context in general, and deserves to be imported to the psychiatric context as well.

9

CONCLUSION

Our journey is near its end. I have discussed many if not most of the issues involving forced treatment of the mentally ill—civil commitment, involuntary medication and other treatment, and restraints and seclusion. I have put these issues in the context of how doctors and lawyers tend to differ about these matters, what the nature of mental illness is, and what the justifications for treating the mentally ill differently are.

Apart from my substantive recommendations, I have made some meta-points throughout that I wish to bring together here. In this conclusion I discuss three issues: first, the reasons I have adduced for thinking that no one can be a principled paternalist or autonomy protector—value impositions pervade this process; second, the value choices I have recommended in a nutshell, and how they compare to those we typically make in this context; and third, my recommendation that we treat the mentally ill as much like the healthy as possible, allowing departures only so far as substantive impairments require them.

First, we have seen reason to believe that no one can be a principled paternalist or autonomy theorist.[1] My discussion in this book has underscored the latter, but the former is equally true: nobody would dream of authorizing, say, a doctor to force treatment of some kind on a perfectly competent, unimpaired person solely because that would be in his best interests. Imagine that the illness was not very severe and the treatment rather unpleasant. Imagine further that it is nevertheless in the person's best interests to have it, by most accounts of what is good for people. Surely we would be horrified if intervention were allowed here. But a principled paternalist would be forced to allow such treatment, because we know it to be in the best interests of the patient. No one would take that position.

216

But why could someone not be a principled autonomy protector? Everyone who believes that incompetence and incompetence alone allows us to override a person's choice is arguably a principled autonomy protector.[2] The problem, as Duncan Kennedy (1982) pointed out a number of years ago, is that there are occasions when most people would want to force choice even though the person forced was not incompetent, and he gives a number of examples.

I have a stronger claim to make: even people who maintain in a principled way that only incompetent people should have their choices overridden are not principled autonomy protectors. The way to see this is to see in how many different ways we impose our values when we decide who will and who will not be able to choose for themselves. The reason this is important is that an autonomy theorist wants to reserve value choices to the decisionmaker herself when she is making a self-regarding choice: she should be presumed to know what is best for herself.

But our own value choices pervade the process of deciding who gets to decide. Most obviously, when we decide to intervene and impose a choice is a value question.[3] Must the person be incompetent or is impairment enough? Do other conditions, such as serious danger to self or others, have to be met? Values and interests must be balanced in order to make these decisions. This book has largely been about how we should see the balances.

So much is obvious. Perhaps less obvious is that the very notion of mental illness is thoroughly pervaded by value choices: deviations from the norm are inescapable when we make a judgment that someone is ill. Recall my discussion of the mental illness vignettes in chapter 2. To the extent that being mentally ill is part of a predicate allowing forced choice, we are imposing our value judgments here, too—in the very concept of mental illness.

In addition, to say that only incompetent choices should be overridden implicates all the value judgments that the very concept of competency involves. Arriving at a competency standard is a thoroughly normative undertaking. We must decide what abilities are necessary. We must decide what *levels* of those abilities are to be required. We must necessarily constrain the person's choice to decide on how she shall decide, that is, by what methods. We must at a certain point constrain the kinds of beliefs she may hold. This is imposing a value choice, inasmuch as she may see differently than her evaluators how best to arrive at the truth. The concept of competency is itself thoroughly value-laden.

Another value question involved with competency is whether we should vary the level—a thoroughly normative question. I have suggested two levels—incompetency and impairment—and the latter raises value questions of its own. How impaired is impaired enough? Why aren't features of decisionmaking that we call impaired merely idiosyncratic or eccentric ways of deciding? Why do we get to impose our values?

Indeed, to speak to both incompetency and impairment, the very concept of an ability involves norms and values, as we saw in the context of mental illness judgments. One is considered disabled only to the extent that the absence of a trait prevents us from doing something we want. And one is considered able only to the extent that the presence of the trait enables us to do something we want. But people can have different preferences about these things—different values. One might value being able to lie in bed for months if one considers that a worthy goal—and so consider that an ability. And one might devalue being able to work and so consider the ability to work a disability. People of course don't do that for the most part; but the point is that, even though certain values are widely shared, they *are* values.

Other value questions are involved too: should we allow self-binding? Should we prefer in the self-binding context the healthy self or the unhealthy self? Should we allow people to change their minds in the self-binding context when they have self-bound to no treatment but now want it? To the extent that we do, we are imposing value choices: we are preferring the healthy self, who makes what we think the healthy choice, to the unhealthy.

Another value question raised in this general area is what criteria we should use when we are authorized to decide for another. Should we do what he's said he wants in the past? What we think he would want? What we think best for him? Deciding this question involves an imposition of our values.

In short, there can be no principled autonomy theorist. Certainly everyone imposes his values sometimes when a person is making a self-regarding choice—everyone wants to disable some people some of the time, for example, those who are incompetent. More important, there are no principled autonomy theorists among those who more moderately impose only the value that they will let people decide for themselves provided they are competent. Values thoroughly pervade the process. What this means is that we must think through the value choices necessarily made and not fool ourselves that a commitment to "autonomy" or "competency" can answer all the hard questions.

This leads me to my second task: to discuss the value choices I recommend that we, as a society, make in this context. I do not rehearse all of the specific recommendations made in the different contexts (civil commitment, right to refuse treatment, and restraints and seclusion). Rather, I note that the recommendations I have made are both *more* and *less* autonomy-protective than current law, in a number of ways. I am more skeptical about what should be called mental illnesses than most doctors. In the civil commitment context, I require not only danger to others but *serious* danger to others, coupled with other things not required under current law—for example, impairment and not being oneself. I am more autonomy-protective in the restraints and seclusion context in ruling out most mechanical restraints, limiting seclusion, and giving patients some choice about which emergency modality they would like. Perhaps most important, I am more autonomy-protective in spelling out a low standard for competency; only the most seriously disabled will meet this standard.

On the other hand, my recommendations are also more paternalistic than current laws. For one thing, they allow for forced hospitalization and treatment the first time a person has come to the attention to treaters in a psychotic state. For another, they provide for the concept of self-paternalism by allowing people to self-bind to treatment (hospitalization and medication) even when they would not ordinarily meet the criteria for these measures and even when they are not incompetent when it comes time to impose the choice. This greater paternalism is justified in both cases because we have reason to believe that the non–mentally ill self—the "true" self (or at least the self we choose to prefer)—will be grateful for our intervention.

One might say that preferring the healthy self is to favor autonomy, and not paternalism, on the ground that the healthy self is the more autonomous. So intervening in these contexts enhances future autonomy. The reader will recall that this is essentially the doctor's typical view in this context. I, however, think it more honest frankly to admit that our actions are paternalistic, even if they do enhance future autonomy and allow the true self to do the choosing in the self-binding context. Self-binding has been rightly referred to as a form of self-paternalism—but paternalism it remains. Nevertheless, I feel comfortable in preferring the nonimpaired self to the impaired self, however much it involves an imposition of our values.

The third thing I wish to point out is my effort in this book to treat the mentally ill without bias and in a nondiscriminatory way. I looked carefully at why we should treat the mentally ill differently, if we should. And I found that there is no good reason to do so solely by virtue of their mental illness. There is good reason to treat, say, the incompetent differently, but many mentally ill people are not incompetent. Thus I took a careful look at each context I discussed and made an effort to arrive at a standard that we could in good conscience apply to the healthy, however likelier the ill would be to evince the characteristics captured by the standard.

In the civil commitment context, for example, I focused on the impairment and not-being-oneself aspects of mental illness, in addition to the kinds of risks nonhospitalization would pose, and arrived at a standard that could conceivably apply to a physically ill person too in similar circumstances. And I proposed a general standard for when anyone who was impaired could have choice taken away from her. In the right-to-refuse-medication context I used precisely the same standard that is applied to the non–mentally ill: only the incompetent could be medicated involuntarily absent an emergency. In the restraints-and-seclusion context I allowed only such interventions as would be permissible outside a hospital in the case of the healthy. That made me question whether tying someone spread-eagled to a bed as a result of danger to self should ever be allowed.

In addition, my definitions of incompetence and impairment paid close attention to the healthy. For instance, decisionmaking is impaired in many people who are not mentally ill, and I took care to arrive at a standard of incompetence that did not unfairly discriminate against the mentally ill who share these mild impairments. I also allowed that people other than the mentally ill could meet my definition of "impaired" (as they could my definition of "incompetent"). Finally, I allowed for self-binding in the mental health context as it is currently allowed in the physical health context. And provided the second choice was impaired, I allowed it to be ignored—a principle applicable to the healthy no less than the ill.

Mentally ill people have for too long been terrorized by the system, neglected, and discriminated against. I hope in this book to have come to a rational scheme for their treatment in contexts in which they are unwilling—one that does not add further to their mistreatment. It remains for someone to write a book—and do the lobbying—that will obtain for the mentally ill treatment they ask for and they are now refused by others.

INTRODUCTION

1. Serious criminality is also highly stigmatized, although in many sectors of life less so than mental illness. Certainly many people would rather be convicted of a crime and spend time in prison than be found mentally ill and spend time in a hospital. And most members of society simply assume that those who commit really serious crimes are also mentally ill.

CHAPTER ONE

1. It is widely held in the literature that lawyers tend to favor principles of autonomy, whereas doctors tend to favor principles of paternalism. See, e.g., Annas and Densberger 1984; Blackburn 1990; Brooks 1986; Roth 1986; and Slovenko 1989. For an important empirical study of lawyers vs. psychiatrists (and law and medical students) in evaluating psychiatric patients' ability to give informed consent, see Kaufmann et al. 1981.

2. One might simply refer to the doctor's and the lawyer's judgments or predictions, rather than their fears and fantasies. But I think "fears and fantasies" is more accurate. I use the word "fantasy" much as a psychoanalyst does: it is a belief that seems compelling but may or may not accord with reality and may say more about the person holding the fantasy than about the object of the fantasy. I think it is correct to call these considerations, as held by the doctor and lawyer, "fantasies."

3. Some commentators reserve the term "competency" for a legal finding that the person is or is not in a position to make a decision, whereas they use "capacity" to refer to the clinical judgment that the person is or is not in such a position. I use the terms interchangeably here, on the grounds that a legal finding (if made only by a clinician) is a predicate to visiting any legal consequences on a patient such as withdrawal of the right to refuse treatment. And those are the contexts with which we are concerned in this book.

CHAPTER TWO

1. See also, e.g., Szasz 1960, 1961, 1974, 1977, 1994, and 1998.

2. Among those critiquing Szasz were Ausubel 1961; Fox 1985; Kubie 1974; Moss 1968; Reiss 1972; Sander 1969; Schoenfeld 1976; and Thorne 1966. Among those agreeing with Szasz or Szasz-like positions were Balance, Hirschfield, and Bingmann 1970; Haskar 1977; Vatz and Weinberg 1994; and Widiger and Trull 1985. For an author struggling with what the definition of disease should be, contra Szasz, see Pies 1979. For a

historical account of similarities and differences between Szasz and Feuchtersleben, see Laor 1982.

3. See, e.g., Begelman 1971; Bentall and Pilgrim 1993; Brown 1991; Dammann 1997; Evison 1990; Gorenstein 1984; Hall 2000; Hobbs 1998; Megone 1998; Moore 1975, 1984; Reznek 1991; Svensson 1995; and Vatz and Weinberg 1994.

4. Indeed, liberty is valuable because it is presumed to serve not only people's best interests but society's. If we are forced to conform to some norm on the threat of being labeled mentally ill, we quash not only criminality and other negative deviance but also genius. Indeed, many of society's geniuses have been labeled mad on the basis of idiosyncratic beliefs that turned out to be true. They were prescient, not crazy. Deviance, then, can be enormously beneficial. That it is hard to distinguish deviancy from craziness is troubling, to say the least.

5. I do not mean to say that false beliefs *are* false by their very deviance, only that, as a matter of epistemology and not ontology, we deem many beliefs false by virtue of their deviance. That is, I am not arguing that because no one has a hotline to the truth, it therefore follows that truth simply means the majority view or the consensual view. All I really mean to say is that we can rarely know the "Truth" to a certainty and that we often rely on what the majority believes even though we cannot prove definitively that the majority's belief is true. It must also be conceded that we don't rely *exclusively* on what others think and that we make an effort to give reasons for, and argue about, our views. Yes—but it nevertheless remains that we sometimes discriminate against certain beliefs, and readily accept other beliefs, primarily because of what others believe.

6. For other difficult cases—and they are legion—consider alcoholics and sex offenders. Are they mentally ill or simply making bad, unproductive choices? There is considerable controversy about whether such groups, particularly the latter, are ill.

7. This is the common way to refer to the *Diagnostic and Statistical Manual of Mental Disorders*, 4th ed. (text revision) (American Psychiatric Association 2000), the bible of diagnosis of the American Psychiatric Association.

8. One could suggest that the issue is not causation but compulsion. Many choices of the mentally ill are characteristically hard choices, and thus constrained in some way, but many do not seem to be so. Unless we are prepared to say that one can be compelled (in a "hard choice" sense) without being aware of it, which is rather implausible, this view is not adequate to the task of distinguishing mental illness from deviancy.

9. A number of commentators address Szasz's argument that values hopelessly infect our judgments of mental illness, some noting that physical illnesses also involve value judgments. See, e.g., Ausubel 1961; Bentall and Pilgrim 1993; Dammann 1997; Evison 1990; Megone 1998; and Thorne 1966.

10. Note that the negative valuation is important; low blood pressure is a deviation from a norm, but it is a good thing and so not an illness. Consider also genius intelligence. Value judgments are critical to the illness determination. Thus Szasz cannot invoke the notion that physical illnesses involve a deviation from a biological or anatomical norm whereas mental illnesses involve a deviation from a social and ethical norm. In both cases value judgments that relate to the quality of life are implicitly made. (Of course Szasz might, by referring to biological or anatomical norms, be simply duplicating his claim that illnesses are physiological. We have already seen why that claim is problemati-

cal. And it seems plausible that Szasz also thinks that this deviation is less problematical than a deviation from an ethical and social norm.)

11. Take, for example, a person with a cleft palate or similar physical handicap.

12. I thank an anonymous reader for the University of Chicago Press for this reconstruction.

CHAPTER THREE

1. A few states—Georgia, North Dakota, Oregon (under some prongs), Pennsylvania (under some prongs), and Vermont—continue to have that standard. At least one commentator endorses this standard and seeks to have it adopted on a more widespread basis (see Treffert 1985). On file I have a review of the law in this area as of 1999, as in the other areas I discuss; this review is available on request.

2. Actually, there are about twenty variations on states' civil-commitment statutes, but most refer to dangerousness to self or others and grave disability. These variants fall into five basic patterns: danger to self or others; danger and grave disability; danger and/or inability to decide on treatment; in need of care or treatment; the person is dangerous or commitment is the least restrictive alternative. In most of these patterns, there are statutes that refer solely to the criterion on which I focus (danger to self or others) and statutes that include additional requirements (e.g., the patient is in need of treatment or commitment is the less restrictive alternative).

3. Commentators who explore the philosophical or policy underpinnings of stricter or more liberal commitment criteria, as well as process features of our laws, include Aviram 1990; Bishop and Olders 1992 (letter); Brouillette and Paris 1991; "Civil Commitment" (note) 1995; Erlinder 1993; Kaufman 1988; King 1990–91; Lamb 1989; Lee 1994; Miller 1985; Morissette 1992 (letter); Pincus 1995; Schopp and Quattrocchi 1995; Stone 1985, 1987; Swanson et al. 1997 (discussing outpatient commitment); Turkheimer and Parry 1992; and Tyler 1992.

Commentators who suggest certain reforms of the civil commitment standard or process include Appelbaum 1992; Bagby 1988; Bloom and Faulkner 1987; Brouillette and Paris 1991; Chiafullo 1994; Dawson 1996; Hermann 1986; Howse 1988; Keilitz 1988; Lamb 1989; Parry and Beck 1990; Price 1994; Treffert 1985; and Turkheimer and Parry 1992. Certain commentators explicitly endorse the current predominant standard and reject the idea that we need reform (e.g., Fisher, Pierce, and Appelbaum 1988; and Leong and Silva 1989).

Certain of these proposals, as well as current law and its application here and abroad, are critiqued in, e.g., Appelbaum 1992; Brouillette and Paris 1991; Dawson 1996; Dorfman 1993; Durham and Pierce 1986; Hiday and Smith 1987; McFarland et al. 1989; Pincus 1995; and Turkheimer and Parry 1992.

For discussions of the National Center for State Courts' guidelines for involuntary commitment, see, e.g., Appelbaum 1988; Appelbaum and Roth 1988; and Wexler 1988.

For discussions of the Stone/APA Model Statute, see, e.g., Price 1994; Stone 1985, 1987; Hoge et al. 1988; and Hoge, Appelbaum, and Greer 1989. The last three articles mention that the Stone/APA criteria seem to lead to fewer civil commitments than do the current dangerousness criteria.

For discussions of the commitment criteria in other countries, see, e.g., Aviram 1990; Bagby 1988; Brouillette and Paris 1991; Howse 1988; Lecompte 1995; Price 1994; and Segal 1989.

On the history of civil commitment laws, see, e.g., Bloom and Williams 1994; Fisher and Pierce 1985; Hughes 1986; Miller 1985; and Turkheimer and Parry 1992.

4. There is at least one exception to our commitment to not preventively detain those dangerous to others. In 1987, the Supreme Court decided that preventive confinement of dangerous arrestees pending trial is permissible. To state the rule in this way, however, gives a misleading impression, for the Court has allowed preventive detention only when there is clear and convincing evidence that no release conditions "will reasonably assure . . . the safety of any other person and the community." In addition, the arrestee must have been accused of the most serious crimes (crimes of violence, offenses for which the sentence is life imprisonment or death, or serious drug offenses) or be a certain kind of repeat offender. He is entitled to a prompt detention hearing, and the maximal length of the detention is limited by the Speedy Trial Act. Our general societal commitment not to confine offenders for mere dangerousness prior to their conviction of a crime is somewhat compromised by this holding, but the inroads represented by this holding are not great. See also the Supreme Court's recent ruling on sexually violent predators, *Kansas v. Hendricks*. On civil commitment of such people, see, e.g., Brooks 1992. Note that in this case there was a mental abnormality predicate in addition to the dangerousness.

5. See LaFave and Scott 1986, at 7.8(a). For a psychiatric account of suicide assessment and intervention, see, e.g., Jacobs 1999. For a discussion of suicide and civil commitment, see Siegel 1987.

6. See, e.g., Brown and Paine 1993; Delaney 1991; Gostin 1993b, 1997; and Harvard Law Review Editors 1974, 1990.

7. An extremely thoughtful and widely cited article in the *Harvard Law Review* discusses this issue (see Harvard Law Review Editors 1974), as does Stephen Morse's persuasive 1982 article, *A Preference for Liberty: The Case Against the Involuntary Commitment of the Mentally Disordered*.

8. It is a truism that even involuntary commitment to a mental health facility does not equate with incompetence. See, e.g., *In re the Mental Health of K.K.B.*, 609 P.2d 747 (Okla. 1980); *New York City Health and Hospitals Corp. v. Stein*, 335 N.Y.S.2d 461 (1972); *Rivers v. Katz*, 504 N.Y.S.2d 74 (1986); *Rogers v. Commissioner of the Department of Mental Health*, 458 N.E.2d 308 (Mass. 1983); *In the Matter of Rosa M.*, 597 N.Y.S.2d 544 (1991); and *Winters v. Miller*, 446 F.2d 65 (2d Cir. 1971). And the MacArthur-funded Treatment Competency studies found that approximately 75 percent of hospitalized schizophrenic patients were not significantly impaired (let alone incompetent) on each measure (when the measures were aggregated, 50 percent scored as impaired) (Grisso and Appelbaum 1995b).

9. See, e.g., Dworkin 1995, 1988, 1993; Frankfurt 1971; Haworth 1986; Shapiro 1973; Tobin 1995; and Winick 1992.

10. See the diagnostic criteria for most Axis I disorders in American Psychiatric Association 2000 (text revision).

11. Some states have a diminished-capacity standard in the criminal law, but none has a diminished-responsibility standard, although, as Arenella 1977 argues, the first tends in practice to become the second. Even when people raise a successful diminished-capacity

defense, they still receive *some* punishment—their choices are deemed sufficiently worthy of respect for that.

12. That mental illness may transform one's character is clear from descriptions of the major Axis I disorders. See American Psychiatric Association 2000.

13. See Saks 1991, 1993.

14. For a comprehensive review of whether mental illness predisposes people to violence and of how accurate predictions of violence are, see Monahan (2002), the dean of dangerousness studies. For comprehensive citation of the literature on the same issues, see Kress 2000. For early work on predicting violence, see Monahan 1981; and for more recent studies, see, e.g., Harris and Rice 1997; Lidz, Mulvey, and Gardner 1993; Litwack 1994; Monahan and Steadman 1994; Steadman et al. 1993; and Steadman et al. 1998. See also Stone and Stromberg 1975 and Cocozza and Steadman 1975–76 for reviews of the earlier research and Reisner and Slobogin 1999, at 453–58 and 653–55, for a review of the recent research. Early studies made the two-of-three false positives finding, although some more recent studies are finding somewhat better prediction rates—in fact, somewhat better than chance. In addition, early studies found no greater risk of violence for the mentally impaired than what could be accounted for by arrest history. Some are now finding a modest increase in risk, although some current studies find that schizophrenics tend to be less dangerous than the general public. More particularly, current studies tend to show that most mentally ill individuals are no more dangerous than the general public but that a small group of symptomatic people are more dangerous. Studies tend to show that past violence is the best predictor of future violence and that concurrent substance abuse, in both the mentally ill and the non–mentally ill, increases the risk of violence. For an important recent study growing out of the MacArthur-funded research, see Steadman et al. 1998. For a critique of the methodology and findings of this study, see Satel and Jaffe 1998. For more specialized studies, see, e.g., Beauford, McNiel, and Binder 1997; Monahan et al. 1993; and Teplin, Abram, and McClelland 1994.

15. This was the theory behind a right to treatment for the civilly committed in the Court of Appeals in *O'Connor v. Donaldson*, 493 F.2d 507 (5th Cir. 1974), but Justice Burger's concurring opinion (422 U.S. 563 [1975]) took issue with it.

16. See, e.g., Farina 1998; Link et al. 1987; Markowitz 1998; Nagler 1990; Reda 1996; Socall and Holtgraves 1992; and Winick 1995. Many court cases dealing with mental health law refer to the stigma attached to the diagnosis of a mental condition as well as to the need for treatment of the condition. Two prominent Supreme Court cases are *Addington v. Texas*, 441 U.S. 418, 426 (1979) and *Vitek v. Jones*, 445 U.S. 480 (1980). See also, e.g., *Altman v. Hofferber*, 28 Cal. 3d 161, 178 (1980); *Doe v. Provident Life and Accident Insurance Co.*, 176 F.R.D. 464, 468 (E.D. Pa. 1997); *Jones v. State*, 447 N.E.2d 353, 356 (Ind. App. 1985); and *Conservatorship of Susan T.*, 36 Cal. Rptr. 2d 40 (1994). Other stigmatized conditions also often coexist with mental illness. See, e.g., Phelan et al. 1997.

17. The most famous work on the topic is Erving Goffman's *Asylums* (1961). For articles on this and related topics—e.g., efforts to counteract the institutionalization of long-stay patients—see Kaminsky 1998; Smith 1998; Sood, Baker, and Bledin 1996; Timko et al. 1993; and Young, Forbes, and Hirdes 1994.

18. See, e.g., Czajkowski and Chesney 1990; and Winick 1991, 1992. On the other hand, there is some evidence that coerced and noncoerced hospitalized patients receive equal benefits, e.g., Addington and Holley 1989; Gove and Fain 1977; Nicholson, Eken-

228 . NOTES TO PAGES 54-63

stam, and Norwood 1996; and Nicholson and Horn 1986. On the efficacy of coerced treatment for drug abusers, see, e.g., Farabee, Prendergast, and Anglin 1998. A certain percentage of patients change from involuntary to voluntary status in their hospitalization;
see, e.g., Cuffel 1992; Nicholson 1988; and Spensley et al. 1974; this lends support to the
idea that some people are grateful for their hospitalization and benefit from it even when
it is involuntary.

19. The reader will note that many of these costs also do not obtain when the person
is *not* mentally ill.

20. See *Humphrey v. Cady,* 405 U.S. 504 (1972).

21. I thank Ken Kress for this analogy.

22. It is widely stated that doctors prefer to make a Type I error—to find illness when
none is really present—rather than to fail to find illness when it *is* present. Perhaps the
most famous study showing this is Rosenhan 1973. See also Davis 1976, commenting on
the Rosenhan study and noting the same proclivity in psychiatric diagnosticians.

23. This is actually to speak somewhat loosely. What I really mean is the first psychotic
break that comes to the attention of a psychiatrist who believes that intervention in the
form of hospitalization is necessary. Later I speak of the "first psychotic break or its functional equivalent." It is simply too cumbersome to keep repeating all the qualifications.

24. Note that such a standard does not seem foreclosed by *O'Connor v. Donaldson,*
which said that confinement *without more* was constitutionally impermissible absent danger to self or others; perhaps with treatment civil commitment would be permissible.
See, e.g., Behnke 1999.

25. It is of course conceivable that the person will be no healthier; indeed, he may remain seriously impaired. But then we should not commit him on later occasions for treatment purposes because the treatment has been shown to be ineffective for him, not because his healthy self has decided against it.

26. For instance, Warner 1994, 193-94, says that the incidence rate (the rate of new
cases in a given time period, usually a year) for treated schizophrenia in the United States
is 0.5 per 1,000. It is even lower in England—0.2 per 1,000.

27. See Jamison 1995.

28. This raises the interesting question of what we would and should do if involuntary confinement of smokers during nicotine withdrawal did result in the cure of their addiction. Most people would probably volunteer to be locked up in that case, but even for
those who would not, perhaps there is reason to think that intervention would be a good
social policy. Yet we now, in some places, confine alcoholics and drug abusers involuntarily so that they can be helped to withdraw from alcohol and other drugs. See, e.g., Goldberg 1995; Conn. Gen. Stat. 1998; Colo. Rev. Stat. 1997; and Mass. Gen. Laws Ann. 1999.
That we do not do so with smokers suggests that we think the immediacy, likelihood,
and gravity of the harms counsel a different action. We also might be less convinced of
true decisional impairment in the case of smokers than in the case of the mentally ill or
substance-addicted.

29. Studies discussing and sometimes confirming Stone's "thank you theory" of civil
commitment include Beck and Golowka 1988. The other studies on patient satisfaction
should be divided into those that questioned only voluntary patients, those that questioned both voluntary and involuntary patients, and those that questioned only involun-

tary patients. The results may be different; there is considerable evidence that involuntary patients are much less happy about their treatment, e.g., Gillig et al. 1990; Kalman 1983; and Sullivan and Spritzer 1997. At least one study found that voluntary and involuntary patients were comparable in terms of satisfaction; see Spensley, Edwards, and White 1980. Interestingly, one study found that patients who did and who did not want treatment were equally ill as measured by the Brief Psychiatric Rating Scale; see Grad and Lindenmayer 1977. Note also that the various studies don't always measure the same thing; some measure satisfaction, some whether the patient thinks he has been helped, some whether the patient would recommend treatment to a friend, some whether he would seek treatment in the future. Not all of these necessarily amount to retrospective gratitude for being committed or a belief that being committed, on balance, was something the patient was glad happened.

There is considerable evidence that voluntary patients are satisfied with their treatment. See, e.g., Oxley 1977, which, on follow-up among parents and their boys, found high satisfaction with an average three-year stay in a residential treatment center; and Sullivan and Spritzer 1997, which found that active users of a community mental health center were more satisfied than less active users (12 percent of high users were dissatisfied, compared to 34 percent of low users). For studies that look at both voluntary and involuntary patients' satisfaction with their treatment, see, e.g., Gillig et al. 1990, which found that 63 percent of patients going to a psychiatric emergency room found that the visit met their needs, 77 percent felt that the care they received was good to excellent, and 86 percent would refer a friend; but note that only 23 percent of the involuntary patients agreed to participate in the study, and only 7 percent of those who participated expressed satisfaction. See also Spensley, Edwards, and White 1980, which found that 50 percent of the involuntary patients contacted one month after discharge expressed satisfaction with their treatment; the results were comparable with those for voluntary patients. See also Nicholson, Ekenstam, and Norwood 1996, which found that of voluntary and involuntary patients surveyed, 93.9 percent thought their hospital stay and treatment was helpful; 79.3 percent said it left them feeling better.

For a review of studies of satisfaction in voluntary patients, patients participating in research, patients who are teaching subjects, and patients who have been civilly committed, see Kalman 1983, which found fairly high satisfaction in general but much less among patients who had been civilly committed. Bradford, McCann, and Merskey 1986 found among "lucid and coherent" patients who had been involuntarily committed and were still in the hospital that 58 percent felt that their hospitalization was appropriate, 81 percent said that it had helped, and 54 percent expressed a willingness to return if necessary. On the other hand, when given the opportunity to make a general comment regarding their stay, only 35 percent made positive statements, with 47 percent replying negatively and the rest saying they had nothing more to say. See also Edelsohn and Hiday 1990, which reported that 46.5 percent of committed patients reported it helpful six months later, with only 19.8 percent reporting it harmful; in addition, a slight majority (54 percent) said that their hospitalization was helpful and necessary; three-fourths said that if they became sick and dangerous they would want to be committed. See also Hiday 1992b, which found that three-fourths of the patients surveyed were positive about their outpatient commitment. Mossman and Hart 1993 questioned "hypothetical consumers" about the prospect of involuntary confinement and found that more than one-fourth im-plicitly preferred being attacked to undergoing a three-day hospitalization in a public psy-chiatric facility. Medical students' aversion was almost as great.

30. See, e.g., Bustillo, Lauriello, and Keith 1998; Cutting et al. 1983; Lehman and Steinwachs 1998a, 1988b; Mueser and Tarrier 1998; Munich 1997; and Schulz et al. 1998. For other disorders, see, e.g., Coryell et al. 1995. For a study of the consequences of untreated anxiety and depressive disorders, see Schonfeld et al. 1997. For a study of un-treated disorders of a variety of kinds, see Winokur and Tsuang 1996. For a study of some of the costs of untreated anxiety disorder, see Candilis and Pollack 1997.

31. This figure is quite conservative, given that in one study, more than 93 percent of the patients thought their treatment helpful. I rely on the lower figure (found in other studies) for three reasons: first, because the 93 percent figure comes from a study of vol-untary as well as involuntary patients, and although those who completed the study ex-pressed the same sentiments whether they were voluntary and involuntary, one-fifth of the potential subjects refused to participate and one-fifth were excluded, both groups con-taining more involuntary patients and more seriously disturbed patients; second, because the patients were surveyed about whether they found their treatment helpful, which is somewhat different from saying they were grateful that they received it (the 50 percent figure also is about that, however); and third, because I wish to be conservative, in order to make the argument more interesting.

32. See, e.g., Cuffel 1992; Nicholson 1988; and Spensley et al. 1974.

33. There are a number of empirical studies of issues other than consumer attitudes that bear on how we think about civil commitment. For instance, there are studies of atti-tudes of other actors in the system, such as judges, police, psychiatrists, investigators, and family members. See, e.g., Husted 1995; McFarland et al. 1989, 1990; and Husted and Nehemkis 1995.

Related to consumer attitudes are views by patients of the coerciveness of their hospi-talization (as well as its effects on outcome). See, e.g., Hiday 1992b; Monahan et al. 1995; and Nicholson, Ekenstam, and Norwood 1996. Note that the first and last come to oppo-site conclusions on whether the perception of coercion is correlated with involuntary sta-tus. For a comprehensive treatment of coercion based on the MacArthur-funded research, see Dennis and Monahan 1996.

A group of important studies focuses on the effects of adopting narrower or broader commitment criteria. For an in-depth study of changes in the law in one jurisdiction (New Jersey) and the role of various factors and actors in bringing about the changes, see Aviram and Weyer 1996. For studies of the effect of narrower criteria, see, e.g., Appelbaum 1992; Bagby et al. 1991; La Fond and Durham 1994; Lecompte 1995; Leiber and Anderson 1993; and Mahler, Co, and Dinwiddie 1986. For studies of the effect of broader commitment criteria, see, e.g., Durham and Pierce 1986; Fisher and Pierce 1985; Hasebe and McRae 1987; La Fond and Durham 1994; Miller 1992b; and Pierce, Durham, and Fisher 1985. An interesting finding of the studies of broader commitment criteria is that the number of voluntary patients goes way down with broader criteria. In addition, more are commit-ted as gravely disabled. Finally, in some (but not all) studies the use of commitment rises sharply. For a study on a methodology for predicting the effects of changes in civil com-mitment laws, see Faulkner et al. 1986a.

Another group of studies discusses the ability to reliably and validly apply the civil commitment criteria, how the criteria are applied in fact, and results of the application of the criteria in terms of who is committed. See, e.g., Bagby et al. 1991; Bursztajn et al. 1986; Faulkner et al. 1986b, 1987; Hiday 1990; Hiday and Smith 1987; Hoge, Appelbaum, and Greer 1989; Holstein 1987; McNeil and Binder 1986, 1987; McNeil, Binder, and Greenfield 1988; Segal 1989; Segal, Watson, and Nelson 1985, 1986a, 1986b; Segal et al. 1988a, 1988b, 1988c. Another study classifies commitment criteria among the states as more and less stringent, and shows that there are fewer admissions in states with more stringent criteria; see Ross, Rothbard, and Schinnar 1996.

Some related studies compare the application of the commitment criteria in different locales. See, e.g., Rubin et al. 1996 and Segal 1989. Other studies look at the features of the hearing process itself that could lead to more or less accurate decisionmaking. See, e.g., Pincus 1995. In one study a hearing officer who is also a law professor reflected on what made him decide as he did during a significant period or time doing civil commitment hearings, see Morris 1988. One of the studies cited above measures detention time and costs, see Faulkner et al. 1987. Other studies cited above also examine the probability of release at different stages of the process. See, e.g., Faulkner et al. 1986b, 1987. Other studies look at the characteristics of patients, voluntary and involuntary, who come to the emergency room as well as what they want and how happy they are with their treatment. See, e.g., Gillig et al. 1990; Rabinowitz et al. 1996. Other studies measure the quality of care in the ER. See, e.g., Sateia et al. 1990; interestingly, this study did not find that satisfaction was a good measure of outcome. Another study found that, among those seeking treatment, the largest factor determining what patients requested in the emergency room was what the patients had received in the past, see Grad and Lindenmayer 1977.

Finally, one interesting study concerns itself with limitations of current empirical studies of civil commitment and how to improve them, see Appelbaum 1985.

34. As I argue in chapter 4, I mean for the one free shot of hospitalization to include one free shot of medication. So the patient is likely to benefit therapeutically.

35. On the dangerousness standard, see, e.g., Brouillette and Paris 1991; Hiday 1990; Hiday and Smith 1987; McNeil and Binder 1986, 1987; McNeil, Binder, and Greenfield 1988; Mills 1988; Morissette 1992; Rachlin 1987; Segal et al. 1988a, 1988b, 1988c; Segal, Watson, and Nelson 1986a, 1986b; and Siegel 1987. Some of the findings are that a patient's impulsiveness is the most important determinant of his being found dangerous; people who are more ill are in fact more dangerous; courts apply the dangerousness criterion broadly; the nondangerous have not been abandoned by the system; and short-term predictions of dangerousness are fairly reliable.

Note that doctors rarely are found liable for wrongful civil confinement (see Appelbaum 1995; Knapp and VandeCreek 1987) as a result of a false positive prediction of dangerousness, suggesting that, given their intense fears of a false negative prediction of violence, the commitment standard should bend over backwards to be protective of patients' rights.

36. Perhaps this is too strong. Perhaps serious mayhem against oneself, such as blinding or emasculating oneself, should also count even if the person is not treatable. I leave this issue for others but wish subsequent references to this standard implicitly to include the caveat that serious mayhem should perhaps be excepted, too.

37. See, e.g., Bessho 1995; Bayer and Dupuis 1995; Gostin 1993a, 1995; Reilly 1993. For recent newspaper articles, see, e.g., Barbanel 1991; Coleman 1995; Emmons 1994; Navarro 1993; and Piller 1993. For a sampling of statutes, see, e.g., Ariz. Rev. Stat. Ann. 1993; West's Ann. Calif. Codes 1996; and Vernon's Ann. Mo. Stat. 1996.

38. Other reasons are that their partners can protect themselves against infection—again going to the likelihood of harm—and that we can try to induce appropriate behavior through tort law and criminal law.

39. This discussion has important implications for a topic somewhat outside the scope of this book: the criminal law. In most places the criminal law excuses people only if they are completely incompetent to commit a crime—"insane." Even diminished-capacity jurisdictions allow formal mitigation only if the mens rea for the crime is not met. But my recommendation in the civil-commitment context suggests that states should adopt a *diminished-responsibility* statute when the criminal is impaired as a result of his mental illness. England, for example, has a diminished-responsibility homicide statute; see *Halsbury's Statutes* 1957. For commentary on this act, see, e.g., Dell 1984; Mackay 1995, 1999; and Sullivan 1994. The reason for this recommendation is that, although civilly committing the impaired, dangerous mentally ill is a benefit to the patient, it also involves a cost. If we are going to impose this cost because the patients are less able to control themselves, we should not then require them to take full responsibility when they do fail to control themselves. Fairness requires no less.

40. Some jurisdictions do include danger to property. See, e.g., 4 Kan. Stat. Ann. sec. 59-2946 (f)(3) (1998); Utah Code Ann. 62A-12-234, sec. 3 (1997); and V.I. Code Ann. tit. 19, pt. III, chap. 31, sec. 722 (b) (1998). An exception to the view in the text might be made for extreme property damage likely to cause retaliation; this would be under the "danger to self" prong (see note 35). And of course danger to property that threatens serious injury to others—e.g., arson—would also be excepted. Indeed, such activity clearly is a danger to others and not only to property.

41. I would not, however, require an "overt act" before allowing predictions of violence. For one thing, the concept tends to become meaningless as applied; virtually every symptom of mental illness has been construed as an overt act. Second, although legitimate overt acts tend to help make better predictions of violence—again, the past is the best predictor of the future—there are enough cases in which one can predict serious violence without an overt act (and will overpredict serious violence with an overt act) that I recommend against such a standard. For sources on the overt act requirement, see, e.g., Cornwell 1996; Drumheller 1984; Groethe 1977; and Simpson 1984. For statutes, see, e.g., 16A Minn. Stat. Ann. sec. 253B.02 Sud. 17 (1998); Wisc. Stat. Ann. sec. 51.20 (1)(a)(2)(b) (1999). There are approximately ten states that currently have an overt act requirement; see Reisner, Slobogin, and Rai 1999.

42. The evidence is actually not that clear. Compare, e.g., Hiday 1991 and 1992a with Bittman and Convit 1993.

43. I make this argument as I think certain proponents of treatment would make it, but I actually think it somewhat beside the point to ask which is the bigger problem—treatment of the unwilling or failure to treat those who are willing. As I say in the introduction, I am unaware of empirical evidence on this point, and I'm not certain how one would study this question. In my view, both problems are immense and need attention.

44. The new methods of delivering treatment may be contributing more to the insufficiency of care than are strict civil-commitment statutes. On managed care in the mental health sector, see, e.g., Petrila 1995. On privatization of mental health treatment, see, e.g., Wisor 1993.

45. See, e.g., Silver 1988, describing this phenomenon in New York. I have heard the same claim by professionals involved with the system in Los Angeles. Note that this may happen not only in the public sector but in the very sphere I mentioned in note 44: managed care may pay for inpatient hospitalization only if the patient meets civil commitment criteria. As I say in the text with regard to the public sector, the issues of civil commitment and treatment should be separated; the mentally ill who wish treatment should be entitled to treatment regardless of whether they are civilly committable.

46. See *Bouvia v. Superior Court*, 225 Cal. Rptr. 297 (1986); and *Thor v. Superior Court*, 21 Cal. Rptr. 357 (1993). (Note that the latter involved a prisoner, a context in which state interests are likelier to prevail.)

47. For discussions of the lack of a legal remedy for physicians' wrongfully overriding patients' desires for lifesaving treatment to be withdrawn or not given (as in the case of do-not-resuscitate orders), see, e.g., Danis et al. 1991; Hackleman 1996; Knapp and Hamilton 1992; Malloy 1998; Orentlicher 1992; and Peters 1998. Most of these articles discuss approvingly a so-called wrongful living cause of action, a concept introduced by A. Samuel Oddi 1986. For an example of a commentator who does not believe a wrongful living form of action should be recognized, see Milani 1997. For a typical case saying that being caused to stay alive is not a compensable injury, see, *Anderson v. St. Francis–St. George Hospital*, 671 N.E.2d 225 (Ohio 1996).

48. On DNRs in intensive care units, see Jayes et al. 1993.

49. The cases are decided in a variety of ways, although most give lip service to the view that competent patients can refuse lifesaving treatment. Some of these cases uphold the right of the patient to refuse. Some deny the patient the right on the ground that there are dependent minors. Others deny the patient the right on the ground that, in extremity, he has become incompetent, and his choice can't now be respected; if competent, he might have chosen to live. And some deny the right on the ground that, although it is against the patient's religion as he conceives it for him to accept the blood himself, he will not be damned if a transfusion is ordered over his objection. For legal discussions of Jehovah's Witnesses refusing blood transfusions, see, e.g., Bamonte and Bierman 1992; Russell and Wallace 1989. For a more medically oriented treatment, see Muramoto 1998a, 1998b. For a response from a Jehovah's Witness who is chair of the Hospital Liaison Committee for Jehovah's Witnesses, Luton, Bedfordshire, see Malyon 1998.

50. Frail or physically ill elderly people receive assistance or are forced into homes without their consent and when they are not mentally ill. On problems concerning the voluntariness of nursing-home admissions, see, e.g., Robin Estrin, *Los Angeles Times*, 7 February 1999, at A15; Kapp 1998; and Kazin 1989. See also Yee et al. 1999 on assisted living situations.

51. This is not to say that he has actually to accede to treatment. See chapter 4.

52. Again, certain other irreversible injuries, such as blinding oneself, should also perhaps be allowed even absent treatability.

53. A growing literature on self-mutilation takes as given that self-mutilation, as such,

is generally not accompanied by suicidal intent. See, e.g., Briere and Gil 1998; Favazza 1998; Fulwiler et al. 1997; and Soloff et al. 1994. On self-mutilation, see further Crawford and Wessely 1998 and Kehrberg 1997. For discussions in the popular media, see, e.g., Through the looking glass 1998; Hall 1999; Thomas 1998; and Turner 1997.

54. There are difficult questions about when a person who cuts himself is indeed at significant risk of serious harm. What if he cuts in a dangerous place, not knowing what is dangerous? What if he is not being forthright when he says he has no intention of killing or seriously wounding himself? What if his behavior escalates in a way that is unpredictable to him?

The mental health professional will need to use clinical judgment here. Past behavior, as in the case of danger to others, is extremely important. Different professionals will have different fantasies and different risk averseness to false positives and false negatives in this context.

55. Of course, there might be less restrictive alternatives to hospitalization; perhaps a visiting nurse could come to his house or he could be placed in a halfway house.

56. In some cases, perhaps particularly with chronic patients, intensive outpatient programs addressing the risk seem the best course; see, e.g., Goldfinger 1990; and Kelly 1997. On the incidence of high-risk behavior among severely mentally ill women, as well as their perception of the importance of the HIV risk, see Weinhardt, Carey, and Carey 1998.

57. On civil commitment and homelessness, see, e.g., Bassuk and Lamb 1986; Kaufman 1988; Lamb 1989; Lamb and Lamb 1990a, 1990b, 1992; Lamb, Bachrach, and Kass 1992; and Ludwig 1991.

58. Some jurisdictions have statutes that refer to incompetency. See, e.g., statutes in Arizona, Delaware, Florida, Idaho, Iowa, Kansas, Maryland, New York, South Carolina, Texas, and Utah. Commentators also often want to include incompetency as a prong of a commitment statute or as a necessary condition for the application of all of the prongs. For instance, the Stone/APA proposal is of this kind; see, e.g., Stone 1985, 1987. For other comments, see, e.g., Hermann 1986; and Price 1994.

59. This is the so-called substituted judgment doctrine—what would the person have wanted if competent?—as contrasted with the "best interests" standard—what is best for him? This doctrine has application in many contexts, most prominently the right to die. On the doctrine, its history, support for it, criticisms of it, and proposals for new standards, see, e.g., Annas 1984; Buchanan and Brock 1986, 1989; Ciccone et al. 1990; Delaney 1991; Elliott and Elliott 1991; Gigliotti and Rubin 1991; Gutheil and Appelbaum 1980, 1983, 1985; Harmon 1990; Hermann 1990; Lebit 1992–93; Martyn 1994; Orentlicher 1994; Robertson 1991; Tonelli 1997; and Weber 1985. A recent symposium on Maryland's Health Care Decision Act, which includes a provision for substitute decisionmaking, can be found in "Trends in health care decisionmaking" 1994.

60. Deciding this question would require a showing either that his prior expressed preferences favor hospitalization or that what we know about what he thinks suggests that he would want hospitalization. The latter would be true only if hospitalization is clearly in his interests—if he will benefit from the treatment in the hospital, it is the least restrictive alternative, the damaging stigmatizing consequences can be contained, and it will not lower his self-esteem too much.

61. I discuss this example briefly in Saks 1991.

CHAPTER FOUR

1. For accounts of the different psychotropic medications and their risks and benefits, see, e.g., Janicak et al. 1997; Pies 1998; and Schatzberg and Nemeroff 1998.

2. The tardive dyskinesia risk, most prominent in the older antipsychotics, is quite serious. For estimates of its prevalence in those treated with neuroleptics (i.e., antipsychotics), see, e.g., Jeste and Caligiuri 1993 (24 percent); Miller et al. 1995 (prevalence rate of 3.7 percent in an Austrian hospital in 1982 and 12.7 percent in those still in the hospital, with 11.4 percent who did not have it in 1982 showing it in 1992); Tarsy and Baldessarini 1984 (10–15 percent); and Woerner et al. 1991 (13.3 percent among patients at a voluntary hospital versus 36.1 percent among patients at a state hospital).

3. There are many accounts of the issues involved in a right to refuse psychotropic medication. The most compelling doctrinal accounts of the right to refuse include Bruce Winick's 1997 massive tome (for a review, see Menninger 1998) and, for earlier accounts, Beyer 1980; Brooks 1986; and Litman 1982. For a symposium on the right to refuse, including doctrinal, theoretical, and empirical articles, see *Behavioral Sciences and the Law*, vol. 4, no. 3 (1986).

For theoretical accounts of a right to refuse—including some doctrinal discussions and some commentators clearly opposed to such a right—see, e.g., Appelbaum 1988 (rights-driven and treatment-driven policies); Appelbaum and Gutheil 1979, 1981 (implications of a right to refuse); Brakel and Davis 1991 (opposing an expansive right to refuse); Brooks 1986 (discussing costs and benefits of right to refuse); Cichon 1992 (history and analysis of a right to refuse); Clayton 1987 (a good review of theoretical and policy issues involved in a right to refuse); Hermann 1990 (account of constitutional bases of a right to refuse); Hickman, Resnick, and Olson 1982 (discussion of issues involved in a right to refuse by military personnel); Hogan 1987 (general discussion of issues related to a right to refuse); Knepper 1996 (a legal versus a medical model); Perlin 1993 (sanism and the right to refuse); Sadoff 1975 (ethical issues implicated in the right-to-refuse context); Shapiro 1973 (framework provided); Slovenko 1992 (the legal landscape surrounding the right to refuse); Toth 1989 (theoretical, doctrinal, and policy issues surrounding the right to refuse); Van Hall et al. 1991 (the right to refuse may go too far); and Wear and Brahams 1991 (ethical issues laid out in the context of English law).

Other commentators address more explicitly the pros and cons of particular laws governing the right to refuse, as found, for example, in important cases. See, e.g., Brian 1992 (discussing *Washington v. Harper*, 494 U.S. 210 [1990]); Cichon 1992 (discussing *Washington v. Harper*); Gostin 1983 (discussing the law on the right to refuse in England); Hewitt 1990 (discussing *Washington v. Harper*); Hogan 1987 (discussing *Rivers v. Katz*); Jaychuk, Manchanda, and Galbraith 1991 (discussing the Ontario Mental Health Act); Knepper 1996 (discussing federal law and an Illinois case, *In re C.E.*, 641 N.E.2d 34 [Ill. 1994]); Ledwith 1990 (discussing *Jones v. Gerhardstein*, 416 N.W.2d 883 [Wis. 1987]); Marshall 1987 (discussing *In re Schuoler*, 723 P.2d 1103 [Wash. 1986], on the right to refuse ECT); Sindel 1991 (discussing *Washington v. Harper*); Weatherhead 1988 (discussing the right to refuse in Canada); and Zito, Craig, and Wanderling 1991 (discussing *Rivers v. Katz*).

Other commentators make particular recommendations for a different substantive or procedural standard than the one they are discussing. See, e.g., Appelbaum 1988 (recommending a treatment-driven model rather than a rights-driven model); Gostin 1983 (recommending, among other things, a multidisciplinary panel in the context of English right-to-refuse law); Hickman, Resnick, and Olson 1982 (interest in the military of return-ing a patient to active duty quickly, recommending an internal appeal process); Hogan 1987 (recommending, among other things, a substituted-judgment standard when the patient is found incompetent to refuse); Ledwith 1990 (recommending use of Ulysses' contracts in the context of a discussion of Wisconsin right-to-refuse law); Prehn 1990 (dis-cussing different procedural options); Toth 1989 (recognizing that a limited right to re-fuse is not enough, that the patient must be able to appreciate the risks and benefits of the medication, and that ambiguities in standards should be cleared up by those authorized to do so); and Zito, Craig, and Wanderling 1991 (preferring a treatment-driven adjudica-tion process before court application, pointing out problems with the *Rivers v. Katz* approach).

Many commentators recount the history of a right to refuse in this country. For some examples, see Brian 1992; Brooks 1986; Cichon 1992; and Weatherhead 1988.

For discussions of a right to refuse in Canada and England, see, e.g., Jaychuk, Man-chanda, and Galbraith 1991 (Canada); Wear and Brahams 1991 (England); and Weather-head 1988 (Canada). For a discussion of the right to refuse in the military, see, e.g., Grant and Resnick 1989.

Related to the topic of a right to refuse treatment is the topic of informed consent to psychiatric care, including intensive therapy. Here the issue is not so much the patient's right to make the decision as his or her right to be informed—and what that encom-passes—before making the decision. For discussions of this issue see, e.g., Dyer and Bloch 1987; Sullivan, Martin, and Handelsman 1993; and Wenning 1993.

Another related body of literature, which is quite vast, is on the right to refuse lifesav-ing treatment. Some of this literature is discussed in chapter 3. For some other examples of treatments of this topic, see Ciccone 1990; McCartney 1979; Strasser 1994–95; Sulli-van and Younger 1994; and Uddo 1992.

4. I discuss outpatients below.

5. Neuroleptic malignant syndrome, though rare, can result in death. Tardive dyskine-sia can also be quite problematic for patients. Risk increases with lifetime dose, and esti-mates of prevalence rates suggest that it occurs quite often. See note 2 above on tardive dyskinesia.

6. Similarly, the showing of danger that does justify involuntary medication now requires a greater imminence—and perhaps severity—than that required for civil commitment.

7. See, e.g., Chesley 1983; and Levit 1992.

8. If treatment is consensual, patients are likelier to continue their treatment regimen; and of course patients who comply with their treatment regimens do better clinically—in all areas of health. See, e.g., Groth, Wilder, and Young 1994 (compliance with the treat-ment regimen for patients with mallet finger injuries leads to excellent outcomes more often than in noncompliant patients—61.5 percent versus 9.1 percent) and Mattson and Del Boca 1998 (compliance with treatment for alcoholism is associated with a better out-come). But compare Goodyer, Miskelly, and Milligan 1995 (treatment compliance in the case of chronic stable heart failure produced only a small beneficial effect). See also the notes on better outcomes for psychiatric patients who are consensually treated discussed in chapter 3.

9. Patients who change their minds and decide to discontinue medication may do so

for a variety of reasons. Most problematically, they may be decompensating without there being visible signs of this; as a result, they may be losing their judgment or may be seduced by the primary or secondary gains of the illness. Patients may also self-bind to no treatment at the point of discontinuing their medication because they fear that "weakness" or the discomforts of returning illness will make them give up trying to stay off medication. They may think that if they are *forced* to stay off the medication, they will be able to weather the discomfort and return to their healthy state.

10. I speak in this chapter of such abstract ideas as autonomy. But aren't there powerful reasons for denying patients a right to refuse on the grounds of what it will do to them, their treatment, and their hospitalization—and consequently others' hospitalization? At the outset of right-to-refuse litigation, psychiatrists were predicting massive exercise of the right to refuse leading hospitals to become, once again, snake pits. Lengths of stay would be drastically increased, use of restraints and seclusion would dramatically rise, incidents of violence would rise sharply, and the costs would be astronomical.

Most of this has not come to pass. Empirical studies have shown very minimal persistent refusal, little increase in violent episodes and use of restraints and seclusion, equivocal results on delays in treatment, and equivocal results on lengths of stay. In addition, there have been positive effects on medication practices, such as more involvement of the patient in his treatment and a decrease in inappropriate delegation of medication decisions. For some of the empirical studies, see, e.g., Binder and McNiel 1991 (impact of *Riese v. St. Mary's Hospital* on an acute inpatient unit; fears not borne out, with little changing); Carey, Jones, and O'Toole 1990 (impact on nurses of treatment refusal); Ciccone et al. 1990 (impact of *Rivers v. Katz*); Farnsworth 1991 (effects on forensic hospital in Minnesota before and after *Jarvis v. Levine*); Hoge, Gutheil, and Kaplan 1987 (impact of *Rogers v. Commissioner* on hospitals in Massachusetts; all petitions filed in an eighteen-month period reviewed; few petitions denied, yet great cost for the process); Miller et al. 1989 (impact of *Jones v. Gerhardstein* on a forensic patient population); Panzano and Rubin 1995 (impact of right-to-refuse law on "events" in hospital; and of looking cross-sectionally or longitudinally); Rachlin 1989 (impact of *Rivers v. Katz* on county hospital in New York); Sauvayre 1991 (study of all forty court cases of a maximum-security forensic hospital in New York after *Rivers v. Katz*, finding that little changed); Wettstein 1999 (reviewing some of the empirical literature); and Zito, Craig, and Wanderling 1991 (impact of *Rivers v. Katz* in all New York state adult psychiatric and forensic facilities during a one-year period; studied all applications to medicate during that period). Some studies, on the other hand, find greater morbidity in refusers, e.g., a greater likelihood to receive restraints or seclusion. See, e.g., Kasper et al. 1997 (study in Virginia, where physicians have authority to override refusal); and Rodenhauser, Schwenkner, and Khamis 1987 (maximum security hospital; refusers, e.g., had significantly longer hospital stays). See also Appelbaum and Hoge 1986 (reviewing studies and presenting a mixed picture).

As noted, the effect of right-to-refuse laws on whether there is serious delay in initiating treatment has been equivocal. Compare Rachlin 1989 (no long delay) and Binder and McNiel 1991 (same) with Farnsworth 1991 (long delays) and Bloom et al. 1988 (same).

Studies of the rate of refusal under a right-to-refuse regime include Appelbaum and Hoge 1986; Binder and McNiel 1991; Ciccone et al. 1990; Miller et al. 1989; Rachlin 1989; Sellwood and Tarrier 1994; and Zito, Craig, and Wanderling 1991.

Studies of the rate at which refusals are upheld include Appelbaum and Hoge 1986

238 · NOTES TO PAGES 91-92

(reviewing literature showing different rates of overrides); Binder and McNiel 1991 (refusals upheld in 1 percent of the cases); Bloom et al. 1988 (none upheld); Farnsworth 1991 (security hospital; post-*Jarvis* nonemergency patients had refusals upheld in 7 percent of cases; post-*Jarvis* emergency patients had no refusals upheld); Hoge, Gutheil, and Kaplan 1987 (4 percent of refusals upheld); Ledwith 1990 (70–80 percent of civil refusals settle, with one-third of the remainder upheld); Rachlin 1989 (no refusals upheld); Sauvayre 1991 (refusals upheld 20 percent of the time); and Urrutia 1994 (27.5 percent of refusals upheld).

Others studied the demographic and other features associated with refusal or noncompliance. See, e.g., Appelbaum and Hoge 1986; Kasper et al. 1997; Ruffalo, Garabedian-Ruffalo, and Pawlson 1985; Sellwood and Tarrier 1994; Young, Zonana, and Shepler 1986; and Zito, Craig, and Wanderling 1991.

One might think that the right-to-refuse movement has been a monumental failure, given the small percentage of patients who refuse and the even smaller percentage who, on review, have their refusals upheld. This conclusion, however, is unwarranted. First, for those whose refusals are upheld the right is extremely important. They care a lot. Second, the right-to-refuse movement has promoted better medication practices. Third, it has given patients the ability to negotiate with their caregivers about type and dose of medication, among other things. Finally, the percentage of refusals upheld is misleading, because doctors may send to review only cases in which they are likely to prevail, so they may be informally permitting many more patients to refuse than court records indicate. In any case, the right to refuse is an extremely important statement of our commitment to the dignity of the mentally ill, quite apart from empirical effects it has had.

11. For accounts of problems with outpatient commitment (such as enforcement), proposed or current solutions, or results of the application of outpatient commitment to patient populations, see, e.g., Appelbaum 1986; Geller 1986; Hiday 1996; Keilitz 1990; Lefkovitch, Weiser, Levy 1993; Munetz et al. 1996; and Swanson et al. 1997. And see below for further citations.

12. Note that some outpatient commitment statutes (such as Iowa's) require the patient to be incompetent, but most do not. Those statutes, however, require more than incompetence; I believe that that is enough, provided the substituted judgment determination leads to a decision to medicate. Also, some jurisdictions (such as California) permit medication in the community of the incompetent not under outpatient commitment (OPC) statutes but under guardianship statutes. This makes a lot of sense to me.

Note further that a common formulation in some statutes is that the patient lacks the ability or has limited ability to make informed decisions to seek or to comply voluntarily with recommended treatment. This language sounds in incapacity, but it is predetermined what the "right choice" is—to seek and comply with treatment—which a more sound capacity doctrine leaves to the patient herself to decide. Here noncompliance is practically equated with incapacity, which is a problematic position. On the other hand, if the intent of this language is simply to pick out patients who are noncompliant, then that is perfectly appropriate.

13. There is by now a considerable literature on involuntary outpatient commitment. Perhaps the most thoughtful and comprehensive account is that of Ken Kress 2000. For theoretical studies, see, e.g., Scheid-Cook 1991; Stein and Diamond 2000; Swanson et al.

1997; and Tavolaro 1992. For accounts that discuss the costs and benefits of OPC, see, e.g., Bloom 1986; Fulop 1995; Geller 1986; Gutterman 2000; Hoge and Grottole 2000; Leong 1987; Mulvey, Geller, and Roth 1987; Smith 1995; Swanson et al. 2000; and Wilk 1988a, 1988b. For accounts of the three different varieties of OPC, see e.g., McCafferty and Dooley 1990; Slobogin 1994; and Wilk 1988a. For accounts of deciding to whom OPC should apply, see, e.g., Appelbaum 1986; Brooks 1997; *Mental and Physical Disability Law Reporter* 1986; Mulvey, Geller, and Roth 1987; and Wilk 1988a. Some commentators would apply it only to the incompetent; see, e.g., Hoge and Grottole 2000; Munetz, Geller, and Frese 2000; others require that the patient accede voluntarily to the OPC; see, e.g., Brooks 1997. Why patients do comply is an open question. Some think it may have to do with a general respect for the law; see, e.g., Lefkovitch, Weiser, and Levy 1993, whereas others cite the case of patients who are misled about the coercive power of the state under this rubric; see, e.g., Geller 1986. (On misperceptions of patients about OPC generally, see, e.g., Borum et al. 1999.) In terms of sanctions for noncompliance, some discuss forcing medication (see, e.g., Appelbaum 1986; Keilitz and Hall 1985; and Miller and Fiddleman 1984), others, return to the hospital (see, e.g., Miller 1992a; and Mulvey, Geller, and Roth 1987). Some explicitly discuss hospitalization on a lower showing than that for civil commitment (see, e.g., Miller 1992a); others discuss the need for ample process if the patient is to be returned to the hospital (see, e.g., Slobogin 1994). (At least one author has urged that periodic review of OPC is needed; see *Mental and Physical Disability Law Reporter* 1986.) In terms of sanctions, enforcement problems with OPC are discussed frequently. See, e.g., Appelbaum 1986; Fulop 1995; Geller 1986; Miller 1988; Miller and Fiddleman 1984; and Wilk 1988b. Certain studies review the laws on OPC (see, e.g., Keilitz and Hall 1985; McCafferty and Dooley 1990; Miller 1988; and Torrey and Kaplan 1995); others review the empirical studies (see, e.g., Draine 1997 [discussing methodological issues, too]; Miller 1988; Swartz et al. 1995 [good treatment of methodological issues, e.g., separating out aggressive case management]; Swartz et al. 1997 [discussing methodological limitations of earlier studies]; and Wilk 1998a). Some commentators report on their own studies; see, e.g., Hiday and Goodman 1982; Hiday and Scheid-Cook 1987; Miller 1992 (reviewing the experience of a state); Policy Research Associates 1998; Swanson et al. 2000; Swartz et al. 1999; and Van Putten, Santiago, and Berren 1988. Other commentators present individual case studies; see, e.g., Geller 1986; Lefkovitch, Weiser, and Levy 1993; and Schneider-Braus 1986. Certain commentators have a comparative perspective, looking at other countries; see, e.g., Davies 2000; Lefkovitch, Weiser, and Levy 1993. The empirical studies report on a variety of outcomes. For instance, some discuss a future increase in the voluntary use of services by those formerly committed to OPC; see, Hiday and Scheid-Cook 1997; Van Putten et al. 1988. Others write about a decrease in future hospital admissions and lengths of stay; see, e.g., Fernandez and Nygard 1990; Munetz et al. 1996. Other outcomes generally are discussed in the individual empirical studies (see above; see also Scheid-Cook 1991). And data on the use of OPC are discussed in Torrey and Kaplan 1995. Certain commentators discuss alternatives to OPC, such as conditional release and the use of guardians; see, e.g., Torrey and Kaplan 1995; and some prefer efforts at aggressive outpatient services that are provided voluntarily; see, e.g., Fulop 1995 and Tavolaro 1992.

14. Commentators actually divide outpatient commitment into three varieties: condi-

tional discharge, alternate placement, and preventive commitment. The first involves putting conditions on discharge from the hospital. The second involves the same standard for inpatient as outpatient commitment—e.g., danger to self or others. One wonders why a dangerous patient should be permitted to be at large. Some jurisdictions allow that such patients may be committed to outpatient status if the evidence of their dangerousness is less strong or the kind of danger is less serious. But one then wonders why such patients should be subject to inpatient *or* outpatient commitment. In any case, if the patient meets the inpatient commitment standard, one can hardly quarrel with giving the patient a less restrictive alternative. The third variety is the most controversial, because it widens the field of those who may be coerced. It also, however, offers some promise.

15. Constitutional questions, of course, could arise, inasmuch as one might be civilly committing, without more, a nondangerous person who could survive safely in the community on her own or with the help of willing and responsible family or friends. And *O'Connor v. Donaldson* seems to preclude this result. But *Donaldson* did not address the issue of the permissibility of such commitment for the sake of inducing a patient to take the medications that would allow her to remain safely in the community—and that, only during one course of outpatient commitment. Because that issue was not addressed, we do not know how the Court would decide. And there are certainly arguments that this would be a permissible deprivation of liberty under the limited conditions specified in the text.

16. Another alternative is simply forcibly to medicate the noncompliant patient in the community. Because I think involuntary hospitalization is less restrictive than involuntary medication, however, I would not favor this course. Perhaps more important, it is clear that giving the patient a choice is less restrictive than forcing compliance, although the choice is a hard one.

17. There have been some discussions of reasons for or factors associated with patients' refusal or noncompliance. See, e.g., Appelbaum and Hoge 1986 (reviewing literature and finding that illness-based reasons are more important than reasons based on side effects); Breen and Thornhill 1998 (dividing reasons into medication-specific factors, patient-specific factors, and practitioner-specific factors); Brown 1986 (factors influencing refusal as well as reasons for refusal); Forman 1993 (positive and negative reasons for noncompliance are related to lack of insight); Hummer and Fleischhacker 1996 (extrapyramidal symptoms can lead to noncompliance); Mattson and Del Boca 1998 (demographic, psychological, and personal characteristics of clients, therapist attributes, and treatment context features, in the case of alcoholics); Prehn 1990 (patient is unable to comprehend, fails to do so, or has legitimate difference of opinion about need for medication); Ruffalo, Garabedian-Ruffalo, and Pawlson 1985 (mentions demographic variables, sociopsychologic variables, cultural background, socioeconomic status, personal motivation, potential barriers to health care, and the physician-patient relationship); and Wettstein 1999 (dividing refusals into those related to the physician-patient relationship and those based on treatment, illnesses or symptoms, religion, and secondary gain). (See also note 23 below on commentators exploring the psychodynamic bases of medication refusal.)

18. See note 31 below and accompanying text for citations to the complaint and for an answer to it.

19. See, e.g., Brown 1986 ("in psychiatry it is often held that drug reluctance is primarily a form of symptomatic behavior, involving hostility, acting out, and paranoid delusions," 85); and Rodenhauser, Schwenkner, and Khamis 1987 (dividing reasons for refusal

into categories of "illness-related" and "rational," and finding that some that I would put in the latter category belong to the former).

20. I am not suggesting that, once a patient begins medication, he should always be on medication. Most patients will want to try to discontinue medication after a reasonable period of good health. Some patients will turn out not to need the medication on a long-term basis. Similarly, even after it appears clear that the patient has a real need for the medication, it may make sense to try to discontinue it in a deliberate way once every three or four years. The patient's illness course might have changed. But most people, at least those on the antipsychotics and mood stabilizers, will need to remain on treatment indefinitely. In any case, I speak below primarily of refusals by people who do need to be on the medication and should not, if we have their best interests in mind, be refusing. (This is not to say that we should not respect their refusals.)

21. See note 17 above.

22. These would clearly be incompetent. They would also be the kinds of reasons that would not survive forcible medication and so would *argue* for forcible medication.

23. Other commentators discuss, among others, such psychodynamic reasons for refusal as I note in the text. See, e.g., Breen and Thornhill 1998; Brown 1986; Demyttenaere 1997; and Fenton, Blyler, and Heinssen 1997.

24. The concept of resistance has a long history in the psychoanalytic literature, beginning with Freud. For a contemporary account, see, e.g., Wolstein 1983.

25. See, e.g., Miller 1997.

26. There are, of course, some discussions in the literature of this issue — some referring to psychotherapeutic approaches, some to more psychosocial approaches. See, e.g., Breen and Thornhill 1998; Demyttenaere 1997; Draine and Solomon 1994; Fenton, Blyler, and Heinssen 1997; Kuipers 1996; Ruffalo, Garabedian-Ruffalo, and Pawlson 1985; Van Heeringen et al. 1995a; Wettstein 1999; and Young, Zonana, and Shepler 1986. For an example of a controlled study demonstrating the effectiveness of "compliance therapy" on psychotic patients, see Kemp et al. 1996.

27. There is a counterargument here: the patient may discontinue the medication because he feels confident of success this time, not because he prefers psychosis to being on medication.

28. See, e.g., Breen and Thornhill 1998 (20–50 percent of any patient population is likely to be at least partially noncompliant; in psychotic disorders, rates run as high as 80 percent, in depressive disorders, 60 percent); Brown 1986 (24–63 percent of outpatients and 15–33 percent of inpatients take less than prescribed amounts of anti-psychotic drugs, but mental patients are apparently "better patients" than medical patients: the rate for general noncompliance for chronic medical conditions usually begins at 50 percent and increases with duration of treatment); Buckalew and Buckalew 1995 (reviews literature on compliance and discusses own study, finding only 25 percent fully compliant); Cramer et al. 1989 (patients with epilepsy took only an average of 76 percent of their medication as prescribed when carefully monitored; proposes new method of medication monitoring, the Medication Event Monitor System, and shows its superiority to other typical approaches); Miller 1997 (around 50 percent noncompliance with medications for chronic diseases such as hypertension); Ruffalo, Garabedian-Ruffalo, and Pawlson 1985 (reviewing literature, mentioning 50 percent figure); Stephenson et al. 1993 (compliance approximately 50 percent for those who remain in care; with antibiotic therapy, declines to less than

25 percent for completion of the therapy); Wettstein 1999 (average compliance rate for antidepressant medication 65 percent; for antipsychotic medication, 58 percent; for "medical treatments generally is erratic," 174); and Young, Zonana, and Shepler 1986 (comprehensive review of data concerning rates of noncompliance). For an account of difficulties in actually measuring compliance and methods for doing so better, see, e.g., Cramer 1995. See also Stephenson et al. 1993 (clinical measures for judging noncompliance found wanting in almost every study).

29. Although we have seen that they also may well *be;* we should not rule that possibility out.

30. The one possible exception to the above is denial of mental illness. This may be more prevalent in certain mental illnesses than others and in mental rather than physical illness. And there is some reason to think that denial is characteristic of certain mental illnesses. Whether we should think of denial as an understandable psychological defense or as a symptom of an illness is unclear and, as the next paragraph suggests, may not matter much anyway. Some commentators (see, e.g., Kress 2000) make much of the idea that denial may have neurophysiological correlates. But surely *everything* mental does, so I'm not sure how far this observation takes us.

31. See, e.g., Appelbaum and Gutheil (1981), who studied the reasons patients refuse and so concluded. See also Sherlock (1986), who makes the point in the context of informed consent to medical treatment generally.

32. See, e.g., Brakel and Davis (1991), who note that of the thirty law review articles on psychotropic medication, twenty would be classified as "vitriolically 'anti-drug.'" Perhaps the most so is Plotkin 1977, but others exist as well.

33. For an account by psychiatrists of legal and judicial rhetoric of psychotropic drugs as mind-controlling, and responses to that charge, see Appelbaum and Gutheil 1979. For a further prominent example of an article making the arguments given in the text against the charge of mind control, see Gutheil and Appelbaum 1984. Another article, by a lawyer-doctor team, attempts to educate the legal community about the true properties of psychotropic medication, arguing for a much greater power to impose medication on psychiatric patients. See Brakel and Davis 1991.

34. See, e.g., Taylor 1999 (which also evinces concern about the possible overuse of Prozac for the wrong reasons); and "Prozac (Fluoxetine Hydrochloride) tablet to be available June 1." This drug is currently available in more than 100 countries (PR Newswire). Prozac has also been prescribed for more than seventeen million Americans. See the Prozac web site, at http://www.prozac.com/general.htm.

CHAPTER FIVE

1. I use "restraint" here to refer to any emergency measures taken to contain violence, including seclusion, mechanical restraints, and physical restraint—holding someone back or down. Some of the articles discuss both seclusion and restraints, and these I will cite under both.

I have on file a compendium of statutory and case law on seclusion and restraints as of 1999. For some of the classic articles on seclusion and restraints, see the works collected in Tardiff 1984. For psychiatric articles and books favorable to the use of seclusion and restraints, see the pieces cited in Saks 1986, footnote 32. Legal discussions of seclusion and restraints occur in Roth 1985; Saks 1986; and Wexler 1983.

2. There is also arguably an emergency exception, which I discuss in chapter 6.

3. See, e.g., the statistics on this issue cited in Heilbrun et al. 1995.

4. On mechanical restraint in nonpsychiatric hospitals for, say, the brain-injured or the elderly, see, e.g., Edlund, Goldberg, and Morris 1991; Lever et al. 1994; Mion, Minnick, and Palmer 1996; and Tinetti et al. 1991.

The Joint Commission on Accreditation of Healthcare Organizations (JCAHO) has written Proposed Revisions to the Joint Commission Restraint Standards Applicable to Non-Psychiatric Patients June 1998, governing use of restraints in the case of non-psychiatric patients.

At the other end of the age-spectrum, certain commentators discuss restraints and seclusion particularly in the case of children and adolescents. See, e.g., Angold and Pickles 1993; Atkins and Ricciuti 1992; Earle and Forquer 1995; Fassler and Cotton 1992; Irwin 1987; Measham 1995; Morgan, Fulliton, and Nabors 1993; and Tsemberis and Sullivan 1988.

5. For discussions of costs, typically costs in terms of physical well-being, see, e.g., Bornstein 1985; Mitchell and Varley 1990; and Thompson 1986.

6. See, e.g., Mitchell and Varley 1990, mentioning studies showing such an effect.

7. Important costs to psychological and dignitary well-being can be seen in surveys of patients' reactions to seclusion. See, e.g., Chamberlin 1985; Eriksson and Westin 1995; Mann, Wise, and Shay 1993; Mason 1993; McElroy 1985; Morgan, Fulliton, and Nabors 1993; Morrison and Lehane 1995; Outlaw and Lowery 1994; Richardson 1987; Soloff, McEvoy, and Ganguli 1989; and Tsemberis and Sullivan 1998.

Interestingly (and not surprisingly), staff have a very different perception of the costs and benefits of seclusion. See, e.g., de Cangas 1993; Klinge 1994; Mason 1993; McElroy 1985; Muir-Cochrane 1996; Outlaw and Lowery 1994; and Tsemberis and Sullivan 1998.

8. Note that the JCAHO has promulgated rules that allow seclusion and restraints only in response to danger. Nevertheless, not all institutions are JCAHO-approved; the JCAHO may come to change its rules; and it is worthwhile to try to tease out just when we think seclusion and restraints are justifiable. My proposal in the case of seclusion allows more use of it than does the JCAHO; my proposal in the case of restraints, less. Note also that Congress has been holding hearings on restraint as a result of the deaths reported in the *Hartford Courant* (see below), and many jurisdictions have fairly restrictive restraint and seclusion laws (see the compendium of laws on file with author). These, however, are often more honored in the breach than in the observance.

9. Many clinicians claim that seclusion is therapeutic—e.g., Soloff, McEvoy, and Ganguli 1989; Tsemberis and Sullivan 1988—but to my knowledge there are no controlled studies, and some commentators admit that there is little or no evidence of its efficacy. See, e.g., Crespi 1990; Irwin 1987; Measham 1995; and Soloff, McEvoy, and Ganguli 1989.

10. Various commentators divide the rationales for seclusion differently; I select the ones in the text for convenience of exposition. See, e.g., Fassler and Cotton 1992; Hopton 1995; Mason 1993; Richardson 1981; Soloff, McEvoy, and Ganguli 1989; and Whittington and Mason 1995.

There is other important literature on seclusion and its uses as well. For instance, commentators discuss why seclusion is used when it is used in a given place. See, e.g., Atkins and Ricciuti 1992; Hafner et al. 1989; Heilbrun et al. 1995; Morrison and Lehane

1996; and Richardson 1981. Commentators also discuss the incidence and duration of seclusion episodes in various hospitals. See, e.g., Angold and Pickles 1993; Atkins and Ricciuti 1992; Betemps, Buncher, and Oden 1992; Betemps, Somoza, and Buncher 1993; Bornstein 1985; Crenshaw and Francis 1995; Earle and Forquer 1995; Fassler and Cotton 1992; Hafner et al. 1989; Heilbrun et al. 1995; Mann, Wise, and Shay 1993; Mitchell and Varley 1990; Morrison 1990a, 1990b; and Morrison and Lehane 1995. Commentators also discuss attributes of patients that may lead them to be high users of seclusion. See, e.g., Angold and Pickles 1987; Atkins and Ricciuti 1992; de Cangas 1993; Dickerson et al. 1994; Earle and Forquer 1995; Morrison and Lehane 1995; Morrison 1990a, 1990b. Others look at whether other interventions or conditions (e.g., token economies, menstruation) lead to a greater or lesser incidence of seclusion. See, e.g., Chiles, Davidson, and McBride 1994; Dickerson et al. 1994; and Van Heeringen et al. 1995b. In addition, certain commentators make very specific recommendations regarding the use of seclusion. See, e.g., Fassler and Cotton 1992; Hopton 1995; and Roper et al. 1985.

11. Thomas Gutheil, followed widely, alleges that seclusion is therapeutic for patients with out-of-control behavior, pathological intensity in relationships, and hyperaesthesia. Seclusion, then, functions as containment, isolation, and decrease in sensory stimuli. See Gutheil 1978. Gutheil also had some observations on the law's view of seclusion in the Boston State Hospital case; see Gutheil 1980.

12. See, e.g., Tardiff 1992, noting that in cases of delirium restraints may be preferable to seclusion in that destimulation may lead to a worsening of the patient's clinical state.

13. See Tsemberis and Sullivan 1988.

14. Consider breast cancer surgeries. More and less radical surgeries have been very carefully studied, for when something is especially invasive, mutilating, or barbaric, we scrutinize it most carefully for therapeutic need and efficacy.

15. At least according to this rationale. See below.

16. See the citations on prediction of violence in chapter 3.

17. I discuss below how to understand the concept of a less restrictive alternative— and whether patients should have some say in deciding which modality is less restrictive for *them*.

18. For one prominent example, see the so-called Hart-Devlin debate, Devlin 1965 and Hart 1963. For a discussion of the debate, see Stewart 1999.

19. At least, it is not enough in most cases; see below.

20. Many statutes prohibit seclusion and restraints as punishment. See the compendium of cases and statutes as of 1999 on file with author.

21. Perhaps those standing in loco parentis of children can "punish" in this sense too, although the punishment here is arguably intended as a form of specific deterrence rather than retribution.

22. Both are traditional aims of this course of action—as is the incapacitation of which I approved earlier—but an intervention is still not punishment unless we think the person did wrong and deserves punishment.

23. See, e.g., Skinner 1971, 1974, 1978.

24. See note 7 above.

25. See, e.g., McElroy 1985.

CHAPTER SIX

1. For a discussion of costs of mechanical restraints in the case of both psychiatric and medical patients, see Moss and La Puma 1991.

2. See, e.g., Carlson and Holm 1993; Hopton 1995; and Mitchell and Varley 1990.

3. Evidently restraints deaths are not studied systematically by researchers or agencies of the government (New York is an exception). The editors of the *Hartford Courant* ran a five-part story discussing this issue; it was they who uncovered the 142 deaths and who commissioned the Harvard research. Their series of articles recounted chilling stories of reported deaths, a disproportionate number among young people (26 percent of the deaths involved patients aged seventeen or younger, although they made up less than 15 percent of the psychiatric hospital population). A teenage girl refuses to give up a picture of her family. She is tackled to the ground and placed in a hold, face-down. And then she dies. Middle-aged people also often died. Death was caused by aspirating one's vomit, heart problems brought on by the restraints, strangulation, and assorted other causes. The *Courant* has compiled a database of restraints deaths, to be found at www.courant.com/news/special/restraint/data.stm.

Many of these deaths are not reported to the authorities, the *Courant* found; the scenes are cleaned up before the authorities arrive when they are reported; and families are given misinformation about what happened. Coroners rarely rule these deaths homicides, and even when they do, staff members plead to trivial offenses. Coroners also often don't rule that the death was related to the restraints, when it often obviously is.

The *Courant* interviewed patients about their experiences with restraints; they routinely reported negative feelings ("confused, angry, and afraid"). The newspaper also noted research uncovering the same. It noted prolonged use of restraints, as well as other problems, such as staff members not making frequent checks of patients. In general, staff training was thought to be wholly inadequate in many places.

Another interesting dimension of the *Courant* articles was the experience reported in Tennessee, which showed that "with strong leadership, the physical restraint of patients can be minimized—indeed, nearly eliminated—safely and without exorbitant cost." New York was reported to have reduced its restraint rate as well. Note finally that not all the deaths reported on in the *Courant* and other newspapers involved mechanical restraints. Some involved physical restraint or seclusion.

For the *Courant* articles, see David Altimari et al., "11 Months, 23 Dead Series: Deadly Restraint," October 11, 1998; David Altimari, "People Die and Nothing Is Done," October 14, 1998; Kathleen Megan and Dwight F. Blint, "Little Training, Few Standards, Poor Staffing Put Lives at Risk," October 12, 1998; Eric M. Weiss, "A Nationwide Pattern of Death," October 11, 1998; Eric M. Weiss, "A Powerful Industry Blocks Reform in California, Governor Vetoes Proposed Restraint Regulations," October 13, 1998; Eric M. Weiss, "From 'Enforcer' to Counselor," October 15, 1998; Eric M. Weiss, "Group Calls for Reform in Use of Restraints: Mental Health Providers React to Reports of 142 Deaths in Facilities," October 24, 1998; Eric M. Weiss, "Lawsuit Filed Against Elmcrest over Death of 11-Year-Old," October 14, 1998; Eric M. Weiss, "Two Connecticut Deaths, Two Questionable Investigations," October 11, 1998; Eric M. Weiss, "Unlocking the Secret of a Daughter's Death: No Justice," October 14, 1998; Eric M. Weiss and Dave Altimari, "Patients Suffer in a System without Oversight," October 13, 1998; and "Lessons Unheeded,

Lives Lost," January 31, 1999. An "All Things Considered" program in which Eric Weiss was interviewed occurred on October 12, 1998.

Over the years other city newspapers have reported restraints deaths in their areas. See, e.g., Bill Baskervill, "Mental Patient Spent Final Month in Solitary Torment," *The Associated Press* (Virginia), June 16, 1997; Mark J. Magyar, "Mental Patient's Death Becomes a Symbol," *The Record* (northern New Jersey), April 21, 1987; Mary Jo Patterson, "Mental Patient Death Followed Abuse Charges: Complaints Grow at Brisbane," *The Star-Ledger* (Newark, N.J.), January 13, 1998; Alisa Wabnik and Rhonda Bodfield, "State Discards Compliance Plan at Desert Hills," *The Arizona Daily Star,* April 2, 1998; and "We Can Afford to Do Better," *The Record* (northern New Jersey), April 27, 1987.

The New York State Commission on Quality of Care has been studying restraints practices in New York psychiatric hospitals. In September 1994 it reported that the use of restraints and seclusion had almost doubled during the past decade and had been associated with more than one hundred deaths. They also reported that the largest survey of former patients in the literature found that patients who were restrained or secluded overwhelmingly stated that these interventions were used illegally and that they were often poorly treated, abused, or injured when restrained or secluded. See New York State Commission on Quality of Care 1994, 1995. See also New York Office of Mental Health 1993.

4. This finding applies to both restraints and seclusion and is widely reported in the literature, based on both studies and on anecdotal evidence. Some of the variance is explained by conditions on the ward, e.g. overcrowding, and some of it is explained by differences in staff and staff policy. See, e.g., Atkins and Ricciuti 1992; Bornstein 1985; Brooks et al. 1994; Carlson and Holm 1993; Crenshaw and Francis 1995; de Cangas 1993; Earle and Forquer 1995; Forquer et al. 1996; Hafner et al. 1989; Heilbrun et al. 1995; Irwin 1987; Mason 1993; Morrison 1990a, 1990b; Morrison and Lehane 1995; Muir-Cochrane 1996; Roper et al. 1985; Thompson 1986; Tsemberis and Sullivan 1988; and Whittington and Mason 1995.

Restraint and seclusion practices also vary widely across countries. For instance, England has a lower seclusion rate than America and a practically nonexistent mechanical restraints rate, at least as of fifteen years ago. See, e.g., Angold and Pickles 1993; Hafner et al. 1989; Lever et al. 1994; Morrison 1990a; Morrison and Lehane 1996; Pfeffer 1995; Saks 1986; Soloff, McEvoy, and Ganguli 1989; and Thompson 1986.

5. See Way 1986; Way and Banks 1990. This is a very large-scale study of restraint and seclusion practices in New York. The finding concerning duration of the restraint or seclusion was that system-wide the two most frequent order lengths were four hours (56 percent) and two hours (34 percent). Indeed, 73 percent of the facilities surveyed used one of these order lengths almost exclusively. Finally, patients weren't always kept in for the length of the order written. The median number of hours was 2 with a mean of 2.5. In 61 percent of the episodes the time actually spent was 2 hours or less. It would thus appear that making longer stays in seclusion or restraints burdensome procedurally may induce shorter restraint episodes.

6. See, e.g., Eriksson and Westin 1995; and Outlaw and Lowery 1994. Staff members often have different perceptions of restraints. See, e.g., Klinge 1994. Another study noted differences in patients and staff in reasons (internal or external) that restraint was used. See Outlaw and Lowery 1994.

7. See, e.g., Sheline and Nelson 1993; and Soliday 1985.

8. A number of different studies on restraints exist. For a discussion of the rationale for restraining people, see, e.g., Hopton 1995. In addition, the rationales discussed above for seclusion are arguably relevant for restraints, too, and have been drawn on in my discussion. For a study of why restraints are used when they are used, see Heilbrun, et al. 1995. For studies of the incidence and duration of restraints, see, e.g., Betemps, Buncher, and Oden 1992; Betemps, Somoza, and Buncher 1993; and Crenshaw and Francis 1995. For discussions of high and low users of restraints, see, e.g., Betemps, Buncher, and Oden 1992; Betemps, Somoza, and Buncher 1993; and Dickerson et al. 1994. For studies of the effect of other interventions or conditions on restraint use, see, e.g., Carlson and Holm 1993; Chiles, Davidson, and McBride 1994; and Dickerson et al. 1994. For recommendations for restraints policies, see, e.g., Roper et al. 1985.

9. See, e.g., Swett, Michaels, and Cole 1989 (speaking of physical restraint). Other commentators note that there is little evidence of efficacy (see, e.g., Crespi 1990) or that there is little evidence that one control mechanism is more therapeutic than another (see, e.g., Measham 1995). For further citations on the therapeutic efficacy view, see Saks 1986, section I.A ("Casting Doubt on Treatment Efficacy: The British Experience").

10. See Moss and La Puma (1991), who also note that restraints have never been proved effective in clinical practice and should be considered a nonvalidated therapy requiring consent by the patient if competent or by his or her proxy if incompetent.

11. It is a suggestion I made in Saks 1986, but I now think it does not go far enough.

12. See Way 1986; Way and Banks 1990.

13. See, e.g., Eriksson and Westin 1995.

14. See, e.g., Saks 1986, recommending that patients be given a choice among emergency modalities. See also Measham 1995, suggesting that a child's collaboration in choosing a management technique should be encouraged.

15. Apart from physical restraint, I would want all hospitals to have available all reasonable modalities.

16. Whether the same rule should apply to the incompetent patient who would have made this choice if competent I leave to another time.

17. Also, we should arguably honor patients' changes of mind about emergency modalities even at the time of the emergency if the choice is between equally effective modalities and there is no added danger in doing something different than expected. But this would not apply to the choice under consideration now—namely, medication refusal—for which I would require a competent choice.

CHAPTER SEVEN

1. A compendium of the statutory and case law on this question as of 1999 is on file with the author.

2. See, e.g., Macklin 1982, at 360. For commentators recognizing that competency varies from one context to the next, see, e.g., Roth, Meisel, and Lidz 1977. For a commentator applauding the law's context-specific view as against the medical, more general, view, see Freedman 1981.

3. See, e.g., Freud 1901; Kahneman 1994; Katz 1984; Mann 1994; Redelmeier, Rozin, and Kahneman 1993; and Tversky and Kahneman 1986.

4. In saying this I do not mean to suggest that choosing a competency standard is *completely* normative, merely that it is *in large part* normative. Choosing such a standard

also depends on empirical findings, such as what impairments lead to substandard decisions, what abilities people actually use when they are deciding, and how psychiatric impairments can impact decisional ability. For another recognition of the normative dimensions of capacity findings, as well as a discussion of those dimensions, see Weisstub 1988.

5. The MacArthur researchers have written a number of articles describing their development of the three MacArthur research instruments, their treatment competence instrument (the MacCAT-T), and their clinical research competence instrument (the Mac-
CAT-CR), as well their application to patient populations and matched controls. See, e.g.,
Appelbaum and Grisso 1988, 1995a, 1995b, 1997; Grisso et al. 1995; Grisso and Appelbaum 1995a, 1995b; Berg, Appelbaum, and Grisso 1996. They have also recently published a book on the MacCAT-T; see Grisso and Appelbaum 1998. And they have written
an article on the application of their instruments to the research context; see Berg and
Appelbaum 1999. They also have copies of the manuals for their different instruments,
which are available on request from them.

There is a considerable literature devoted to the MacArthur instruments, for instance,
an entire volume of *Psychology, Public Policy, and Law* (vol. 2, 1996). See, e.g., the articles
therein by Kirk and Bersoff 1996; Perlin and Dorfman 1996; Slobogin 1996; and Winick
1996b and 1996c. See also Grisso and Appelbaum's 1996 response to their critics. See
also Saks 1999 and Saks and Behnke 1999 for critiques of the MacArthur instruments.

Other instruments for measuring treatment competence have been discussed in the
literature. On the Hopkins Competency Assessment Test, see, e.g., Barton et al. 1996;
Janofsky, McCarthy, and Folstein 1992; Lavin 1992; and Sales 1992. On the Competency
Interview Schedule, see, e.g., Bean et al. 1994, 1996. On a vignette procedure for mea-
suring treatment competency, see, e.g., Marson et al. 1994; Marson et al. 1995a, 1995b,
1996, 1997a, 1997b. On the Structured Clinical Interview for Competency Incompetency
Assessment Testing and Ranking Inventory, see Tomoda et al. 1997. On the Competency
Questionnaire, see Billick et al. 1996. On the Nova Scotia questionnaire of assessment
of competency to consent to or refuse treatment, see Morrison 1987. On the Measure of
Competency to Render Informed Treatment Decisions, see Weithorn 1982. On an instrument for measuring competency in the mentally retarded, see Morris et al. 1993. For a
proposed method for assessing treatment capacity in the context of Canadian law, see
Weisstub 1988.

There are also a number of important studies of the application of these various instruments, or of a clinical competency interview, to patients or groups of patients of varying kinds. In addition to the MacArthur studies of patients' capacities mentioned above
(see Appelbaum and Grisso 1997; Grisso and Appelbaum 1995; Grisso et al. 1995), there
are other articles using other measures or methods. See, e.g., Banja and Auerbach 1988;
Barton et al. 1996; Bean et al. 1994, 1996; Beck and Parry 1992; Bentivegna and Garvey
1990; Billick et al. 1996; Hoffman and Srinivasan 1992; Katz et al. 1995; Kelly 1987;
Kloezen, Fitten, and Steinberg 1988; Marson et al. 1994, 1995a, 1995b, 1996, 1997a,
1997b; Myers and Barrett 1986, 1987; Rosenfeld 1992; Roth et al. 1982; Stern 1994; Sullivan, Ward, and Laxton 1992; Wear and Brahams 1991; and Weinstock, Copelan, and
Bagheri 1994. For a discussion of a law professor's year-long experience doing competency hearings in the right-to-refuse-medication context, see Morris 1995. For a discussion of some methodological problems with studies of patient competency, see, e.g., Weis-

stub 1988. For a discussion of a competence paradigm, see, e.g., Bocknek 1990. For a bibliography on competency, see Zaubler, Viederman, and Fins 1996.

6. See, e.g., Berg, Appelbaum, and Grisso, 1996, 385–87; Grisso and Appelbaum, 1998, chap. 7.

7. See, e.g., Berg, Appelbaum, and Grisso, 1996, 380–81. Indeed, the authors suggest that there are *empirical* grounds to aggregate the standards because they pick out different groups. Actually, however, it is a *normative* issue whether we should aggregate the standards given that they pick out different groups, depending on whether we think the capacities judged are important to competency.

8. The researchers say that they have based their instruments on standards found in the courts. But the language the courts have used is very ambiguous and does not clearly lead to the investigators' selection of measures. Some courts speak about the rationality of the patient's choice. See, e.g., *Osgood v. District of Columbia*, 567 F. Supp. 1026, 1031 (D.C. Cir. 1983); *In re Mental Commitment of M.P.*, 500 N.E.2d 216 (Ind. Ct. App. 1986); and *United States v. Charters*, 829 F.2d 479, 496 (4th Cir. 1987). But is this meant to imply a judgment about the reasonableness of the outcome (the so-called reasonable result standard)? About the intactness of the patient's reasoning processes (what is measured by MacArthur's TRAT)? About the soundness of the beliefs underlying his choice (what is measured by MacArthur's POD)? The language of the courts is simply very unclear in many instances. For a discussion of the lack of clarity of the courts' statements on this matter, see Saks 1991, 977–84. In addition to this problem, relying on the courts is no substitute for one's own normative analysis—and is itself a normative choice.

9. See Saks 1999 and Saks and Behnke 1999 on the interpretation of, and problems with, the MacArthur schema.

10. We may want to reserve the term "incompetent" for people who are suffering from some disability and are not simply ignorant. Although well-known philosophers have justified paternalism in the face of ignorance (recall John Stuart Mill's broken bridge example), the law may prefer to reserve the appellation "incompetent" for those who lack abilities and not simply knowledge. There may be practical reasons for doing this—for example, we often do not know the truth, so we want assurances that the person is under some disability and so likelier to be self-deceived. And these practicalities may not speak to what we *would* do if we *could* always know the truth. If so, perhaps in an ideal universe, all ignorance would amount to incompetency. Whatever we decide in the real world, surely most people would want, in the example above, to be disabled from deciding for themselves—whatever we call it when we so do—and to have benign others decide for them.

11. A number of commentators have addressed the need for such abilities. See, e.g., Macklin 1983; Pavlo, Bursztajn, and Gutheil 1987; and President's Commission for the Study of Ethical Problems 1982. I myself am skeptical about incorporating them in an incompetency standard. See Saks 1993.

12. A number of commentators have proposed or adopted particular standards for treatment competency. See, e.g., Abernethy 1984; Annas and Densberger 1984; Banja and Auerbach 1988; Beck 1978; Beck and Parry 1992; Benesch 1989; Buchanan and Brock 1986; Bursztajn et al. 1991; Callahan and Hagglund 1995; Checkland and Silberfeld 1996; Drane 1984; Draper and Dawson 1990; Galen 1993; Ganzini and Lee 1993;

Hanson et al. 1994; Hawkins 1996; Hipshman 1987; Hoffman 1980, 1988; Jones and Keywood 1996; Kaplan and Price 1989; Kirk and Bersoff 1996; Lippert and Stewart 1988; Mahler and Perry 1988; Marson et al. 1994; Matthews 1987; Morrison 1987; Pearce 1994; Pomerantz and de Nesnera 1991; Redding 1993; Roth, Meisel, and Lidz 1977; Schwartz and Blank 1986; Searight 1992; Sherlock 1984; Snyder 1994; Stern 1994; Valentine, Waring, and Giuffrida 1992; Venesy 1995; Weisstub 1988; and Wolff 1990.

Some commentators address medical patients and medical treatments—including life-sustaining treatment—generally, whereas others address specifically psychiatric patients. For the former, see, e.g., Annas and Densberger 1984; Callahan and Hagglund 1995; Draper and Dawson 1990; Evans 1995; Fowles and Fox 1995; Hanson et al. 1994; Hawkins 1996; Kaplan and Price 1989; Katz et al. 1995; Kelly 1987; Liberman 1985; Lippert and Stewart 1988; Mahler and Perry 1988; Mahler, Perry, and Miller 1990; Marson et al. 1996, 1998a, 1998b; Marzen and Avila 1995; Myers and Barrett 1986, 1987; Pearce 1994; Sherlock 1984; Snyder 1994; Steinberg, Fitten, and Kachuck 1986; Weinstock, Copelan, and Bagheri 1984; and Weisstub 1988.

Some commentators focus on the competency of children and adolescents. See, e.g., Alderson 1992; Evans 1995; Hawkins 1996; Parker and Dewar 1992; Redding 1993; Weisstub 1988; and Weithorn 1982. For a commentator focusing on the mentally retarded, see Morris et al. 1993.

Some of the discussions occur in the context of countries other than the United States, such as England and Canada. See, e.g., Burra, Kimberley, and Miura 1980; Draper and Dawson 1990; Evans 1988; Gallop 1988; Hoffman 1988; Hoffman and Srinivasan 1992; Jones and Keywood 1996; Kline 1988; Liberman 1985; Lippert and Stewart 1988; Morrison 1987; Parker and Dewar 1992; Pearce 1994; Stern 1994; Valentine, Waring, and Giuffrida 1992; Wear and Brahams 1991; and Weisstub 1988.

For citations to earlier articles that address these issues, see Saks 1991, esp. note 9, in addition to the articles discussed in this text.

For my other earlier work on treatment competency, see Saks 1993, 1999; and Saks and Behnke 1999.

13. For a more detailed critique, see Saks 1999; and Saks and Behnke 1999.

14. Studies show reliability and validity of psychiatric diagnosis to be somewhat limited, though better than in the past. See, e.g., Buysse et al. 1994 ("kappa values for sleep disorder diagnoses fell in the moderate to poor range," 1359); Fennig et al. 1994 (regarding level of agreement in facility and research diagnoses in first-admission psychotic patients, Public facilities demonstrate the lowest level of agreement, community facilities an intermediate level, and the university hospital the best overall agreement); Perry 1992 (diagnosis of personality disorders on structured instruments resulted in improved diagnostic reliability within each method; "[h]owever, comparisons of any two instruments used with the same subject reveal more diagnostic disagreement than agreement on average," 1651); and Vitiello et al. 1990 (showing that "reliability of child psychiatric diagnoses is unsatisfactory and that the validity of both structured and unstructured interviews is problematic," 66–67).

15. I also argue elsewhere that belief in a serious delusion distorts reality in a way that belief that it is *not* a delusion—is not a product of mental illness—does not. See Saks 1991, 991.

16. Appelbaum and Grisso 1992, 54 (emphasis in original).

17. In the MacCAT-T, the MacArthur researchers allow a patient to receive a full score if he says he expects to be in the bottom 10 percent because previous treatments have failed for him. But the patient may also have other reasons—maybe even superstitious ones—for thinking that treatment will fail now and he will be in the bottom 10 percent. Once again, he may be right—and many people are pessimistic about treatment (see below).

18. There are three additional measures on the POD that are equally problematic (although they do not contribute to the patient's score at present): the patient must acknowledge the side effects of the medication (maybe they don't and won't affect her); the patient must think her treaters have the benign motive of helping her (does it patently distort reality to believe that some do it for the money or prestige?); and the patient must acknowledge the need for hospital treatment (her doctor may be wrong—she may be one of the ones who regress in the hospital and one of the ones who rise to the demands of treatment in the community).

19. In addition to overstating the presence of incompetency by treating denial in the wrong way (on which see below), the POD may also, at times, *understate* the presence of incompetency by focusing too exclusively on disavowal of what one's doctor believes and not enough on the degree of distortion that the belief represents. Take the patient who admits he has the condition his doctor says he has and agrees with his prognosis with and without treatment. This person would receive a full score on the POD. But suppose he also believes that he has the condition his doctor says he has because aliens are manipulating his neurotransmitters from afar and that taking the medication will enrage the aliens and cause them to destroy the earth—even though he thinks it will cure his illness. Again, this person would receive a full score on the POD. But is he really competent to refuse treatment? Do we not want to look for patently false beliefs (see below) and not simply disagreement with what one's doctor says?

20. Note that most (if not all) patently false beliefs will be delusions, so the questions raised above about delusions remain apt. These are issues that deserve further study.

21. See, e.g., *In re Estate of Yett*, 606 P.2d 1174, 1176 (Or. Ct. App. 1980); and *In re Meagher's Estate*, 375 P.2d 148, 150 (Wash. 1962). See also *Insane Delusions as Invalidating a Will*, 175 ALR 868, 964 (1948).

22. I discuss this also in Saks 1991, 988–92, although my view since then has been tempered somewhat; see below.

23. See Saks 1991, 990, for some sources supporting this claim.

24. See studies cited above on the limited reliability and validity of psychiatric diagnosis. Courts including the Supreme Court have also commented on the uncertainty of psychiatric diagnosis; see, e.g., *Ake v. Oklahoma*, 470 U.S. 68 (1985) ("Psychiatry is not, however, an exact science, and psychiatrists disagree widely and frequently on what constitutes mental illness, on the appropriate diagnosis to be attached to given behavior and symptoms, on cure and treatment, and on likelihood of future dangerousness," 81). See also Goodman 1986, 721 (citing courts decrying the inexactitude of psychiatry). And see Almy 1984 (reviewing literature, as well as studies, on the inexactitude of psychiatric diagnosis).

25. To the extent that organic mental illnesses can be established by physical tests, patients should arguably have to accept them. This is one context, then, in which the analysis for, say, demented patients may be very different than the analysis for, say, schizophrenia.

26. With any physical illness there are issues that may adversely affect our certainty about the diagnosis. How reliable is the test for the illness? Could anything have gone awry between the test and its interpretation? Even if the test is reliable, how valid is it in identifying symptoms? And how certain is it that these physical findings mean there is an illness? Cannot the patient admit that he has these physical signs but say that they do not amount to an illness but are only deviant physical findings? Nevertheless, there are some tests for some illnesses that are extremely reliable and valid. In addition, it may be the right response here, too, that so long as one admits the symptoms one doesn't have to take the next step and admit to the illness. See below.

27. Another point to bear in mind is that even certain doctors and psychologists have similar views about mental illness; Szasz, for instance, denies that any nonorganic mental illness is real. See, e.g., Szasz 1974, 1978. It would be surprising to discover an oncologist similarly denying the existence of cancer.

28. The exception would be denial based on patently distorted beliefs, for example, "little men in the sky are causing me to suffer to save the world."

29. The exception is in the "one free shot" scenario; I have endeavored to justify relaxing the conditions in this scenario in the relevant places in the text.

30. The reader will recall that for "first-time" breaks I allow involuntary hospitalization and medication for a time. So how is this standard different? Should I not use "psychotic" or "impaired" in both cases? Actually, the terms are not coextensive, see text below, although there is a good deal of overlap. In addition, the reader will also recall that I allow people with first-time breaks to be treated on a much lower standard than would justify forced intervention for "impairment"; hence the standard for when impairment justifies intervention, namely, the risk of serious, perhaps irreversible, harm.

31. A number of commentators recommend a sliding-scale approach to competency determinations. See, e.g., Buchanan and Brock 1986; Drane 1984, 1985–86; Marzen and Avila 1995; Rappeport 1986; Schwartz and Blank 1986; Searight 1992; Valentine, Waring, and Giuffrida 1992; Venesy 1995; Weisstub 1988; and Winick 1991. The MacArthur researchers also recommend a sliding-scale approach, as does the President's Commission on Making Health Care Decisions.

Some commentators criticize, or raise problems with, a sliding-scale approach. See, e.g., Eth 1985; Kloezen, Fitten, and Steinberg 1988; Mahler and Perry 1988 (which prefers the Hundert approach); Saks 1991, 1999; and Saks and Behnke 1999.

Others make a variety of other recommendations in the treatment competency context (I mean to refer to things other than what the standard should be, articles about which were cited above). See, e.g., Abernethy 1984; Alderson 1992; Appelbaum and Roth 1981; Benesch 1989; Brown 1986; Burra, Kimberley, and Miura 1980; Callahan and Hagglund 1995; Caplan 1985; Culver and Gert 1990; K. Evans 1988; J. L. Evans 1995; Galen 1993; Gallop 1988; Hawkins 1996; Ho 1995; Hoffman 1988; Jones and Keywood 1996; Kapp and Mossman 1996; Kirk and Bersoff 1996; Kline 1988; McCrary and Walman 1990; Mahler, Perry, and Miller 1990; Morrison 1987; Parker and Dewar 1992; Pavlo, Bursztajn, and Gutheil 1987; Pearce 1994; Pomerantz and de Nesnera 1991; Steinberg, Fitten, and Kachuck 1986; Venesy 1995; Walkow 1994; Watson 1984; and Weisstub 1988.

32. Sometimes, it is true, we take the precise opposite position—e.g., letting adolescents make birth control decisions because the consequences are *so* important. For discussions of whether or when minors should have this right, see, e.g., Best 1983; Peiris 1987;

Rodman and Griffith 1982; Silber 1982; It seems unlikely we this tack because we think one needs less capacity for more important decisions—say because it is more dignity-impairing to take away important choices or because one will have to live oneself with the more serious consequences. Rather, it seems we allow such choices to people of lesser capacity because the policy implications of not doing so are so important—e.g., the consequences for the children and for society in having to care for these children; and because the usual competent decisionmakers (parents, in this case) are not as available for a variety of reasons to make the choice for their children.

33. "This choice is somewhat problematic, so we raise the bar a little; that choice is very problematic, so we raise the bar a lot." Of course, in both cases the evaluator gets to say that and to say why a choice is problematic based on his own values, rather than a standard speaking to the nature of the necessary harm as in the text.

34. I myself have designed a new instrument to measure "appreciation," which I am now studying empirically with my colleagues. See Saks et al. 2002. And there are other instruments available too; see note 5 above. My colleagues and I review the existing instruments in an article under preparation.

CHAPTER EIGHT

1. There have been many descriptions of self-binding mechanisms in the medical context. For two such descriptions, particularly in the psychiatric context, see Appelbaum 1991; and Dixon 1992. A number of articles discuss the Patient Self-Determination Act (PSDA). See, e.g., Bursztajn 1993; Marta 1993; and Swisher 1991. For a prospective study in the case of advance directives for life-sustaining care, see Pickard and Patrick 1991. For statutes and case law on self-binding in the mental health context as of 1999, see the compendium on file with author.

2. Commentators have debated the advisability of advance directives in both the psychiatric and the ordinary medical context. For articles debating the pros and cons of ADs, see, e.g., Backlar 1995; Brock 1993; Buchanan 1988; Churchill 1989; Dresser 1982, 1984, 1992; Macklin 1987; Moorhouse and Weisstub 1996; Radden 1992; Rosenson and Kasten 1991; Winick 1996a; and Winston and Winston 1982.

Articles studying the use of ADs, both in actuality and in prospect (by using a vignette procedure), have arrived at interesting results. See, e.g., Backlar and McFarland 1996; Diamond et al. 1989; Ganzini et al. 1994; Reilly, Teasdale, and McCullough 1994; and Zweibel and Cassel 1989. For a case study, see Epstein et al. 1994.

3. Articles that focus on self-binding to psychiatric treatment or to no psychiatric treatment include Appelbaum 1982, 1991; Backlar 1995; Backlar and McFarland 1996; Brock 1993; Cuca 1993; Dixon 1992; Dresser 1992; Macklin 1987; Perling 1993; Radden 1992; Rosenson and Kasten 1991; Winick 1996; and Winston and Winston 1982.

Other articles discuss self-binding in the medical context more generally, but in the case of specific populations of patients, such as the depressed elderly. See, e.g., Ganzini et al. 1992 (depressed psychiatric inpatients and do-not-resuscitate orders); Ganzini et al. 1994 (depressed); Ganzini, Lee, and Heintz 1994 (patients with borderline personality disorder); Marta 1993 (depressed elderly and the PSDA); Shamoo and Irving 1993 (depressed elderly); and Swisher 1991 (psychiatric patients and the PSDA).

4. I don't mean to be too glib, because of course it is possible that what the patient would have wanted if competent now is different from his prior competent choice. Never-

theless, that choice in most cases will be the best evidence of what the patient would have wanted if competent.

5. See Dresser 1984, among others of her articles on the topic.

6. If he did face a danger to his life, he would be civilly committable by the ordinary route.

7. On the other hand, we do allow "specific performance" in some cases, even though this requires actions that may be most aversive to the person who must specifically perform. For instance, if you sign a contract to sell your house, you generally must sell it even if you change your mind; you can't just pay the prospective buyer damages. Thus, all contracts and promises analogies cut both ways—there are examples on both sides. This is just a very complicated issue.

8. At least I was not impaired according to the definition I gave above. I was somewhat impulse-ridden, at least as regards the cookies, but probably not enough to justify a finding of impairment. Even if I had been, there are other reasons not to impose my prior self's choice—namely, that this is simply not an important enough case to justify acting paternalistically. See below.

9. A number of commentators make recommendations in the Ulysses-contract context, some to do with procedural protections and others with other matters, such as changes in the law to allow advance directive legislation to apply to the psychiatric context or recommendations for working more effectively with proxies. See, e.g., Bursztajn 1993; Cuca 1993; Dubler 1995; Ganzini et al. 1992; Moorhouse and Weissstub 1996; Perling 1993; and Swisher 1991.

10. I would allow civil commitment if the patient meets the other commitment criteria, particularly if she is dangerous to others but also probably if she is significantly dangerous to herself or gravely disabled, for the reasons given in chapter 4. That is, only if she is incompetent to decide on hospitalization would I allow a prior self-bound choice arguably to prevail. See below.

11. For a wrinkle on this scenario, see below.

12. Admittedly, we accept favoring the nonimpaired self, but that is autonomy-protective according to some theories—we are preferring the more autonomous self. In addition, choosing selves is different from actually making the choices of concern to people; the latter is the most shame-producing and dignity-impairing kind of intervention, because one is saying one knows best about a substantive matter of concern in someone's life.

13. The reader will recall that in the civil commitment context I counted receipt of treatment as an added benefit, and indeed it is hard not to so count it. Here I press the autonomy position harder to see where it takes us. As it turns out, there are reasons to think that the patient could receive treatment in these circumstances that do not obtain in the case of civil commitment. I confess that there is a part of me that thinks this a good outcome.

14. In the same way, of course, someone self-binding to treatment should be alerted to the case of the later current self declining and explicitly asked what should be done in that case.

15. The example above of psychosurgery is another case of the same.

CHAPTER NINE

1. I do not mean to suggest the approach discussed here is without reasons. The point is that these reasons are not *purely* autonomy-protective or *purely* paternalistic. The position I endorse—and suggest that the vast majority of people would endorse—cannot rely exclusively on autonomy or paternalism principles. In short, there are no principled autonomy theorists or paternalists, but this does not mean that the approach we take is unprincipled.

2. One could go further and say that even imposing a condition of competency makes one not a *principled* autonomy protector. But then by "autonomy" one would mean "freedom to take any self-regarding action whatever, no matter what condition one was in." Autonomy then becomes coterminous with negative liberty concerning self-regarding actions. And this is an implausible concept of autonomy.

What I try to show in the text is that even taking a more moderate position on autonomy requires value choices above and beyond setting a standard requiring that the exercise of choice be meaningful (say, because one is not incompetent). As I try to show, for example, the concepts of mental illness and competency themselves require value choices that should arguably be reserved to the decisionmaker herself if one were a principled autonomy protector.

3. The interlocutor says "when the person is incompetent," but it is worth spelling out that there are different possibilities, and which we choose depends on balancing values and interests.

Abernethy, Virginia. 1984. Compassion, control, and decisions about competency. *American Journal of Psychiatry* 141:53–58.

Addington, Donald, and Heather L. Holley. 1989. A comparison of voluntary with remanded schizophrenics. *Canadian Journal of Psychiatry* 34:89–93.

Alderson, P. 1992. In the genes or in the stars: Children's competence to consent. *Journal of Medical Ethics* 18:119–24.

Almy, Thomas B. 1984. Psychiatric testimony: Controlling the "ultimate wizardry" in personal injury actions. *Forum* 19:233–67.

American Psychiatric Association. 2000. *Diagnostic and statistical manual of mental disorders*, 4th ed. (text revision). Washington, D.C.: American Psychiatric Association.

American Psychiatric Association Joint Commission on Public Affairs, Sub-Committee, eds. 1980. *A psychiatric glossary*. 5th ed. Boston: Little, Brown.

Angold, Adrian, and Andrew Pickles. 1993. Seclusion on an adolescent unit. *Journal of Child Psychology and Psychiatry and Allied Disciplines* 34:975–89.

Annas, George J. 1984. The case of Mary Hier: When substituted judgment becomes sleight of hand. *Hastings Center Report* 14:23–25.

Annas, George J., and Joan E. Densberger. 1984. Competence to refuse medical treatment: Autonomy vs. paternalism. *University of Toledo Law Review* 15:561–96.

Appelbaum, Paul S. 1982. Can a subject consent to a Ulysses contract? Commentary. *Hastings Center Report* 12:27–28.

———. 1985. Empirical assessment of innovation in the law of civil commitment: A critique. *Law, Medicine and Health Care* 13:304–9.

———. 1986. Outpatient commitment: The problems and the promise. *American Journal of Psychiatry* 143:1270–72.

———. 1988. The right to refuse treatment with antipsychotic medications: Retrospect and prospect. *American Journal of Psychiatry* 145:413–19.

———. 1991. Advance directives for psychiatric treatment. *Hospital and Community Psychiatry* 42:983–84.

———. 1992. Civil commitment from a systems perspective. *Law and Human Behavior* 16:61–74.

———. 1995. Civil commitment and liability for violating patients' rights. *Psychiatric Services* 46:17–18.

Appelbaum, Paul S., and Thomas Grisso. 1988. Assessing patients' capacities to consent to treatment. *New England Journal of Medicine* 319:1635–38.

———. 1992. Manual for perceptions of disorder. Typescript.

———. 1995a. The MacArthur Treatment Competence Assessment Tool—Clinical Research. Typescript.

———. 1995b. The MacArthur Treatment Competence Study: I. Mental illness and competence to consent to treatment. *Law and Human Behavior* 19:105–26.

———. 1997. Capacities of hospitalized, medically ill patients to consent to treatment. *Psychosomatics* 38:119–25.

Appelbaum, Paul S., and Thomas G. Gutheil 1979. The Boston State hospital case: "Involuntary mind control," the Constitution, and the "right to rot." *American Journal of Psychiatry* 137:720–23.

———. 1981. "Rotting with their rights on": Constitutional theory and clinical reality in drug refusal by psychiatric patients. *Bulletin of the American Academy of Psychiatry and the Law* 7:306–15.

Appelbaum, Paul S., and Steven K. Hoge. 1996. The right to refuse treatment: What the research reveals. *Behavioral Sciences and the Law* 4:280–92.

Appelbaum, Paul S., and Loren H. Roth. 1981. Clinical issues in the assessment of competency. *American Journal of Psychiatry* 138:1462–67.

———. 1988. Assessing the NCSC guidelines for involuntary civil commitment from the clinician's point of view. *Hospital and Community Psychiatry* 39:406–10.

Arenella, Peter, 1977. The diminished capacity and diminished responsibility defenses: Two children of a doomed marriage. *Columbia Law Review* 77:827–65.

Atkins, Marc S., and Alexander Ricciuti. 1992. The disproportionate use of seclusion in a children's psychiatric state hospital. *Residential Treatment for Children and Youth* 10:23–33.

Ausubel, David P. 1961. Personality disorder is disease. *American Psychologist* 16:254–66.

Aviram, Uri. 1990. Care or convenience? On the medical-bureaucratic model of commitment of the mentally ill. *International Journal of Law and Psychiatry* 13: 165–77.

Aviram, Uri, and Robert A. Weyer. 1996. Changing trends in mental health legislation: Anatomy of reforming a civil commitment law. *Journal of Health, Politics, Policy and Law* 21:771–805.

Backlar, Patricia. 1995. The longing for order: Oregon's medical advance directive for mental health treatment. *Community Mental Health Journal* 31:103–8.

Backlar, Patricia, and Bertson. H. McFarland. 1996. A survey on use of advance directives for mental health treatment in Oregon. *Psychiatric Services* 47:1387–89.

Bagby, R. Michael. 1988. The deprofessionalization of civil commitment. *Canadian Psychology* 29:234–36.

Bagby, R. Michael, Judith S. Thompson, Susan E. Dickens, and Michiko Nohara. 1991. Decision making in psychiatric civil commitment: An experimental analysis. *American Journal of Psychiatry* 148:28–33.

Balance, William D., Paul P. Hirschfield, and Wolfgang C. Bingmann. 1970. Mental illness: Myth, metaphor, or model. *Professional Psychology* 1:133–37.

Bamonte, Jennifer L., and Cathy Bierman. 1992. *In re Dubreuil:* Is an individual's right to refuse a blood transfusion contingent on parental status? *Nova Law Review* 17:517–47.

Banja, J. D., and V. S. Auerbach. 1988. Competence to consent to medical treatment among neurologically impaired persons: The competency interview. *Archives of Physical Medicine and Rehabilitation* 69:716.

Barbanel, Josh. 1991. Rise in tuberculosis forces review of dated methods. *New York Times*, 10 July.

Barton, Dennis C., Harminder S. Mallik, William B. Orr, and Jeffery S. Janofsky. 1996. Clinicians' judgment of capacity of nursing home patients to give informed consent. *Psychiatric Services* 47:956–60.

Bassuk, Ellen L., and H. Richard Lamb. 1986. Homelessness and the implementation of deinstitutionalization. *New Directions for Mental Health Services San Francisco* 30: 7–14.

Bayer, Ronald, and Laurence Dupuis. 1995. Tuberculosis, public health, and civil liberties. *Annual Review of Public Health* 16:307–26.

Bazelon, David. 1986. The right to a partisan psychiatric expert: Might indigency preclude insanity? *New York University Law Review* 61:703–37.

Bean, Graham, Shizuhiko Nishisato, Neil A. Rector, and Graham Glancy. 1994. The psychometric properties of the competence interview schedule. *Canadian Journal of Psychiatry* 39:368–76.

———. 1996. The assessment of competence to make a treatment decision: An empirical approach. *Canadian Journal of Psychiatry* 41:85–92.

Beauford, James E., Dale E. McNiel, and Renée L. Binder. 1997. Utility of the initial therapeutic alliance in evaluating psychiatric patients' risk of violence. *American Journal of Psychiatry* 154:1272–76.

Beck, James C. 1987. Right to refuse antipsychotic medication: Psychiatric assessment and legal decision-making. *Mental and Physical Disability Law Reporter* 11: 368–72.

———. 1988. Determining competency to assent to neuroleptic drug treatment. *Hospital and Community Psychiatry* 39:1106–8.

Beck, James C., and Edward A. Golowka. 1988. A study of enforced treatment in relation to Stone's "Thank You" Theory. *Behavioral Sciences and the Law* 6:559–66.

Beck, James C., and John W. Parry. 1992. Incompetence, treatment refusal, and hospitalization. *Bulletin of the American Academy of Psychiatry and the Law* 20: 261–67.

Begelman, D. A. 1971. Misnaming, metaphors, the medical model, and some muddles. *Psychiatry* 34:38–58.

Behnke, Stephen H. 1999. *O'Connor v. Donaldson:* Retelling a classic and finding some revisionist history. *Journal of the American Academy of Psychiatry and the Law* 27: 115–26.

Benesch, Katherine. 1989. Legal issues in determining competence to make treatment decisions. *New Directions for Mental Health Services* 41:97–105.

Bentall, Richard P., and David Pilgrim. 1993. Thomas Szasz, crazy talk and the myth of mental illness. *British Journal of Medical Psychology* 66:69–76.

Bentivegna, Santo W., and Kathleen Garvey. 1990. Applications of Hartman's competency to consent and right to refuse treatment concepts. *American Journal of Forensic Psychology* 8:25–34.

Berg, Jessica Wilen, and Paul S. Appelbaum. 1999. Subject's capacity to consent to neurobiological research. In *Ethics in psychiatric research: A resource manual for human subjects' protection*, edited by Howard A. Pincus, Jeffery A. Lieberman, and Sandy Ferris. Washington, D.C.: American Psychiatric Association.

Berg, Jessica Wilen, Paul S. Appelbaum, and Thomas Grisso. 1996. Constructing competence: Formulating standards of legal competence to make medical decisions. *Rutgers Law Review* 48:345–96.

Bessho, David M. 1995. Health hospitalization for tuberculosis: Ensure due process for persons involuntarily hospitalized. *Georgia State University Law Review* 12:247–51.

Best, Marilyn. 1983. Unemancipated minors' rights of access to contraceptives without parental consent or notice—the squeal rule and beyond. *Oklahoma City University Law Review* 8:219–50.

Betemps, Elizabeth J., C. Ralph Buncher, and Mary Oden. 1992. Length of time spent in seclusion and restraint by patients at 82 VA medical centers. *Hospital and Community Psychiatry* 43:912–14.

Betemps, Elizabeth J., Eugene Somoza, and C. Ralph Buncher. 1993. Hospital characteristics, diagnoses, and staff reasons associated with use of seclusion and restraint. *Hospital and Community Psychiatry* 44:367–71.

Beyer, Stephan. 1980. Madness and medicine: The forcible administration of psychotropic drugs. *Wisconsin Law Review* no. 3: 497–567.

Billick, Stephen B., Peter W. Naylor, Matthew R. Majeske, and Woodward Burget III. 1996. A clinical study of competence in psychiatric inpatients. *Bulletin of the American Academy of Psychiatry and the Law* 24:505–11.

Binder, Renee L., and Dale E. McNiel. 1991. Involuntary patients' right to refuse medication: Impact of the *Riese* decision on a California inpatient unit. *Bulletin of the American Academy of Psychiatry and the Law* 19:351–57.

Bishop, M., and H. Olders. 1992. Alternatives to civil commitment. *Canadian Journal of Psychiatry* 37:223.

Bittman, Betsy J., and Antonio Convit. 1993. Competency, civil commitment, and the dangerousness of the mentally ill. *Journal of Forensic Sciences* 38:1460–66.

Blackburn, Catherine E. 1990. The "therapeutic orgy" and the "right to rot" collide: The right to refuse antipsychotic drugs under state law. *Houston Law Review* 27: 447–513.

Bloom, Joseph D. 1986. The *Tarasoff* decision, dangerousness and mandated outpatient treatment. *International Journal of Offender Therapy and Comparative Criminology* 30:vii–x.

Bloom, Joseph D., and Larry R. Faulkner. 1987. Competency determinations in civil commitment *American Journal of Psychiatry* 144:193–96.

Bloom, Joseph D., and Mary H. Williams. 1994. Oregon's civil commitment law: 140 years of change. *Hospital and Community Psychiatry* 45:466–70.

Bloom, Joseph D., Mary H. Williams, Sally L. Godard, and Larry R. Faulkner. 1988. The influence of the right to refuse treatment on pre-commitment patients. *Bulletin of the American Academy of Psychiatry and the Law* 16:5–9.

Bocknek, Gene. 1990. Extending Masterpasqua's competence paradigm. *American Psychologist* 45:1176–77.

Bornstein, Philipp E., 1985. The use of restraints on a general psychiatric unit. *Journal of Clinical Psychiatry* 46:175–78.

Borum, Randy, Marvin Swartz, Sharon Riley, Jeffrey Swanson, Virginia Aldigé Hiday, and Ryan Wagner. 1999. Consumer perceptions of involuntary outpatient commitment. *Psychiatric Services* 50:1489.

Bradford, B., S. McCann, and Harold Merskey. 1986. A survey of involuntary patients' attitudes towards their commitment. *Psychiatric Journal of the University of Ottawa* 11:162–65.

Brakel, Samuel Jan, and John M. Davis 1991. Taking harms seriously: Involuntary mental patients and the right to refuse treatment. *Indiana Law Review* 25:429–73.

Breen, Robert, and Joshua T. Thornhill. 1998. Noncompliance with medication for psychiatric disorders—reasons and remedies. *Disease Management* 6:457–71.

Brian, Jeanette. 1992. The right to refuse antipsychotic drug treatment and the Supreme Court: *Washington v. Harper. Buffalo Law Review* 40:251–82.

Briere, John, and Eliana Gil. 1998. Self-mutilation in clinical and general population samples: Prevalence, correlates, and functions. *American Journal of Orthopsychiatry* 68:609–20.

Brock, Dan W. 1993. A proposal for the use of advance directives in the treatment of incompetent mentally ill persons. *Bioethics* 7:247–56.

Brooks, Alexander D. 1986. The right to refuse antipsychotic medications: Law and policy. *Rutgers Law Review* 39:339–76.

———. 1992. The constitutionality and morality of civilly committing violent sexual predators. *University of Puget Sound Law Review* 15:709–54.

———. 1997. Outpatient commitment for the chronically mentally ill: Law and policy. *New Directions for Mental Health Services* 36:117–28.

Brooks, Kathryn L., Jane S. Mulaik, Maggie P. Gilead, and Betty S. Daniels. 1994. Patient overcrowding in psychiatric hospital units: Effects on seclusion and restraint. *Administration and Policy in Mental Health* 22:133–44.

Brouillette, Marie-Josee, and Joel Paris. 1991. The dangerousness criterion for civil commitment: The problem and a possible solution. *Canadian Journal of Psychiatry* 36:285–89.

Brown, Lowell C., and Shirley J. Paine. 1993. Thunder from California: The *Thor* decision and the ever-expanding right to die. *HealthSpan* 10:13–17.

Brown, Phil. 1986. Psychiatric treatment refusal, patient competence, and informed consent. *International Journal of Law and Psychiatry* 8:83–94.

Brown, Robin G. 1991. Thomas Szasz, mental illness and psychotherapy. *British Journal of Psychotherapy* 7:283–94.

Buchanan, Allen. 1988. Advance directives and the personal identity problem. *Philosophy and Public Affairs* 17:277–302.

Buchanan, Allen, and Dan W. Brock. 1986. Deciding for others. *Milbank Quarterly* (supp. 2) 64:17–94.

———. 1989. *Deciding for others: The ethics of surrogate decisionmaking.* Cambridge: Cambridge University Press.

Buckalew, L. W., and N. M. Buckalew. 1995. Survey of the nature and prevalence of patients' noncompliance and implications for intervention. *Psychological Reports* 76:315–21.

Burra, P., R. Kimberley, and K. Miura. 1980. Mental competence and consent to treatment. *Canadian Journal of Psychiatry* 25:251–53.

Bursztajn, Harold. J. 1993. From PSDA to PTSD: The Patient Self-Determination Act and post-traumatic stress disorder. *Journal of Clinical Ethics* 4:71–74.

Bursztajn, Harold J., Thomas G. Gutheil, Mark Mills, Robert M. Hamm, and Archie Brodsky. 1986. Process analysis of judges' commitment decisions: A preliminary empirical study. *American Journal of Psychiatry* 143:170–74.

Bursztajn, Harold J., Herndon P. Harding, Thomas G. Gutheil, and Archie Brodsky. 1991. Beyond cognition: The role of disordered affective states in impairing competence to consent to treatment. *Bulletin of the American Academy of Psychiatry and the Law* 19:383–88.

Burt, Robert. 1979. *Taking care of strangers*. New York: Free Press.

Bustillo, Juan R., John Lauriello, and Samuel J. Keith. 1999. Schizophrenia: Improving outcome. *Harvard Review of Psychiatry* 6:229–40.

Buysse, David J., Charles F. Reynolds, Peter J. Hauri, Thomas Roth, et al. 1994. Diagnostic concordance for DSM-IV sleep disorders: A report from the APA/NIMH DSM-IV field trial. *American Journal of Psychiatry* 151:1351–60.

Callahan, Charles D., and Kristopher J. Hagglund. 1995. Comparing neuropsychological and psychiatric evaluation of competence in rehabilitation: A case example. *Archives of Physical Medicine and Rehabilitation* 76:909–12.

Candilis, Philip J., and Mark H. Pollack. 1997. The hidden costs of untreated anxiety disorders. *Harvard Review of Psychiatry* 5:40–42.

Caplan, Arthur L. 1985. Let wisdom find a way. *Generations* 10:10–14.

Carey, Naomi, Susan L. Jones, and Anita W. O'Toole. 1990. Do you feel powerless when a patient refuses medication? *Journal of Psychosocial Nursing and Mental Health Services* 28:19–25.

Carlson, Janene M., and Margo B. Holm. 1993. Effectiveness of occupational therapy for reducing restraint use in a psychiatric setting. *American Journal of Occupational Therapy* 47:885–89.

Chamberlin, Judi. 1985. An ex-patient's response to Soliday. *Journal of Nervous and Mental Disease* 173:288–89.

Checkland, David, and Michel Silberfeld. 1996. Mental competence and the question of beneficent intervention. *Theoretical Medicine* 17:121–34.

Chesley, Richard A. 1983. The increasingly disparate standards of recovery for negligently inflicted emotional injuries. *University of Cincinnati Law Review* 52:1017–37.

Chiafullo, Louis A. 1994. Innocents imprisoned: The deficiencies of the New Jersey standard governing the involuntary commitment of children. *Seton Hall Law Review* 24:1507–48.

Chiles, John A., Peter Davidson, and Dennis McBride. 1994. Effects of Clozapine on use of seclusion and restraint at a state hospital. *Hospital and Community Psychiatry* 45:269–71.

Churchill, L. R. 1989. Trust, autonomy, and advance directives. *Journal of Religion and Health* 28:175–83.

Ciccone, J. Richard, John F. Tokoli, Colleen D. Clement, and Thomas E. Gift. 1990. Right to refuse treatment: Impact of *Rivers v. Katz*. *Bulletin of the American Academy of Psychiatry and the Law* 18:203–15.

Cichon, Dennis E. 1992. The right to "just say no": A history and analysis of the right to refuse antipsychotic drugs. *Louisiana Law Review* 53:283–426.

Civil commitment and the "great confinement" revisited: Straightjacketing individual rights, stifling culture (note). 1995. *William and Mary Law Review* 36:1769–1805.

Clayton, Ellen W. 1987. From *Rogers* to *Rivers:* The rights of the mentally ill to refuse medication. *American Journal of Law and Medicine* 13:7–52.

Cocozza, Joseph J., and Henry J. Steadman. 1975–76. The failure of psychiatric predictions of dangerousness: Clear and convincing evidence. *Rutgers Law Review* 29:1084–1101.

Coleman, Brenda C. 1995. Resurgence of tuberculosis called a worldwide crisis. *Los Angeles Times*, 29 January.

Cornwell, John Kip. 1996. Confining mentally disordered "super criminals": A realignment of rights in the nineties. *Houston Law Review* 33:651–730.

Coryell, William, Jean Endicott, George Winokur, Hagop Akiskal, David Solomon, Andrew Leon, Timothy Mueller, and Tracie Shea. 1995. Characteristics and significance of untreated major depressive disorder. *American Journal of Psychiatry* 152:1124–29.

Cramer, Joyce A. 1995. Relationship between medication compliance and medical outcomes. *American Journal of Health-System Pharmacists* 52:27–29.

Cramer, Joyce A., Richard H. Matson, Mary L. Prevey, Richard D. Scheyer, and Valinda L. Ovellette. 1989. How often is medication taken as prescribed? *Journal of the American Medical Association* 261:3273–77.

Crawford, M. J,. and S. Wessely. 1998. Does initial management affect the rate of repetition of deliberate self harm? *British Medical Journal* 317:985.

Crenshaw, Wesley B., and Saul S. Francis. 1995. A national survey on seclusion and restraint in state psychiatric hospitals. *Psychiatric Services* 46:1026–31.

Crespi, Tony D. 1990. Restraint and seclusion with institutionalized adolescents. *Adolescence* 25:825–29.

Cuca, Roberto. 1993. Ulysses in Minnesota: First steps toward a self-binding psychiatric advance directive statute. *Cornell Law Review* 78:1152–86.

Cuffel, Brian J. 1992. Characteristics associated with legal status change among psychiatric patients. *Community Mental Health Journal* 28:471–82.

Culver, Charles M., and Bernard Gert. 1990. The inadequacy of incompetence. *Milbank Quarterly* 68:619–43.

Cutting, John, Manfred Bleuler, Luc Ciompi, T. J. Crow, David Abrahamson, and D. Tantam. 1983. Schizophrenic deterioration. *British Journal of Psychiatry* 143:77–84.

Czajkowski, Susan M., and Margaret A. Chesney. 1990. Adherence and the placebo effect. In *The handbook of health behavior change*, 409–23. New York: Springer.

Dammann, Eric J. 1997. "The myth of mental illness": Continuing controversies and their implications for mental health professionals. *Clinical Psychology Review* 17:733–56.

Danis, Marion, Leslie I. Southerland, Joanne M. Garrett, Janet L. Smith, Frank Hielema, C. Glenn Pickard, David M. Egner, and Donald L. Patrick. 1991. A prospective study of advance directives for life-sustaining care. *New England Journal of Medicine* 324:882–88.

Davies, Stefan. 2000. Involuntary out-patient commitment and supervised discharge. *British Journal of Psychiatry* 177:183.

Davis, Douglas A. 1976. On being detectably sane in insane places: Base rates and psychodiagnosis. *Journal of Abnormal Psychology* 85:416–22.

Dawson, John. 1996. Psychopathology and civil commitment criteria. *Medical Law Review* 4:62–83.

de Cangas, Jose P. C. 1993. Nursing staff and unit characteristics: Do they affect the use of seclusion? *Perspectives in Psychiatric Care* 29:15–22.

Delaney, Jeffrey J. 1991. Specific intent, substituted judgment and best interests: A nationwide analysis of an individual's right to die. *Pace Law Review* 11:565–641.

Dell, Susanne. 1984. Murder into manslaughter, the diminished responsibility defence in practice. Institute of Psychiatry Maudsley Monographs, no. 27. New York: Oxford University Press.

Demyttenaere, Koen. 1997. Compliance during treatment with antidepressants. *Journal of Affective Disorders* 43:27–39.

Dennis, Deborah L., and John Monahan. 1996. Coercion and aggressive community treatment. In *A new frontier in mental health law*. New York: Plenum.

Devlin, Patrick. 1965. *The enforcement of morals*. New York: Oxford University Press.

Diamond, Eric L., James A. Jernigan, Ray A. Moseley, and Valerie Messina. 1989. Decision-making ability and advance directive preferences in nursing home patients and proxies. *Gerontologist* 29:622–26.

Dickerson, Faith, Norman Rangel, Frederick Parente, and John Boronow. 1994. Seclusion and restraint, assaultiveness, and patient performance in a token economy. *Hospital and Community Psychiatry* 45:168–70.

Dixon, Gayle. 1992. The Minnesota advance psychiatric directive: Protecting patient decision-making. *Minnesota Medicine* 75:33–34.

Dorfman, Deborah A. 1993. Through a therapeutic jurisprudence filter: Fear and pretextuality in mental disability law. *New York Law School Journal of Human Rights* 3:805–24.

Draine, Jeffrey. 1997. Conceptualizing services research on outpatient commitment. *Journal of Mental Health Administration* 24:306–15.

Draine, Jeffrey, and Phyllis Solomon 1994. Explaining attitudes toward medication compliance among a seriously mentally ill population. *Journal of Nervous and Mental Disease* 182:50–54.

Drane, James F. 1984. Competency to give an informed consent: A model for making clinical assessments. *Journal of the American Medical Association* 252:925–27.

———. 1985–86. The many faces of competency. *Hastings Center Report* 15–16:17–21.

Draper, Ronald J., and David Dawson. 1990. Competence to consent to treatment: A guide for the psychiatrist. *Canadian Journal of Psychiatry* 35:285–89.

Dresser, Rebecca S. 1982. Ulysses and the psychiatrists: A legal and policy analysis of the voluntary commitment contract. *Harvard Civil Rights–Civil Liberties Law Review* 16:777–854.

———. 1984. Bound to treatment: The Ulysses contract. *Hastings Center Report* 14:13–16.

———. 1992. *Autonomy revisited: The limits of anticipatory choices*. Baltimore: Johns Hopkins University Press.

Drumheller, Betty L. 1983–84. Constitutionalizing civil commitment: Another attempt— *In re Harris,* 98 Wash. 2d 276, 654 P 2d 109 (1982). *Washington Law Review* 59:375–99.

Dubler, Nancy Neveloff. 1995. The doctor-proxy relationship: The neglected connection. *Kennedy Institute of Ethics Journal* 5:289–306.

Durham, Mary L., and Glenn L. Pierce. 1986. Legal intervention in civil commitment: The impact of broadened commitment criteria. *Annals of the American Academy* 484:42–69.

Dworkin, Gerald. 1988. *The theory and practice of autonomy.* Cambridge: Cambridge University Press.

———. 1993. Thomas Hill, Jr., Autonomy and self-respect. *Philosophical Quarterly* 43:378–79.

———. 1995. Review of *Liberations from self: A theory of personal autonomy,* by Bernard Berofsky. *Journal of Philosophy* 94:212–16.

Dyer, Allen R., and Sidney Bloch. 1987. Informed consent and the psychiatric patient. *Journal of Medical Ethics* 13:12–16.

Earle, Kathleen A., and Sandra L. Forquer. 1995. Use of seclusion with children and adolescents in public psychiatric hospitals. *American Journal of Orthopsychiatry* 65:238–44.

Edelsohn, Gail A., and Virginia Aldigé Hiday. 1990. Civil commitment: A range of patient attitudes. *Bulletin of the American Academy of Psychiatry and the Law* 18:65–77.

Edlund, Matthew J., Richard J. Goldberg, and Philip L. P. Morris. 1991. The use of physical restraint in patients with cerebral contusion. *International Journal of Psychiatry in Medicine* 21:173–82.

Elliott, Carl, and Britt Elliott. 1991. From the patient's point-of-view: Medical-ethics and the moral imagination. *Journal of Medical Ethics* 17:173–78.

Emmons, Steve. 1994. A new war on TB: Myths and poor medical care have allowed tuberculosis to make a comeback, but O.C. health officials are ready to get tougher in their battle against this potential killer. *Los Angeles Times,* 9 January.

Epstein, Stephen A., Eduina Martins, Margaret A. Crowley, and Marie F. Pennanen. 1994. The use of an advance directive in consultation-liaison psychiatry: A case report. *International Journal of Psychiatry in Medicine* 24:371–76.

Eriksson, Kirstin I., and C. G. Westrin. 1995. Coercive measures in psychiatric care. *Acta Psychiatrica Scandinavica* 92:225–30.

Erlinder, C. Peter. 1993. Minnesota's Gulag: Involuntary treatment for the "politically ill." *William Mitchell Law Review* 19:99–159.

Estrin, Robin. 1999. Housing wishes of elderly often ignored needs: A Brandeis University study reports that millions of senior citizens are placed in adult day programs or nursing homes against their will. *Los Angeles Times,* 7 February.

Eth, Spencer. 1985. Competency and consent to treatment. *Journal of the American Medical Association* 253:778–79.

Evans, Jennifer. L. 1995. Are children competent to make decisions about their own deaths? *Behavioral Sciences and the Law* 13:27–41.

Evans, Kenneth G. 1988. Mental competence, treatment and substitute consent: A lawyer's perspective. *Health Law in Canada* 8:96–99.

Evison, Ian S. 1990. Between the priestly doctor and the myth of mental illness. In *Religious and ethical factors in psychiatric practice,* edited by Don S. Browning and Thomas Jobe. Chicago: Nelson Hall.

Farabee, David, Michael Prendergast, and M. Douglas Anglin. 1998. The effectiveness of coerced treatment for drug-abusing offenders. *Federal Probation* 62:3–10.

Farina, Amerigo. 1998. Stigma. In *Handbook of social functioning in schizophrenia,* edited by Kim Tornvall and Nicholas Tarrier. Boston: Allyn and Bacon.

Farnsworth, Michael G. 1991. The impact of judicial review of patients' refusal to accept antipsychotic medications at the Minnesota Security Hospital. *Bulletin of the American Academy of Psychiatry and the Law* 19:33–42.

Fassler, David, and Nancy Cotton. 1992. A national survey on the use of seclusion in the psychiatric treatment of children. *Hospital and Community Psychiatry* 43:370–74.

Faulkner, Larry R., Bentson H. McFarland, Joseph D. Bloom, and Thomas O. Stern. 1986a. A methodology for predicting the effects of changes in civil commitment decision making. *Bulletin of the American Academy of Psychiatry and the Law* 14:71–80.

———. 1986b. A method for quantifying and comparing civil commitment processes. *American Journal of Psychiatry* 143:744–49.

———. 1987. Methodology for the analysis of civil commitment detention times and costs. *Bulletin of the American Academy of Psychiatry and the Law* 15:359–70.

Favazza, Armando R. 1998. The coming of age of self-mutilation. *Journal of Nervous and Mental Disease* 186:259–68.

Feinberg, Joel. 1985. *Offense to others.* New York: Oxford University Press.

Fennig, Shmuel, Thomas J. Craig, Marsha Tanenberg-Karant, and Evelyn J. Bromet. 1994. Comparison of facility and research diagnoses in first-admission psychotic patients. *American Journal of Psychiatry* 151:1423–29.

Fenton, Wayne S., Crystal R. Blyler, and Robert K. Heinssen. 1997. Determinants of medication compliance in schizophrenia: Empirical and clinical findings. *Schizophrenia Bulletin* 23:637–51.

Fernandez, Gustavo A., and Sylvia Nygard. 1990. Impact of involuntary outpatient commitment on the revolving-door syndrome in North Carolina. *Hospital and Community Psychiatry* 41:1001–4.

Fisher, William H., and Glenn L. Pierce. 1985. Civil commitment reform: Context and consequences. *Psychiatric Quarterly* 57:217–29.

Fisher, William H., Glenn L. Pierce, and Paul S. Appelbaum. 1988. How flexible are our civil commitment statutes? *Hospital and Community Psychiatry* 39:711–12.

Forman, Lisa. 1993. Medication: Reasons and interventions for noncompliance. *Journal of Psychosocial Nursing and Mental Health Services* 31:23–25.

Forquer, Sandra L., Kathleen A. Earle, Bruce B. Way, and Steven M. Banks. 1996. Predictors of the use of restraint and seclusion in public psychiatric hospitals. *Administration and Policy in Mental Health* 23:527–32.

Fowles, G. P., and B. A. Fox. 1995. Competence to consent to treatment and informed consent in neurobehavioral rehabilitation. *Clinical Neuropsychologist* 9:251–57.

Fox, Michael A. 1985. Is mental illness a myth? *South Atlantic Quarterly* 84:280–93.

Frankfurt, Harry G. 1971. Freedom of the will and the concept of a person. *Journal of Philosophy* 68:5–20.

Freedman, Benjamin. 1981. Competence, marginal and otherwise. *International Journal of Law and Psychiatry* 4:53–72.

Freud, Sigmund. 1986. *The psychopathology of everyday life* (1901). Standard edition, vol. 6.

Fulop, Naomi J. 1995. Involuntary outpatient civil commitment: What can Britain learn from the U.S. Experience? A civil liberties perspective. *International Journal of Law and Psychiatry* 18:291–303.

Fulwiler, Carl, Catherine Forbes, Susan L. Santangelo, and Marshall Folstein. 1997. Self-mutilation and suicide attempt: Distinguishing features in prisoners. *Journal of the American Academy of Psychiatry and the Law* 25:69–77.

Galen, Kenneth D. 1993. Assessing psychiatric patients' competency to agree to treatment plans. *Hospital and Community Psychiatry* 44:361–64.

Gallop, Ruth. 1988. Mental competence, treatment and substitute consent: A nurse's perspective. *Health Law in Canada* 8:94.

Ganzini, Linda, and Melina A. Lee. 1993. Authenticity, autonomy, and mental disorders. *Journal of Clinical Ethics* 4:58–61.

Ganzini, Linda, Melinda A. Lee, and Ronald T. Heintz. 1994. The capacity to make decisions in advance and borderline personality disorder. *Journal of Clinical Ethics* 5:360–64.

Ganzini, Linda, Melinda A. Lee, Ronald T. Heintz, and Joseph D. Bloom. 1992. Do-not-resuscitate orders for depressed psychiatric inpatients. *Hospital and Community Psychiatry* 43:915–19.

Ganzini, Linda, Melinda A. Lee, Ronald T. Heintz, Joseph D. Bloom, and Darien S. Fenn. 1994. The effect of depression treatment on elderly patients' preferences for life-sustaining medical therapy. *American Journal of Psychiatry* 151:1631–36.

Geller, Jeffrey L. 1986. The quandaries of enforced community treatment and unenforceable outpatient commitment statutes. *Journal of Psychiatry and Law* 14 (spring–summer): 149–58.

Gigliotti, Gary A., and Jeffrey Rubin. 1991. The right to refuse treatment: An application of the economic principles of decision-making under uncertainty. *International Journal of Law and Psychiatry* 14:405–16.

Gillig, Paulette M., Paula Grubb, Robert Kruger, Aimee Johnson, James R. Hillard, and Nancy Tucker. 1990. What do psychiatric emergency patients really want and how do they feel about what they get? *Psychiatric Quarterly* 61:189–96.

Goffman, Erving. 1961. *Asylums.* New York: Doubleday.

Goldberg, Judith A. 1995. Due process limitations on involuntary commitment of individuals who abuse drugs or alcohol. *Boston University Law Review* 75:1481–1506.

Goldfinger, Stephen M. 1990. Psychiatric aspects of AIDS and HIV infection. *New Directions for Mental Health Services* 48:83–95.

Goodman, Mark P. 1986. The right to a partisan psychiatric expert: Might indigency preclude insanity? *New York University Law Review* 61:1–32.

Goodyer, L. I., F. Miskelly, and P. Milligan. 1995. Does encouraging good compliance improve patients' clinical condition in heart failure? *British Journal of Clinical Practice* 49:173–76.

Gorenstein, Ethan E. 1984. Debating mental illness: Implications for science, medicine, and social policy. *American Psychologist* 39:50–56.

Gostin, Lawrence O. 1983. Compulsory treatment in psychiatry: Some reflections on self-determination, patient competency and professional expertise. *Poly Law Review* 7: 86–93.

———. 1993a. Controlling the resurgent tuberculosis epidemic. *Journal of the American Medical Association* 269:255–61.

———. 1993b. Drawing a line between killing and letting die: The law, and law reform, on medically assisted dying. *Journal of Law, Medicine and Ethics* 21:94–101.

———. 1995. Tuberculosis and the power of the state: Toward the development of rational standards for the review of compulsory public health powers. *University of Chicago Law School Roundtable* 2:219–45.

———. 1997. Deciding life and death in the courtroom: From Quinlan to Cruzan, Glucksberg, and Vacco—A brief history and analysis of constitutional protection of the "right to die." *Journal of the American Medical Association* 278:1523–28.

Gove, Walter R., and Terry Fain. 1977. A comparison of voluntary and committed psychiatric patients. *Archives of General Psychiatry* 34:669–76.

Grad, Gary J., and Jean-Pierre Lindenmayer. 1977. The psychiatric emergency room: A study of patient treatment requests. *Social Psychiatry* 23:132–39.

Grant, William H., and Phillip J. Resnick. 1989. Right of active duty military personnel to refuse psychiatric treatment. *Behavioral Sciences and the Law* 7:339–54.

Grisso, Thomas, and Paul S. Appelbaum. 1992. Manual for understanding treatment disclosures. Typescript.

———. 1995a. Comparison of standards for assessing patients' capacities to make treatment decisions. *American Journal of Psychiatry* 152:1033–37.

———. 1995b. The MacArthur Treatment Competence Study: III. Abilities of patients to consent to psychiatric and medical treatments. *Law and Human Behavior* 19:149–74.

———. 1995c. MacArthur Competence Assessment Tool—Treatise. Typescript.

———. 1996. Values and limits of the MacArthur Treatment Competence Study. *Psychology, Public Policy, and Law* 2:167–81.

———. 1998. *MacArthur Competence Assessment Tool for Treatment.* Florida: Professional Resource Press.

Grisso, Thomas, Paul S. Appelbaum, Edward P. Mulvey, and Kenneth Fletcher. 1995. The MacArthur Treatment Competence Study: II. Measures of abilities related to competence to consent to treatment. *Law and Human Behavior* 19:127–48.

Groethe, Reed. 1977. Overt dangerous behavior as a constitutional requirement for involuntary civil commitment of the mentally ill. *University of Chicago Law Review* 44:562–93.

Groth, Gail N., Dawn M. Wilder, and V. Leroy Young. 1994. The impact of compliance on the rehabilitation of patients with mallet finger injuries. *Journal of Hand Therapy* 7:21–24.

Gutheil, Thomas G. 1978. Observations on the theoretical bases for seclusion of the psychiatric inpatient. *American Journal of Psychiatry* 135:325–28.

———. 1980. Restraint versus treatment: Seclusion as discussed in the Boston State Hospital case. *American Journal of Psychiatry* 173:718–19.

Gutheil, Thomas G., and Paul S. Appelbaum. 1980. Substituted judgment and the physician's ethical dilemma: With special reference to the problem of the psychiatric-patient. *Journal of Clinical Psychiatry* 41:303–5.

———. 1983. Substituted judgment: Best interests in disguise. *Hastings Center Report* 13:8.

———. 1984. "Mind control," "synthetic sanity," "artificial competence," and genuine confusion: Legally relevant effects of antipsychotic medication. *Hofstra Law Review* 12:77–120.

———. 1985. The substituted judgment approach: Its difficulties and paradoxes in mental health settings. *Law, Medicine, and Health Care* 13:61–64.

Gutterman, Jennifer. 2000. Waging a war on drugs: Administering a lethal dose to
    Kendra's Law. *Fordham Law Review* 68:2401–44.
Hackleman, Tricia Jonas. 1996. Violation of an individual's right to die: The need for a
    wrongful living cause of action. *University of Cincinnati Law Review* 64:1355–81.
Hafner, R. J., J. Lammersma, R. Ferris, and M. Cameron. 1989. The use of seclusion:
    A comparison of two psychiatric intensive care units. *Australian and New Zealand
    Journal of Psychiatry* 23:235–39.
Hall, Dee J. 1999. "The emotions . . . take control"; TV show focuses on Wisconsin teens'
    self-mutilation. *Wisconsin State Journal,* 9 February.
Hall, Olivia. 2000. Mental illness, treatment, and medical ethics. B.A. thesis, University
    of Brighton.
Hanson, Laura C., Marion Danis, and Nora L. Keenan. 1994. Impact of patient
    incompetence on decisions to use or withhold life-sustaining treatment. *American
    Journal of Medicine* 97:235–41.
Harmon, Louise. 1990. Falling off the vine: Legal fictions and the doctrine of substituted
    judgment. *Yale Law Journal* 100:1–71.
Harris, Grant T., and Marnie E. Rice. 1997. Risk appraisal and management of violent
    behavior. *Psychiatric Services* 49:1168–76.
Hart, H. L. A. 1963. *Law, liberty, and morality.* New York: Vintage.
Harvard Law Review Editors. 1974. Developments in the law: Civil commitment of the
    mentally ill. *Harvard Law Review* 87:1190–1406.
———. 1990. Medical technology and the law. *Harvard Law Review* 103:1519–1676.
Hasebe, Tad, and John McRae. 1987. A ten-year study of civil commitments in
    Washington state. *Hospital and Community Psychiatry* 38:983–87.
Haskar, William. 1977. The critique of "mental illness": Conceptual and/or ethical crisis?
    Journal of Psychology and Theology 5:110–24.
Hawkins, Susan D. 1996. Protecting the rights and interests of competent minors in
    litigated medical treatment disputes. *Fordham Law Review* 64:2075–2132.
Haworth, Lawrence. 1986. *Autonomy: An essay in philosophical psychology and ethics.*
    New Haven, Conn.: Yale University Press.
Heilbrun, Kirk, Glenn G. Galloway, Victor E. Shoukry, and David Gustafson. 1995.
    Physical control of patients on an inpatient setting: Forensic vs. civil populations.
    Psychiatric Quarterly 66:133–45.
Hermann, Donald H. 1986. Barriers to providing effective treatment: A critique of
    revisions in procedural, substantive, and dispositional criteria in involuntary civil
    commitment. *Vanderbilt Law Review* 39:83–106.
———. 1990. Autonomy, self determination, the right of involuntarily committed
    persons to refuse treatment, and the use of substituted judgment in medication
    decisions involving incompetent persons. *International Journal of Law and Psychiatry*
    13:361–85.
Hewitt, Mary L. 1990. The revolving door of mentally ill inmates who refuse
    antipsychotic medications. *Creighton Law Review* 24:341–70.
Hickman, Franklin J., Phillip J. Resnick, and Kathryn B. Olson. 1982. Right to refuse
    psychotropic medication: An interdisciplinary proposal. *Mental and Physical Disability
    Law Reporter* 6:122–30.

Hiday, Virginia Aldigé. 1990. Dangerousness of civil commitment candidates: A six-month follow-up. *Law and Human Behavior* 14:551–67.

———. 1991. Arrest and incarceration of civil commitment candidates. *Hospital and Community Psychiatry* 42:729–34.

———. 1992a. Civil commitment and arrests: An investigation of the criminalization thesis. *Journal of Nervous and Mental Disease* 180:184–91.

———. 1992b. Coercion in civil commitment: Process, preferences, and outcome. *International Journal of Law and Psychiatry* 15:359–77.

Hiday, Virginia Aldigé, and Rodney R. Goodman. 1982. The least restrictive alternative to involuntary hospitalization, outpatient commitment: Its use and effectiveness. *Journal of Psychiatry and Law* 10 (spring): 81–96.

Hiday, Virginia Aldigé, and Teresa L. Scheid-Cook. 1987. The North Carolina experience with outpatient commitment: A critical appraisal. *International Journal of Law and Psychiatry* 10:215–32.

Hiday, Virginia Aldigé, and Lynn N. Smith. 1987. Effects of the dangerousness standard in civil commitment. *Journal of Psychiatry and Law* 15 (fall): 433–54.

Hipshman, Lawrence. 1987. Defining a clinically useful model for assessing competence to consent to treatment. *Bulletin of the American Academy of Psychiatry and the Law* 15:235–45.

Ho, V. 1995. Marginal capacity: The dilemmas faced in assessment and declaration. *Canadian Medical Association Journal* 152:259–63.

Hobbs, Angela. 1998. Commentary on "Aristotle's function argument and the concept of mental illness." *Journal of Philosophy, Psychiatry, and Psychology* 5:209–13.

Hoffman, Brian F. 1980. Assessing competence to consent to treatment. *Canadian Journal of Psychiatry* 25:354–55.

———. 1988. Competency to consent to psychiatric treatment. *Health Law in Canada* 8:100.

Hoffman, Brian F., and J. Srinivasan. 1992. A study of competence to consent to treatment in a psychiatric hospital. *Canadian Journal of Psychiatry* 37:179–82.

Hogan, Carla. 1987. The involuntarily committed patient's qualified right to refuse psychotropics in New York. *Albany Law Review* 51:333–68.

Hoge, Michael A., and Elizabeth Grottole. 2000. The case against outpatient commitment. *Journal of the American Academy of Psychiatry and the Law* 28:165–70.

Hoge, Steven K., Paul S. Appelbaum, and Alexander Greer. 1989. An empirical comparison of the Stone and dangerousness criteria for civil commitment. *American Journal of Psychiatry* 146:170–75.

Hoge, Steven K., Thomas G. Gutheil, and Eric Kaplan. 1987. The right to refuse treatment under *Rogers v. Commissioner:* Preliminary empirical findings and comparisons. *Bulletin of the American Academy of Psychiatry and the Law* 15:163–69.

Hoge, Steven K., Gary Sachs, Paul S. Appelbaum, Alexander Greer, and Christopher Gordon. 1988. Limitations on psychiatrist's discretionary civil commitment authority by the Stone and dangerousness criteria. *Archives of General Psychiatry* 45:764–69.

Holstein, James A. 1987. Mental illness assumptions in civil commitment proceedings. *Journal of Contemporary Ethnography* 16:147–75.

Hopton, John. 1995. Control and restraint in contemporary psychiatric nursing: Some ethical considerations. *Journal of Advanced Nursing* 22:110–15.

Howse, Robert 1988. Civil commitment as preventive detention: The constitutionality of the Ontario Mental Health Act. *University of Toronto Faculty of Law Review* 47:173–90.

Hughes, John S. 1986. Isaac Ray's "Project of a Law" and the 19th century debate over involuntary commitment. *International Journal of Law and Psychiatry* 9:191–200.

Hummer, Martina, and W. Wolfgang Fleischhacker. 1996. Compliance and outcome in patients treated with antipsychotics: The impact of extrapyramidal syndromes. *CNS Drugs* 5:13–20.

Husted, June R., and June R. Nehemkis. 1995. Civil commitment viewed from three perspectives: Professional, family, and police. *Bulletin of the American Academy of Psychiatry and the Law* 23:533–46.

Irwin, Martin. 1987. Are seclusion rooms needed on child psychiatric units? *American Journal of Orthopsychiatry* 57:125–26.

Jacobs, Douglas G., ed. 1999. *The Harvard Medical School guide to suicide assessment and investigation*. San Francisco: Jossey-Bass.

Jamison, Kay R. 1995. *An unquiet mind: A memoir of moods and madness*. New York: Random House.

Janicak, Philip G. 1997. *Principles and practice of psychopharmacotherapy*. Baltimore: William and Wilkins.

Janofsky, Jeffrey S., Richard J. McCarthy, and Marshal F. Folstein. 1992. The Hopkins Competency Assessment Test: A brief method for evaluating patients' capacity to give informed consent. *Hospital and Community Psychiatry* 43:132–36.

Jaychuk, G., R. Manchanda, and D. A. Galbraith. 1991. Consent to treatment: Loophole in the Ontario Mental Health Act. *Canadian Journal of Psychiatry* 36:594–96.

Jayes, Robert L., Jack E. Zimmerman, Douglas P. Wagner, Elizabeth A. Draper, and William A. Knaus. 1993. Do-not-resuscitate orders in intensive care units. *Journal of the American Medical Association* 270:2213–17.

Jeste, Dilip V., and Michael P. Caligiuri. 1993. Tardive dyskinesia. *Schizophrenia Bulletin* 19:303–15.

Joint Commission on Accreditation of Health Care Organizations. 1998. *Written and proposed revisions to the Joint Commission restraint standards applicable to non-psychiatric patients*. [Web site no longer available.]

Jones, Michael A., and Kirsty Keywood. 1996. Assessing the patient's competence to consent to medical treatment. *Medical Law International* 2:107–47.

Kahneman, Daniel. 1994. New challenges to the rationality assumption. *Journal of Institutional and Theoretical Economics* 150:18–36.

Kalman, Thomas P., 1983. An overview of patient satisfaction with psychiatric treatment. *Hospital and Community Psychiatry* 34:48–54.

Kaminsky, Irene. 1998. An assessment of young men previously in residential treatment: Is the past prologue? *Residential Treatment for Children and Youth* 16:67–82.

Kaplan, Harold R., and Benjamin J. Sadock. 1998. *Kaplan and Sadock's synopsis of psychiatry*. Philadelphia: Williams and Wilkins.

Kaplan, Kenneth H., and Marilyn Price. 1989. The clinician's role in competency evaluations. *General Hospital Psychiatry* 11:397–403.

Kapp, Marshall B. 1998. The "voluntary" status of nursing facility admissions: Legal, practical and public policy implications. *New England Journal on Criminal and Civil Confinement* 24:1–35.

Kapp, Marshall B., and Douglas Mossman. 1996. Measuring decisional capacity: Cautions on the construction of a "capacimeter." *Psychology, Public Policy, and Law* 2:73–95.

Kasper, John A., Steven K. Hoge, Thomas Feucht-Haviar, Jorge Cortina, and Bruce Cohen. 1997. Prospective study of patients' refusal of antipsychotic medication under a physician discretion review procedure. *American Journal of Psychiatry* 154:483–89.

Katz, Jay. 1984. *The silent world of doctor and patient.* New York: Free Press.

Katz, Mark, Susan Abbey, Anne Rydall, and Frederick Lowy. 1995. Psychiatric consultation for competency to refuse medical treatment: A retrospective study of patient characteristics and outcome. *Psychosomatics* 36:33–41.

Kaufman, Mark S. 1988. "Crazy" until proven innocent? Civil commitment of the mentally ill homeless. *Columbia Human Rights Law Review* 19:333–67.

Kaufmann, Caroline L., Loren H. Roth, Charles W. Lidz, and Alan Meisel. 1981. Informed consent and patient decisionmaking: The reasoning of law and psychiatry. *International Journal of Law and Psychiatry* 4:345–61.

Kazin, Cathrael, 1989. "Nowhere to go and chose to stay": Using the tort of false imprisonment to redress involuntary confinement of the elderly in nursing homes and hospitals. *University of Pennsylvania Law Review* 137:903–27.

Kehrberg, Corinne. 1997. Self-mutilating behavior. *Journal of Child and Adolescent Psychiatric Nursing* 3:10–35.

Keilitz, Ingo. 1988. An introduction to the National Center for State Courts' Guidelines for Involuntary Civil Commitment: A workable framework for justice and practice. *Hospital and Community Psychiatry* 39:398–402.

———. 1990. Empirical studies of involuntary outpatient civil commitment: Is it working? *Mental and Physical Disability Law Reporter* 14:368–79.

Keilitz, Ingo, and Terry Hall. 1985. State statutes governing involuntary outpatient civil commitment. *Mental and Physical Disability Law Reporter* 9:378–97.

Kelly, Jeffrey A. 1997. HIV risk reduction interventions for persons with severe mental illness. *Clinical Psychology Review* 17:293–309.

Kelly, K. V. 1987. Competency and treatment refusal. *Psychosomatics* 28:494.

Kemp, Roisin, Peter Hayward, Grantley Applewhaite, Brian Everitt, and Anthony David. 1996. Compliance therapy in psychotic patients: Randomised controlled trial. *British Medical Journal* 312:345–47.

Kennedy, Duncan. 1982. Distributive and paternalist motives in contract and tort law, with special reference to compulsory terms and unequal bargaining power. *Maryland Law Review* 41:563–658.

King, Patricia. 1991–92. Rights within the therapeutic relationship. *Journal of Law and Health* 6:31–60.

Kirk, Trudi, and Donald N. Bersoff. 1996. How many procedural safeguards does it take to get a psychiatrist to leave the lightbulb unchanged? A due process analysis of the MacArthur Treatment Competence Study. *Psychology, Public Policy, and Law* 2:45–72.

Kline, Stephen A. 1988. Mental competence, treatment and substitute consent: A psychiatrist's perspective. *Health Law in Canada* 8:92–93.

Klinge, Valerie. 1994. Staff opinions about seclusion and restraint at a state forensic hospital. *Hospital and Community Psychiatry* 45:138–41.

Kloezen, Sandra, L. Jaime Fitten, and Alan Steinberg. 1988. Assessment of treatment decision-making capacity in a medically ill patient. *Journal of the American Geriatrics Society* 36:1055–58.

Knapp, Samuel, and Leon VandeCreek. 1987. A review of tort liability in involuntary civil commitment. *Hospital and Community Psychiatry* 38:648–51.

Knapp, William C., and Fred Hamilton. 1992. "Wrongful living": Resuscitation as tortious interference with a patient's right to give informed refusal. *Northern Kentucky Law Review* 19:253–76.

Knepper, Kathleen. 1996. The importance of establishing competence in cases involving the involuntary administration of psychotropic medications. *Law and Psychology Review* 20:97–137.

Korr, Wynne S. 1988. Outpatient commitment: Additional concerns. *American Psychologist* 43:748–49.

Kress, Ken. 2000. An argument for assisted outpatient treatment for persons with serious mental illness illustrated with reference to a proposed statute for Iowa. *Iowa Law Review* 85:1269–1386.

Kubie, Lawrence S. 1974. The myths of Thomas Szasz. *Bulletin of the Menninger Clinic* 38:497–500.

Kuipers, Elizabeth. 1996. The management of difficult to treat patients with schizophrenia, using non-drug therapies. *British Journal of Psychiatry* 169:41–51.

LaFave, Wayne R., and Austin W. Scott Jr. 1986. *Criminal law,* 2d ed. St. Paul, Minn.: West Group.

La Fond, John Q., and Mary L. Durham. 1994. Cognitive dissonance: Have insanity defense and civil commitment reforms made a difference? *Villanova Law Review* 39:71–122.

Lamb, H. Richard. 1989. Involuntary treatment for the homeless mentally ill. *Notre Dame Journal of Law, Ethics and Public Policy* 4:269–80.

Lamb, H. Richard, Leona L. Bachrach, and Frederick I. Kass. 1992. *Treating the homeless mentally ill: A task force report.* Washington, D.C.: American Psychiatric Association.

Lamb, H. Richard, and Doris M. Lamb. 1990a. Factors contributing to homelessness among the chronically and severely mentally ill. *Hospital and Community Psychiatry* 41:301–5.

———. 1990b. Will we save the homeless mentally ill? *American Journal of Psychiatry* 147:649–51.

———. 1992. Perspectives on effective advocacy for homeless mentally ill persons. *Hospital and Community Psychiatry* 43:1209–12.

Lamm, Michael. 1992. The Hopkins Competency Assessment Test: A brief method for evaluating patients' capacity to give informed consent: Comment. *Hospital and Community Psychiatry* 43:647–48.

Laor, Nathaniel. 1982. Szasz, Feuchtersleben, and the history of psychiatry. *Psychiatry* 45:316–24.

Lavin, Michael. 1992. "The Hopkins Competency Assessment Test: A brief method for evaluating patients' capacity to give informed consent": Comment. *Journal of Hospital and Community Psychiatry* 43:646–47.

Lebit, Lynn E. 1992–93. Compelled medical procedures involving minors and incompetents and misapplication of the substituted judgments doctrine. *Journal of Law and Health* 7:107–30.

Lecompte, D. 1995. The paradoxical increase in involuntary admissions after the revision of the civil commitment law in Belgium. *Medicine and the Law* 14:53–57.

Ledwith, Delila M. J. 1990. *Jones v. Gerhard-Stein:* The involuntarily committed mental patient's right to refuse treatment with psychotropic drugs. *Wisconsin Law Review,* 1367–98.

Lee, Susan. 1994. *Heller v. Doe:* Involuntary civil commitment and the "objective" language of probability. *American Journal of Law and Medicine* 20:457–77.

Lefkovitch, Y., M. Weiser, and A. Levy. 1993. Involuntary outpatient commitment: Ethics and problems. *Medicine and Law* 12:213–20.

Lehman, Anthony F., William T. Carpenter Jr., Howard H. Goldman, and Donald M. Steinwachs. 1995. Treatment outcomes in schizophrenia: Implications for practice, policy, and research. *Schizophrenia Bulletin* 21:669–75.

Lehman, Anthony F., and Donald M. Steinwachs. 1998a. At issue: Translating research into practice: The Schizophrenia Patient Outcomes Research Team (PORT) treatment recommendations. *Schizophrenia Bulletin* 24:1–10.

———. 1998b. Pattern of usual care for schizophrenia: Initial results from the Schizophrenia Patient Outcomes Research Team (PORT) client survey. *Schizophrenia Bulletin* 24:11–20.

Leiber, Michael J., and Sean Anderson. 1993. A comparison of pre-reform and post-reform civil commitment decisionmaking in Dane County, Wisconsin. *Criminal and Civil Confinement* 20:1–25.

Leong, Gregory B. 1987. Letter to the editor: Outpatient civil commitment. *American Journal of Psychiatry* 144:694–95.

Leong, Gregory B., and J. Arturo Silva. 1989. Civil commitment. *Hospital and Community Psychiatry* 40:192.

Lever, Judith, A., David W. Molloy, D. Joan Eagle, Gail Butt, Michel Bedard, Pat Millar, and Tricia Stiles. 1994. Use of physical restraints and their relationship to medication use in patients in four different institutional settings. *Humane Medicine Journal* 10:17–27.

Levit, Nancy. 1992. Ethereal torts. *George Washington Law Review* 61:136–92.

Liberman, Ellen. 1985. Mental competency and medical treatment in Ontario. *Health Law in Canada* 6:32.

Lidz, Charles W., Edward P. Mulvey, and William Gardner. 1993. The accuracy of predictions of violence to others. *Journal of the American Medical Association* 269:1007–11.

Link, Bruce G., Francis T. Cullen, James Frank, and John F. Wozniak. 1987. The social rejection of former mental patients: Understanding why labels matter. *American Journal of Sociology* 92:1461–1500.

Lippert, Gerard. P., and Donna. E. Stewart. 1988. The psychiatrist's role in determining competency to consent in the general hospital. *Canadian Journal of Psychiatry* 33:250–53.

Litman, Jessica. 1982. A common law remedy for forcible medication of the institutionalized mentally ill. *Columbia Law Review* 82:1720–51.

Litwack, Thomas R. 1994. Assessments of dangerousness: Legal, research, and clinical developments. *Administration and Policy in Mental Health* 21:361–77.

Ludwig, The Honorable Edmund V. 1991. The mentally ill homeless: Evolving involuntary commitment issues. *Villanova Law Review* 36:1085–1111.

Mackay, R. D. 1995. *Mental condition defenses in the criminal law: Diminished responsibility and infanticide.* Oxford: Clarendon.

———. 1999. The abnormality of mind factor in diminished responsibility. *Criminal Law Review* (February): 117–25.

Macklin, Audrey. 1982. Some problems in gaining informed consent from psychiatric patients. *Emory Law Journal* 31:345–74.

———. 1987. Bound to freedom: The Ulysses contract and the psychiatric will. *University of Toronto Faculty Law Review* 45:37–68.

Macklin, Ruth. 1983. Treatment refusals: Autonomy, paternalism, and the "best interests" of the patient. In *Ethical questions in brain and behavior,* edited by D. Pfaff. New York: Springer.

Mahler, Howard, Bun Tee Co Jr., and Stephen Dinwiddie. 1986. Studies in involuntary civil commitment and involuntary electroconvulsive therapy. *Journal of Nervous and Mental Disease* 174:97–106.

Mahler, John, and Samuel W. Perry. 1988. Assessing competency in the physically ill: Guidelines for psychiatric consultants. *Hospital and Community Psychiatry* 39:856–61.

Mahler, John, Samuel Perry, and Frank Miller. 1990. Psychiatric evaluation of competency in physically ill patients who refuse treatment. *Hospital and Community Psychiatry* 41:1140–41.

Malloy, S. Elizabeth Wilborn. 1998. Beyond misguided paternalism: Resuscitating the right to refuse medical treatment. *Wake Forest Law Review* 33:1035–91.

Malyon, David. 1998. Transfusion-free treatment of Jehovah's Witnesses: Respecting the autonomous patient's motives. *Journal of Medical Ethics* 24 (6): 376–81.

Mann, Lee S., Thomas N. Wise, and Laurel Shay. 1993. A prospective study of psychiatry patients' attitudes toward the seclusion room experience. *General Hospital Psychiatry* 15:177–82.

Mann, Traci. 1994. Informed consent for psychological research: Do subjects comprehend consent forms and understand their legal rights? *Psychological Science* 5:140–43.

Markowitz, Fred E. 1998. The effects of stigma on the psychological well-being and life satisfaction of persons with mental illness. *Journal of Health and Social Behavior* 39:335–47.

Marshall, [?]. 1987. Right to refuse psychiatric treatments. *Mental and Physical Disability Law Reporter* 11:24–26.

Marson, Daniel C., Anjan Chatterjee, Kellie K. Ingram, and Lindy E. Harrell. 1996. Toward a neurologic model of competence: Cognitive predictors of capacity to consent in Alzheimer's disease using 3 different legal standards. *Neurology* 46:666–72.

Marson, Daniel C., Maureen P. Dymek, Linda W. Duke, and Lindy E. Harrell. 1997. Subscale validity of the Mattis Dementia Rating Scale. *Archives of Clinical Neuropsychology* 12:269–75.

Marson, Daniel C., Lauren Hawkins, Bronwyn McInturff, and Lindy E. Harrell. 1997.

Cognitive models that predict physician judgments of capacity to consent in mild Alzheimer's disease. *Journal of the American Geriatrics Society* 45:458–64.

Marson, Daniel C., Kellie K. Ingram, Heather A. Cody, and Lindy E. Harrell. 1995a. Assessing the competence of patients with Alzheimer's disease under different legal standards: A prototype instrument. *Archives of Neurology* 52:949–54.

———. 1995b. Neuropsychologic predictors of competence in Alzheimer's disease using a rational reasons legal standard. *Archives of Neurology* 52:955–59.

Marson, Daniel C., Frederick A. Schmitt, Kellie K. Ingram, and Lindy E. Harrell. 1994. Determining the competence of Alzheimer patients to consent to treatment and research. *Alzheimer Disease and Associated Disorders* 8:5–18.

Marta, Jan. 1993. The PSDA and geriatric psychiatry: A cautionary tale. *Journal of Clinical Ethics* 4:80–81.

Martyn, Susan R. 1994. Substituted judgment, best interests, and the need for best respect. *Cambridge Quarterly of Healthcare Ethics* 3:195–208.

Marzen, Thomas J., and Daniel Avila. 1995. Will the real Michael Martin speak up! Medical decisionmaking for questionably competent persons. *University of Detroit Mercy Law Review* 72:833–71.

Mason, Tom. 1993. Seclusion theory reviewed—a benevolent or malevolent intervention? *Medicine, Science, and the Law* 2:95–102.

Matthews, Martha A. 1987. Suicidal competence and the patient's right to refuse lifesaving treatment. *California Law Review* 75:707–58.

Mattson, Margaret E., and Frances K. Del Boca. 1998. Compliance with treatment and follow-up protocols in project MATCH: Predictors and relationship to outcome. *Alcoholism: Clinical and Experimental Research* 22:1328–39.

McCafferty, Gerry, and Jeanne Dooley. 1990. Involuntary outpatient commitment: An update. *Mental and Physical Disability Law Reporter* 14:277–87.

McCartney, James R. 1979. Refusal of treatment: Suicide or competent choice. *General Hospital Psychiatry* 1:338–43.

McCrary, S. Van, and A. Terry Walman. 1990. Procedural paternalism in competency determination. *Law, Medicine and Health Care* 18:108–13.

McElroy, Evelyn M. 1985. Consumers of psychiatric services and staff: Worlds apart on the issue of seclusion. *Journal of Nervous and Mental Disease* 173:287.

McFarland, Bentson H., Larry R. Faulkner, Joseph D. Bloom, Roxy J. Hallaux, and J. Donald Bray. 1989. Investigators' and judges' opinions about civil commitment. *Bulletin of the American Academy of Psychiatry and the Law* 17:15–24.

———. 1990. Family members' opinions about civil commitment. *Hospital and Community Psychiatry* 41:537–40.

McNiel, Dale E., and Renée L. Binder. 1986. Violence, civil commitment, and hospitalization. *Journal of Nervous and Mental Disease* 174:107–11.

———. 1987. Predictive validity of judgments of dangerousness in emergency civil commitment. *American Journal of Psychiatry* 144:197–200.

McNiel, Dale E., Renée L. Binder, and Thomas K. Greenfield. 1988. Predictors of violence in civilly committed acute psychiatric patients. *American Journal of Psychiatry* 145:965–70.

Measham, Toby J. 1995. The acute management of aggressive behavior in hospitalized children and adolescents. *Canadian Journal of Psychiatry* 40:330–36.

Megone, Christopher. 1998. Aristotle's function argument and the concept of mental illness. *Philosophy, Psychiatry, and Psychology* 5:187.

Menninger, Karl, II. 1998. The right to refuse mental health treatment. *Journal of Legal Medicine* 19:455–61.

Mental and Physical Disability Law Reporter. 1986. Case law developments: Civil commitment. Vol. 10, various issues.

Milani, Adam A. 1997. Better off dead than disabled? Should courts recognize a "wrongful living" cause of action when doctors fail to honor patients' advance directives? *Washington and Lee Law Review* 54:149–228.

Miller, Carl H., Iwan Simioni, Harald Oberbauer, Josef Schwitzer, et al. 1995. Tardive dyskinesia prevalence rates during a ten-year follow-up. *Journal of Nervous and Mental Disease* 183:404–7.

Miller, Nancy Houston. 1997. Compliance with treatment regimens in chronic asymptomatic diseases. *American Journal of Medicine* 102:43–49.

Miller, Robert D. 1985. Involuntary civil commitment: Legal versus clinical paternalism. *New Directions for Mental Health Services* 25:13–24.

———. 1988. Outpatient civil commitment of the mentally ill: An overview and an update. *Behavioral Sciences and the Law* 6:99–118.

———. 1992a. An update on involuntary civil commitment to outpatient treatment. *Hospital and Community Psychiatry* 43:79–81.

———. 1992b. Need-for-treatment criteria for involuntary civil commitment: Impact in practice. *American Journal of Psychiatry* 149:1380–84.

Miller, Robert D., Michael R. Bernstein, Gregory J. Van Rybroek, and Gary J. Maier. 1989. The impact of the right to refuse treatment in a forensic patient population: Six-month review. *Bulletin of the American Academy of Psychiatry and the Law* 17:107–19.

Miller, Robert D., and Paul B. Fiddleman. 1984. Outpatient commitment: Treatment in the least restrictive environment? *Hospital and Community Psychiatry* 35:147–51.

Mills, Mark J. 1988. Civil commitment: The relationship between perceived dangerousness and mental illness. *Archives of General Psychiatry* 45:770–72.

Mion, Lorraine C., Ann Minnick, and Robert Palmer. 1996. Physical restraint use in the hospital setting: Unresolved issues and directions for research. *Milbank Quarterly* 74:411–33.

Mitchell, Jeff, and Christopher Varley. 1990. Isolation and restraint in juvenile correctional facilities. *Journal of the American Academy of Child and Adolescent Psychiatry* 29:251–55.

Monahan, John. 1981. *Predicting violent behavior: An assessment of clinical techniques.* Beverly Hills, Calif.: Sage.

———. 2002. The scientific status of research on clinical and actuarial predictions of violence. In *Modern scientific evidence: The law and science of expert testimony* (2d ed.), edited by D. Faigman, D. Kaye, M. Saks, and J. Sanders, 1:423–45. St. Paul, Minn.: West Publishing.

Monahan, John, Paul S. Appelbaum, Edward P. Mulvey, Pamela Clark Robbins, and Charles W. Lidz. 1993. Ethical and legal duties in conducting research on violence: Lessons from the MacArthur Risk Assessment Study. *Violence and Victims* 8:387–96.

Monahan, John, Steven K. Hoge, Charles Lidz, Loren H. Roth, Nancy Bennett, William Gardner, and Ed Mulvey. 1995. Coercion and commitment: Understanding involuntary mental hospital admission. *International Journal of Law and Psychiatry* 18:249–63.

Monahan, John, and Henry J. Steadman. 1994. *Violence and mental disorder: Developments in risk assessment.* Chicago: University of Chicago Press.

Moore, Michael S. 1975. Some myths about "mental illness." *Archives of General Psychiatry* 32:1483–97.

———. 1984. *Law and psychiatry: Rethinking the relationship.* New York: Cambridge University Press.

Moorhouse, Anne, and David N. Weisstub. 1996. Advance directives for research: Ethical problems and responses. *International Journal of Law and Psychiatry* 19:107–41.

Morgan, Sam B., William Fulliton, and Laura Nabors. 1993. Adolescents' perceptions of acceptability of inpatient treatments: Does exposure to the treatment make a difference? *Residential Treatment for Children and Youth* 10:85–99.

Morissette, L. 1992. Preventive detention of the mentally ill [letter]. *Canadian Journal of Psychiatry* 37:223–24.

Morris, C. Donald, John H. Niederbuhl, and Jeffrey A. Mahr. 1993. Determining the capability of individuals with mental retardation to give informed consent. *American Journal on Mental Retardation* 98:263–72.

Morris, Grant H. 1988. Civil commitment decisionmaking: A report on one decisionmaker's experience. *Southern California Law Review* 61:291–351.

———. 1995. Judging judgment: Assessing the competence of mental patients to refuse treatment. *San Diego Law Review* 32:343–435.

Morrison, Denis. 1987. Criteria used by physicians to assess competency to consent to treatment. *Health Law in Canada* 8:9.

Morrison, Paul. 1990a. A multidimensional scalogram analysis of the use of seclusion in acute psychiatric settings. *Journal of Advanced Nursing* 15:59–66.

———. 1990b. The use of environmental seclusion in psychiatric settings: A multidimensional scalogram analysis. *Journal of Environmental Psychology* 10:353–62.

Morrison, Paul, and Michael Lehane. 1995. Staffing levels and seclusion use. *Journal of Advanced Nursing* 22:1193–1202.

———. 1996. A study of the official records of seclusion. *International Journal of Nursing Studies* 33:223–35.

Morse, Stephen. 1982. A preference for liberty: The case against involuntary commitment of the mentally disordered. *California Law Review* 70:54–106.

Moss, Gene R. 1968. Szasz: Review and criticism. *Psychiatry* 31:184–94.

Moss, Robert J., and John La Puma. 1991. The ethics of mechanical restraints. *Hastings Center Report* 21:22–25.

Mossman, Douglas, and Kathleen J. Hart. 1993. How bad is civil commitment? A study of attitudes toward violence and involuntary hospitalization. *Bulletin of the American Academy of Psychiatry and the Law* 21:181–94.

Mueser, Kim T., and Nicholas Tarrier. 1998. *Handbook of social functioning in schizophrenia.* Boston: Allyn and Bacon.

Muir-Cochrane, Eimear. 1996. An investigation into nurses' perceptions of secluding patients on closed psychiatric wards. *Journal of Advanced Nursing* 23:555–63.

Mulvey, Edward P., Jeffery L. Geller, and Loren H. Roth. 1987. The promise and peril of involuntary outpatient commitment. *American Psychologist* 42:571–84.

Munetz, Mark R., Jeffery L. Geller, and Frederick J. Frese. 2000. Commentary: Capacity-based involuntary outpatient treatment. *Journal of the American Academy of Psychiatry and the Law* 28:145–48.

Munetz, Mark R., Thomas Grande, Jeffrey Kleist, Gregory A. Peterson. 1996. The effectiveness of outpatient civil commitment. *Psychiatric Services* 47:1251–53.

Munich, Richard L. 1997. Contemporary treatment of schizophrenia. *Bulletin of the Menninger Clinic* 61:189–221.

Muramoto, Osamu. 1998a. Bioethics of the refusal of blood by Jehovah's Witnesses: Part 1: A novel. *Journal of Medical Ethics* 24:223–30.

———. 1998b. Bioethics of the refusal of blood by Jehovah's Witnesses: Part 2: A novel. *Journal of Medical Ethics* 24:295–301.

Myers, Beverle, and Curtis L. Barrett. 1986. Competency issues in referrals to a consultation-liaison service. *Psychosomatics* 27:782–89.

———. 1987. Competency and treatment refusal: Reply. *Psychosomatics* 28:494.

Nagler, Mark, ed. 1990. *Perspectives on disability*. Palo Alto, Calif.: Health Markets Research.

Navarro, Mireya. 1993. Confining tuberculosis patients: Weighing rights vs. health risks. *New York Times*, 21 November.

New York State Commission on Quality of Care for the Mentally Disabled. 1994 and 1995. *Restraint and seclusion practices in New York state psychiatric facilities, and voices from the frontline: Patients' perspectives of restraint and seclusion use, NYS Law, Regulation, and Policy.* Albany: New York State Commission on Quality of Care for the Mentally Disabled.

New York State Office of Mental Health, Task Force on Restraint and Seclusion. 1993. *Report of the Task Force on Restraint and Seclusion.* Albany: New York State Office of Mental Health.

Nicholson, Robert A. 1988. Characteristics associated with change in the legal status of involuntary psychiatric patients. *Hospital and Community Psychiatry* 39:424–29.

Nicholson, Robert A., Carolyn Ekenstam, and Steve Norwood. 1996. Coercion and the outcome of psychiatric hospitalization. *International Journal of Law and Psychiatry* 19:201–17.

Nicholson, Robert A., and Joseph M. Horn. 1986. A discriminant analysis of committed and voluntary psychiatric patients. *Journal of Psychiatry and Law* 14:159–76.

Oddi, Samuel. 1986. The tort of interference with the right to die: The wrongful living cause of action. *Georgetown Law Journal* 75:625–65.

Orentlicher, David. 1992. The illusion of patient choice in end-of-life decisions. *Journal of the American Medical Association* 267:2101–4.

———. 1994. The limitations of legislation. *Maryland Law Review* 53:1255–1305.

Outlaw, Freida Hopkins, and Barbara J. Lowery. 1994. An attributional study of seclusion and restraint of psychiatric patients. *Archives of Psychiatric Nursing* 8:69–77.

Oxley, Genevieve B. 1977. Involuntary clients' responses to a treatment experience. *Social Casework* 58:607–14.

Panzano, Phyllis C., and William V. Rubin. 1995. Lost in the shuffle: The influence of patient classification scheme on views about the relationship between refusal of medication and involvement in important hospital-based outcomes. *Psychiatric Quarterly* 66:147–62.

Parker, Stephen, and John Dewar. 1992. Medical treatment for a mental disorder—consent—"Gillick competence"—child who is a ward of court. *Journal of Social Welfare and Family Law* 2:143–51.

Parry, John W., and James C. Beck. 1990. Revisiting the civil commitment/involuntary treatment stalemate using limited guardianship, substituted judgment and different due process considerations: A work in progress. *Mental and Physical Disability Law Reporter* 14:102–7.

Pavlo, Anne-Marie, Harold Bursztajn, and Thomas G. Gutheil. 1987. Christian Science and competence to make treatment choices: Clinical challenges in assessing values. *International Journal of Law and Psychiatry* 10:395–401.

Pearce, John. 1994. Consent to treatment during childhood: The assessment of competence and avoidance of conflict. *British Journal of Psychiatry* 165:713–16.

Peiris, G. L. 1987. The *Gillick* case: Parental authority, teenage independence and public policy. In *Current legal problems*, edited by Roger Rideout and Jeffrey Jowell, 93–122. London: Stevens and Sons.

Perlin, Michael L. 1993. Decoding right to refuse treatment law. *International Journal of Law and Psychiatry* 16:151–77.

Perlin, Michael L., and Deborah A. Dorfman. 1993. Sanism, social science, and the development of mental disability law jurisprudence. *Behavioral Sciences and the Law* 1:47–66.

———. 1996. Is it more than "dodging lions and wastin' time"? Adequacy of counsel, questions of competence, and the justice process in individual right to refuse treatment cases. *Psychology, Public Policy, and Law* 2:114–36.

Perling, Lester J. 1993. Health care advance directives: Implications for Florida mental health patients. *University of Miami Law Review* 48:193–228.

Perry, Clifton B. 1985. A problem with refusing certain forms of psychiatric treatment. *Social Science and Medicine* 20:645–48.

Perry, J. Christopher. 1992. Problems and considerations in the valid assessment of personality disorders. *American Journal of Psychiatry* 149:1645–53.

Peters, Philip G., Jr. 1998. The Illusion of autonomy at the end of life: Unconsented life support and the wrongful life analogy. *UCLA Law Review* 45:673–97.

Petrila, John. 1995. Who will pay for involuntary civil commitment under capitated managed care? An emerging dilemma. *Psychiatric Services* 46:1045–48.

Pfeffer, J. M. 1995. Physical restraints of patients in a psychiatric hospital. *Medicine, Science, and the Law* 4:361.

Phelan, Jo, Bruce G. Link, Robert E. Moore, and Ann Stueve. 1997. The stigma of homelessness: The impact of the label "homeless" on attitudes toward poor persons. *Social Psychology Quarterly* 60:323–37.

Pickard, David M. Egner, and Donald L. Patrick. 1991. A prospective study of advance directives for life-sustaining care. *New England Journal of Medicine* 324:882–88.

Pierce, Glenn L., Mary L. Durham, and William H. Fisher. 1985. The impact of broadened civil commitment standards on admissions to state mental hospital. *American Journal of Psychiatry* 142:104–7.

Pies, Ronald. 1979. On myths and countermyths. *Archives of General Psychiatry* 36:139–44.

———. 1998. *Handbook of essential psychopharmacology.* Washington, D.C.: American Psychiatric Press.

Piller, Ruth. 1993. Judge orders homeless man confined, treated for tuberculosis. *Houston Chronicle,* 23 June.

Pincus, William Hoffman. 1995. Civil commitment and the "Great Confinement" revisited: Straightjacketing individual rights, stifling culture. *William and Mary Law Review* 36:1771–1817.

Plotkin, Robert. 1977. Limiting the therapeutic orgy: Mental patients' right to refuse treatment. *Northwestern University Law Review* 72:461–525.

Policy Research Associates, Inc., for New York City Department of Mental Health, Mental Retardation and Alcoholism Services. 1998. *Final report: Research study of the New York City involuntary outpatient commitment pilot program.* Delmar, N.Y.: Policy Research Associates.

Pomerantz, Andrew S., and Alexander de Nesnera. 1991. Informed consent, competency, and the illusion of rationality. *General Hospital Psychiatry* 13:138–42.

Prehn, Robert A. 1990. Medication refusal: Suggestions for intervention. *Psychiatric Hospital* 21:37–40.

President's Commission for the Study of Ethical Problems in Medicine and Biomedical and Behavioral Research. 1982. *Making health care decisions.* Washington, D.C.: President's Commission for the Study of Ethical Problems in Medicine and Biomedical and Behavioral Research.

Price, David P. T. 1994. Civil commitment of the mentally ill: Compelling arguments for reform. *Medical Law Review* 2:321–52.

Prozac (Fluoxetine Hydrochloride) tablet to be available June 1; scored tablet to provide physicians, patients with more convenient dosing. 1999. PR Newswire Association, Inc., www.prnewswire.com, 18 May.

Rabinowitz, Jonathan, Michael Slyuzberg, Itamar Salamon, Sharron Dupier, Robert S. Kennedy, and Robert Steinmuller. 1996. Who comes to the psychiatric emergency room and how they are helped. *Administration and Policy in Mental Health* 23:425–37.

Rachlin, Stephen. 1987. Redefining dangerousness for civil commitment. *Hospital and Community Psychiatry* 38:884–86.

———. 1989. Rethinking the right to refuse treatment. *Psychiatric Annals* 19:213–22.

Radden, Jennifer. 1992. Planning for mental disorder: Buchanan and Brock on advance directives in psychiatry. *Social Theory and Practice* 18:165–86.

Rappeport, Jonas. 1986. Treating schizophrenia "legally." *Psychiatric Annals* 16:542–46.

Reda, Sawsan. 1996. Public perception of discharged psychiatric patients: A community survey. *International Journal of Social Psychiatry* 42:220–29.

Redding, Richard E. 1993. Children's competence to provide informed consent for mental health treatment. *Washington and Lee Law Review* 50:695–753.

Redelmeier, Donald A., Paul Rozin, and Daniel Kahneman. 1993. Understanding patients' decisions: Cognitive and emotional perspectives. *Journal of the American Medical Association* 270:72–76.

Reilly, Rebecca B., Thomas A. Teasdale, and Laurence B. McCullough. 1994. Projecting patients' preferences from living wills: An invalid strategy for management of dementia with life-threatening illness. *Journal of the American Geriatrics Society* 42:997–1003.

Reilly, Rosemary G. 1993. Combating the tuberculosis epidemic: The legality of coercive treatment measures. *Columbia Journal of Law and Social Problems* 27:101–27.

Reisner, Ralph, and Christopher Slobogin. 1990. *Law and the mental health system: Civil and criminal aspects.* 2d ed. St. Paul, Minn.: West Group.

Reisner, Ralph, Christopher Slobogin, and Arti Rai. 1999. *Law and the mental health system: Civil and criminal aspects.* 3d ed. St. Paul, Minn.: West Group.

Reiss, Steven. 1972. A critique of Thomas S. Szasz's myth of mental illness. *American Journal of Psychiatry* 128:1081–85.

Reznek, Lawrie. 1991. *The philosophical defense of psychiatry.* London: Routledge.

Richardson, Betty Kehl. 1987. Psychiatric inpatients: Perceptions of the seclusion-room experience. *Nursing Research* 36:234–38.

Robertson, Edward D. 1991. *Personal autonomy and substituted judgment: Legal issues in medical decisions for incompetent patients.* Corpus Christi, Tex.: Diocesan.

Rodenhauser, Paul, Charles E. Schwenkner, and H. J. Khamis. 1987. Factors related to drug treatment refusal in a forensic hospital. *Hospital and Community Psychiatry* 38:631–37.

Rodman, Hyman, and Saralyn B. Griffith. 1982. Adolescent autonomy and minors' legal rights: Contraception and abortion. *Journal of Applied Developmental Psychology* 3:307–18.

Roper, Janice M., Adam Coutts, Janet Sather, and Rosella Taylor. 1985. Restraint and seclusion. *Journal of Psychosocial Nursing and Mental Health Services* 23:18–23.

Rosenfeld, Barry D. 1992. Decisionmaking competence of the mentally ill: A longitudinal analysis of treatment decisionmaking. Ph.D. diss., University of Virginia.

Rosenhan, David L. 1973. On being sane in insane places. *Science* 179:250–58.

Rosenson, Marilyn K., and Agnes M. Kasten. 1991. Another view of autonomy: Arranging for consent in advance. *Schizophrenia Bulletin* 17:1–7.

Ross, Ruth E., Aileen B. Rothbard, and Arie Schinnar. 1996. A framework for classifying state involuntary commitment statues. *Administration and Policy in Mental Health* 23:341–56.

Roth, Loren H. 1985. *Clinical treatment of the violent person.* Rockville, Md.: National Institute of Mental Health.

———. 1986. The right to refuse psychiatric treatment: Law and medicine at the interface (The 1985 Jonas Robitscher Memorial Lecture in Law and Psychiatry). *Emory Law Journal* 1:139–61.

Roth, Loren H., Charles W. Lidz, Alan Meisel, Paul H. Soloff, Kenneth Kaufman, Duane G. Spiker, and F. Gordon Foster. 1982. Competency to decide about treatment or research: An overview of some empirical data. *International Journal of Law and Psychiatry* 5:29–50.

Roth, Loren H., Alan Maisel, and Charles W. Lidz. 1977. Tests of competency to consent to treatment. *American Journal of Psychiatry* 134:279–84.

Roth, Martin, and Robert Bluglass, eds. 1985. *Psychiatry, human rights and the law.* New York: Cambridge University Press.

Rubin, William V., Mary Beth Snapp, Phyllis C. Panzano, and Janie Taynor. 1996. Variation in civil commitment processes across jurisdictions: An approach for monitoring and managing change in mental health systems. *Journal of Mental Health Administration* 23:375–88.

Ruffalo, Richard L., Susan M. Garabedian-Ruffalo, and L. Gregory Pawlson. 1985. Patient compliance. *American Family Physician* 31:93–100.

Russell, Geraldine Koeneke, and Donald Wallace. 1989. Jehovah's witnesses and the refusal of blood transfusions: A balance of interests. *Catholic Lawyer* 4:361–81.

Sadoff, Robert L. 1975. Risks of state and private hospital psychiatrists in involuntary hospitalization in re: Right to treatment. *Bulletin of the American Academy of Psychiatry and the Law* 3:32–37.

Saks, Elyn R. 1986. The use of mechanical restraints in psychiatric hospitals. *Yale Law Journal* 95:1836–57.

———. 1991. Competency to refuse treatment. *North Carolina Law Review* 69:945–99.

———. 1993. Competency to refuse psychotropic medication: Three alternatives to the law's cognitive standard. *University of Miami Law Review* 47:689–761.

———. 1999. Competency to decide on treatment and research: The MacArthur Capacity Instruments. In *Research involving persons with mental disorders that may affect decisionmaking capacity*, edited by the National Bioethics Advisory Commission (Commissioned Papers, vol. 2). Rockville, Md.: National Bioethics Advisory Commission.

Saks, Elyn R., and Stephen H. Behnke. 1999. Competency to decide on treatment and research: MacArthur and beyond. *Journal of Contemporary Legal Issues* 10:103–29.

Saks, Elyn R., Laura B. Dunn, Barbara J. Marshall, Gauri V. Nayak, Shahrokh Golshan, and Dilip V. Jeste. 2002. The California scale of appreciation: A new instrument to measure the appreciation component of capacity to consent to research. *American Journal of Geriatric Psychiatry* 10:166–74.

Sales, Gary N. 1992. Assessing competency. *Hospital and Community Psychiatry* 43:646.

Sander, Fred M. 1969. Some thoughts on Thomas Szasz. *American Journal of Psychiatry* 125:1429–31.

Sateia, Michael J., David H. Gustafson, and Sandra W. Johnson. 1990. Quality assurance for psychiatric emergencies: An analysis of assessment and feedback methodologies. *Psychiatric Clinics of North America* 13:35–48.

Satel, Sally, and D. J. Jaffe. 1998. Violent fantasies. *National Review* 50:36–37.

Sauvayre, Pascal. 1991. The relationship between the court and the doctor on the issue of an inpatient's refusal of psychotropic medication. *Journal of Forensic Sciences* 36:219–25.

Schatzberg, Alan F., and Charles B. Nemeroff, eds. 1998. *Textbook of Psychopharmacology.* Washington, D.C.: American Psychiatric Press.

Scheid-Cook, Teresa L. 1991. Outpatient commitment as both social and least restrictive alternative. *Sociological Quarterly* 32:43–60.

Schneider-Braus, Kathleen. 1986. Civil commitment to outpatient psychotherapy: A case study. *Bulletin of the American Academy of Psychiatry and Law* 14:273–79.

Schoenfeld, C. G. 1976. An analysis of the views of Thomas S. Szasz. *Journal of Psychiatry and Law* 4:245–63.

Schonfeld, Warren H., Carol J. Verboncoeur, Sheila K. Fifer, Ruth C. Lipschutz, Deborah P. Lubeck, and Don P. Buesching. 1997. The functioning and well-being of patients with unrecognized anxiety disorders and major depressive disorder. *Journal of Affective Disorders* 43:105–19.

Schopp, Robert F., and Michael R. Quattrocchi. 1995. Predicting the present: Expert testimony and civil commitment. *Behavioral Sciences and the Law* 13:159–81.

Schultz, S. Charles, Robert L. Findling, Lee Friedman, John T. Kenny, Alexandria L. Wise.

1998. Treatment and outcomes in adolescents with schizophrenia. *Journal of Clinical Psychiatry* 59 (supp. 1): 50–56.

Schwartz, Harold I., and Karen Blank. 1986. Shifting competency during hospitalization: A model for informed consent decisions. *Hospital and Community Psychiatry* 37: 1256–60.

Searight, H. Russell. 1992. Assessing patient competence for medical decision-making. *American Family Physician* 45:751–59.

Segal, Steven, 1989. Civil commitment standards and patient mix in England/Wales, Italy, and the United States. *American Journal of Psychiatry* 146:187–93.

Segal, Steven P., Margaret A. Watson, Stephen M. Goldfinger, and David S. Averbuck. 1988a. Civil commitment in the psychiatric emergency room. *Archives of General Psychiatry* 45:748–52.

———. 1988b. Civil commitment in the psychiatric emergency room II. Mental disorder indicators and three dangerousness criteria. *Archives of General Psychiatry* 45:753–58.

———. 1988c. Civil commitment in the psychiatric emergency room III. Disposition as a function of mental disorder and dangerousness indicators. *Archives of General Psychiatry* 45:759–63.

Segal, Steven P., Margaret A. Watson, and L. Scott Nelson. 1985. Equity in the application of civil commitment criteria. *New Directions for Mental Health Services* 28:93–105.

———. 1986a. Consistency in the application of civil commitment standards in psychiatric emergency rooms. *Journal of Psychiatry and Law* 14:125–48.

———. 1986b. Indexing civil commitment in psychiatric emergency rooms. *Annals, AAPSS* (American Academy of Political and Social Sciences) 484:56–69.

Sellwood, W., and N. Tarrier. 1994. Demographic factors associated with extreme non-compliance in schizophrenia. *Social Psychiatry and Psychiatric Epidemiology* 29: 172–77.

Shamoo, A. E., and D. N. Irving. 1993. The PSDA and the depressed elderly: "Intermittent competency" revisited. *Journal of Clinical Ethics* 4:74–80.

Shapiro, Michael. 1973. Legislating control of behavior control: Autonomy and the coercive use of organic therapies. *Southern California Law Review* 47:237–356.

Sheline, Yvette I., and Teresa Nelson. 1993. Patient choice: Deciding between psychotropic medication and physical restraints in an emergency. *Bulletin of the American Academy of Psychiatry and the Law* 21:321–29.

Sherlock, Richard. 1984. Competency to consent to medical care: Toward a general view. *General Hospital Psychiatry* 6:71–76.

———. 1986. Reasonable men and sick human beings. *American Journal of Medicine* 80:2–4.

Siegel, Karolynn. 1987. Suicide and civil commitment. *Journal of Health Politics, Policy and Law* 12:343–60.

Silber, Tomas Jose. 1982. Ethical considerations concerning adolescents consulting for contraceptive services. *Journal of Family Practice* 15:909–11.

Silver, Hedy M. 1988. Voluntary admission to New York City hospitals: The rights of the mentally ill homeless. *Columbia Human Rights Law Review* 19:399–431.

Simpson, David T. 1984. Involuntary civil commitment: The dangerousness standard and its problems. *North Carolina Law Review* 63:241–56.

Sindel, Patricia E. 1991. Fourteenth Amendment: The right to refuse antipsychotic drugs masked by prison bars: *Washington v. Harper. Journal of Criminal Law and Criminology* 81:952–80.

Skinner, B. F. 1971. *Beyond freedom and dignity.* New York: Knopf.

———. 1974. *About behaviorism.* New York: Knopf.

———. 1978. *Reflections on behaviorism and society.* Englewood Cliffs, N.J.: Prentice-Hall.

Slobogin, Christopher. 1994. Involuntary community treatment of people who are violent and mentally ill: A legal analysis. *Hospital and Community Psychiatry* 45:685–89.

———. 1996. "Appreciation" as a measure of competency: Some thoughts about the MacArthur Group's approach. *Psychology, Public Policy, and the Law* 2:18–30.

Slovenko, Ralph. 1989. Commentary: Misadventures of psychiatry with the law. *Journal of Psychiatry and Law* 17:115–56.

———. 1992. The right of the mentally ill to refuse treatment revisited. *Journal of Psychiatry and Law* 20:407–34.

Smith, Carol A. 1995. Use of involuntary outpatient commitment in community care of the seriously and persistently mentally ill. *Issues in Mental Health* 16:275–84.

Smith, Rosalind C. 1998. Implementing psychosocial rehabilitation with long-term patients in a public psychiatric hospital. *Psychiatric Services* 49:593–95.

Snyder, Allen C. 1994. Competency to refuse lifesaving treatment: Valuing the nonlogical aspects of a person's decisions. *Issues in Law and Medicine* 10:299–320.

Socall, Daniel W., and Thomas Holtgraves. 1992. Attitudes toward the mentally ill: The effects of label and beliefs. *Sociological Quarterly* 33:435–45.

Soliday, Stanley M. 1985. A comparison of patient and staff attitudes toward seclusion. *Journal of Nervous and Mental Disease* 173:282–86.

Soloff, Paul H., Judith A. Lis, Thomas Kelly, Jack Cornelius, and Richard Ulrich. 1994. Self-mutilation and suicidal behavior in borderline personality disorder. *Journal of Personality Disorders* 8:257–67.

Soloff, Paul H., Joseph P. McEvoy, and Rohan Ganguli. 1989. Controversies in psychiatry: Is seclusion therapeutic? *Psychiatric Annals* 19:1.

Sood, Samidha, Martyn Baker, and Kenneth Bledin. 1996. Social and living skills of new long-stay hospital patients and new long-term community patients. *Psychiatric Services* 47:619–22.

Spensley, James, James T. Barter, Paul H. Werme, and Donald G. Langsley. 1974. Involuntary hospitalization: What for and how long? *American Journal of Psychiatry* 131:219–23.

Spensley, James, Daniel W. Edwards, and Edward White. 1980. Patient satisfaction and involuntary treatment. *American Journal of Orthopsychiatry* 5:725–27.

Starkey, David, and Barbara A. Leadholm. 1997. Prism: The psychiatric rehabilitation integrated service model—A public psychiatric hospital model for the 1990's. *Administration and Policy in Mental Health* 24:497–508.

Steadman, Henry J., John Monahan, Pamela Clark Robbins, Paul Appelbaum, Thomas Grisso, Dierdre Klassen, Edward Mulvey, and Loren Roth. 1993. From dangerousness to risk assessment: Implications for appropriate research strategies. In *Mental disorder and crime,* edited by Sheilagh Hodgins, 39–62. Newbury Park, Calif.: Sage.

Steadman, Henry J., Edward P. Mulvey, John Monahan, Pamela Clark Robbins, Paul S.

Appelbaum, Thomas Grisso, Loren H. Roth, and Eric Silver. 1998. Violence by people discharged from acute psychiatric inpatient facilities and by others in the same neighborhoods. *Archives of General Psychiatry* 55:393–401.

Stein, Leonard I., and Ronald J. Diamond. 2000. Commentary: A "systems"-based alternative to mandatory outpatient treatment. *Journal of the American Academy of Psychiatry and the Law* 28:159–64.

Steinberg, Alan, L. Jaime Fitten, and Norman Kachuck. 1986. Patient participation in treatment decision-making in the nursing home: The issue of competence. *Gerontologist* 26:362–66.

Stephenson, Barbara J., Brian H. Rowe, R. Brian Haynes, and Gladys Leon. 1993. The rational clinical examination: Is this patient taking the treatment as prescribed? *Journal of the American Medical Association* 269:2779–81.

Stern, Kristina. 1994. Competence to refuse life-sustaining medical treatment. *Law Quarterly Review* 110:541–45.

Stewart, Hamish. 1999. Legality and morality in H. L. A. Hart's theory of criminal law (Symposium on the Jurisprudence of H. L. A. Hart). *SMU Law Review* 1:201–27.

Stone, Alan A. 1985. A response to comments on APA's Model Commitment Law. *Hospital and Community Psychiatry* 36:984–89.

———. 1987. Broadening the statutory criteria for civil commitment: A reply to Durham and La Fond. *Yale Law and Policy Review* 5:412–27.

Stone, Alan A., and Clifford D. Stromberg. 1975. Mental health and law: A system in transition. Rockville, Md.: National Institute of Mental Health, Center for Studies of Crime and Delinquency.

Strasser, Mark. 1994–95. Incompetents and the right to die: In search of consistent meaningful standards. *Kentucky Law Journal* 83:733–98.

Sullivan, G. R. 1994. Intoxicants and diminished responsibility. *Criminal Law Review* (March): 156–62.

Sullivan, Greer, and Karen L. Spritzer. 1997. Consumer satisfaction with CMHC Services. *Community Mental Health Journal* 33:123–31.

Sullivan, Mark D., Nicholas G. Ward, and Audrey Laxton. 1992. The woman who wanted electroconvulsive therapy and do-not-resuscitate status: Questions of competence on a medical-psychiatric unit. *General Hospital Psychiatry* 14:204–9.

Sullivan, Mark D., and Stuart J. Younger. 1994. Depression, competence, and the right to refuse lifesaving medical treatment. *American Journal of Psychiatry* 15:971–78.

Sullivan, Therese, William L. Martin, and Mitchell M. Handelsman. 1993. Practical benefits of an informed-consent procedure: An empirical investigation. *Professional Psychology: Research and Practice* 24:160–63.

Svensson, Tommy. 1995. *On the notion of mental illness: Problematizing the medical-model conception of certain abnormal behavior and mental afflictions.* Aldershot, U.K.: Avebury/Ashgate.

Swanson, Jeffrey W., Marvin S. Swartz, Randy Borum, Virginia A. Hiday, H. Ryan Wagner, and Barbara J. Burns. 2000. Involuntary out-patient commitment and reduction of violent behavior in persons with severe mental illness. *British Journal of Psychiatry* 176:324–31.

Swanson, Jeffrey W., Marvin S. Swartz, Linda K. George, Barbara J. Burns, Virginia A. Hiday, Randy Borum, and H. Ryan Wagner. 1997. Interpreting the effectiveness of involuntary outpatient commitment: A conceptual model. *Journal of the American Academy of Psychiatry and the Law* 25:5–16.

Swanson, Jeffrey W., Miriam C. Tepper, Patricia Backlar, and Marvin S. Swartz. 2000. Psychiatric advance directives: An alternative to coercive treatment? *Psychiatry* 63:160–72.

Swartz, Marvin S., Barbara J. Burns, Linda K. George, Jeffery Swanson, Virginia A. Hiday, Randy Borum, and H. Ryan Wagner. 1997. The ethical challenges of a randomized controlled trial of involuntary outpatient commitment. *Journal of Mental Health Administration* 24:35–43.

Swartz, Marvin, Barbara J. Burns, Virginia A. Hiday, Linda K. George, Jeffrey Swanson, and H. Ryan Wagner. 1995. New directions in research on involuntary outpatient commitment. *Psychiatric Services* 46:381–85.

Swartz, Marvin S., Jeffrey W. Swanson, H. Ryan Wagner, Barbara J. Burns, Virginia A. Hiday, and Randy Borum. 1999. Can involuntary outpatient commitment reduce hospital recidivism? Findings from a randomized trial with severely mentally ill individuals. *American Journal of Psychiatry* 156:1968–75.

Swett, Chester, Jr., Alisa S. Michaels, and Jonathan O. Cole. 1989. Effects of a state law on rates of restraint on a child and adolescent unit. *Bulletin of the American Academy of Psychiatry and the Law* 2:165–69.

Swisher, K. N. 1991. Implementing the PSDA for psychiatric patients: A common-sense approach. *Journal of Clinical Ethics* 2:199–205.

Szasz, Thomas S. 1960. The myth of mental illness. *American Psychologist* 15:113–18.

———. 1961. The uses of naming and the origin of the myth of mental illness. *American Psychologist* 16:59–65.

———. 1974. *The myth of mental illness.* New York: Harper and Row.

———. 1977. *The manufacture of madness: A comparative study of the inquisition and the mental health movement.* Syracuse, N.Y.: Syracuse University Press.

———. 1978. Behavior therapy: A critical review of the moral dimensions of behavior modification. *Journal of Behavior Therapy and Experimental Psychiatry* 9:199–203.

———. 1994. Mental illness is still a myth. *Society* 31:34.

———. 1998. Commentary on "Aristotle's function argument and the concept of mental illness." *Philosophy, Psychiatry, and Psychology* 5:203–7.

Tardiff, Kenneth. 1984. *The psychiatric uses of seclusion and restraint.* Washington, D.C.: American Psychiatric Press.

———. 1992. The current state of psychiatry in the treatment of violent patients. *Archives of General Psychiatry* 49:493–95.

Tarsy, Daniel, and Ross J. Baldessarini. 1984. Tardive dyskinesia. *Annual Review of Medicine* 35:605–23.

Tavolaro, Karen B. 1992. Preventative outpatient civil commitment and the right to refuse treatment: Can pragmatic realities and constitutional requirements be reconciled? *Medicine and Law* 11:249–67.

Taylor, Helen Kirwan. 1999. Health: Should we play with Prozac? Many people who are not depressed are taking "Vitamin P." *Daily Telegraph* (London), 27 April, 20–23.

Teplin, Linda A., Karen M. Abram, and Gary M. McClelland. 1994. Does psychiatric disorder predict violent crime among released jail detainees? A six-year longitudinal study. *American Psychologist* 49:335–42.

Thomas, Karen M. 1998. Trying to cut through the silence. *Dallas Morning News*, 27 May.

Thompson, Peter. 1986. The use of seclusion in psychiatric hospitals in the Newcastle area. *British Journal of Psychiatry* 149:471–74.

Thorne, Frederick C. 1966. An analysis of Szasz' "myth of mental illness." *American Journal of Psychiatry* 123:652–56.

Through the looking glass: One young woman's year-long struggle with self-mutilation and depression. 1998. *Dateline NBC*, 26 October.

Timko, Christine, An-Thu Q. Nguyen, William O. Williford, and Rudolf H. Moos. 1993. Quality of care and outcomes of chronic mentally ill patients in hospitals and nursing homes. *Hospital and Community Psychiatry* 44:241–46.

Tinetti, Mary E., Wen-Liang Liu, Richard A. Marottoli, and Sandra F. Ginter. 1991. Mechanical restraint use among residents of skilled nursing facilities. Prevalence, patterns, and predictors. *Journal of the American Medical Association* 265:468–71.

Tobin, Bernadette. 1995. Did you think about buying her a cat? Some reflections on the concept of autonomy. *Journal of Contemporary Health Law and Policy* 11 (pt. 2): 417–28.

Tomoda, Atsuko, Rie Yasumiya, Takahiro Sumiyama, Kazumi Tsukada, Tatsumo Hayakawa, Kimimori Matsubara, and Toshinori Kitamara. 1997. Validity and reliability of structural interviews for competency and incompetency assessment testing and ranking inventory. *Journal of Clinical Psychology* 53:443–50.

Tonelli, Mark R. 1997. Substituted judgment in medical practice: Evidentiary standards on a sliding scale. *Journal of Law, Medicine and Ethics* 25:22–29.

Torrey, E. Fuller, and Robert J Kaplan. 1995. A national survey of the use of outpatient commitment. *Psychiatric Services* 46:778–84.

Toth, Tonya M. 1989. Refusing psychotropic drugs: Whose day in court? *University of Kansas Law Review* 37:657–77.

Treffert, Darold A. 1985. The obviously ill patient in need of treatment: A fourth standard of civil commitment. *Hospital and Community Psychiatry* 36:259–64.

Trends in health care decisionmaking (symposium). 1994. *Maryland Law Review* 53 (4): 1041–1277.

Tsemberis, Sam, and Cornelius Sullivan. 1988. Seclusion in context: Introducing a seclusion room into a children's unit of a municipal hospital. *American Journal of Orthopsychiatry* 58:462–65.

Turkheimer, Eric, and Charles D. H. Parry. 1992. Why the gap? Practice and policy in civil commitment hearings. *American Psychologist* 47:646–55.

Turner, Janice 1997. Kids who cut: Something's gone wrong in their lives and they take knives or razor blades or lit cigarettes to their bodies. *Toronto Star*, 10 October.

Tversky, Amos, and Daniel Kahneman. 1986. Rational choice and the framing of decisions. *Journal of Business* 59:251–78.

Tyler, Tom R. 1992. The psychological consequences of judicial procedures: Implications for civil commitment hearings. *SMU Law Review* 46:433–45.

Uddo, Basile J. 1992. Federal policy on forgoing treatment or care: Contradictions or consistency? *Law and Medicine* 8:293–308.

Urrutia, Guillermo. 1994. Medication refusal—clinical picture and outcome after use of administrative review. *Bulletin of the American Academy of Psychiatry and the Law* 22:595–603.

Valentine, Mary B., Duff Waring, and David Giuffrida. 1992. Competency and treatment refusal in psychiatric hospitals. *Canada's Mental Health* 40:19–24.

Van Hall, Suzanne F. West, Brenda S. Reid, and Frank A. Uribie. 1991. Refusing psychiatric medications and hospitalization: What "just say no" means to patients and providers. *Whittier Law Review* 1:51–69.

Van Heeringen, C., S. Jannes, W. Buylaert, H. Henderick, and B. De Baquer. 1995a. The management of non-compliance with referral to out-patient after-care among attempted suicide patients: A controlled intervention study. *Psychological Medicine* 25:963–70.

Van Heeringen, Kees, Paul Ducheyne, Paul Schollaert, Robert Verheyen, Kris Goethals, and Stijn Jannes. 1995b. The risk of seclusion and the menstrual cycle in female psychiatric patients. *Journal of Psychosomatic Research* 39:629–32.

Van Putten, Robert A., Jose M. Santiago, and Michael R. Berren. 1988. Involuntary outpatient commitment in Arizona: A retrospective study. *Hospital and Community Psychiatry* 39:953–58.

Vatz, Richard E., and Lee S. Weinberg. 1994. The rhetorical paradigm in psychiatric history: Thomas Szasz and the myth of mental illness. In *Discovering the history of psychiatry,* edited by Mark S. Micale and Roy Porter. New York: Oxford University Press.

Venesy, Barbara A. 1995. A clinician's guide to decision-making capacity and ethically sound medical decisions. *American Journal of Physical Medicine and Rehabilitation* 74:219–26.

Vitiello, Benedetto, Richard Malone, Pamela Roth Buschle, Mary Anne Delaney, and David Behar. 1990. Reliability of DSM-III diagnoses of hospitalized children. *Hospital and Community Psychiatry* 41:63–67.

Walkow, Moujan M. 1994. Informed consent: Legal competency not determinative of person's ability to consent to medical treatment. *Suffolk University Law Review* 28: 271–77.

Warner, Richard. 1994. *Recovery from schizophrenia.* London: Routledge.

Watson, Andrew S. 1984. Compassion, control, and decisions about competency: Comment. *American Journal of Psychiatry* 141:58–60.

Way, Bruce B. 1986. The use of restraint and seclusion in New York state psychiatric centers. *International Journal of Law and Psychiatry* 8:383–93.

Way, Bruce B., and Steven M. Banks. 1990. Use of seclusion and restraint in public psychiatric hospitals: Patient characteristics and facility effects. *Hospital and Community Psychiatry* 4:75–81.

Wear, A. N., and Diana Brahams. 1991. To treat or not to treat: The legal, ethical and therapeutic implications of treatment refusal. *Journal of Medical Ethics* 17:131–35.

Weatherhead, Rebecca. 1988. Psychotropic drug-treatment refusal by competent psychiatric patients. *University of Toronto Faculty Law Review* 47:101–31.

Weber, Walter M. 1985. Substituted judgment doctrine: A critical analysis. *Issues in Law and Medicine* 1:131–59.

Weinhardt, Lance S., Michael P. Carey, Kate B. Carey. 1998. HIV-risk behavior and the public health context of HIV/AIDS among women living with a severe and persistent mental illness. *Journal of Nervous and Mental Disease* 186:276–82.

Weinstock, Robert, Russell Copelan, and Abbas Bagheri. 1984. Competence to give informed consent for medical procedures. *Bulletin of the American Academy of Psychiatry and the Law* 12:117–25.

Weisstub, David N. 1988. *Law and mental health: International perspectives.* New York: Pergamon.

Weithorn, Lois A. 1982. Competency to render informed treatment decisions: A comparison of certain minors and adults. Ph.D. diss., University of Pittsburgh.

Wenning, Kenneth. 1993. Long-term psychotherapy and informed consent. *Hospital and Community Psychiatry* 44:364–67.

Wettstein, Robert M. 1999. The right to refuse psychiatric treatment. *Forensic Psychiatry* 22:173–82.

Wexler, David B. 1983. Seclusion and restraint: Lessons from law, psychiatry, and psychology. *International Journal of Law and Psychiatry* 5 (3–4): 285–94.

———. 1988. Reforming the law in action through empirically grounded civil commitment guidelines. *Hospital and Community Psychiatry* 39:402–5.

Whittington, Richard, and Tom Mason. 1995. A new look at seclusion: Stress, coping and the perception of threat. *Journal of Forensic Psychiatry* 6:285–304.

Widiger, Thomas A., and Timothy J. Trull. 1985. The empty debate over the existence of mental illness: Comments on Gorenstein. *American Psychologist* 40:468–70.

Wilk, Ruta J. 1988a. Implications of involuntary outpatient commitment for community mental health agencies. *American Journal of Orthopsychiatry* 58:580–91.

———. 1988b. Involuntary outpatient commitment of the mentally Ill. *Social Work* 133–37.

Winick, Bruce J. 1991. Competency to consent to treatment: The distinction between assent and objection. *Houston Law Review* 28:15–61.

———. 1992. On autonomy: Legal and psychological perspectives. *Villanova Law Review* 37:1705–77.

———. 1995. The side effects of incompetency labeling and the implications for mental health law. *Psychology, Public Policy, and Law* 1:6–42.

———. 1996a. Advance directive instruments for those with mental illness. *University of Miami Law Review* 51:57–95.

———. 1996b. Foreword: A summary of the MacArthur Treatment Competence Study and an introduction to the special theme. *Psychology, Public Policy, and Law* 2:3–17.

———. 1996c. The MacArthur Treatment Competency Study: Legal and therapeutic implications. *Psychology, Public Policy, and Law* 2:137–66.

———. 1997. *The right to refuse mental health treatment.* Washington, D.C.: American Psychological Association.

Winokur, George, and Ming T. Tsuang. 1996. *The natural history of mania, depression, and schizophrenia.* Washington, D.C.: American Psychiatric Press.

Winston, Martin E., and Sally M. Winston. 1982. Can a subject consent to a Ulysses contract? Commentary. *Hastings Center Report* 12:26–27.

Wisor, Ronald L., Jr., 1993. Community care, competition and coercion: A legal perspective on privatized mental health care. *American Journal of Law and Medicine* 19:145–75.

Woerner, Margaret G., John M. Kane, Jeffrey A. Lieberman, Jose Alvir, Kenneth J. Bergmann, Michael Borenstein, Nina R. Schooler, Sukdeb Mukherjee, John Rotrosen,

Morton Rubinstein, et al. 1991. The prevalence of tardive dyskinesia. *Journal of Clinical Psychopharmacology* 11:34–42.

Wolff, Kevin R. 1990. Determining patient competency in treatment refusal cases. *Georgia Law Review* 24:733–57.

Wolstein, Benjamin. 1983. Transference and resistance as psychic experience. *Contemporary Psychoanalysis* 19:276–94.

Yee, Donna L., John A. Capitman, Walter N. Leutz, and Mark Sceigaj. 1999. Resident-centered care in assisted living. *Journal of Aging and Social Policy* 10:7–26.

Young, Janet E., William F. Forbes, and John P. Hirdes. 1994. The association of disability with long-term care institutionalization of the elderly. *Canadian Journal on Aging* 13:15–29.

Young, John L., Howard V. Zonana, and Lynn Shepler. 1986. Medication noncompliance in schizophrenia: Codification and update. *Bulletin of the American Academy of Psychiatry and the Law* 14:105–22.

Zaubler, Thomas S., Milton Viederman, and Joseph J. Fins. 1996. Ethical, legal, and psychiatric issues in capacity, competency, and informed consent: An annotated bibliography. *General Hospital Psychiatry* 18:155–72.

Zito, Julie M., Thomas J. Craig, and Joseph Wanderling. 1991. New York under the *Rivers* decision: An epidemiologic study of drug treatment refusal. *American Journal of Psychiatry* 148:904–9.

Zweibel, Nancy R., and Christine K. Cassel. 1989. Treatment choices at the end of life: A comparison of decisions by older patients and their physician-selected proxies. *Gerontologist* 29:615–21.

Boston State Hospital case (*continued*)
to preserve therapeutic milieu in, 132,
135–36
Bouvia v. Superior Court, 233n. 46
breast cancer surgeries, 173, 191, 244n. 14
Brief Psychiatric Rating Scale, 183–84
Brown, Joyce (aka Billie Boggs): civil
commitment of, 44–45, 46; possible
commitment of, 56–59; rationalizing
intervention for, 59–60
Burger, Warren E., 227n. 15
Burt, Robert "Bo," 73

California: forced medication standard in,
238n. 12; guardianship statutes in,
238n. 12; mentally ill in jails in, 71;
refusing treatment in, 74
capacity. *See* competence and competency
standard
Cecilia (pseud.), 23, 30
children: decisionmaking of, 199, 247n. 14;
punishment of, 244n. 21; restraint of,
123; seclusion of, 122, 133, 141. *See also*
youth
civil commitment: costs of, 53–55, 64; for
first psychotic break, 55, 56–68, 201,
219–20; forced medication compared
to, 85, 86–89, 92; hearings on vs.
persuasion for, 62; lawyers' ethics in,
15; length of, 67–68; other circumstances leading to, 55, 68–82; outpatient's noncompliance as basis for,
94–95, 240n. 15; patients' satisfaction
with, 228–30n. 29, 230n. 31; refusing
treatment in, 209–15; risk of error and,
52–53, 54–55; self-binding in context
of, 56, 71–72, 80, 81–82, 202–3; standards current in, 45–53, 225nn. 1–2;
standards proposed for, 47–48, 55–56,
194, 219, 220; studies of, 228–30n. 29,
230n. 31, 230–31n. 33. *See also* hospitalization; outpatient commitment
codes of professional ethics, 15, 16, 17
coercion: in medication vs. hospitalization
choice, 93–94; in patient-"requested"
restraints, 163; in self-binding, 207–8

community setting: forced treatment in,
240n. 16; voluntary treatment in, 94–
95. *See also* outpatient commitment
competence and competency standard:
autonomy protection and, 176,
255n. 2; basis for choosing, 247–
48n. 4; capacity levels necessary for,
176, 177, 180–97; capacity of appreciation in, 177; capacity of belief formation
in, 178–79, 180, 182–94; capacity of
expressing a choice in, 177, 178, 179,
180; capacity of knowing desires in,
179–80; capacity of reasoning in, 177,
178, 179, 180, 181–82; capacity of
understanding in, 177, 178, 180–81;
cases on, 226n. 8; in civil-commitment
standard, 47, 81–82; consequentiality
of decision and, 174; courts' language
on, 249n. 8; definition of, 9, 174–76,
223n. 3; denial of mental illness and,
190–94; impairment and, 194–97;
instruments for measuring, 248–
49n. 5; mental illness and, as standard
for confinement, 68–69, 80–82;
normative issues in, 175–77, 217–19;
in patients' choice for/against sedation,
164, 167, 168–72, 247n. 17; in patients'
choice of emergency treatment, 165–
66; in patients' choice of medication,
86–95, 96–103, 105, 107–9, 247n. 17;
in patients' choice of seclusion, 129,
132, 140, 160–61; physical illness and,
73, 74–75, 173–74, 233n. 49; restraints
and, 147, 150, 161–64, 247n. 10; in
state laws, 234n. 58; two-tiered system vs. sliding scale for, 55, 196–200,
218, 253n. 33. *See also* impairment of
abilities; incompetence
compliance/noncompliance: with medication, 100–101, 106–7; with outpatient
commitment, 94–95, 240n. 15; studies of, 108, 241–42n. 28; with ward/
hospital rules, 142–44
Connecticut: restraints practices in, 147–
48
criminal law: diminished-capacity standard

dignity and respect (*continued*)
  harm to self vs. other, 158–59; risk
    of harm to, 53; seclusion as affront to,
    124, 129; self-binding and, 204, 209–
    15; society's commitment to, 22
diminished capacity, 226–27n. 11
diminished responsibility, 226–27n. 11,
  232n. 39
disability: in diagnosis of mental illness,
    37–38; forced medication issues and,
    85, 86; impairment linked to, 206;
    mental illness and, as standard for
    confinement, 68–69, 73–80; physical
    handicaps as, 39; in serious psychotic
    break, 61; skepticism about, 41; use of
    term "incompetent" and, 249n. 10;
    values embedded in determining, 218.
    See also danger to self
distress: in definition of serious psychotic
    break, 61; in diagnosis of mental ill-
    ness, 37–38
doctors. *See* mental health professionals;
  physicians
Donaldson, Kenneth, 1, 44, 45–46
do-not-resuscitate orders. *See* advance
  directives (ADs)
Dresser, Rebecca, 202, 203
drug abuse, 228n. 28
*DSM-IV-TR (Diagnostic and Statistical
  Manual of Mental Disorders*, 4th ed.,
  text revision), 33, 224n. 7

eccentricity. *See* unconventionality
Eighth Amendment, 188
Einstein, Albert, 30
emergency rooms: restraints used in, 155–
  57
emergency situations: definition of, 15; pa-
    tient's choice among emergency treat-
    ments in, 164–67, 219, 247nn. 14, 17;
    patient's choice of seclusion or restraint
    in, 160–64; patient's refusal of medica-
    tion that could avert, 168–72, 247n. 17;
    restraints used in, 121–22
empowerment, 17

England: diminished-responsibility statute
    in, 232n. 39; patients' choices in, 163–
    64; restraint and seclusion practices
    in, 152, 159, 246n. 4
epilepsy, 191
ethics codes, 15, 16, 17

family. *See* friends and relatives
fantasy: false beliefs distinguished from
    unconscious, 187; use of term, 223n. 2
    (ch. 1)
fears and fantasies: of law students, 56; of
    lawyers, 5, 7–11, 13, 60, 63; lawyers'
    and doctors' compared, 11–19; of men-
    tal health professionals, 5–7, 12–13,
    59; use of term, 223n. 2 (ch. 1). *See also*
    autonomy; paternalism
feeding tubes, 74
Feinberg, Joel, 132–33
First Amendment, 109
flexibility of thinking, 34–35, 37
Florida: incompetency standard in,
    234n. 58; involuntary commitment
    in, 44
Florida State Hospital, 44
Foster, Jodie, 26
Fourteenth Amendment, 109
freedom: of beliefs, 182; lawyers' commit-
    ment to, 13; mentation and locomotor,
    87, 97–98, 109; refusing medication
    viewed as, 109; restrictions on physi-
    cal vs. mental, 40; society's commit-
    ment to, 22. *See also* autonomy;
    liberty
friends and relatives: as counterweight to
    hospitalization, 61; on rights of family
    members vs. strangers, 56–59. *See also*
    guardianship

genetic engineering, 117, 118–19
genius intelligence, 224–25n. 10. *See also*
  unconventionality
Georgia: civil-commitment standard in,
  225n. 1
Goffman, Erving, 227n. 17